INSIDERS' GUIDE® TO

CALIFORNIA'S
WINE COUNTRY
A GUIDE TO NAPA AND SONOMA COUNTIES
EIGHTH EDITION

JEAN SAYLOR DOPPENBERG

INSIDERS' GUIDE®

GUILFORD, CONNECTICUT

WITHDRAWN

AN IMPRINT OF THE GLOBE PEQUOT PRESS

The prices and rates in this guidebook were confirmed at press time. We recommend, however, that you call establishments before traveling to obtain current information.

To buy books in quantity for corporate use or incentives, call **(800) 962–0973** or e-mail **premiums@GlobePequot.com**.

INSIDERS' GUIDE®

Text design by Sheryl Kober
Maps by XNR Productions, Inc. © Morris Book Publishing, LLC

ISSN 1539-9923
ISBN 978-0-7627-4915-7

Printed in the United States of America
10 9 8 7 6 5 4 3 2 1

CONTENTS

Directory of Maps

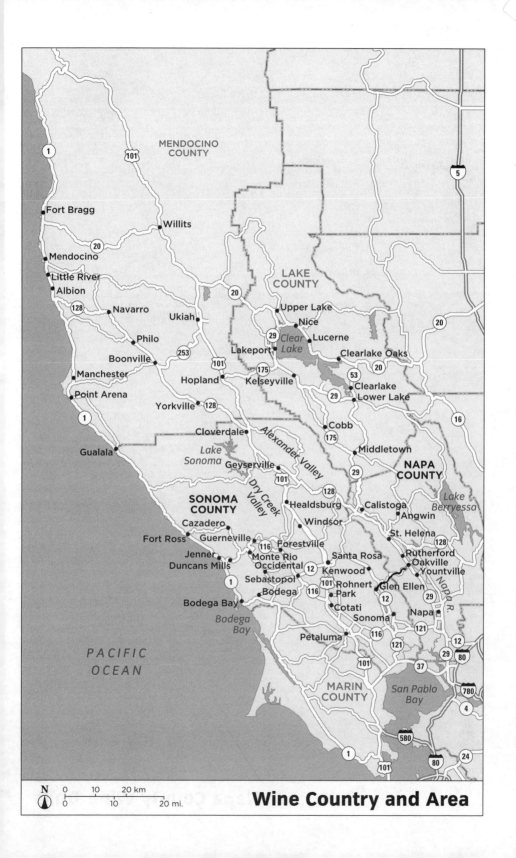

Wine Country and Area

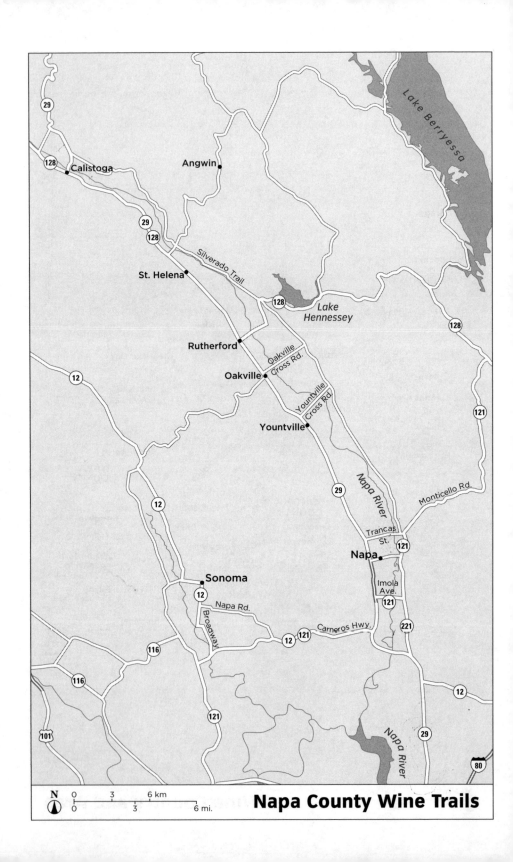

Napa County Wine Trails

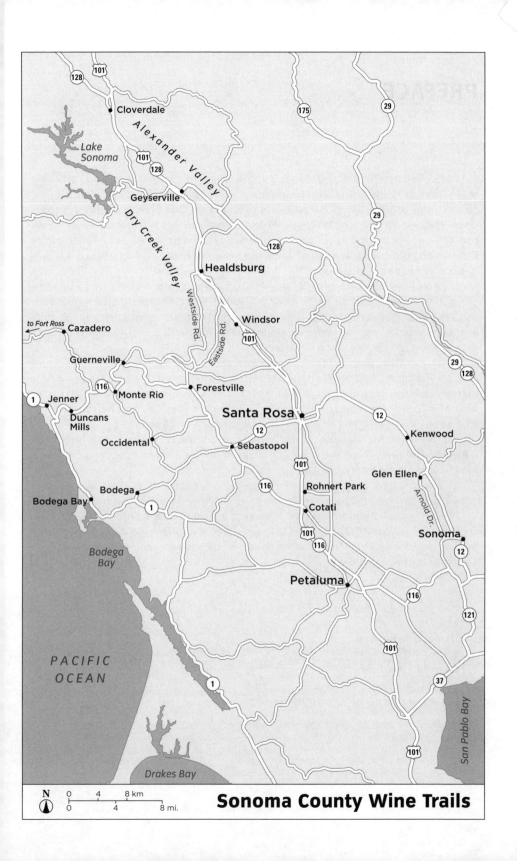

Sonoma County Wine Trails

PREFACE

As I watch one jumbo jet after another making slow descents over my house on their way to landing at San Francisco International Airport, I get a little thrill. More visitors heading to Wine Country? Sure, no doubt a few of the passengers in those planes are vacationers. Gliding overhead before they touch down—securing tray tables and bringing seat backs forward—perhaps they too are anticipating the thrill of finally stepping off the plane and making their way to "Eden to a Wine Grape," as my part of California has been called. I like to think that many of those visitors are toting along this book in their baggage, written by a resident tourist.

There are many Wine Country guides on the market, and all of them will enlighten you to some extent about the region. But the *Insiders' Guide to California's Wine Country* provides information from the perspective of someone who lives in the middle of the action, just a short drive in any direction from all the attractions and cool stuff listed here. I love this part of the state, and I never tire of checking out new places and revisiting tried-and-true favorites.

As you turn these pages, you'll see detailed information on wineries, restaurants, lodgings, shopping, arts and culture, annual events, outdoor recreation, and much more. There's also an overview of the many attractions to be found in nearby San Francisco and ideas for day trips beyond the boundaries of Wine Country. For an extra dash of insight, check out the Insiders' tips, those helpful nuggets of information you won't find in other books. They are flagged with the ℹ symbol.

With the help of the Relocation chapter, you will have practical information close at hand about real estate, retirement, schools, health care—all crucial for new and prospective residents. Try finding information like that in those other guides.

It's your choice, but this guide—page for page—is superior to the others in the volume of data offered about the Northern California region known around the world as Wine Country.

Whether you are visiting Wine Country as a tourist or a settler, *Insiders' Guide to California's Wine Country* welcomes you with open arms. Let us know if the book worked for you. If you discover something we missed, we'd like to know about that too. We update this guide annually, and we want to be as accurate and helpful as possible.

Write to us at:

Insiders' Guide to California's
Wine Country
The Globe Pequot Press
P.O. Box 480
Guilford, CT 06437-0480

You can also visit us on the Web at www.Insiders.com.

ACKNOWLEDGMENTS

Only one author's name appears on the cover of this book, but pulling together so much information is not accomplished without the help and cooperation of scores of friends, acquaintances, and even total strangers. I have nearly as many people to thank for their time and trouble as there are grapes in Wine Country. It's impossible to name them all, but here are several who stand out, in no particular order:

For their true insiders' insight into the wine industry, I thank Clay Gregory, former president of the board of directors of the Napa Valley Vintners Association, and Nick Frey, president of the Sonoma County Winegrape Commission. A special shout-out goes to each of these helpful people (also Wine Country "insiders") who made my life easier and the book richer for their assistance: Nancy Lilly of Wildcat Vineyard (thanks for treating me to one of the most spectacular views I've ever seen), Duskie Estes and John Stewart, Donna Ferguson, Tony and Marcia Babb, Nick Kite, Steve MacRostie, Gerrett Snedaker, and Alan Lemery. I also extend my gratitude to the staffs of the many chambers of commerce and visitor centers around the region, and information provided by the *Napa Valley Register* (particularly Jennifer Huffman) and the *Press Democrat*.

Amy Lyons and Lynn Zelem at Globe Pequot Press kept me inspired, helping to bring this latest edition—my fifth—to print. My husband, Loren, was patient and understanding when piles of writing and research littered the house, and my sister, Jan Blanchard, was gracious about lending some of her photographs for your viewing pleasure. Thanks also to the friends who gave their encouragement and support.

Finally, I can't thank my parents enough for instilling in me a lifelong curiosity about new places and new people. John and Gert's four children shared in their countless drive-all-day vacation adventures in overpacked and overheated station wagons, and I am grateful they always brought me along for the ride.

HELP US KEEP THIS GUIDE UP TO DATE

Every effort has been made by the author and editors to make this guide as accurate and useful as possible. However, many changes can occur after a guide is published—establishments close, phone numbers change, facilities come under new management, etc.

We would love to hear from you concerning your experiences with this guide and how you feel it could be improved and be kept up to date. While we may not be able to respond to all comments and suggestions, we'll take them to heart, and we'll make certain to share them with the author. Please send your comments and suggestions to the following address:

The Globe Pequot Press
Reader Response/Editorial Department
P.O. Box 480
Guilford, CT 06437

Or you may e-mail us at: editorial@GlobePequot.com

Thanks for your input, and happy travels!

HOW TO USE THIS BOOK

Skimming through *Insiders' Guide to California's Wine Country* is a bit like channel surfing with your TV's remote control—you flip here and there, back and forth, looking for something to grab your attention. It might be an interesting name, a familiar place, or an intriguing topic that leaps out and demands closer investigation. Go ahead and land on any page that strikes your fancy, whether it's for a restaurant, winery, or lodging listing. Data-heavy books such as this one are designed for thumbing through. But at some point you might want to find a particular "thing" by region, so it will help to understand the book's structure.

The table of contents indicates the chapter topics, but if any questions remain, a quick peek at chapter introductions should answer them. Beyond that, each chapter is organized geographically, more or less, with Napa County listings first, followed by those of Sonoma County. In general, the listings for hotels, attractions, wineries, and so forth appear in order in the book as you would encounter them while driving in each region, approximately south to north and east to west. (To make the Sonoma County listings more manageable—there are scads of them—I further divided the county into Southern, Northern, Sonoma Coast, and West County/Russian River subheadings.) Refer to the list below for the general order by town and city.

NOTE: Many of Wine Country's world-class eateries are known by name and not necessarily by their location. So I've organized the Restaurants chapter using the same geographical method explained above, then listed the restaurants alphabetically within their respective towns and regions.

NAPA COUNTY

Napa, Yountville, Oakville, Rutherford, St. Helena, Angwin, Lake Berryessa, Calistoga

SONOMA COUNTY

Southern Sonoma

Sonoma, Glen Ellen, Kenwood, Petaluma, Cotati, Rohnert Park, Santa Rosa

Northern Sonoma

Windsor, Healdsburg, Geyserville, Cloverdale, Alexander Valley, Dry Creek Valley, Lake Sonoma, Westside Road

Sonoma Coast

Bodega, Bodega Bay, Jenner, Fort Ross

West County/Russian River

Sebastopol, Occidental, Forestville, Guerneville, Monte Rio, Cazadero, Duncans Mills

Several chapters cover topics that venture beyond Wine Country or otherwise defy a strict county-by-county organization. These include the Golden Gateway (San Francisco) and Day Trips chapters, which focus on more distant destinations. Likewise, the Spectator Sports chapter covers professional teams in and beyond Wine Country and is thus organized by sport. The Flora, Fauna, and Climate chapter and, to some extent, the Getting Here, Getting Around chapter, deal with phenomena that have no respect for county lines and thus have their own unique breakdowns. And the Festivals and Annual Events chapter logically follows a chronological order.

You may notice that some material teeters on the categorical fence that divides chapters, so I have cross-referenced information wherever it made sense, briefly mentioning a related event, activity, or locale where appropriate and referring you to the chapter where it is described in more detail.

For those who wish to extend their stay in Wine Country by becoming a full- or part-time resident, check out the information-packed Relocation chapter. There you will find useful details about real estate, educational opportunities, health care, retirement options, and other important information you should know before—and after—making your move.

I hope the book answers all your questions and raises a few you might not have considered. If you find anything you believe to be inaccurate or misleading, I urge you to let me know.

AREA OVERVIEW

Napa and *Sonoma*—two words synonymous with beauty and the good life. I gaze upon that beauty every day, yet I'm endlessly fascinated by the changing vistas. Trust me, visitors never go away disappointed by the scenery.

Although it is promoted as a nirvana for foodies and wine lovers, this region has much more to offer than its famous agricultural crops. I'm happy to report that it's composed of vibrant small cities, sleepy rural communities, an expansive coastline blissfully free of commercialism, some of the tallest trees in the world, and an endless collection of colorful characters who call it home.

In this chapter, Wine Country is put under the microscope to reveal the cities and towns you'll encounter as a visitor.

NAPA COUNTY

Always rural in nature, Napa County has seen the rise and fall of wheat, cattle, and prunes as the dominant product. For the past three decades, it has been the ultrapremium wine grapes—and the visitors who love them—driving the economy. ("Napa County" and "Napa Valley" are used somewhat interchangeably in this book.)

Though Napa County is the Bay Area's least populated county, the population has increased a bit over the past few years—growing to 133,522 residents, according to the California Department of Finance. The median income of these hardworking folks hovers at $53,184. But we have a good share of celebrity residents too, who earn a bit more. Property owners in Napa Valley and its environs include Francis Ford Coppola (see the Wineries chapter), Robin Williams, Robert Redford, Woody Harrelson, Boz Scaggs, Danielle Steele, David Wolper, racing legend Mario Andretti, baseball legend Tom Seaver, and a legendary survivor of the '60s, Ray Manzarek of the Doors.

Even if they don't commit to buying their very own villa or vineyard, celebs flock to the area for getaway jaunts or special celebrations (the wedding of pop singer Christina Aguilera, for example), the same as you, the probably-not-world-famous visitor. Because of the number of high rollers

and famous faces flitting about, filmmaker/wine baron/longtime resident Coppola once quipped to the local press that he feared Napa Valley was turning into the East Hampton of the West Coast. Yet if you should spot Redford pedaling the Silverado Trail on his bicycle or selecting scones at the Model Bakery, please be discreet.

The southern gateway to Napa Valley is the city of Napa, which, at about 75,900 people, makes up more than half of the county's population. Napa has several gracious, older districts left over from the horse-and-buggy days—the lettered streets known as Old Town, the Fuller Park area south of downtown, and Alta Heights—connected by more down-to-earth neighborhoods. Many of the city's best bed-and-breakfast inns can be found in these areas.

Most of the commercial action (some would call it blight) in Napa is along Soscol Avenue, with the usual chain retail stores and shopping centers, cookie-cutter restaurants, and auto dealerships found in all cities—and the traffic congestion that goes with them.

Meanwhile, downtown Napa continues to undergo major renovation that was triggered by the development and construction of the now closed Copia and a massive flood-control project along the Napa River. Where once it was seen primarily as the commercial core of the valley proper, lacking tourist-oriented amenities, the city of Napa is drawing visitors to new hotels and inns, and new eateries are collecting rave reviews. The city center in general has been spiffed up and transformed, and plans for major new projects seem to be announced every few weeks. One of the biggest under construction in 2008 is called Riverfront, a 2-block-long mixed-use development on Main Street. Also coming soon to downtown Napa—pending those pesky municipal approvals—is a Ritz-Carlton hotel. My, how the neighborhood has changed.

Though Napa owes much of its prosperity to the wine industry, government is the largest employer in the city. Napa is the seat of the county government, and the Napa Valley Unified School District and Napa State Hospital account for hundreds of jobs.

To the north of the city of Napa is Yountville, named after Napa Valley pioneer George Yount (see the History chapter). Though the smallest city (population 3,300) in Napa Valley, it self-proclaims more world-class restaurants per capita than any city in America. I can vouch for that (see the Restaurants chapter). New subdivisions built in the late 1990s increased the population slightly, but this is a town that caters almost exclusively to visitors and their creature comforts. A building moratorium that began in 1999 was lifted in 2005, making way for expansions at some existing hotels, at least one new hotel project, a new community center, and more residential development.

Oakville and Rutherford appear frequently in addresses throughout the book, but usually the reference is to nearby countryside locales. The towns themselves are hardly more than wide spots around Highway 29. This is, however, a beautiful part of the valley—a midway sector where the mountains begin to encroach upon the valley floor.

When most visitors imagine the quintessential Wine Country village, they envision St. Helena, with its gingerbread cottages, canopied sidewalks of a thriving-yet-nostalgic downtown, pocket gardens with not a blade of grass out of place—and only three traffic lights! Though it has its peripheral subdivisions and apartment complexes, the overall look of St. Helena (pronounced Hel-LAY-na) is defined by high-priced neatness (see the Relocation chapter). Much of the housing is pre–World War II, nearly all has been immaculately maintained, and the residential streets in the heart of town are lushly lined with mature trees. About a quarter of the town's approximately 6,000 residents are 65 or older, making it a popular spot for retirees with comfortable bank accounts. Due east of St. Helena is Deer Park, a small community with about 1,800 souls.

The hilltop hamlet of Angwin, up Deer Park Road/Howell Mountain Road off the Silverado Trail, orbits around Pacific Union College. The town's population (heavily Seventh-day Adventist) is mostly college students—approximately 61 percent of the inhabitants here are under age 30.

To the east of Angwin is man-made Lake Berryessa (see the Parks and Recreation chapter). The settlements are on the western and southern shores of the lake, especially along Berryessa-Knoxville Road. The eastern perimeter is virtually inaccessible to any vehicle. Berryessa is not encircled by hotels and restaurants. It has been known more as a spot for vacation homes, though big changes are taking place there.

Calistoga, the northernmost city of Napa Valley, is an iconoclastic slice of California, a burg that sees itself as real and unadulterated even as it supports itself almost entirely through tourist dollars, cornering the spa and mud-bath market. As one local wag likes to describe it, "Calistoga is to pickup trucks what St. Helena is to Range Rovers." The population hovers at around 5,200, with about 28 percent age 65 and older. Wine isn't the only liquid refreshment bottled in Napa Valley: On the east side of Calistoga are two major suppliers of mineral water, Calistoga and Crystal Geyser, and some excellent beers are brewed and bottled at the Calistoga Inn and Silverado Brewing Co., south a bit on Highway 29.

Wine Country Vital Statistics

Napa County population: 133,522

Square miles: 788

Acres in vineyards: 45,275 (total county acreage is 485,120)

Largest city: Napa (population 75,900)

Largest employers: Government, Napa Valley Unified School District, Napa State Hospital, Queen of the Valley Medical Center, St. Helena Hospital, Owens Corning, Foster's Wine Estates

Major colleges: Pacific Union College, Napa Valley College

County sales tax: 7.75 percent

Sonoma County population: 482,034

Square miles: 1,600

Acres in vineyards: 60,000 (total county acreage is 1,050,000)

Largest city: Santa Rosa (population 156,200)

Largest employers: Government, Kaiser Permanente, St. Joseph Health System, Agilent Technologies, Medtronic Vascular, Kendall-Jackson Wine Estates

Major colleges: Sonoma State University, Santa Rosa Junior College, Empire College

County sales tax: 7.75 percent (8.0 percent in Santa Rosa)

Wine Country climate: Mediterranean-like, with mild, moist winters and warm, dry summers

SONOMA COUNTY

i Santa Rosa earned acclaim in 2008 as one of the nation's "greenest" cities, based on a ranking released by *Popular Science* magazine. The city came in at No. 23 among 254 cities nationwide with populations above 100,000.

Encompassing nearly 1,600 square miles from the Pacific coast to the Mayacmas Mountains and San Pablo Bay, Sonoma County is home to approximately 482,034 residents, most of whom live in a relatively narrow corridor along U.S. Highway 101 from Santa Rosa to Petaluma. The rest of the county—approximately 56 percent—is farmland. The farms consist of apple, peach, and plum orchards; livestock rangeland and dairy farms; and of course vineyards.

It's no surprise that grapes and wine are the most prized agricultural commodities, yet agricultural employment accounts for less than 4 percent of the total workforce. The services, retail, and manufacturing sectors by far employ the most people—approximately 62 percent.

Santa Rosa is the county seat and the largest city, with a population of 156,200. In May 2002 *Forbes* magazine ranked the city No. 2 in its list of the top 10 dynamic economic regions in the nation. More recently it was named a top "green" city by *Popular Science* magazine.

Some of the largest employers include such clean industries as Agilent Technologies, St. Joseph Health System, Kaiser Permanente, Kendall-Jackson Wine Estates, Medtronic Vascular, and state and county government offices. As in Napa County and the rest of California, the Hispanic population is booming in Sonoma County (currently at 21 percent). Asian peoples are the second-largest minority (4 percent), followed by African Americans and Native Americans (each at 1 percent).

Santa Rosa's downtown is split in two by US 101—a planning decision that many have long since regretted. To the west of the highway are antiques shops and historic Railroad Square, whose sturdy buildings were constructed of locally quarried stone. Much of this area has been renovated in recent years, and big plans for a huge food and wine center—to rival the same type of marketplace found in San Francisco's Ferry Building—are still on the drawing board. To the east, especially along Fourth Street, are restaurants, coffeehouses, home furnishings stores, and gift shops. The Luther Burbank Home and Gardens (see the Attractions chapter) are also nearby. The core of Santa Rosa has changed little in recent years, with historic streets in the McDonald Avenue district lined with stately, well-kept mansions.

On the southeastern edge of the county is the town of Sonoma. This small enclave of approximately 9,900 residents is largely defined by its historic sites, especially those along the town's eight-acre central plaza (we called them town squares where I grew up). There you'll find the Mission San Francisco de Solano, the Sonoma Barracks, the Swiss Hotel, and several nearby wineries within walking distance (see the Wineries; Hotels, Motels, and Inns; and Bed-and-Breakfast Inns chapters).

North of Sonoma are the tiny hamlets of Glen Ellen and Kenwood. Tucked away from the traffic of Highway 12, Glen Ellen's Main Street is only two blocks long, so you might have to invent an excuse to spend the whole day here. One possibility is Jack London State Historic Park, just west of town (see the Attractions chapter). Kenwood is equally small (population 1,440), but no less charming.

Directly south of Santa Rosa along US 101 are the residential communities of Cotati, Rohnert Park, and Petaluma. The latter is the third-largest town in Wine Country, with more than 57,000 people and regal Victorian-era homes and art deco commercial palaces (such as the McNear Building).

Rohnert Park (population 43,000) is a planned community commonly referred to by locals as the region's Big Box town, having welcomed all manner of chain stores, restaurants, and motels with open arms. Contrasting sharply with that town vision, Cotati (population 7,600) has stubbornly kept some of those same franchise businesses from gaining a foothold within the town borders, particularly fast-food restaurants. It also lays claim to one of only two hexagonal town plazas in America.

North of Santa Rosa is Windsor, once considered little more than an affordable bedroom community, with a population of 26,500. During the past few years, the crumbling downtown area has literally been rebuilt from the ground up with colorful Old West–inspired live/work buildings surrounding a spacious town green.

At the north end of the county is the town of Healdsburg, with a population of 11,700. Like Sonoma, the town has a delightful core centered on its plaza, a classic town square recently freshened up with a brand-new copper-roofed gazebo for staging concerts and other small-town affairs. Around the plaza you can find good food, chic clothing and accessories, art galleries, and a good dose of fine old relics. Wine-tasting rooms also occupy many storefronts around and near the plaza.

Just a short hop north on US 101 from Healdsburg is Geyserville, named for an area northeast of the town where natural steam vents from the earth. These fumaroles, as they are called, are visible from many points in the county, particularly on cool mornings.

Still farther north on US 101 is Cloverdale, a small, picturesque town of 8,700 souls nestled at the far end of the peaceful Alexander Valley, one of the county's prime grape-growing regions. Its downtown area has been rejuvenated, ideal for a pleasant walking experience to stores and restaurants. From this point north, the coast redwoods start to take over, though there are still large expanses of vineyards to be found in Sonoma's northern neighbor, Mendocino County (see the Day Trips chapter for more about these).

Phone Numbers for Visitors

Napa County

The Napa Valley Destination Council
1310 Napa Town Center, Napa
(707) 226-5813
www.legendarynapavalley.com

Napa Chamber of Commerce
1556 First Street, Napa
(707) 226-7455
www.napachamber.org

Yountville Chamber of Commerce
6484 Washington Street, Yountville
(707) 944-0904
www.yountville.com

St. Helena Chamber of Commerce
1010 Main Street, St. Helena
(707) 963-4456, (800) 799-6456
www.sthelena.com

Calistoga Chamber of Commerce
1506 Lincoln Avenue, Calistoga
(707) 942-6333
www.calistogafun.com

Sonoma County

Hispanic Chamber of Commerce of
Sonoma County
3033 Cleveland Avenue, Santa Rosa
(707) 575-3648
www.hcc-sc.com

Sonoma Valley Visitors Bureau
453 First Street E., Sonoma
(707) 996-1090, (800) 996-1090
www.sonomavalley.com

Sonoma Valley Chamber of Commerce
651 Broadway, Sonoma
(707) 996-1033
www.sonomachamber.com

Petaluma Chamber of Commerce
6 Petaluma Boulevard, Petaluma
(707) 762-2785
www.petalumachamber.com

Petaluma Visitors Center
210 Lakeville Street, Petaluma
(707) 769-0429, (877) 273-8258
www.petaluma.org/visitor

Cotati Chamber of Commerce
216 East School Street, Cotati
(707) 795-5508
www.cotati.org

Rohnert Park Chamber of Commerce
6050 Commerce Boulevard, Rohnert
Park
(707) 584-1415
www.rohnertparkchamber.org

Santa Rosa Convention & Visitors
Bureau and California Welcome Center
9 Fourth Street, Santa Rosa
(707) 577-8674, (800) 404-7673
www.visitsantarosa.com

Santa Rosa Chamber of Commerce
637 First Street, Santa Rosa
(707) 545-1414
www.santarosachamber.com

Sonoma County Tourism Bureau
420 Aviation Boulevard, Suite 106,
Santa Rosa
(707) 522-5800, (800) 576-6662
www.sonomacounty.com

Mark West Area Chamber of Commerce
4787 Old Redwood Highway, Santa Rosa
(707) 578-7975
www.markwest.org

continued

Windsor Chamber of Commerce &
Visitors Center
9001 Windsor Road, Windsor
(707) 838-7285
www.windsorchamber.com

Healdsburg Chamber of Commerce &
Visitors Bureau
217 Healdsburg Avenue, Healdsburg
(707) 433-6935, (800) 648-9922
(California only)
www.healdsburg.com

Geyserville Chamber of Commerce
(707) 857-3745
www.geyservillecc.com

Cloverdale Chamber of Commerce &
Visitors Center
105 North Cloverdale Boulevard,
Cloverdale
(707) 894-4470
www.cloverdale.net

Sonoma Coast Visitor Information/
Bodega Bay Area Chamber of Commerce
(707) 875-3866
www.bodegabay.com

Sebastopol Chamber of Commerce
265 South Main Street, Sebastopol
(707) 823-3032
www.sebastopol.org

Monte Rio Chamber of Commerce
(707) 865-1533
www.monterio.org

Forestville Chamber of Commerce
(707) 887-1111
www.forestvillechamber.org

Russian River Chamber of Commerce &
Visitor Center
16209 First Street, Guerneville
(707) 869-9000, (877) 644-9901
www.russianriver.com

Occidental Chamber of Commerce
(707) 874-3279
www.occidental.org

The Alexander Valley south of Cloverdale offers wine tasters a more relaxed alternative to the relative bustle of Napa and Sonoma Valleys. It may not have as many wineries, but it does have some good ones (see the Wineries chapter), and the traffic is comparatively light. In spring, when the winter rains have turned the hills a vivid green, the valley is especially charming—like a wee bit of the rolling Irish countryside.

Another smaller and similarly charming vale is the Dry Creek Valley, which lies west of Alexander Valley above Healdsburg. Here row upon row of vineyards line the rich valley floor and terraces climb up the gentle hillsides. At one time, Dry Creek Valley extended farther to the north, but much of it was submerged when Warm Springs

Dam was built in 1982. The dam gave birth to Lake Sonoma, a recreational area profiled more thoroughly in the Parks and Recreation chapter.

Despite the scarcity of wineries compared with other areas, western Sonoma County offers much to see. Bodega Bay is the gateway to the Pacific Ocean, and where Highway 1 kisses the coast and begins its circuitous trek northward. Much of the Alfred Hitchcock thriller *The Birds* was filmed in 1963 in both Bodega Bay and the slightly inland enclave of Bodega.

The movie featured Bodega's Potter School, a one-room schoolhouse built a century before Hitchcock's cameras rolled into town. Now privately owned and occupied upstairs, the building has a small gift shop as you walk in the front door featuring merchandise emblazoned with images from the film. I'm told it's not uncommon to see visitors running downhill from the school—arms flailing to scare away imaginary crows—to re-create the famous scene from the movie for their companions' camera phones and camcorders.

Bodega Bay is one of the largest fishing ports between San Francisco and Eureka. In September and October the locals like to celebrate what they call "secret summer," when temperatures are relatively mild and the morning fog quickly disperses. The hook-shaped peninsula that shields the harbor from the open sea is Bodega Head. You can drive out on the headland along Westshore Road, which offers brilliant views and access to beaches and cliffs. Even if the weather is clear and sunny, you can usually count on strong winds on the Head.

The town of Jenner lies about 7 miles north of Bodega Bay, at the point where the Russian River meets the sea. Dozens of harbor seals congregate near the town, growing fat on steelhead and other fish that migrate upriver. North of Jenner the coastal settlements are few and far between. Once the easternmost outpost of czarist Russia, Fort Ross is now a state historic park (see the History and Attractions chapters).

Russian geographers will also recognize the name Sebastopol. The Wine Country town with a population of 7,700 that shares this name with the Crimean city is located between Santa Rosa and the coast. Sebastopol rose to prominence on the cores of a billion Gravenstein apples—the delectable fruit that got its start here. The community has honored the revered apple by naming Highway 116, which runs through the heart of town, the Gravenstein Highway, and every summer it hosts the Gravenstein Apple Fair (see the Festivals and Annual Events chapter).

West and north of Sebastopol is the town of Forestville, which serves as a way station for travelers headed to the Russian River and the Pacific coast. Nearby is the all-but-forgotten town of Occidental, perched at the top of a hill in the middle of redwood country. Anchored by a couple of family-style Italian restaurants, it's a quirky town with gift shops and other stores whose main thoroughfare goes by the name Bohemian Highway. Occidental is also where you catch one of the most fascinating and meandering roads in all of Sonoma County: Coleman Valley Road. It's not for white-knuckle drivers, but if you have the time to slow down and soak up the scenery on your way out to the ocean, it's a worthwhile way to get there. The road ends at Highway 1, a few miles north of Bodega Bay. The view as you descend to the coast is breathtaking.

Where the Bohemian Highway meets the Russian River just north of Occidental is the tiny town of Monte Rio, whose freestanding movie theater, the Rio, is covered in colorful murals. Farther to the east along Highway 116 is Guerneville (pronounced GURN-ville). This former lumber capital–cum–summer resort is sometimes referred to as the Gay Riviera, because of the large gay population that lives and weekends here.

While Guerneville is the largest town in the Russian River resort area, Duncans Mills is one of the smallest. Located about 4 miles before Highway 116 joins Highway 1, the town looks much as it did when it was the western terminus of the Northwest Pacific Railroad. A museum recalls the glory days of the beloved choo-choo, and a sprinkling of shops and restaurants provides plenty of distractions.

GETTING HERE, GETTING AROUND

Napa and Sonoma counties are predominantly agricultural areas, so first-time visitors to Wine Country are usually surprised by the large expanse of the region. This section of Northern California is not crisscrossed by fast-moving freeway systems, thank goodness, and it may take more time than you think to get from one place to another. (See the maps at the front of this book to get a feel for the lay of the land and distances between destinations.) The trade-off is spectacular scenery and a slower, more laid-back lifestyle as you wind your way along our highways and byways.

Major Wine Country thoroughfares run north–south, generally along the principal valleys. They are occasionally linked by roads and highways that run east–west, with the latter often traversing the hills and ranges that divide the region. I cover the major highways here, starting with the four primary routes. Unless otherwise stated, all roads mentioned are two-lane highways. In addition to the route descriptions, I've provided information on public and private transportation, including airports, shuttle services, Amtrak and Greyhound, taxis, limousines, and public buses.

One word of advice: Use your common sense when it comes to wine tasting and driving. If you plan to drive to a series of tasting rooms, designate one person to drink in moderation (or literally only "taste"—as in swirl, sniff, sip, and spit) or, preferably, rent a limo and see Wine Country safely and in style. Remember, the legal blood-alcohol threshold in California is 0.08 percent. That is lower than some visitors are accustomed to, and it is possible to be over this limit without feeling particularly buzzed. So play it safe. Don't drink and drive. If you're not sure, you probably are drunk, at least by California Highway Patrol standards. More important, even if you are sober, others on the road might not be.

BY AUTOMOBILE

The Main North–South Arteries

Highway 29

This is the main traffic corridor of Napa Valley for both locals and visitors, and because of that it can get bogged down in certain spots. The highway begins in Vallejo and passes through the town of American Canyon before reaching the city of Napa about 12 miles later. North of Napa, the road quickly becomes a ride in a wine-theme amusement park. It winds through some of the finest wine-grape acreage in America and connects the valley's towns: Yountville, Oakville, Rutherford, St. Helena, and Calistoga. Its shoulders are weighed down by châteaus, fortresses, Victorians, and renowned restaurants. Wine Country heavyweights such as Domaine Chandon and Robert Mondavi are here, and so are great historic wineries like Beringer and Charles Krug (see the Wineries chapter). Highway 29 is also commonly referred to as St. Helena Highway, and you will see it used frequently in addresses, as in this book. You will also see and hear the expression "upvalley" from time to time. This generally refers to the area of the valley north of Yountville.

Highway 29 is four lanes from Vallejo to Yountville; two thereafter. The road makes a sharp right when it gets to Calistoga and proceeds through the mostly vintage downtown. It leaves Calistoga and heads due north, climbing the flank of Mount St. Helena and dropping into the flats of Lake County.

i As you zip along Highway 29 on your way to Napa, watch for a hilltop statue just west of the intersection with Highway 221. Cast in bronze by sculptor Gino Miles, *The Grapecrusher* greets visitors atop a vista point. The sculpture was erected in 1987 to pay tribute to the farmworkers who toil in the vineyards.

Highway 12

Highway 12 travels east–west for most of its length, but it achieves acclaim for a relatively short north–south stretch that runs through the Sonoma Valley. Soon after joining with Highway 29 just below Napa, Highway 12 breaks west, hooking up with Highway 121 and skirting the Carneros Valley before crossing the Napa-Sonoma border. It then splits north to begin its renowned tour past wineries and hot springs and through classic Wine Country towns (and often referred to in addresses as Sonoma Highway through this stretch). It veers west after Kenwood, soon widening to four lanes in east Santa Rosa and continuing through stop-and-go and freeway-style traffic before reaching Sebastopol, where it narrows again to two lanes.

U.S. Highway 101

U.S. Highway 101, also known as the Redwood Highway, doesn't have the charm of Highways 29 or 12. As the major freeway for Sonoma County, it serves commuters, truckers, farmers, and all manner of passersby, who may travel it south to Hollywood or north to Oregon.

US 101 enters Sonoma County about 5 miles south of Petaluma and continues on to Rohnert Park, Santa Rosa, Healdsburg, Cloverdale, and into Mendocino County. The southern Wine Country stretch of US 101—from Petaluma to Windsor—is rather developed and populated, and traffic tends to creep along close to rush hour, but snarls can occur any time of day. This stretch

of the highway has been undergoing a long-overdue widening project that isn't expected to be fully completed until 2010. Throughout Santa Rosa proper, US 101 is being widened to six lanes. Construction to widen this highway to six lanes north of Santa Rosa to Windsor and south of Santa Rosa to Cotati was scheduled to get under way early in 2009.

Highway 1

Highway 1 is a destination unto itself. Though the Sonoma Coast stretch of the highway may not be as celebrated as the Big Sur–Carmel section to the south, it does offer approximately 50 miles of breathtaking coastal landscape, jaw-dropping vistas of the craggy coastline and the ocean to the west, and stands of coast live oak, pine, fir, or coast redwoods to the east.

Snaking its way north through Marin County, Highway 1 cuts over to the ocean at Bodega Bay, about 8 miles after it enters Sonoma County. The highway intersects numerous parks and places to play on its ascent through Wine Country (see the Parks and Recreation chapter). It also is the main artery for the coastal town of Jenner and the Sea Ranch community farther north. You'll notice that the road is often designated as Coast Highway 1.

One note of realism: The Sonoma Coast is not 50 miles you can drive in less than an hour. Highway 1 is a road that requires both hands on the wheel. The route regularly curves up, down, and around. At times your top speed may be 10 miles per hour as you maneuver hairpin turns. If the sometimes roller-coaster drive gives you or your passengers the heebie-jeebies, there are many opportunities to pull over at vista points and into parking areas for the state beaches. Besides, you may want to do a little beachcombing and watch surfers in action.

i Pull over to talk! California law prohibits handheld cell phone use while driving. If you lack a headset or speaker-phone, find a safe place to stop, or call that by-appointment-only winery to arrange a visit before you get behind the wheel.

Other Wine Country Roadways
Highway 121

This highway joins Sonoma with the Lake Berryessa highlands, via Napa. The route is born at Sears Point, site of the famed Infineon Raceway at the southern tip of Sonoma County (see the Spectator Sports chapter). As it heads north through this section, it is sometimes referred to as Arnold Drive in addresses. South of the town of Sonoma it makes a sharp right to join Highway 12 on its way to Napa Valley.

Highway 121 travels through the Carneros grape-growing region, which has only a few wineries but some of the most coveted vineyards in the state. The road intersects Highway 29 and is lured north, but it quickly departs with three sharp turns—right, left, and right again—through the city of Napa. Highway 121 then assumes a winding northeasterly course into the hills before it enters Highway 128 not far from Lake Berryessa.

Highway 128

Best known as the path through the Alexander Valley wine region, Highway 128 is a rambling roadway that periodically hitches northward rides to augment its own northwesterly journey. It enters Napa County from the east, navigating the steep hills that hug Lake Berryessa. It sneaks around the southwest fingers of the lake, then follows Sage Creek west into Napa Valley. When it gets to Rutherford, Highway 128 joins Highway 29 on a northern jaunt through the vineyards. But when Highway 29 makes a right turn into Calistoga, Highway 128 continues northwest, into rustic Knights Valley and then lovely Alexander Valley with its first-rate wineries.

> **i** Coast Highway 1 several miles north of Jenner follows a steep serpentine route—affectionately but unofficially called Dramamine Drive. The highway climbs high up the Coast Range, offering spectacular views of the ocean below.

Highway 128 meets US 101 just north of Geyserville and follows it to Cloverdale. It then breaks away again, heading northwest into Mendocino County.

Highway 116

Highway 116 is the paved shadow of the Russian River for a good part of its length. After connecting Sonoma and Petaluma in southern Sonoma County, it joins with US 101 up to Cotati, then splits off and heads northwest through Sebastopol and Forestville. It's a perfectly nice highway during all that, but Highway 116 really shines just as it reaches Guerneville and follows the river to the coast. The water sparkles, the sunlight blinks through the trees, and the ocean feels just a few curves away.

BY AIR

Three major airports serve Wine Country on its periphery—San Francisco, Oakland, and Sacramento—each of them as inconveniently located as the next. Among the big three profiled here, the Oakland and Sacramento airports are slightly more efficient if you are entering Wine Country through Napa or the town of Sonoma. Figure on 75 to 90 minutes to drive from Oakland or Sacramento to Napa, and about the same from San Francisco to Santa Rosa. Of course San Francisco offers a longer lineup of airlines. Most of the major rental car companies serve all three airports.

Major Airports
SAN FRANCISCO INTERNATIONAL AIRPORT (SFO)
San Francisco
(650) 821-8211, (800) 435-9736
www.flysfo.com

With millions of passengers a year, San Francisco International Airport (SFO) is among the busiest airports in the United States and the world. Located 14 miles south of downtown San Francisco, the airport is surrounded by more than 2,700 acres of undeveloped tidelands. The runways you see today were built on land reclaimed from San Francisco Bay.

Over the past few years the airport was significantly renovated and expanded, at a cost of approximately $3 billion. This includes a 2.5-million-square-foot international terminal that increased the number of gates from 10 to 24; two parking garages; a centralized rental car facility; a BART (Bay Area Rapid Transit) station; and an AirTrain system to move passengers between terminals.

Every major airline carrier, and virtually every smaller carrier with any sort of presence in the western United States, touches down at SFO. If you're in doubt about service from a specific airline, contact the airport or your travel agent.

There are outlets for all the expected rental car companies at the airport. Here are the contact numbers you will need: National, (650) 616-3000; Budget, (650) 877-0998; Dollar, (866) 434-2226; Hertz, (650) 624-6600; Avis, (650) 877-6780; Enterprise, (650) 697-9200; Thrifty, (877) 283-0898; and Alamo, (650) 616-2400.

Parking fees are $1 for 12 minutes, $13 daily in long-term parking, and $33 daily in short-term parking.

OAKLAND INTERNATIONAL AIRPORT (OAK)
Oakland
(510) 563-3300
www.flyoakland.com
www.oaklandairport.com
Oakland International Airport (OAK) is smaller and less ambitious than its neighbor to the west, and that is exactly what makes it more attractive to many Wine Country visitors. With only two terminals and a dozen airlines, it can be a painless experience.

South of downtown Oakland, the airport is at the Hegenberger Road exit from Interstate 880. Once you're inside, there are 14 boarding gates at Terminal One and 8 at Terminal Two, where no gate is farther than 400 feet from the curb. Terminal Two is devoted entirely to Southwest Airlines, which bases hundreds of pilots and flight attendants in Oakland.

Several major and regional airlines service OAK. These include Alaska, Continental, Delta, Horizon, JetBlue, Southwest, United, and US

Airways. Eight car rental companies operate at the airport. Local numbers are Hertz, (800) 654-3131; Avis, (800) 331-1212; Budget, (800) 527-0700; Dollar, (800) 800-4000; National, (800) 227-7368; Thrifty, (800) 847-4389; Fox, (800) 225-4369; and Enterprise, (800) 261-7331. All the parking lots charge $2 for the first 30 minutes, but daily rates vary: It's $32 in the hourly lot, $19 long-term in the daily lot, and $15 in economy.

SACRAMENTO INTERNATIONAL AIRPORT (SMF)
Sacramento
(916) 929-5411
www.sacairports.org
It used to be that politicians shuttling back and forth between their constituents and the state capital created most of the traffic at Sacramento International Airport (SMF), about 10 miles north of downtown Sacramento (and accessible from Interstate 5). But this is now one of the busiest airports in the nation, and a terminal that opened in 1996 effectively doubled the size of the facility.

Fourteen major air carriers serve the Sacramento airport—Air Canada, Alaska, American, Continental, Delta, Frontier, Hawaiian, Horizon, JetBlue, Mexicana, Northwest, Southwest, United, and US Airways. Several of the usual rental car agencies can provide you with wheels at SMF. Phone numbers are Hertz, (800) 654-3131; Avis, (800) 331-1212; Budget, (800) 763-2999; National, (800) 227-7366; Alamo, (800) 327-9633; Dollar, (800) 800-4000; and Enterprise, (800) 736-8227. Depending on the garage, parking runs about $1 for the first hour, $2 per hour thereafter in the hourly lot, with a maximum of $26 a day. The daily lots charge $7 to $12 per day.

CHARLES M. SCHULZ–SONOMA COUNTY AIRPORT
2200 Airport Boulevard, Santa Rosa
(707) 565-7240
www.sonomacountyairport.com
This airport was renamed in 2000 to honor the late Charles Schulz, of Peanuts fame, who lived in Santa Rosa for several decades. A $3 million upgrade of the runways and main taxiways was

completed in 2001, and renovations continue. An ambitious $84 million expansion plan was announced in 2007 to accommodate growth over several years and build longer runways. Also in 2007, the airport began regular commercial service again, with round-trip Horizon Air flights daily to Los Angeles, Seattle, and Las Vegas on comfortable, 74-passenger jets.

Meanwhile, private planes are always welcome, and 20 hangars were built in 2001 to accommodate them. There are no landing fees, though the overnight rate is $6 to $25, and the monthly rate can range from $42 to $175 (depending on wingspan). This airport is also a commercial balloon launch and landing site—an added bonus!

A "Snoopy Store" gift shop, stocked with apparel and accessories bearing the Peanuts character in his Flying Ace persona, was scheduled to open in 2008. The Sky Lounge Steakhouse and Raw Bar serves breakfast, lunch, and dinner.

The airport is about 7 miles north of downtown Santa Rosa, 2.2 miles west of US 101 on Airport Boulevard. Hertz, (800) 654-3131 or (707) 528-0834; Enterprise, (707) 570-3600 or (800) RENT-A-CAR; and Avis, (800) 331-1212 or (707) 571-0465, offer rental car services at this airport. The daily rate for long-term parking is $6, or it's $36 per week.

Smaller Wine Country Airports

The region includes several smaller airports open to private planes. I start with a description of the larger of these airports, then follow with an alphabetical listing of the most accessible, with numbers you can call for details. Figure on no landing fees and inexpensive overnight charges.

NAPA COUNTY AIRPORT
2030 Airport Road, Napa
(707) 253-4300
www.napacountyairport.org
Perhaps the most elaborate of the small airports, Napa County's offers Bridgeford Flying Service and Jonesy's Famous Steakhouse, both in

business here for more than 50 years. The building of this airport was the result of the attack on Pearl Harbor, when an air defense field was first constructed at this site in 1942. Ironically, Japan Air Lines has maintained a multimillion-dollar pilot training facility on the grounds since 1971.

When Auction Napa Valley and the major road races at Infineon Raceway take place, this airport is at its busiest with a flurry of private jets arriving and departing. With numerous corporate jets based here, there's a long waiting list for hangar space. The airport is 1 mile west of the intersection of Highways 12 and 29. There is no landing fee for private planes. The overnight fee is $5 for a single-engine plane, $8 for a double-engine, and $20 for a commercial plane.

ANGWIN AIRPORT
100 Angwin Avenue, Angwin
(707) 965-6219

CLOVERDALE MUNICIPAL AIRPORT
220 Airport Road, Cloverdale
(707) 894-1895

HEALDSBURG MUNICIPAL AIRPORT
1580 Lytton Springs Road, Healdsburg
(707) 433-3319

PETALUMA MUNICIPAL AIRPORT
601 Sky Ranch Road, Petaluma
(707) 778-4404

SONOMA SKY PARK
21870 Eighth Street E., Sonoma
(707) 996-2100

SONOMA VALLEY AIRPORT
23980 Arnold Drive, Sonoma
(707) 938-5382

Airport Shuttles

If you enter Wine Country via San Francisco International Airport, Oakland International Airport, or the Sonoma County Airport, you don't have to be stranded at the baggage carousel. The following carriers specialize in transportation between these airports. It's customary to tip your shuttle driver, particularly if he or she stows and retrieves your bags for you.

Napa County

EVANS AIRPORT SERVICE
4075 Solano Avenue, Napa
(707) 255-1559
www.evanstransportation.com
Evans Airport Service, long the prime mode of getting to SFO from Napa (or vice versa), goes to OAK too. Evans has eight daily departures to San Francisco and five daily runs to Oakland. The fare is $29 one-way from Evans's large, patrolled lot, but children younger than 13 ride for half price. They can also arrange pickups from about 25 Napa Valley hotels and inns, for $45 one-way, with 24-hour notice. To get to Evans take Highway 29 to Trower Avenue and go west 1 miniblock to Solano Avenue, the frontage road. Turn right and look for the first building past the fire station. Parking is $5 per day. An extensive array of charters and wine tours can also be arranged (see California Wine Tours in this chapter). You will notice their attractive vans and motor coaches frequently throughout Wine Country.

Sonoma County

SONOMA COUNTY AIRPORT EXPRESS
5807 Old Redwood Highway, Santa Rosa
(707) 837-8700, (800) 327-2024
www.airportexpressinc.com
The Airport Express makes 15 daily runs from the Sonoma County Airport to San Francisco International Airport and 10 runs daily to Oakland International Airport. There are three intermediate pickup/drop-off points: Days Inn at 3345 Santa Rosa Avenue, the DoubleTree Hotel at 1 DoubleTree Drive in Rohnert Park, and the Petaluma Fairgrounds at 175 Fairgrounds Drive in Petaluma. The one-way fare to either airport is $30 for adults, $28 for seniors, and free for kids under 12. Long-term parking at the Sonoma County Airport is $6 per day, parking is free for 72

hours at the DoubleTree lot, and secured parking at the Petaluma site costs $4 per day.

SONOMA AIRPORTER
18346 Sonoma Highway, Sonoma
(707) 938-4246, (800) 611-4246
www.sonomaairporter.com
The Airporter makes six daily runs (five on Saturday) from Sonoma Valley to SFO, with a connection in San Rafael. The nine-passenger vans will pick you up practically anywhere in Sonoma, Boyes Hot Springs, Glen Ellen, Kenwood, or Oakmont and deposit you at your terminal about one hour and 40 minutes later. The one-way fare is $50 for adults, $35 for children 2 to 11 (free for infants with an adult chaperone). Service to OAK is not provided at this time.

BY BUS/TRAIN

AMTRAK
1275 McKinstry Street, Napa
(800) 872-7245
www.Amtrak.com
No, the Napa Valley Wine Train, as described in this chapter's close-up, doesn't connect to an Amtrak line. The nearest Amtrak station to Wine Country is in Martinez, about 30 miles southeast of Napa. Amtrak runs buses from Napa, Petaluma, Rohnert Park, Santa Rosa, Healdsburg, and Cloverdale that will drop you off at an Amtrak station or deliver you from a station (even farther away from Wine Country, but still in the Bay Area, are stations in Oakland/Emeryville and San Jose). The fee varies with destination but generally is reasonable. From Martinez the rail line can take you practically anywhere in the country. Call Amtrak for details.

GREYHOUND BUS LINES
435 Santa Rosa Avenue, Santa Rosa
(707) 545-6495, (800) 231-2222
www.greyhound.com
Greyhound's only true Wine Country station is in Santa Rosa. Other towns—Napa, Petaluma, and Sonoma included—are flag stops. That means

they have infrequent but regular pickups at specific corners and parking lots. Call for details.

PUBLIC TRANSPORTATION

Public buses and vans might not be a viable
option for a week of exploring and wine tasting,
but they are handy for specific errands. And for
those of you who live here or stay with friends
for any significant time, they can be a blessing.
The Wine Country has an extensive network of
intercity and intracity public vehicles, many of
which are connected by a transfer system. Only
basic information is provided below; please call
for more details.

Napa County

THE VINE (NAPA VALLEY TRANSIT)
1151 Pearl Street, Napa
(707) 251-2800, (800) 696-6443,
www.nctpa.net/vine.cfm
The VINE is a multiline municipal bus service
within Napa Valley. Five lines are within the city
of Napa and its environs; a sixth runs all the
way from Vallejo to Calistoga (this was formerly
known as the Napa Valley Transit, and locals
might still refer to it as NVT). The basic fare in
town is $1.25 for adults (more for the longer
route), $1.00 for students, and 60 cents for seniors
and the disabled. All the buses are accessible by
wheelchairs and have bicycle racks. Daily service
is offered, but weekend schedules are slightly
more limited.

Sonoma County

GOLDEN GATE TRANSIT (SANTA ROSA TO SAN FRANCISCO)
Pioneer Way and Industrial Drive
(707) 541-2000, (415) 455-2000
www.goldengate.org
Golden Gate Transit (GGT) is a comprehensive
network that connects San Francisco with that
amorphous region known as the North Bay. Most
of the routes end in Marin County, but several
continue north into Sonoma County. There are
service points in the Sonoma Valley, Petaluma,

Cotati, Rohnert Park, Santa Rosa, and Sebastopol.
The basic adult fares vary from $7.60 to $8.40 one-
way to or from San Francisco to Sonoma County,
depending on where you embark. Kids, seniors,
and the disabled ride for about half price. (Fares
are cash only, and you must have exact change.)
Once in San Francisco you get transfer privileges
for the Bay Area Rapid Transit system (BART) and
the San Francisco Municipal Railway (Muni). Call
for schedule information and locations of GGT's
nine park-and-ride lots in Wine Country.

HEALDSBURG MUNICIPAL TRANSIT
401 Grove Street, Healdsburg
(707) 431-3324
http://healdsburgtransit.org
This in-city bus has only one route, but it tries its
damnedest to hit every corner in town, making
almost 60 stops. The busier pickup points get
hourly service between 8:30 a.m. and 4:30 p.m.
The standard adult fare is $1.25, falling to 75
cents for students and 60 cents for seniors and
the disabled.

PETALUMA TRANSIT
555 North McDowell Boulevard, Petaluma
(707) 778-4460
Three routes serve downtown Petaluma and its
surroundings. Buses generally run every hour
between 6:30 a.m. and 6:00 p.m. with a con-
densed schedule on Saturday and no service on
Sunday. Adults and students ride for $1, seniors
and the disabled for 50 cents, and children five
or younger for free. Discounted monthly and
multiride passes are available.

SANTA ROSA CITYBUS
Second and B Streets, Santa Rosa
(707) 543-3333, (707) 543-3926 (TDD)
This network offers 13 convenient routes within
the Santa Rosa city limits plus free transfers to
Golden Gate Transit or Sonoma County Transit.
Most CityBuses operate from 6:00 a.m. to 8:00 p.m.
Monday through Friday, 8:00 a.m. to 5:30 p.m. on
Saturday, and 10:00 a.m. to 5:00 p.m. on Sunday.
The fares are $1 for adults, 75 cents for students,

50 cents for seniors, and free for children five or younger. Monthly passes are available.

SONOMA COUNTY TRANSIT
(Petaluma to Cloverdale)
355 West Robles Avenue, Santa Rosa
(707) 576-7433, (800) 345-7433
www.sctransit.com
Sonoma County Transit (SCT) serves an area bounded by Petaluma to the south, Sonoma to the east, Cloverdale to the north, and Occidental to the west, with most of the action in the vicinity of US 101. Basic adult fares run from $1.15 to $3.10, depending on distance. Kids get a small discount, while seniors and the disabled ride for half price. SCT offers transfers to Santa Rosa CityBus, Golden Gate Transit, and the Sonoma County municipal transit systems that lie within a designated area. Most buses run from 5:00 a.m. to 10:30 p.m. during the workweek and 7:00 a.m. to 7:00 p.m. on weekends.

BY LIMOUSINE

You see so many stretch limos in some parts of Wine Country that you'll swear the Academy Awards are at the next intersection. During a recent spin through Napa Valley on a holiday weekend, I lost count of the number of limos on the road and idling in winery parking lots, chauffeurs leaning patiently against the shiny vehicles, waiting for their passengers to emerge from tasting rooms. This comforts me, because it means there are fewer tipsy drivers behind the wheels of rental cars. It just makes good sense to leave the driving to someone who hasn't lifted a wineglass to his or her lips all afternoon. If no one in your group volunteers for designated-driver duties, a limousine will escort you from winery to winery, freeing you up to act silly and for a few brief hours feel like a movie star.

The chauffeurs are knowledgeable about the region and its vintages, and can provide you with as little or as much information as you desire while rolling through the countryside. Most limo businesses prefer not to quote rates until you call, because the variables—type of car, size of party,

day of the week, distance, and so on—are multiple. Many feature special tours to particular Wine Country regions for a fixed per-person rate, with a complimentary glass of sparkling wine to jumpstart your journey. In general there's usually a three- to four-hour minimum, and basic rates can start at $60 and go up. Fuel surcharges may also apply, and tip your driver generously—please.

Here's a sampling of services offered by a few regional limo companies. To avoid confusion, this category isn't divided by county. Most of these providers routinely crisscross the two counties to satisfy the whims of their customers. Many will also take you beyond Wine Country if your heart desires, or for more practical reasons, such as to and from the major airports. Exceptions are noted in the descriptions.

ANTIQUE TOURS
(707) 226-9227
www.antiquetours.net
After 20 years in business, this company still stands out for one simply luxurious reason: its small fleet of restored 1947 Packard convertible limos, which can accommodate up to seven passengers. Little did you know that postwar Packards were equipped with stereos, ice drawers, and air-conditioning. Rates begin at $130 per hour for two to three passengers, with a five-hour minimum. Gourmet picnic lunches can also be added.

BEAU WINE TOURS
(800) 387-2328, (707) 938-8001
Sit back and leave the driving to Beau. Their drivers know the region up, down, and sideways and will whisk you off on a customized tour, along with gourmet lunches. A town car can be yours for $65 per hour, with more luxurious limos running about $90. A stretch Hummer, if that's your thing, is $165 per hour.

CALIFORNIA WINE TOURS
4075 Solano Avenue, Napa
22455 Broadway, Sonoma
(800) 294-6386
www.californiawinetours.com
These operators deserve mention for their

extensive wine knowledge and detailed suggestions. This full-service transportation company offers just about everything from intimate sedan- and stretch-limo service, to minibuses and custom vans, to deluxe motor coaches for larger events and tours. (The company has partnered with Evans Airport Service—see the listing in this chapter—to expand its fleet and offer more touring options to visitors.) For those who wish to ride "green," California Wine Tours maintains a fleet of luxury hybrid vehicles. They can add light breakfasts, lunches, wine, and snacks to your journey, and provide complimentary high-speed wireless Internet on the Prius sedan. The options for tours are many and varied. For instance, a personalized sparkling-wine cellar tour of Domaine Carneros, Gloria Ferrer, and Artesa wineries starts at $50 per hour in a green vehicle. Pour the bubbly!

CELEBRITY LIMOUSINE
(707) 552-7752
www.celeblimo.com
What's a limo without a flat-screen TV and crystal stemware? Celebrity has the luxury sedan or stretch vehicle you're seeking. Private tour packages for up to eight passengers (five-hour minimum) begin at $299; seven-hour trips run $399.

NAPA VALLEY CROWN LIMOUSINE
(800) 286-8228
www.napalimo.com
The proprietors of this service have plenty of experience in the tourist biz. Before getting behind the wheel, they ran a bed-and-breakfast inn and a tourist information office, so their winery knowledge is superior. Basic eight-passenger rentals are $65 an hour during the week, $75 an hour on weekends.

NAPA VALLEY TOURS & TRANSPORTATION
(707) 251-9463 (WINE)
www.nvtt.net
The usual choices apply here: sedans, stretch limos, vans, buses, mini coaches, land yachts, and the S Class Mercedes. Group tours start at $59 per person. This carrier can arrange special

tours of smaller, family-run wineries more off the beaten path, and add a picnic lunch to enhance the experience.

NAPA WINERY SHUTTLE
(707) 257-1950
www.wineshuttle.com
Sip, swish, and spit all you wish, then leave the driving to these folks. Though not a luxury limo experience, this shuttle service operates much like one but for fewer bucks. Providing door-to-door pickups and drop-offs at just about any Napa Valley hotel or bed-and-breakfast inn, the cheerful drivers chauffeur you to a series of wineries, with pit stops at a couple of restaurants. Upon request, they can personalize your journey, and pick up and deliver your wine purchases too. The service's fleet of white, 14-passenger, nonsmoking vans is top of the line, with plush interiors for extra comfort. The drivers, all longtime valley residents, provide interesting commentary and history as you glide worry-free from one place to the next. A full-day excursion with unlimited stops runs about $60 per person.

PACIFIC LIMOUSINE
(707) 792-1500, (877) 333-3613
www.pacificlimo.com
Pacific has been operating since 1994. The charge is $55 per hour for a town-car limo. The flat rate to either San Francisco International or Oakland International Airport is $180.

PURE LUXURY
(800) 626-5466 (LIMO)
www.pureluxury.com
www.pureluxurywinetours.com
Pure Luxury will take you anywhere in Wine Country, for any reason: wine tours, weddings, airport transportation—you name it. Call to customize a tour, whether for two in a tricked-out sedan or for 35 in a comfortable shuttle bus. A five-hour tour of the Alexander Valley runs $79 per person; a Sonoma Valley tour with lunch is $90 per person. A six-person minimum applies for the package tours.

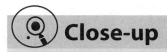

Close-up

Vintage Railroad: All Aboard the Napa Valley Wine Train

The Napa Valley Wine Train moves slowly through vineyards, giving passengers a close view of the scenery while they dine.

COURTESY OF NAPA VALLEY WINE TRAIN

If you spend any significant time driving the length of Napa Valley, you will eventually see it: a chain of exquisite railroad cars, painted "burgundy, champagne gold, and grapeleaf green," rumbling along at a luxuriously unhurried gait. It's the Napa Valley Wine Train, a rolling ringside seat for taking in the scenery of the valley.

The train cars are beautiful, with Honduran mahogany paneling, brass bathroom fixtures, etched glass partitions, crystal chandeliers, and wool carpeting. Norman Roth, the San Francisco–based designer who oversaw the interior design, patterned the cars after early-20th-century classics such as the Venice-Simplon Orient Express and the Andalusian Express, and they aren't far off the mark. (In 1997 the Wine Train added a double-decked dome car, built for the Milwaukee Road Railroad Line in 1947.) Seated in one of the plush seats that swivel 360 degrees, you can point yourself at the window and watch the Wine Country pass by at a leisurely 15 to 20 miles per hour. It's a hypnotic sensation.

The Wine Train Depot is at 1275 McKinstry Street in Napa, near the corner of Soscol Avenue and First Street. Before you board, a Wine Train representative conducts a quickie seminar, explaining how the senses of taste, smell, and touch combine to help you enjoy the experience.

All in all, you'll travel 36 miles from Napa to St. Helena, past two dozen wineries and countless acres of vines. St. Helena is the midpoint, and there is no turnaround loop there. The two engines, connected back-to-back, are moved along parallel tracks to the back of the train, which then becomes the front. And then it's time for you to move too.

Unless you are in the dome car, you will either start with an hors d'oeuvres course in the parlor and move to a dining car for lunch, or eat the first two courses in a dining car, then retire to the parlor for dessert. The food is complemented by some 40 still wines and a small selection of sparkling wines; some are big names, some small, but all are from Napa Valley.

Prices for the Wine Train vary widely, depending on whether you choose lunch, dinner, or brunch, or prefer to dine on the twice-monthly Murder Mystery run. If you opt to sit in the dome car, the price is higher still. But expect to pay from $50 to more than $100 per person for this unique experience, and allow three to four hours to do so.

The Wine Train accepts most credit cards. Smoking is not permitted anywhere on board.

Whenever you ride the Napa Valley Wine Train, and whichever package you choose, reservations are a must. You can call (707) 253-2111 or (800) 427-4124 or visit the Web site at www.winetrain.com.

ROYAL COACH LIMOUSINE SERVICE

(800) 995-7692

www.royalcoachlimousine.com

You have a choice of six- or eight-passenger cars and a range of itineraries. Buses to accommodate 15 to 47 passengers can also be provided. Ask for Matt if you want to customize something special.

i **To toodle around downtown Napa, jump on the free trolley. There's a fixed route and a varied schedule, with several stops for hopping on and off, so check the latest postings at locations around downtown.**

BY TAXI

In Wine Country, "hailing a cab" means saluting a robust Cabernet Sauvignon. Your chances of flagging down a taxi on our roads are statistically smaller than your odds of being trampled by a cow. But there are several companies to get you from curb to curb, which is especially important if you are woozy from indulging in the grape. The standard rate is $3 baseline and $3 per mile thereafter.

In Napa County, you'll find Black Tie Taxi, (707) 259-1000 or (888) 544-8294; Napa Valley Cab, Napa, (707) 257-6444; Taxi Cabernet, St. Helena, (707) 963-2620 or (707) 942-2226; Valley Valet, (707) 942-9009; and Yellow Cab of Napa, (707) 226-3731 or (866) 226-3731.

In Sonoma County, there's A-1 Taxi of Petaluma, (707) 763-3393; A-C Taxi, Santa Rosa, (707) 526-4888; Bill's Taxi Service, Guerneville, (707) 869-2177; George's Taxi/Yellow Cab, Santa Rosa, (707) 546-3322 or (707) 544-4444; Healdsburg Taxi Cab, (707) 433-7088; and Vern's Taxi Service, Sonoma, (707) 938-8885.

HISTORY

The flags of Spain, England, Imperial Russia, Mexico, and the Bear Flag Republic have all flown over Wine Country at one time or another, a testament to the ambition, struggle, victories, and bitter disappointments of numerous explorers and conquerors. But before all the hubbub started, the region was home to Miwok, Pomo, Mayacoma, Yukia, and other indigenous peoples. Early descriptions of their lives evoke visions of a kind of Eden, where food was abundant and the mild climate permitted a life without the burden of clothes.

The gold rush of 1849 is perhaps the most renowned and defining event of Northern California history. The accidental discovery of one tiny nugget in 1848 by James Marshall, a moody carpenter working a sawmill in the Sierra foothills, set off one of the most frenzied mass migrations in history.

California was then newly a part of the United States, having been acquired from the Republic of Mexico—a remote, sparsely populated region cut off from the United States by 1,800 miles of broiling desert and nearly impassable mountain ranges. As news of the California Eldorado spread, hordes of gold seekers stampeded west, while others sailed from the East Coast around South America's Cape Horn. Some came from as far off as Germany, England, Wales, Ireland, and China. By the summer of 1849, more than 100 vessels floated empty in San Francisco Bay, their passengers and crew having forsaken all for a chance in the mines.

Through all this, the various settlers of the region had experimented with growing vines north of San Francisco. However, the area's potential was not fully recognized until a man by the name of Count Agoston Haraszthy arrived on the scene (see the close-up in this chapter). Not long afterward, vineyards began to stretch in neat rows to the horizon. With time, numerous wineries sprang up and the region began to slowly gain international fame as the California Wine Country.

NAPA COUNTY

For 10,000 years or more, the Pomos were the undisputed occupants of the lands of the upper Sonoma and Napa Valleys, on up to Clear Lake and the surrounding lands. They lived an orderly life, with the men carrying on the outdoor work and often specializing in fishing or crafting arrowheads. Marriage was conducted in traditional fashion, and babies were the domain of the women—mothers, grandmothers, aunts, and cousins.

The first white settler in the Napa Valley was George Yount—frontiersman, hunter, trapper, and mountain man. He had left his wife and three children in Missouri in 1832 to drive mules with a pack train to Santa Fe. The job fizzled, but Yount saw no reason to return to Missouri. Instead, his restless feet took him to California's coast, where he trapped beaver for a while. He eventually made his way north in the summer of 1834 to the mission in Sonoma.

Yount was a resourceful man who could do almost anything. In time he became acquainted with the Mexican commandant Mariano Vallejo (who later became General Vallejo), who needed a new roof for his hacienda. Soon Yount was turning out 1,000 shingles a day, and his payment likely came via a 12,000-acre Napa Valley land grant he received with Vallejo's help.

In 1836 Yount set about building a Kentucky-style blockhouse for himself. Then he erected a flour mill and a sawmill, planted wheat and potatoes, and started a small vineyard. Initially he believed that grapes were for eating, not for turning into wine. But Yount's name would eventually live on in Napa Valley history—the town of Yountville was named in his honor.

Soon another settler appeared on the scene—Dr. Edward Bale, a young English surgeon. His marriage to a niece of General Vallejo made him a Mexican citizen, and as such he was given a land grant north of Yount's. Bale established a sawmill to cut timber and a gristmill (still standing and known as Bale Mill) to grind the settlers' grain. The mills became centers of great activity and supplied work for new settlers, but the best was yet to come for Bale. When gold diggers poured into the state, flour became a premium product, and Bale's mill was a gold mine in its own right.

The near-wilderness aspect of the Napa Valley changed dramatically after gold was discovered in the Sierra foothills, 100 miles east of San Francisco, in 1848. The city by the bay, which boasted a population of less than 450, was virtually abandoned in the rush to the gold fields. And although Napa was 40 miles to the north—not exactly on the direct route to the foothills—large numbers of gold seekers did wander off course and find their way into the valley, on foot or on horseback.

Miners also found the valley a popular wintering place when rains drowned the mines. Some stayed in the area. In two years Napa's population tripled to 450. A census two years later showed a jump to 2,116 (including 252 women). In just one decade, wilderness had been transformed into populace.

City on the River

The first town in the valley, founded in 1836, was Napa City—not that it amounted to much. But soon after the discovery of gold, prosperity set in. The chief places of business were saloons, and the method of payment was likely to be gold dust. In fact, the change brought about by gold was amazing.

The only route into town, the Napa River, soon opened the region to the world. The channel was deep, so before long steamboats were plying the river, transporting passengers to San Francisco and Sacramento for a $1 fare, lunch included. But the river's main value was for moving freight. The valley's fertile soil was producing such a profusion of fruits and vegetables that ships lined up daily at the Napa docks to load up for the San Francisco market.

In the outlying Berryessa Valley, some 30 miles inland, wheat grew so abundantly it became an international product. Ships from foreign ports arrived regularly at the Napa embarcadero to load Napa County wheat. The river brought in industry that would last until the end of the century. Lined up along its shores were potteries, iron works, tile factories, and tanneries. The term "napa leather" earned its own listing in the dictionary as "a type of leather resembling the original glove leather made in Napa by tanning sheepskins with a soap and oil mixture."

Many residents prospered beyond their wildest dreams, and by the 1880s Napa had achieved fame for both its charm and vast wealth. That reputation brought in the bankers, who were by no means above ostentation in the building of their great Victorian mansions. Some of those homes still stand today as an architectural reminder of other times.

But it came to an abrupt end. Napa's river traffic was killed by a single structure—a bridge built across the Carquinez Straits between Martinez and Vallejo. That allowed trucks to come into Napa Valley for the first time.

Those Amazing Hot Springs

During the 1860s it became fashionable all over the country to "take the waters." Soaking in hot mineral baths or mineral-rich mud was touted to cure virtually every known ailment. The first entrepreneur to capitalize on these bubbling springs was Sam Brannan, who had become a millionaire selling shovels and picks to miners.

Some of that wealth was spent acquiring 1 square mile of land in the northern valley. It was

Brannan's vision to build an extravagant resort spa that would become a holiday retreat for San Francisco's shamefully rich. He called the place Calistoga—a combination of his fondness for Saratoga Springs and the word California. On the grounds there soon appeared a lavish hotel, 25 gingerbread cottages, an observatory tower, large stables with fine horses, a winery, and a distillery. The benefits of the hot springs, of course, were obvious and needed no further publicity.

In time, another hot springs resort, Napa Soda Springs, was developed 5 miles east of Napa City and took the place of Calistoga in the fickle favor of San Franciscans accustomed to lavish living. Banked against a flower-carpeted hillside, it presented an unequaled view of Napa Valley and San Pablo Bay. A good deal of faith was put in the healing powers of "a course at the springs." According to the report of a Dr. Anderson, the waters were beneficial "in the treatment of chronic metritis and ovaritis, for Bright's disease, acid blood, and dyspepsia."

i The Napa County Historical Society is housed in the Goodman Library in Napa, the oldest library in California still in use for that purpose. In addition to exhibits, there is also a tea room. Located at 1219 First Street downtown, the Historical Society is open to visitors between noon and 4:00 p.m. Tuesday through Saturday.

The Silver Commotion

In the winter of 1858, rumors started percolating that silver had been discovered in the mountains. In no time at all, every unemployed man had turned prospector. Most of those wielding a pick knew nothing of the characteristics of silver ledges, and outcrops of barren rock of any description were equally valuable to their ignorant eyes. Miners hauled their rocks to San Francisco, where reports came back "no silver at all" or "a trace." Fortune quickly turned to folly, and tons of shiny rocks were unloaded by the disenchanted miners to make paving material for the streets of Napa.

Of more serious import were the quicksilver mines that developed in the 1860s in the Mayacmas Mountains that separate the Napa and Sonoma Valleys. Mining quicksilver, or mercury, was a hazardous process, and newspapers of the day were filled with accident stories.

In the 1870s, silver fever struck again. A vein of silver was discovered in the Calistoga hills, and a new town sprang up around the diggings—Silverado City. The hillsides soon were pocked with mining claims, and the city prospered briefly. The vein was short lived, but the town's hotel and mining office became famous, for it was here that Robert Louis Stevenson spent his honeymoon.

It was a strange entourage that straggled into the Napa Valley on a warm May day in 1880—the gaunt, ailing Stevenson; his new bride, Fanny; her 12-year-old son; and a setter-spaniel named Chuchu. They had decided to honeymoon in Calistoga, hoping to cure the Scottish author's lung problems. They arrived at the Springs Hotel, where they lived a short time in a "cottage on the green," but after a couple of weeks they located cheaper quarters. They moved into the assayer's office and the bunkhouse of an abandoned silver mine as squatters, paying no rent.

With a secondhand cookstove and a few household effects pulled up the mountain by a new neighbor who was also a squatter, they settled down for the summer, living the free life of gypsies. Here Stevenson wrote in his journal the notes that became his first literary success, *The Silverado Squatters*.

The Emergence of Fine Wine

Although Yount and Bale were the first to raise grapes in Napa Valley, it seems doubtful either had the inclination to cultivate fine wines. That distinction came to several German immigrants who arrived in the 1870s: Jacob Schram (who barbered by day and planted vines by moonlight), Charles Krug (known as the father of Napa viniculture), Jacob and Frederick Beringer (Jacob was Krug's winemaker until he built his own winery), and Gottlieb Groezinger (his winery stands as Yountville's V Marketplace).

The 1870s marked tremendous growth in the Napa Valley wine industry. Local viticulture clubs began organizing in 1875, with Charles Krug chosen president of the largest. (A note that will come in handy: Generally speaking, we use "viticulture" when talking specifically about the science and practice of growing grapes, and "viniculture" to discuss the process of making wines.) About the same time, the Beringer brothers established their winery, complete with a cellar dug into a hillside by Chinese laborers and reinforced with stone—a feat of advanced architecture as well as masonry. Adding to the growth of the industry was an outbreak of phylloxera (a ravenous louse that eats the plant's roots) in French vineyards. Napa wineries continued to expand, with some 140 wineries producing almost five million gallons of wine.

Unfortunately, this led to overproduction. In the late 1880s growers were all feeling the pinch, and Charles Krug's vineyards and cellar went into receivership. More bad times loomed in the form of a general nationwide depression in 1890. But the blow that brought valley growers to their knees was the discovery that the dreaded, grapevine-ravaging phylloxera—for which there was no cure—had infected the vineyards of the entire area. By the turn of the 20th century, almost every vineyard had been ruined.

Plantings of resistant varieties brought fresh hope. Viticulture looked to be getting back on track. But those bright hopes were dashed by a new cataclysm called Prohibition. For the old-world grape growers, who considered wine the elixir of life, the law was inexplicable madness. The plague of Prohibition lasted for 14 years, from 1920 to 1933. Some vintners survived it by making sacramental or pharmaceutical wines. But for others it would take years to build back their businesses. Still, one thing was clear: There would be no returning to wheat or cattle raising. Napa County was on its way to becoming America's premier wine region.

By 1966 wine was becoming fashionable, not only in California but across the nation. Between 1966 and 1972 wine consumption doubled. Visitors started pouring into the area to look, sample, and buy. By the mid-'70s there were again more than 50 wineries in operation in Napa Valley, and a new promotional technique had been developed—wine tastings. To let the public see how great the product was, vintners opened their doors and uncorked their bottles for sampling. Many offered their cellars for touring.

In the 1980s viticulture became a sort of dream occupation—a creative endeavor that could be both financially rewarding and personally satisfying. New wineries popped up almost overnight, many operated by individuals drawn into the field because they savored living close to the soil. Wineries started gaining public acceptance by offering extra attractions—Shakespearean plays and readings in the caves and Mozart played on expansive green lawns. Wine Country golf courses and croquet courts drew international competition. Cooking classes featured famous chefs. It all drew attention to the work of the winemaker.

SONOMA COUNTY

In 1823 a zealous young Spanish priest, Father Jose Altimira, arrived in California and established the Mission San Francisco de Solano, northernmost in a chain of missions spaced a day's journey apart along California's coast. This mission was the only one to be dedicated after Mexico overthrew Spanish rule earlier that year. In fact, not everyone in the mission hierarchy thought it was a good idea. But Altimira was nothing if not enthusiastic, and he convinced his colleagues it would be a better climate than San Francisco for the Native American converts.

The mission was doomed from the start. A decree was passed down from the Mexican government that all church properties would be "secularized" (that is, confiscated). In 1834 a young lieutenant, Mariano Vallejo, was sent from Monterey to seize all mission property and dispose of grain fields and thousands of head of cattle, sheep, and horses. It was outright thievery carried out under the guise of eminent domain.

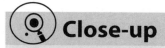

The Father of California Viticulture

Although many early settlers had started vineyards north of San Francisco, the first individual to recognize the area's potential for growing fine wine grapes was Count Agoston Haraszthy.

A flamboyant man who may or may not have been a true aristocrat, Haraszthy fled political turmoil in his native Hungary to seek his fortunes in America. His first endeavor in the New World was founding Sauk City, Wisconsin, where he built homes, mills, and stores; planted hops; and started a vineyard. The town remains to this day.

Once weary of that project, he headed to California along the Santa Fe Trail. He arrived at the gold fields on horseback, an argonaut in silken shirt, red sash, and velvet hat, seeking whatever opportunities might exist. Haraszthy was working as an assayer at the San Francisco mint when General Vallejo heard of the man's interest in viticulture. Vallejo invited him to Sonoma in 1856, whereupon Haraszthy quickly recognized the potential of Sonoma's soil. Convinced that grapes could prosper without irrigation, he sailed for Europe and returned with 300 varieties of grape cuttings, the basis for his 6,000-acre vineyards.

The winery he built was of massive stones, with cellars dug into the hillsides. For himself, he built a grand Pompeian-style villa. His fame spread quickly, and vintners from other parts of California, as well as those newly arrived from Europe, came to him for advice and for cuttings. It created something of a "grape rush" in the Sonoma and Napa Valleys.

But by 1868 the count was again restless and decided to turn his enthusiasm to raising sugar in Nicaragua. He left his two sons (who had married Vallejo daughters) to run the winery business. They never saw their father again, for he vanished mysteriously in the jungle. According to legend, he fell from a tree into a river and was devoured by crocodiles.

The villa he built in Sonoma was destroyed by the passage of time, but in the 1980s townsfolk built a replica next to the first vineyards he planted. Both are there to see today. Find it on Castle Road east of Sonoma, on your way to Bartholomew Park Winery.

A modern replica of Agoston Haraszthy's Sonoma home is on the outskirts of that town. JEAN SAYLOR DOPPENBERG

i In the late 1950s Pacific Gas & Electric Company selected Bodega Bay as the site for a nuclear power plant. The project was eventually abandoned in 1964, but not before construction had already begun. Fortunately, the idea has never been resurrected.

The mission's converts—turned loose to fend for themselves—were likely to have been grateful. They didn't much like Altimira, a cold and impersonal man, and they didn't care for the Spanish or the Mexicans, who were sometimes oppressive. In any case, the Mexican government had another, more serious reason to send an emissary into the territory—to discourage foreign invaders. Trappers were arriving in ever-increasing poaching forays over the Sierra Nevada, and some were staying on as settlers. And on the north coast Russian settlers had arrived from Alaska.

Meanwhile, young Lieutenant Vallejo brought his beautiful, cultured wife, Francisca Benicia, to this rough, untamed land and set up house in the abandoned mission. In one of its 37 rooms, their first daughter was born. In time, Vallejo set about creating the town of Sonoma. Using a pocket compass, he laid out an eight-acre plaza around which the town would rise. The plaza would serve as a promenade area for the populace as well as a parade ground where young soldiers could drill and practice their horsemanship. At the same time, Vallejo was preoccupied with developing a 66,000-acre ranch in the grasslands of Petaluma Valley, some 10 miles away. Built as a defense against intruders, the structure's walls were 3 feet thick, braced by redwood beams. It became a second home for the growing Vallejo family, which eventually numbered 15 children.

Some 2,000 American Indians (most of them transfers from the mission ranks) answered roll call daily in the courtyard before going to work making saddles and boots. These products were marketed to settlers or shipped to coastal communities as far south as San Blas, Mexico. Though it all seemed like a sustainable arrangement,

trouble was brewing behind the scenes. That trouble was the Bear Flag Republic.

The Bear Flag Rebellion

"About half past five in the morning of Sunday, June 14, a group of desperados surrounded the house of General Vallejo and arrested him," wrote his sister. "Vallejo, dressed in the uniform of a general, was the prisoner of this group of rough-looking men, some wearing on their heads caps made with the skins of coyotes or wolves. . . . Shoes were to be seen on the feet of 15 or 20 among the whole lot."

The issues surrounding this drama were complex. England, France, and the United States were each vying for the California territory, which Mexico was sure to relinquish (whether by force or purchase). General Vallejo argued in favor of American rule, while his rivals, General Pio Pico of Los Angeles and General Jose Castro of Monterey, strongly preferred the English or French to the Americans. Adding to this tense situation was the unexpected arrival in Monterey of Lieutenant John Charles Frémont of the U.S. Topographical Service, a surveyor purportedly on a mission to map a more direct route to the Pacific. Frémont rode in accompanied by a contingent of 62 armed U.S. cavalry.

Frémont did not hesitate in inciting the Mexican generals, going so far as to raise the Stars and Stripes over his camp. After some fierce posturing but no real fighting, Frémont moved north to Oregon. Following his departure, rumors began circulating that the Mexicans were about to evict all Americans from California. The story incited rage among local settlers, having been lured to California by the Mexican government's promise of land. They decided to take matters into their own hands.

Thirty-three renegade malcontents went to the Sonoma presidio to dispose of the Mexicans. Along the way they hastily fashioned a flag for the new republic, made of a woman's red flannel petticoat and a length of unbleached muslin. For their emblem they used berry juice to paint on it the picture of a bear (it looked more like a pig) and the words *California Republic.* The ever-cordial Vallejo brought up some wine for the group, and they spent some time in convivial conversation. But in the end, he was carried off to Sutter's Fort in Sacramento, where Vallejo's friend John Sutter reluctantly jailed him.

The California Republic lasted 26 days. On July 9, 1846, U.S. Navy Lieutenant Joseph Revere lowered the bear flag and replaced it with the American Stars and Stripes. Vallejo was released from jail August 6. He had been away no more than a month, but in that time his horses and cattle had been stolen and his fields stripped of grain.

The New State of California

The months that followed the rebellion brought mass confusion. Nobody knew who was in charge. A group of military volunteers known as Company C from New York City's Bowery arrived. But since there wasn't much for the soldiers to do (unless they wanted to stoop to manual labor), they improved their leisure by riding spirited horses, hunting waterfowl, and staging cruel bear-and-bull fights in a makeshift stadium behind their barracks.

The discovery of gold suddenly shifted everyone's attention. Settler and soldier alike left Sonoma to the womenfolk. The village sank into stagnation. Vallejo, on the other hand, wasn't too bad off. He had seen what was coming and had hedged his bets. While serving Mexico loyally (virtually without pay), he had also taken steps to ingratiate himself with the United States. In time he actually became a California senator.

But Vallejo's plans of becoming a prominent American somehow went awry. Lawsuit after lawsuit went against him, and his land empire disappeared. He slipped deeper into debt. One by one his dreams vanished. He did manage to hold on to his Sonoma home, Lachryma Montis, and here his wife—once pampered—sold dried fruit and chili peppers for the San Francisco market. In old age Vallejo became a symbol of the link between an idealized Mexican era and the Yankee-dominated present. In his unfailing dignity and hospitality, he seemed to personify all that was best about the past.

By the mid-1860s Sonoma had become almost totally neglected. There were no trees, and the plaza had degenerated. A fire in 1866 destroyed much of what the settlers had built. Some of the early pioneers responded by organizing a Pioneer Society of 340 members to revitalize the town. They planted trees, built fences, and cleaned up the plaza (appointing one member to be in charge of keeping livestock out of that area of town). Gradually the town took on a more respectable look, though the society itself fizzled out.

About 1888 many Italian immigrants came to quarry cobblestones for the streets of San Francisco. Among them was Samuele Sebastiani, who quickly recognized the possibilities for growing wine grapes. In no time at all he was supplying the demand of the growing Italian community for wine and making a name for his winery. Today the strong Italian influence remains in and around Sonoma.

One of Vallejo's mandates when he took over as commandant was to ensure that lands north of San Francisco were settled. At the time, this northern frontier was a lonesome wilderness, and Vallejo had some trouble convincing any of his fellow Californians to apply for grants. But he had plenty of relatives, so most of them fell heir to large tracts. In 1837 he convinced his widowed mother to leave her San Diego adobe and travel 700 miles to an area near Santa Rosa Creek. She packed up her nine children and seven-trunk wardrobe and built the Cabrillo adobe, the first bona fide home in the Santa Rosa Valley. In time it became the nucleus of a settlement.

Santa Rosa

In 1854 the town of Santa Rosa was little more than a trading post. A few small businesses and houses had sprung up along the creek, and the town had a representative in the state senate. That man was William Bennett, another former Missourian, and his ambition was to snatch the county seat from Sonoma. To help voters make up their minds on the issue, he hosted a big

Fourth of July barbecue attended by, according to one historian, "the lame, the halt and blind if they could influence a vote." Not surprisingly the vote went in favor of Santa Rosa. At daybreak a group of Santa Rosans, fearing Sonoma wouldn't release the county records, hired a wagon and raced to Sonoma, grabbed the records, and raced back to Santa Rosa.

Reporting the hijacking, the *Sonoma Bulletin* editor wrote, "We are only sorry they did not take the adobe courthouse too . . . its removal would have embellished our plaza." Within three years, according to the newly launched *Sonoma Democrat*, Santa Rosa had grown to 100 buildings. After the arrival of the railroad in 1870, the town's population exploded to 6,000.

About this time a shy, trim New Englander named Luther Burbank opened a nursery in the town and began experimenting on flowers, fruits, and vegetables. His uncanny talent for interpreting the results of his experiments earned him the lasting title of "plant wizard."

A wizard of a different sort next appeared in town—spiritualist-sage Thomas Harris, a man of magnetic personality and piercing eyes "like revolving lights." In the outlying area called Fountain Grove, Harris established the esoteric Brotherhood of New Life, a colony of communal living that separated its members from their spouses (and their cash) to await their celestial mates in another world. Harris claimed these other worlds were revealed to him during his conversations with the angels. It was left to a female reporter to provide the impetus to drive Harris from the gates of his Eden. She joined the group long enough to write a lurid exposé that sent the preacher packing.

The infamous 1906 earthquake that leveled San Francisco also struck Santa Rosa—nearby Petaluma, Santa Rosa's then rival, escaped virtually unscathed. The courthouse collapsed, and downtown buildings suffered devastating damage. Nearly 100 people died in the rubble, but the city's spirit survived. Although some residents did head for other parts, many townsfolk simply rolled up their sleeves and began to rebuild.

> **i** Take a brief walking tour of Petaluma's historic Victorian homes beginning on Fifth Street at A Street, and continuing on Liberty Street, switching over to Sixth Street, up D Street, and then down Fifth Street.

Petaluma

Before the advent of the railroads in the mid-1880s, rivers were the principal means of shipping goods inland. In the Petaluma River, steamboats—introduced to California during the gold rush—operated regularly during the 1850s, hauling wool, butter, cream, eggs, and live chicks down the twisting tidal river to San Francisco Bay. By the 1890s Petaluma was the third-busiest waterway in the state.

But it was neither the river nor steamboats that gave Petaluma its enduring fame. In the 1880s, it became known as the Egg Basket of the World when the first practical chicken incubator was invented there and marketed on a mass scale. Immigrants from Europe thronged to Petaluma to set up hundreds of hatcheries and thousands of chicken-feed mills. As many as 600 million eggs per year were shipped to worldwide points. But chicken-related prosperity declined in the 1930s due to high feed costs. Leghorn hens were replaced by Holstein cows. Today the Petaluma countryside is mostly dairy land.

Jack London in Glen Ellen

Glen Ellen, 9 miles north of Sonoma, lies in an area forested with oak, madrone, redwood, and buckeye trees. Author Jack London came to this countryside in 1903 at the invitation of friends who owned the Wake Robin Lodge. There, at age 30, he met their vivacious niece, Charmian. Instantly attracted to each other, the couple spent their days riding horseback and having sprightly conversations. They were perfectly matched, adventurous individuals, and London stayed on to marry Charmian.

At first they lived at her family's lodge, but London fell in love with the land locally known as the Valley of the Moon. He started accumulating property until he had a 1,500-acre tract, and here the Londons lived in a simple white house. He called the place Beauty Ranch, and it was there he wrote most of his prodigious output of books. London's success as an author had initially been spurred by the appearance of a Yukon story in *Atlantic Monthly* magazine and confirmed by publication of *The Call of the Wild* when he was 22.

Within eight years he was America's highest-paid author. In his short lifetime he wrote 54 books, 1,300 articles, and 188 short stories, some translated into 30 languages. His house overflowed with guests—scientists, actresses, writers, and socialites. And exuberance marked just about everything London did. He took up scientific farming and designed a pigpen that gave each pig family an apartment. Later, he took a long sea voyage with Charmian on a ship he designed himself.

But London's most wondrous dream was Wolf House, his 26-room mansion, an imposing affair of redwood and huge stone blocks, with arched windows opening onto forested slopes and offering views of the entire valley. London wrote, "It will last one-thousand years, God willing." But one midnight in August 1913, billows of black smoke filled the sky as a raging fire burned out of control. The author watched silently from a nearby hill as his dream crumbled to the earth. London never quite recovered from the calamity. Three years later he died at age 40. The official cause was uremic poisoning, but rumors persisted it was suicide. The magnificent ruins of Wolf House, as well as all of Beauty Ranch, live on as a California state park.

Northern Sonoma County

The Pomo tribe lived for centuries in what is now northern Sonoma County. In 1841 Mexico granted a portion of their domain to a New England sea captain, Henry Fitch (nobody consulted the Pomos, of course), who had eloped with General Vallejo's sister. But Fitch, having received such an excellent dowry, saw no reason to live out his life in such a lonely land. He hired Cyrus Alexander to manage a ranch there with immense herds of cattle. The names of both men live on as landmarks—Fitch Mountain looms over the town of Healdsburg and to the east lies Alexander Valley, Cyrus's payment for work on the ranch.

Healdsburg itself bears the name of Harmon Heald, a disenchanted forty-niner who arrived on the scene in 1852 and claimed land for a town site. He surveyed the town and sold lots for $15 apiece around a central plaza. By the end of the decade, Healdsburg had a population of 500.

Russian River and Western Sonoma County

Called *Slavyanka* (Slavic girl) by Russian settlers during their tenure in California, the Russian River flows from the hilly regions above Hopland, past Cloverdale, Healdsburg, Guerneville, Duncans Mills, and finally Jenner, where it meets the Pacific. The Russians explored the length of the river basin—a territory the Spanish had largely ignored—initially to scout out a suitable settlement site and thereafter to occasionally chase down otter. They saw the area for what it was, a rich river valley dense with towering virgin redwood stands, bounded by fertile plains, and awash with fish. But the Russians abandoned their foothold in California before ever establishing a settlement upriver, leaving the region behind for others to exploit.

When the first American loggers arrived in the Russian River valley, they could hardly believe what they saw. The trees were enormous, some measuring as wide as 23 feet in diameter and 300 feet in height. The first sawmill opened in the valley in 1861, with others springing up soon thereafter. Stumptown, renamed Guerneville in 1870 after lumberman George Guerne, was the region's logging epicenter.

The trees offered the woodsmen a rich bounty for a time. Around the turn of the 20th century, however, many trees had been harvested, and the mills began to close. In an effort to shore up profits, the Northwest Pacific Railroad—which had been servicing the mills—began to promote the Russian River area as a tourist destination.

Urban vacationers from San Francisco and other parts were soon hopping aboard trains in droves to escape to the region—with the railroad cars rolling right onto a ferryboat for the ride across the Golden Gate. Hotels and resorts sprang up, as did bevies of summer cottages. In the 1930s revelers boogied all night at the Rio Nido Inn to the sounds of Benny Goodman's clarinet and Ozzie Nelson's band.

Another popular local name also harks back to a Russian source. Settlers at Fort Ross introduced the Gravenstein apple to the county in the mid-19th century. In 1883 Nathaniel Griffin demonstrated that "Gravs" could be grown commercially, and he was dubbed "Grandfather of the Gravenstein." The apple became popular in the county because of its exceptional flavor and early ripening. The fruit was so well liked that locals inaugurated an annual celebration—the Gravenstein Apple Festival—in 1910 in its honor. The festival continues to be held today.

Other western Sonoma towns include Valley Ford, Bloomfield, Forestville, and Occidental. The latter was first settled by Bill Howard, who had survived a shipwreck off New York, malaria in Africa, and a revolution in Brazil. He and a sawmill operator lured a railroad into the territory and after that success built the whole town of Occidental in four months. Italian woodcutters from Tuscany worked the forests, and a few opened restaurants where a traditional Italian feast could be had for two bits. Today, Occidental is still the place to go for Italian dinners; it is also a hub for artists and environmental activists.

The Sonoma Coast

For almost 60 miles along the jagged coastline, Sonoma County's Highway 1 (called Coast Highway 1 in many locales) snakes through rangeland and small towns that lie between the Coast Range and the Pacific. Centuries ago Miwok and Pomo tribes fished these coastal waters. Later, Russians and the Aleut hunters they brought down from Alaska harvested otter here—to near extinction—in nimble kayaks called baidarkas. The hunters skillfully negotiated their small craft through the surf and swells of the rugged coastline, occasionally seeking refuge in one of the few protected coves hidden among the bluffs. Bodega Bay, near Sonoma County's southern border, was one of the few places where larger ships could safely drop anchor. It thus wasn't long before the bay became a shipping center, dispatching lumber and agricultural products to San Francisco and beyond.

Bodega Bay became famous as the site where Alfred Hitchcock filmed his classic thriller *The Birds*. A wall-size photo at Bay View Restaurant at the popular Inn at the Tides (see the Hotels, Motels, and Inns chapter) commemorates Hitchcock's work.

GOLDEN GATEWAY

An icon of the American West, San Francisco lives up to its legends. The classic old cable cars really do climb halfway to the stars (or at least as far as Nob Hill). Luminous fog does swirl around the Golden Gate Bridge. At eventide the golden glow of the setting sun glints from the windows of Alcatraz Island, making the old prison seem almost romantic, as errant sailors tack home against the late and misty sky. And taquerias in the Mission District, dim sum eateries in Chinatown, Italian coffeehouses in North Beach, to name just a few, make up a fascinating and tasty cultural mélange. Even the frequently chilling summer weather and traffic-snarled streets fail to diminish the multicultural excitement and avant-garde aura that pervade this town. It's a city with an irrepressible spirit, a noble grande dame on a hilltop throne, proud and resilient after the terrible earthquake of 1906 and the Loma Prieta temblor of 1989. So . . . if you had only two days in San Francisco (called "The City" by locals), what places should you not miss? Everyone's tastes are different, but here are a few sites that most folks are sure to enjoy.

Nob Hill, at the top of California and Sacramento Streets, with its posh hotels, private clubs, and smart addresses, retains much of the glamour and gentility it possessed at the end of the 19th century, when men who had made fortunes in silver erected grand mansions for the world to envy on these unobstructed, commanding heights.

i **The Ferry Building at the foot of Market Street is a food lover's paradise. There are farmers' markets, a tea shop, and numerous purveyors offering everything from chocolate to oysters (www.ferrybuilding marketplace.com).**

Fisherman's Wharf, with its picturesque views, pungent aromas, street performers, steaming crab pots, and fine restaurants, draws many visitors—it's all hustle and bustle during the summer tourist season (www.fishermanswharf.org). Fishing boats bob alongside the wharf, while seagulls float overhead and sea lions bask and bark on large rafts moored at the wharf's edge. Local gourmets (and commoners alike) consider West Coast Dungeness crab among the best seafood

in the world. Walkaway crab cocktails are sold from the sidewalk, along with clam chowder and sourdough bread, and it's pleasant to nibble on a little seafood while watching the fishing boats return, with the sea lions barking their welcomes. Parking is available in public lots along Beach and North Point Streets.

Check out the Hyde Street Pier and look at the tall 19th-century ships permanently berthed there. Ghirardelli Square, a short walk uphill on Hyde Street, is one of San Francisco's most successful attempts to hang on to the transient past (www.ghiradellisq.com). Until 1964 it was a crumbling, abandoned factory that had once turned out Civil War uniforms and later served as a chocolate factory where Domingo Ghirardelli made cocoa. Within the rambling complex are a dozen places to eat and an assortment of interesting shops and galleries.

The Cannery at Del Monte Square, just down the street on Leavenworth, is where Del Monte once tinned fruit (www.delmontesquare.com). Now it's a delightful and original collection of sprightly shops, art galleries, and restaurants; a place to buy, say, Sarah Jessica Parker's clothing line, Bitten (at Steve & Barry's). Often there's entertainment in the courtyard—small combo bands, magicians, and jugglers.

Alcatraz Island, once the end of the line and the beginning of hopelessness for federal prisoners, is now part of a national park (www.nps.gov/alcatraz). It can be reached by boats that leave several times a day from Pier 41 at Fisherman's Wharf. A cell-block tour gives insight into life behind bars for men like Al Capone and Machine Gun Kelly, who lived out their days here without visitors.

An excellent audio tour narrated by former guards and inmates is full of fascinating anecdotes about some of the more notorious criminals, escape attempts, and the prison riot of 1946. Plan on staying at least a couple hours on the island to soak in the history, and dress warmly. Same-day tickets are available at Pier 41 (you'll run into long lines in summer), or you can get them in advance by calling (415) 981-7625.

The renovated Union Square, the heart of the city's shopping district, now offers more green spaces, light sculptures by R. M. Fischer, and a stage large enough to accommodate an orchestra. The underground parking garage beneath the square, the first in the world, was originally built during World War II to serve as a bomb shelter. Around the square or close by are Saks Fifth Avenue, Macy's, Neiman Marcus, Dior, Williams-Sonoma, the Apple Store, and a Virgin Megastore.

Chinatown is just a short walk up Grant Avenue from Union Square. This "city within a city" is home to arguably more Chinese than any other place outside of Asia (www.sanfranciscochinatown.com). It's packed with open-air markets, a variety of bakeries, restaurants, temples, souvenir shops, and, yes, people. Grant Avenue is touristy, but Stockton Street, a block west of Grant, offers a real taste of Chinatown. Tearooms, temples, Chinese schools, and shops lining the streets offer exotic produce and delicacies such as yellow croaker salted fish, and dried papaw, fish peel, and black fungus. In Portsmouth Square you may find elderly Chinese playing mah-jongg, or fascinating tai chi classes under way.

For a rare treat, stop for a dim sum lunch at one of the restaurants offering this unusual fare.

i | Making reservations can frequently be a challenge in San Francisco's world-famous restaurants and trattorias. But if you can't get a table, ask the concierge if you can be served at the bar. There you can often sample from the menu while partaking in San Francisco's No. 1 pastime, people watching.

Servers wheel different carts around the room, each offering a unique cornucopia of delights—some of it mysterious, all of it delicious. They call out their particular specialty in Chinese, and you order whatever you like. (Some restaurants sell their more popular items, such as steamed pork buns, in to-go bakery-style cases for those who want to savor this delicacy on the run.)

Between Chinatown and Fisherman's Wharf is North Beach, the Italian district of the city. Pasta, provolone, and dark, rich espresso are in abundance here, as are a wide variety of cafes, galleries, small theaters, and nightclubs. Beat poets Jack Kerouac, Allen Ginsberg, and William Burroughs chose North Beach as their principal hangout, contributing to San Francisco's international reputation as a funky, hip literary city. In 1953 Lawrence Ferlinghetti, then a struggling poet who later became a Beat legend, opened City Lights Books at 261 Columbus Avenue (www.citylights.com). It has since become one of the city's most cherished landmarks as well as a leader among the many feisty independent booksellers that have staked their claim in the Bay Area. For the full Beat experience, wander through the little store's voluminous stacks, then take 10 steps across Jack Kerouac Alley to lift a tall, cool one at Vesuvio's—a legendary watering hole that still draws the city's more colorful creative types.

If you're into museums, you'll appreciate the world-class offerings in San Francisco. The Asian Art Museum (www.asianart.org) reopened in 2003 in the Civic Center, filling 40,000 square feet of gallery space with $4 billion worth of Asian treasures. Rivaling that is the even newer de Young Museum in Golden Gate (www.famsf. org/deyoung), which opened in 2005 to much fanfare. From its nine-story-high observation tower, there are sweeping views of San Francisco and Golden Gate Park. And the San Francisco Museum of Modern Art, at 151 Third Street, can always be counted on for spectacular and sometimes downright peculiar shows (www.sfmoma. org). A museum of a different sort, the California Academy of Sciences (www.calacademy.org), opened in fall 2008 in Golden Gate Park near the deYoung Museum. This remarkable building houses a planetarium, an aquarium, a rain forest, a coral reef, and penguins and alligators, topped off by a living roof that spans more than two acres. Designed by famed architect Renzo Piano, it is said to be the largest structure of its kind in the world to use all "green" construction techniques and materials.

ℹ️ **Though it seems as if it's been around forever, the fortune cookie is not an ancient Asian delicacy. Local legend claims invention of the cookie in San Francisco about a century ago by Makota Hagiwara, who was a gardener at the Japanese Tea Garden in Golden Gate Park.**

Get the feel of the Pacific Ocean along the Great Highway. Start at Point Lobos Avenue and the Great Highway, then visit Cliff House, a once-famous resort that overlooks the ocean and nearby Seal Rock (www.cliffhouse.com). From there, the long windswept strand of Ocean Beach stretches to the great sand dunes to the south. Leave your bathing suit at the hotel, and stay out of the roiling surf, where the southbound tidal currents traveling at 12 mph have a habit of swallowing swimmers and surfers alike.

Along this highway you'll discover an entrance to Golden Gate Park, the city's great green retreat, bordered by the Great Highway, Lincoln Way, and Stanyan and Fulton Streets. When the park was built in 1887, it included 730 acres of dunes and 270 acres of arable land. Today, its 1,000 acres are lush with meadows, lakes, and 5,000 varieties of shrubs, flowers, and trees. Within its borders you can also visit a plant conservatory that looks a lot like Kew Gardens in London.

When you get hungry in San Francisco, you're never too far from a restaurant. In fact, there's one on nearly every corner. It's hard to make recommendations, but keep in mind that there are more than 3,000 eating and drinking establishments in the city. Wherever you decide to dine, you're not likely to be disappointed.

When the sun begins its slow descent into the ocean and the late afternoon fog snakes its tendrils over the hills and into the bay (it looks eerie, but it really does that), the city takes on a more romantic feel. San Francisco may be a sightseer's paradise during the day, but it is also a great place to spend an evening. Live entertainment can be found any night of the week, but for some soulful gospel music stop in at Biscuits and Blues, 401 Mason Street (www. biscuitsandblues.com), or head to the new San Francisco outpost of Yoshi's, at 1330 Fillmore Street. The original Yoshi's opened years ago in Oakland and still packs 'em in. The musical lineup can be eclectic at both clubs, with big-name acts like Dr. John and the Pat Metheny Trio. If comedy is more to your liking, an evening of stand-up at Punch Line, 444 Battery Street (www. punchlinecomedyclub.com) will tickle your funny bone. One of the best comedy shows in town is the long-running Beach Blanket Babylon (www. beachblanketbabylon.com) at Club Fugazi, 678 Beach Blanket Babylon Boulevard. It's wacky and ever-changing—skewering whatever and whoever has recently shaken up pop culture.

Of course, this listing of attractions only scratches the surface. It is said that everyone who visits San Francisco wants to come back again. The guy who wrote "I Left My Heart in San Francisco" knew what he was talking about. So there will be plenty more to enjoy on a return trip. It would be nice, for instance, to take in the Cable Car Barn and Museum on Washington and Mason Streets (www.cablecarmuseum.org) to see the historic old paraphernalia and glimpse the innards of these machines in action. (Just how does that cable car work anyway?) Kids and parents alike should see the Exploratorium, Marina Boulevard and Lyon Street, which contains more than 600 interactive science exhibits (www.exploratorium.edu).

The city's Victorian architecture is almost as famous as its cable cars. Handsome and slightly irrational, painted brightly in all combinations of colors, these structures are certainly unique. Some of the best can be seen in Pacific Heights, particularly on these streets: Vallejo, Broadway, Pacific, Jackson, Washington, Pierce, and Scott, generally in blocks between 1600 and 3000.

i San Francisco's Presidio National Park has left its military history behind for good. The huge green space's most famous new tenant is the 23-acre Letterman Digital Arts Center, where movie and special effects mogul George Lucas moved most of the operations of Industrial Light & Magic and the gaming division of his empire, LucasArts, in 2005.

One thing visitors should keep in mind is that San Francisco weather is, well, unlike what you would expect. True, temperatures don't often vary outside a range of 50 to 70 degrees, summer or winter. But sometimes January and February can be the sunniest, most glorious months. On the other hand, summer can be so cold that tourists who mistakenly thought California called for tank tops and flip-flops huddle in doorways to keep warm. Mark Twain reportedly once said, "The coldest winter I ever spent was a summer in San Francisco." So you may want to have that sweater or jacket handy if you're walking about. What is the best time of year to visit? Locals will tell you the most pleasant months are September and October.

Much like Manhattan and some quaint and compact European cities, San Francisco is best enjoyed by walking its many neighborhoods. Besides, driving a car in San Francisco—and then trying to park it here and there—can be an exercise in futility. But if you must drive, be prepared for the traffic idiosyncrasies you will encounter.

In negotiating the city by automobile, be aware of red-light-running fools, and expect traffic jams at any hour. On-street parking is virtually nonexistent—at best scarce—and those who overstay their legal welcome are subject to heavy fines and might even be clamped with "the boot," which immobilizes the vehicle. An impounded car is endless trouble to retrieve.

Fortunately there are a number of public parking facilities; one of the handiest offering underground parking is at Union Square. In hilly San Francisco, it is illegal to park a car on most hills (technically, those exceeding a grade of 3 percent) without setting your parking brake and turning the wheels into the curb. When parking uphill the wheels must be "heeled," with the inside front tire resting securely against the curb. Parking downhill, tires must be "toed"—turned in. Complicated enough for you? I recommend turning over your keys to the valet to park the car when you first arrive at your hotel and forgetting about it until you're ready to leave town. You'll be glad you did.

So if you have only a day or, heaven forbid, even less, and you're still wondering what to do, my advice is this: Go out and simply walk. That's what I like to do, and I discover something new and memorable every time. Enjoying yourself comes easily here. It costs nothing to breathe the fragrance of a vendor's flowers on Union Square, hike up Telegraph Hill (where rowhouses climb steep slopes), take in the breathtaking view from Coit Tower at the crest, stroll through Chinatown or Little Italy, or photograph the busy fleet at Fisherman's Wharf. And don't worry, you will be back.

FLORA, FAUNA, AND CLIMATE

Upon arriving in the Santa Rosa area in 1875, famed horticulturist Luther Burbank could barely contain his excitement, declaring "this is the chosen spot of all earth as far as Nature is concerned." When I moved to Wine Country more than two decades ago, I discovered that gardening nearly year-round is one benefit of living here. I'm pretty certain that's also what drew Luther to the region (read more about his legacy in the Attractions chapter), inspired as he was by the bucolic scenery and the mild Mediterranean climate. There's no doubt about it—this area is spilling over with natural gifts. Every season reveals a different facet of the landscape. In spring a kaleidoscope of wildflowers lines the roadsides, with the hills and mountains wrapped in emerald green. In summer the grapevines practically beam with verdant life. In fall the fields are quilted with bright patches of red and orange. And in winter, always wet but not too harsh, a misty hush descends on the hills and valleys, with wisps of fog adding mystery. Beyond the Wine Country's ever-changing beauty lies a fascinating natural history, too. Though it's impossible to summarize all there is to tell, here's a sampling of salient geologic, climatic, and ecological features.

GEOLOGY

A hundred million years ago, the Wine Country area was exceptionally poor as a grape-growing region because all of it was under water. It took a lot of tectonic activity—movement of the massive plates that together form the earth's crust—to swing Napa, Sonoma, and environs eastward onto dry land. It was all part of the succession of north–south "island arcs" that violently, if patiently, crashed into the North American continent and sent California on the way to its modern-day topography, which includes the prominent Mayacmas Mountains—which divide Sonoma and Napa Counties—and the steep Coast Range.

Of course, the movement hasn't exactly stopped altogether, and you can feel the effects every now and then. I'm talking about earthquakes. The renowned San Andreas system (a massive network of strike-slip faults that forms the border between the Pacific and North American tectonic plates) runs the length of Sonoma and Mendocino Counties, sometimes on the mainland and sometimes beneath the sea. Several smaller, generally north–south faults lurk beneath Wine Country, including the Rodgers Creek Fault, which caused some destruction in Santa Rosa with a 1969 quake that measured 5.7 on the Richter scale.

Things could be worse. In fact, they used to be. Much of the region was the scene of frightful volcanic activity three million to four million years ago. Those eruptions, combined with unrelenting seismic activity, have given California's North Coast ranges a highly complex geologic profile. And this is of more than theoretical interest, for two of the lures that historically have drawn people to the region are direct results of geology.

The most obvious of these is geothermal activity. Sonoma and Napa Counties are pierced by fault "pipelines" that send water heated by magma 8 miles below the earth's surface percolating upward. In the Calistoga area you can pay to gawk at a burst of hot water (at the Old Faithful Geyser) or to soak in the stuff (at the many spas). And around one section of the Sonoma–Lake County border, geothermal sites are even used to generate electricity. In fact, the Geysers steam field weighs in as the world's largest complex (19 units) of geothermal power plants.

But the peculiar North Coast geology has spawned a lot more than mud baths. The second regional drawing card with its roots in plate tectonics is the mighty grapevine.

SOIL

Soils reflect the rocks they used to be, so it makes sense that an area of convoluted geology will contain many types of soil. And because soil composition greatly affects the chemistry of a growing grape, it follows that precisely where you plant your vines has a lot to do with the quality of your wine.

The soil within a single vineyard can vary substantially. Red soil tends to produce soft wine; light, "fluffy" soils are known for hard, austere wines; and gravelly ground, which has a hard time holding water, tends to result in earthy wines. Moreover, wine made from hillside grapes usually is riskier and more robust than valley wine, because the grapes are smaller and therefore have a higher skin-to-pulp ratio. (The intense flavor is in the skin.) And some of the best vineyard soil in Napa Valley is found on the Oakville and Rutherford "benches"—broad, nutrient-rich alluvial fans that have been washed from the Mayacmas Mountains.

Of course, all of this is gross oversimplification. You'll find more information on the whole business of "appellations"—slightly varied microclimates that produce grapes and yield wines with specific, refined characteristics—in the Wineries chapter, but sorting out such details is what separates a successful vintner from the rest of us guzzlers. The point is that, in a manner of speaking, the Cabernet Sauvignon you're savoring today has been in the works for about 100 million years.

i The Chalk Hill grape-growing appellation in Sonoma County is named for its light-colored soil. It's not chalk at all, but a white volcanic ash.

CLIMATE

Northern California is one of five regions in the world that enjoys a Mediterranean climate, characterized by warm, dry summers and mild, moist winters. While the area's geographic location helps to shape its climate—Santa Rosa is about par with Athens on the latitude scale—local environmental influences are also important. Weather varies dramatically throughout the region, and you can often find a huge difference in conditions just by driving a few miles.

To understand what causes Wine Country weather, think of the Pacific Ocean as a giant climate-control device, set on Mild. In general, the farther you stray from salt water, the hotter your summers will be and the colder your winters. Temperature variations along the coast are minuscule, and river towns such as Guerneville and Napa also are fairly mild. Though coastal winter nights are cooler, they don't often see temperatures drop lower than 40. There is also morning summer fog and evening sea breezes.

That is in stark contrast to places such as Calistoga, where hilly terrain serves as a barrier to ocean influences and it can be uncomfortably still and hot in summer months. When it's hot, however, it qualifies as "dry heat." Californians tend to consider that phrase a meaningless cliché, but long-suffering midwesterners and easterners can immediately feel the difference. A 100-degree day is a test no matter how you look at it, but the night air has a chance to cool considerably when humidity is low.

Rainfall too varies across Wine Country, with the coastal towns usually receiving more inches of precipitation than those in inland valleys. Regardless of volume, however, you can expect most of the rain between November and February, with residual storms in March and April. Summer and fall downpours are rare.

In general, spring and autumn are the best months to visit. The weather is exceptional, and there is added color from wildflowers or turning leaves. Summer temperatures in Sonoma County usually edge into the mid-80s, but the nights are still comfortable (even chilly sometimes), with the mercury falling into the 50s.

> ℹ️ **The Napa Registry of Significant Trees was founded in 1995 to protect special trees on private properties in perpetuity until their natural death. To be listed on the registry, the tree must have historic significance and high public visibility, be native to Napa Valley, and be extraordinarily beautiful.**

FLORA

Luther Burbank was right: Just about anything can and does grow here. So I won't try to construct any sort of comprehensive list of flora—it would be voluminous. I can, however, state a few generalities.

Two types of ecosystem—oak woodland and chaparral—dominate the rolling hills of Napa and Sonoma Counties. It's impossible to drive along U.S. Highway 101 or Highway 29 without noticing the stolid oak trees, but the collection includes many varieties. Coast live oaks are perhaps the most impressive, with a single tree able to spread its branches up to 130 feet. These trees prefer moist locations, such as creek bottoms and north slopes. Canyon live oaks, with their exceptionally hard wood, thrive on steep hillsides. Blue oaks like hot, dry slopes, and California black oaks pop up on mesas with deep soil and gentle slopes.

Chaparral, made up of shrubs such as manzanita, ceanothus, and toyon, is more closely associated with the hills of Southern California, but it is prevalent here too. It is an environment inhospitable to humans and designed to burn—many of its plant species have highly flammable oils in their bark, and the underbrush can be thorny and impenetrable.

The standout citizen of the damp, misty Coast Range forests is the coast redwood, the tallest tree in the world. Though Sonoma County has several preserves devoted to redwoods (see the Parks and Recreation chapter), the biggest of all are found in Humboldt County (see the Big Trees section of the Day Trips chapter). You might also stumble on a redwood in steep, darker canyons along Wine Country streams. Other dominant trees include the ponderosa pine, with its arrow-straight trunk; the Pacific madrone, whose gnarled trunk will creep 50 feet horizontally to find sunlight; and the Douglas fir, the Western Hemisphere's premier lumber tree.

No matter which Wine Country microclimate you're in, you are likely to see wildflowers if your timing is sound. Somewhere between February and June, depending on elevation and intensity of sunlight, literally hundreds of shrubs and herbs burst into bloom. The most eye-catching include the California poppy—the bright orange state flower that pops up just about anywhere—and mustard, which lays a breathtaking yellow carpet in the early spring vineyards (and inspires all sorts of reverent celebrations—see the Festivals and Annual Events chapter). Other native wildflowers to look for include orchids, irises, monkey flowers, Indian paintbrushes, golden bushes, wild roses, lupines, violets, shooting stars, fiddlenecks, lilies, wild onions, and buttercups.

> ℹ️ **Rub marks left by the long-extinct Columbian mammoth can be found in rocks at Duncans Landing along the Sonoma Coast. Archaeologists and geologists believe the huge beasts routinely rubbed their backs on the rocks. The 10-ton behemoths roamed the Bay Area as late as 12,000 years ago.**

FAUNA

It isn't exactly a jungle out here, but keen observers will spy a wide range of furry, feathered, or fishy creatures in Wine Country. Drive the scenic routes at dusk in summer and fall and you are likely to see the omnipresent black-tailed deer nibbling scrub oak or buckbrush in the meadows. You are even more likely to see skunks, raccoons, and opossums, though it might be in the form of roadkill. They are among the most common of the region's mammals, especially in semideveloped areas. The more mountainous areas are home to black bears, mountain lions, bobcats, coyotes, bats, diminutive gray foxes, porcupines, badgers, feral pigs, and even the occasional ring-tailed cat or tule elk. Many of them are nocturnal and all are elusive, but they are out there, trying to stay downwind of humans. Once in a while, however, a bear or bobcat wanders into the eastern city limits of Santa Rosa, nestled along the western side of the Mayacmas Mountains, in search of some easy food and water. A mountain lion even startled commuters one afternoon when it strolled onto US 101—a jungle of a different sort—in the middle of the city. Though these sightings are rare, it serves to remind us that we are surrounded by wild and unpredictable beauty.

i A great place to observe seals is at the mouth of the Russian River in Jenner. If you want to climb down to the beach to get a close-up photo, you must stay at least 100 yards from the animals. Getting too close can result in a fine, so bring a good zoom lens.

The rugged coastal areas have their own communities: seals and sea lions on the rocks; river otters in the estuaries; and gray whales offshore, migrating southward from the Bering Sea to Baja California between December and April. The nutrient-rich waters of the coastal areas also teem with benthic life, including eight species of the highly desirable—and highly endangered—abalone. River otters are found in much of Wine Country's freshwater. The reptile and amphibian crowd includes alligator lizards, pond turtles, king snakes, rubber boas, skinks, and the ones you need to watch out for: western rattlesnakes.

The local waterways—primarily the Napa and Russian Rivers—are dominated by anadromous fish, that is, species that travel from the sea to spawn in freshwater. The three big fish in Wine Country (as in most of Northern California) are chinook salmon, coho salmon, and steelhead—the latter are basically rainbow trout that have learned to migrate. Most of the good lake fishing is for bass (smallmouth and largemouth) and catfish, though none of them are native sons. (See more on rivers, lakes, and fishing in the Parks and Recreation chapter.)

Audubon Society chapters are active throughout the region, and they have plenty to catalog. There are swallows and swifts, American robins, northern mockingbirds, woodpeckers and warblers, finches and flycatchers. There are at least six species of hawk and seven species of owl, including the northern spotted, that rather harmless old-growth percher despised by a generation of loggers.

Golden eagles (the nation's largest raptor, with a wingspan of up to 7 feet), ospreys, kestrels, and peregrine falcons ride the thermals along high bluffs and cliff faces. Peregrines, with a maximum flight speed of 275 mph, have been known to overtake small airplanes. Herons and egrets poke about in swampy spots, such as the Napa-Sonoma Marshes Wildlife Area, south of those two towns, and we have a varied collection of ducks and geese. And if jet lag and ambitious wine tasting have you feeling dehydrated and fatigued, don't fret too much about those California turkey vultures circling overhead. It's nothing personal—the hefty, red-faced scavengers are quite populous in Wine Country.

HOTELS, MOTELS, AND INNS

Once upon a time, finding an exceptional hotel in Wine Country was a challenge. Today the challenge is having to choose between the many new and upgraded hotels, motels, and inns that have opened within the past few years. Still more luxury hotels are in the planning stages, including a 351-room Ritz-Carlton resort in Napa. In 2008, two other downtown Napa hotels were under construction: the 160-room Westin Verasa and 141-room AVIA Napa, targeted to open their doors in the fall of 2008 and spring of 2009, respectively. In Sonoma County, two new luxury hotels are planned for Healdsburg.

In this chapter you'll find lodging options from the widely known chains (Best Western, Marriott, Hilton, and Super 8, for instance) to special places that defy the standard definition of a hotel, motel, or bed-and-breakfast inn (Milliken Creek Inn, Hotel D'Amici, and Duchamp Hotel, to name a few). All of these lodgings are well equipped to provide you with a good night's sleep, but most go beyond with amenities that make your stay more comfortable and enjoyable. Some are full-service hotels that can be as charming as B&Bs (but with more amenities), and some are less expensive, basic motel rooms. Many could even qualify for mention in the Spas and Resorts chapter.

OVERVIEW

Unless stated otherwise, assume that hotels, motels, and inns accept major credit cards. Pets are usually not welcome, but don't be afraid to ask—some places cater to both two- and four-legged creatures. A few facilities set aside rooms for their guests who smoke, but most are entirely smoke-free environments. In addition, high-speed wireless Internet access is now commonplace at the larger hotels and motels, and some of the elegant inns have added this service too. Always inquire about these specifics when calling for information.

Hotels, motels, and inns are listed using the south-to-north geographical sequence explained in the How to Use This Book chapter. I start with Napa Valley accommodations, followed by those in Sonoma County. Afterward, I list agencies specializing in vacation rentals.

Price Code

The following price guidelines are based on the approximate cost of a one-night, weekend, double-occupancy stay. Keep in mind that rates change with the seasons, and summer rates sometimes jump significantly above off-season rates. Many properties also offer a range of lodgings and amenities, from modest rooms to luxury cottages, with widely varying prices. These approximations do not include tax, gratuities, or other amenities such as spa services or room service.

$	Less than $110
$$	$111 to $150
$$$	$151 to $170
$$$$	$171 to $225
$$$$$	More than $226

NAPA COUNTY

GAIA NAPA VALLEY HOTEL & SPA　$$$$
3600 Broadway Street (Highway 29),
American Canyon
(707) 674-2100, (888) 798-3777
www.gaiahotelnapavalley.com
www.spagaia.com
If you're passionate about "green" living, Gaia may

appeal to you. New in 2006, it is Napa Valley's first environmentally sustainable hotel, certified Gold LEED (Leader in Energy and Environmental Design). Every detail is environmentally conscious, from the recycled tiles and granite used in guest rooms to the chemical-free landscaping, and everything in between. The 132 rooms have high-def TVs, microwaves, refrigerators, and complimentary high-speed Internet access. (Check out the Romance Package, which includes a sprinkling of rose petals in your room—a nice "green" touch.) A full-service spa and a restaurant are on-site. Gaia is located in American Canyon, approximately 11 miles south of downtown Napa, so allow extra time to get to upvalley destinations.

EMBASSY SUITES NAPA VALLEY $$$$$
1075 California Boulevard, Napa
(707) 253-9540, (800) 362-2779
www.embassysuites.com
A group of three-story canary and burgundy buildings, the Embassy Suites offers a nice combination of corporate know-how and Wine Country charm. There are indoor and outdoor pools, wet and dry saunas, swans in the mill pond, and a soaring lobby with terra-cotta tiles and parlor chairs. Every guest unit is a two-room suite with extra pullout sofa, wet bar, and microwave. The tariff includes a full, cooked-to-order breakfast and an afternoon Manager's Reception with complimentary drinks. The on-site restaurant, Rings, is a steakhouse serving traditional American cuisine.

NAPA VALLEY MARRIOTT $$$$
3425 Solano Avenue, Napa
(707) 253-8600, (800) 228-9290
www.napavalleymarriott.com
The 274-room hotel (including several suites) is just off Highway 29, north of the Trancas Street/ Redwood Road exit. Each room has individual climate control, in-room pay movies, iron and ironing board, a work desk, and voice mail. The Harvest Cafe, specializing in steaks and California vegetables, serves breakfast and dinner; Character's Sports Bar & Grill serves lunch and cocktails.

Amadeus spa offers massages, exfoliations, body treatments, and facials. (See the Web site at www .spame.com.) The Marriott also has a heated outdoor pool and Jacuzzi, lighted tennis courts, and a fitness center.

HILTON GARDEN INN $$$$
3585 Solano Avenue, Napa
(707) 252-0444, (877) STAY-HGI
www.hiltongardeninn.com
Designed for business and leisure travelers, this 80-room hotel has all the amenities you expect from a Hilton property. All rooms (and 18 suites) have refrigerators, microwaves, and coffeemakers. Each room features an ergonomic Herman Miller chair at a large work desk, and the on-site business center is available 24 hours a day. The location has easy access to Highway 29, too.

MILLIKEN CREEK INN $$$$$
1815 Silverado Trail, Napa
(707) 255-1197, (800) 835-6112
www.millikencreekinn.com
In its short life, this "boutique inn" set on the Napa River has become one of the valley's most luxurious and popular retreats for couples wanting to get away from it all. It's only five minutes to downtown Napa's restaurants, yet you will feel far removed from city life. More than a bed-and-breakfast, but not a hotel, this inn is in a class by itself. Luxurious and inviting, it's in a tranquil setting, thanks to the natural expanse of the river wherever you look. Enhancing the grounds are gardens, fountains, Adirondack chairs, and even a waterfall and koi pond.

The innkeepers have many years of experience in the upscale hotel industry, and it shows in their attention to detail. The 12 guest rooms are elegantly noncluttered, in what they call "British campaign" design. But these rooms have modern amenities such as DVD players (there's a lending library of 200 movie titles), well-appointed minibars, high-speed Internet, and in-room continental breakfast service. There's even a pillow menu—soft or firm, feather or foam? Massage and spa treatments, along with private yoga classes, are offered on-site.

NAPA RIVER INN $$$$$
500 Main Street, Napa
(707) 251-8500, (877) 251-8500
www.napariverinn.com

When the historic Napa Mill and Hatt Building were renovated along the Napa River in 2000, this hotel was the result. It offers luxury accommodations in 58 guest rooms and suites in various themes—from nautical to "California rustic" to vintage 1800s. All rooms feature large TVs, refrigerators, and in-room coffee. Many rooms have fireplaces, river views, and balconies. (Rumor has it this hotel is haunted, but in a good way.) A full-service spa is nearby for use by guests, and restaurants and shops are handy right next door in the refurbished Hatt Market building. Pets are welcome here for $25 per night and treated as VIPs. All rooms are nonsmoking.

WINE VALLEY LODGE $$
200 South Coombs Street, Napa
(707) 224-7911, (800) 696-7911
www.winevalleylodge.com

South of downtown Napa, close to Highway 121, the mission-style lodge has 54 guest rooms including deluxe suites suitable for families. There is a heated pool in the motor court and complimentary continental breakfast with Belgian waffles. Ask about the photos of Elvis Presley and Marilyn Monroe in the breakfast room.

RIVER TERRACE INN $$$$
1600 Soscol Avenue, Napa
(707) 320-9000, (866) NAPA-FUN
www.riverterraceinn.com

Most of the 106 rooms and suites at this hotel in downtown Napa have balconies with either Napa River or Napa Valley views, 10-foot ceilings, king-size beds, whirlpool tubs, DVD/CD players, rich linens, minibars, and wireless Internet access. The private spa provides in-room massages, facials, hydrotherapy, and body treatments for individuals or couples. An outdoor pool and 24-hour full fitness room complete the body-pampering extras. A complimentary breakfast buffet is available each morning in the River Terrace Cafe, which offers light meals and salads

at lunchtime and nightly dinner specials. There's also a wine bar, where many local boutique wines are poured. And if you need a place to properly store that special bottle of Cabernet Sauvignon until you're ready to uncork it, the hotel provides a wine storage unit upon request.

BEST WESTERN INN AT THE VINES $$$
100 Soscol Avenue, Napa
(707) 257-1930, (877) 846-3729
www.innatthevines.com

Best Western offers few surprises, which is probably why it's one of America's most popular chains. The Napa version has 68 rooms, including 8 suites. All rooms have cable TV and refrigerators. There is a heated pool and spa, a meeting room for up to 50 people, and a 24-hour Denny's restaurant on the property. This is a nonsmoking hotel.

HAWTHORN INN & SUITES $$$$
314 Soscol Avenue, Napa
(707) 226-1878, (800) 527-1133
www.napavalleyinns.com

One of Napa's newer hotels is this 60-room, three-story structure that focuses on comfort, with a nod to business travelers. The rooms have high-speed Internet access, irons and ironing boards, microwaves, refrigerators, and executive chairs with oversize desks. Business services, a daily newspaper, a hot breakfast buffet, and a boardroom for meetings are also available. The deluxe suites have in-room spa tubs. Vacationers who like a little exercise will appreciate the hotel's swimming pool and spa, as well as the fitness center.

Napa Valley Downtown

TRAVELODGE $$$
853 Coombs Street, Napa
(866) 520-5948
www.travelodge.com

If location is everything, the Travelodge has it all. The downtown Napa locale puts you in close proximity to shopping and restaurants, and it's four blocks from the Wine Train depot (see the Getting Here, Getting Around chapter). The 45-room motel, recently renovated and upgraded, has a heated pool, and each unit comes with a two-line phone with a fax port, individual air-conditioning, and Italian marble vanities.

CHARDONNAY LODGE $
2640 Jefferson Street, Napa
(707) 224-0789
www.chardonnaylodge.net

The lodge offers convenient Napa centrality and beds of various proportions. The 20 rooms are air-conditioned and have phones and cable TV. Renovated in 2007, the rooms are decorated in wine themes. There's a vineyard and a rose garden, along with topiary trees and iron benches for watching the world go by.

THE JOHN MUIR INN $$$
1998 Trower Avenue, Napa
(707) 257-7220, (800) 522-8999
www.johnmuirnapa.com

I can't imagine John Muir, the naturalist who wandered through the Sierra Nevada range, staying here at the intersection of Trower Avenue and Highway 29. But the inn that bears his name is a solid midprice choice with a courtyard swimming pool and whirlpool spa, conference room, 24-hour front desk, and free continental breakfast. About one-quarter of the 60 rooms have kitchenettes, and some have wet bars or private spas. Children 13 and younger stay free. The entire property is a smoke-free environment.

YOUNTVILLE INN $$$$$
6462 Washington Street, Yountville
(707) 944-5600, (800) 972-2293
www.yountvilleinn.com

This rambling hotel has seven buildings and 51 bright and spacious rooms. Most units have a fieldstone fireplace, French doors leading to a patio, a wood-beamed ceiling, and a refrigerator. All guests in this nonsmoking hotel receive free continental breakfast. The inn also has a heated pool and spa and is near the Vintners Golf Club (see the Parks and Recreation chapter). Should you be mixing business with pleasure,

the elegantly comfortable Club Room facilitates groups of up to 30 people.

NAPA VALLEY RAILWAY INN $$$
6523 Washington Street, Yountville
(707) 944-2000
www.napavalleyrailwayinn.com

This is probably the best lodgings deal in the tony town of Yountville. Sure, the curious might come clomping down the boardwalk between the two sets of railcars, hoping for a look inside the rooms, but this is where I'd opt to stay in Yountville, if only for the novelty of it. The rooms, all in historic railroad cars on the original track of the Napa Valley Railroad, are luxuriously appointed and filled with light. It's a short walk to the world-class restaurants and just steps to the shops at V Marketplace. Guests also have complimentary use of a nearby fitness center, in case you don't do enough walking while you're exploring the town.

VINTAGE INN $$$$$
6541 Washington Street, Yountville
(707) 944-1112, (800) 351-1133
www.vintageinn.com

This elegant, country-style inn is spread out on a large, landscaped lot. It has 80 units—basic rooms, minisuites, and villas—divided between the outer court and the more protected inner court. Most have patios or balconies. All of them have fireplaces and come with a complimentary continental breakfast buffet, including California sparkling wine. Vintage Inn offers room service, a 60-foot lap pool and hot tub, tennis courts, bike rentals in the summer, and a private limousine service. The inn also has executive conference facilities that can handle 20 to 200 people.

NAPA VALLEY LODGE $$$$$
2230 Madison Street, Yountville
(707) 944-2468, (888) 455-2468
www.woodsidehotels.com/napa

If you've ever stayed at one of Woodside Hotels' Northern California establishments, you'll be keen to reserve a spot at this 55-room hotel at the north end of Yountville. The exterior incorporates classic Tuscan-style architecture, with arched loggias, iron railings, and limestone details. Woodside is known for its gracious service and amenities, and Napa Valley Lodge is right in step—from the 400-book lending library and hearth in the lobby to the free champagne buffet breakfast to the Spanish-tile double vanities, duvet bed coverings, and reproduced vintage tapestries in the rooms. About three-fourths of the units have fireplaces, and all feature a balcony or terrace with views of vineyard or pool and gardens. In addition to the pool, the hotel has a spa, a redwood sauna, and a small exercise room.

RANCHO CAYMUS INN $$$$$
1140 Rutherford Cross Road, Rutherford
(707) 963-1777, (800) 845-1777
www.ranchocaymus.com
If Father Junipero Serra had built a really fancy mission to impress the folks back home in Spain, it might have looked like this. Rancho Caymus, a couple blocks east of Highway 29 on Rutherford Cross Road (aka Highway 128), carries off the hacienda motif flawlessly, from the adobe-looking stucco to the tile roof. The rough-hewn white oak and pine beams were salvaged from an 80-year-old barn in Ohio; the parota wood chairs, tables, and dressers are from Guadalajara; and the wool rugs and wall hangings were made by indigenous Ecuadorians. A central, tiled courtyard brims with flowers and small trees. Most of the 26 nonsmoking units have fireplaces and a split-level layout, and 5 of them have kitchenettes. Continental breakfast is included.

EL BONITA MOTEL $$$$
195 Main Street, St. Helena
(707) 963-3216, (800) 541-3284
www.elbonita.com
The old neon sign and poolside layout point to this motel's roots as a classic 1950s roadside motor hotel, but there have been upgrades galore since then. The 42 rooms are nicely furnished and painted in subdued gray-green tones. About two-thirds have microwaves and

refrigerators. Some allow pets for a small fee. There is a fireplace in the lobby, and each guest receives a continental breakfast. Flowers and fountains proliferate in the lawn areas, while the pool is complemented by a sauna and a Jacuzzi. For quieter rooms away from the highway traffic, ask for the Homestead building.

HARVEST INN $$$$$
1 Main Street, St. Helena
(707) 963-WINE, (800) 950-8466
www.harvestinn.com
The inn's reception building, the Main Lodge, is built to evoke the English countryside, with its corkscrew brick chimneys and oak-paneled great room. But rustic this place isn't. It is a sprawling, manicured complex that specializes in (but isn't limited to) corporate functions, with conference facilities accommodating as many as 60 captains of industry. Set between Sutter Home Winery and Sulphur Springs Avenue on the southern fringe of St. Helena, and bordering a sizable vineyard, Harvest Inn has 74 nonsmoking rooms—the result of a recent expansion. Most of them have king beds, brick fireplaces, wet bars, and dressing vanities, and some have patio balconies. There are two heated pools and whirlpool spas on the grounds, and all guests are served continental breakfast. Spa services are also available in the Garden Spa Sanctuary.

THE WINE COUNTRY INN $$$$$
1152 Lodi Lane, St. Helena
(707) 963-7077, (888) 465-4608
www.winecountryinn.com
This hard-to-categorize accommodation does a good job of blending the comforts of a bed-and-breakfast with the convenience of a small hotel. The Wine Country Inn offers a full buffet breakfast, afternoon appetizers and wine tasting, distinctive rooms filled with hand-picked antiques, a large pool and Jacuzzi, a well-trained staff, and easy parking. No matter how the inn is defined, Lodi Lane, about 2 miles north of St. Helena, is hard to beat for serenity. Immediately to the east is a working vineyard; almost all of the 20 rooms

have private patios or balconies that practically sit on the trellises. Most units have fireplaces, and some even have private hot tubs. There are also four suites and five cottages. The hotel, popular with honeymooners, caters to adults rather than to families with children, and there are no in-room TVs here.

THE INN AT SOUTHBRIDGE $$$$$
1020 Main Street, St. Helena
(707) 967-9400, (800) 520-6800
www.innatsouthbridge.com

This upscale St. Helena hotel looks something like a winery, with its earth tones and creeping vines. The resemblance is no coincidence, as architect William Turnbull Jr. is known for his winery design. The Inn at Southbridge has 21 ample rooms, each with a vaulted ceiling, fireplace, sisal-style carpets, and down comforter. French doors open onto a private balcony overlooking the courtyard. The rooms are set up for corporate clients, with high-speed Internet access. The inn has a lap pool and a full-service health club with steam, weights, and stationary bikes.

HOTEL ST. HELENA $$$$
1309 Main Street, St. Helena
(707) 963-4388, (888) 478-4355
www.hotelsthelena.net

This restored hotel in the heart of downtown is quintessential St. Helena: immaculate, charming, and not cheap. It was an upscale hotel when it was built back in 1881, but it soon deteriorated into a second-floor flophouse over the local Montgomery Ward. Now it has recaptured and redefined its glory. At ground level are shops and a flowery arcade, plus a wine and coffee bar in the lobby. Upstairs are 18 antiques-filled rooms painted in combinations of subdued tones: burgundy, mauve, chocolate, dark tan, and pale gold. Fourteen of the rooms have private baths, some with old claw-foot tubs. A large continental breakfast is included in the price, as well as complimentary wine in the afternoon. This is a nonsmoking property.

CALISTOGA INN $$
1250 Lincoln Avenue, Calistoga
(707) 942-4101
www.calistogainn.com

For a no-frills (OK, maybe a couple of frills), ambience-thick stay in Calistoga, try the Calistoga Inn, an old western-style hotel that dates from 1882. The 18 second-floor rooms, connected by a creaking wood-floored hallway, sit over a restaurant and microbrewery/bar (see the Restaurants and Nightlife chapters). Each room has a sink and a queen bed (one room has two twin beds), but there are central, shared bathrooms and showers, and no in-room TVs. Continental breakfast is included; brunch, for an extra charge, is available on weekends.

MOUNT VIEW HOTEL $$$$
1457 Lincoln Avenue, Calistoga
(707) 942-6877, (800) 816-6877
www.mountviewhotel.com

This is the closest Calistoga comes to the Ritz-Carlton. The mission revival building, now a National Historic Landmark, was constructed in 1919 and served the area for years as the European Hotel, haunt of literary bigwigs and first ladies. (It is said that Mrs. Herbert Hoover planted the roses in the garden.) An elegant lobby takes you to either the hotel or Mount View Spa; both are run separately and found separately in this book. BarVino Wine Bar is right next door (see the Restaurants chapter). The hotel has 32 rooms, suites, and cottages, the latter being detached units (with private spa tubs) out by the pool. The other rooms are on the second floor, and some have antique furnishings. Continental breakfast is delivered to your room. No smoking is allowed anywhere on this property.

HOTEL D'AMICI $$$$
1436 Lincoln Avenue, Calistoga
(707) 942-1007
www.hoteldamici.com

If Calistoga had luxury apartment suites, they'd look something like this. Hotel d'Amici is downtown, perched on the second floor of a 1936 building once known as Green Hotel. (The "secret door" is just to the right of the Flatiron Grill entrance.) The hotel has four spacious, well-appointed rooms, two of which share a balcony over Lincoln Avenue, making them coveted spaces during the Fourth of July and its Silverado Parade (see the Festivals and Annual Events chapter). All have private baths, and continental breakfast is delivered to your door. The owners also run Rutherford Grove Winery. You pick up your keys there (1673 Highway 29 in Rutherford) and get a complimentary wine tasting.

CLARION COLLECTION LODGE AT
CALISTOGA $$$$
1865 Lincoln Avenue, Calistoga
(707) 942-9400, (877) 424-6423
www.clarionhotel.com

Only in Calistoga would the Clarion have a mineral-water swimming pool and whirlpool tub. It also has a sauna and steam room. Each of the 55 rooms (including a 2-room suite) features individual temperature control, cable TV, coffeemakers, and hair dryers. Continental breakfast is included in the price.

STEVENSON MANOR INN $$$$
1830 Lincoln Avenue, Calistoga
(707) 942-1112
www.stevensonmanor.com

This motel is affiliated with Best Western. Stevenson Manor has a pool, a sauna, and a gazebo-sheltered central courtyard. The 34 rooms are done in subdued shades of green and burgundy. Four have private whirlpool baths, and seven are warmed by fireplaces; all of them are equipped with refrigerators, microwaves, and coffeemakers. All rooms are nonsmoking.

SONOMA COUNTY

Southern Sonoma

LEDSON HOTEL $$$$$
480 First Street E., Sonoma
(707) 996-9779
www.ledsonhotel.com

This is quite likely Sonoma County's smallest luxury hotel. Opened in 2003 and overlooking the Sonoma Plaza, Ledson Hotel was created by the owners of Ledson Winery (see the Wineries chapter), who know a lot about constructing unique properties. The hotel's six guest rooms are on the second floor; on the first floor is Harmony Lounge, a wine bar featuring a menu of small plates expertly paired with Ledson wines, and live music on occasion. Each elegant guest room has its own personality, plus king beds, whirlpool tubs, fireplaces, and balconies. Modern amenities include surround-sound TVs and high-speed Internet access. Three rooms overlook the plaza (try to reserve one of these for people-watching).

EL DORADO HOTEL $$$$
405 First Street W., Sonoma
(707) 996-3220, (800) 289-3031
www.eldoradosonoma.com

On the northwest corner of Sonoma Plaza, the El Dorado has had a checkered history as a government office, college, winery, and hotel. Salvador Vallejo, brother of Gen. Mariano Vallejo, built the adobe in the early 1840s; subsequently, it was occupied by Bear Flag Party members (see the History chapter) as well as Gen. John C. Frémont during the opening days of the Mexican War. Today its 23 rooms and four bungalows have an aura of casual elegance. It's definitely the right choice for those who want to revel in the plaza's historical ambience. Some rooms face the plaza and have balconies looking onto it below. Other rooms face onto a garden courtyard and overlook flowers and trees. All have private baths. The El Dorado Kitchenette has an assortment of delicious takeaway breakfast and lunch offerings; the hotel's sit-down restaurant is El Dorado Kitchen. There's a pleasant stone courtyard for dining al fresco under a large fig tree.

EL PUEBLO INN $$$
896 West Napa Street, Sonoma
(707) 996-3651, (800) 900-8844
www.elpuebloinn.com

Built of adobe brick, this is the classic L-shaped motel of the 1950s. With a large, heated swimming pool, whirlpool, exercise room, and garden courtyard around the 53-room complex, it is an excellent location for either families or couples. Cribs are available, and there's a coffeemaker, hair dryer, and refrigerator in each room, plus cocoa and biscotti for the kids. Continental breakfast is included.

SONOMA HOTEL $$$$
110 West Spain Street, Sonoma
(707) 996-2996, (800) 468-6016
www.sonomahotel.com
Situated on the northwest corner of Sonoma Plaza, this fine old hotel was originally a town hall built in the 1880s. Rooms are furnished with antique furniture and one, the Vallejo Room, has a bedroom suite of carved rosewood once owned by Gen. Mariano Vallejo's family (see the History chapter). All rooms are furnished in keeping with the 19th century, and all have been given names to match their decor—Bear Flag room, Yerba Buena, and Italian Suite. In one of the rooms, author/poet/actress Maya Angelou holed up to write her third novel. All 16 rooms have private baths and air-conditioning. Breakfast is served in a quaint foyer that retains the original fireplace and stained-glass windows. At street level is the Girl & the Fig restaurant (see Restaurants chapter).

BEST WESTERN SONOMA
VALLEY INN $$$$$
550 Second Street W., Sonoma
(707) 938-9200, (800) 334-5784
www.sonomavalleyinn.com
This hotel was built in 1987, but it has been designed in California mission-style architecture to match the ambience of the town's early Mexican heritage. One of its great assets is its location: It's only two blocks from the city's plaza (see the Shopping chapter), yet away from city hubbub with rooms that face onto an inner courtyard. Most of the 73 rooms, which were recently redecorated, have patios or decks for outdoor privacy. The spacious rooms feature either a fireplace or a Jacuzzi. New to this hotel is Spa Gratitude, which offers a varied menu of treatments. A laundry room is available, and continental breakfast is

delivered to your room. Children 16 and younger stay free, and your dog is welcome, too, for an extra fee. The hotel's event center can accommodate up to 170 people.

GAIGE HOUSE $$$$
13540 Arnold Drive, Glen Ellen
(707) 935-0237, (800) 935-0237
www.gaige.com
www.thompsonhotels.com
Once a humble little inn, this elegant Italianate Victorian, restored from its original 1880s construction, has gone upscale as a boutique hotel. Gaige House has a prime location at the edge of the village of Glen Ellen in the heart of the Sonoma Valley. It has 23 rooms altogether, some in the main house and newer suites around the grounds. Most of the decor property-wide is contemporary Asian.

The signature lodging in the main house is the Gaige Suite, a sunny corner room with large windows on two sides and a huge private deck overlooking the pool and gardens. The bathroom in this suite is to die for: besides being mammoth, it has a soaking tub for two with headrests and a shower that wouldn't look out of place in a museum of modern art. Outside the main house, I like the Woodside suite, with its private fountain and creekside table for two. In 2006 the inn added eight fabulous spa Zen suites with private gardens, granite soaking tubs, and dual showerheads.

The lushly landscaped three-acre setting includes a large swimming pool and Jacuzzi. Spa services are offered; inquire at the time of booking. A two- or three-course breakfast is served for an extra charge; lunch and dinner are not available. Flashlights are provided for guests to make the short walk to restaurants after dark. This property is now part of the small Thompson Hotels group of hip boutique hotels.

SHERATON SONOMA COUNTY HOTEL $$$$
745 Baywood Drive, Petaluma
(707) 283-2888, (800) 325-3535
www.starwoodhotels.com
Opened in 2002, this marina-front hotel featuring

Asian architectural details has 180 guest rooms, including 3 suites. (The grand staircase is a stunner.) The setting is convenient to U.S. Highway 101, yet the hotel offers views of adjacent protected wetlands along the Petaluma River, about 300 acres' worth. The rooms are decorated in earth tones and include state-of-the-art phone systems in addition to the usual amenities you would expect from a Sheraton. Meeting spaces total nearly 10,000 square feet, including a 4,300-square-foot grand ballroom. Begin your day in the fitness center, equipped with men's and women's saunas and outdoor swimming pool and spa. End your day dining at Tolay, the hotel restaurant.

QUALITY INN $$
5100 Montero Way, Petaluma
(707) 664-1155, (866) 407-4959
www.winecountryqi.com
Built in 1985, the hotel features seven clustered Cape Cod–style buildings nestled amid landscaped grounds and redwood arbors planted with grapes. Its 109 guest rooms include 36 with in-room spas and 4 two-room suites with private spas. Some rooms have kitchenettes. The outdoor pool is surrounded by a large sundeck with an adjacent sauna. Its location near Adobe Creek Golf & Country Club and its Robert Trent Jones Jr.–designed course makes it appealing to golfers (see the Golf section of the Parks and Recreation chapter), and shoppers will be glad to know it's only a mile to Petaluma Village Premium Outlets. A full continental breakfast is served.

DOUBLETREE HOTEL $$$$
1 DoubleTree Drive, Rohnert Park
(707) 584-5466, (800) 222-TREE
www.doubletree.com
Set on 22 acres between two golf courses, the hotel evokes Sonoma County's Spanish heritage with tile roofs and arched windows. For business travelers, the DoubleTree offers every convenience and amenity necessary for meetings and full conferences, including 18,000 square feet of conference space; it's also conveniently located

near US 101 and offers express bus service to the San Francisco airport. But those on business will also find, as do great numbers of tourists, that it's a very enjoyable resort, with 245 luxurious guest rooms and suites, a restaurant, a pool and spa, and live entertainment.

HYATT VINEYARD CREEK HOTEL,
SPA & CONFERENCE CENTER $$$$
170 Railroad Street, Santa Rosa
(707) 284-1234
www.vineyardcreek.hyatt.com
This hotel in downtown Santa Rosa opened in 2002. The $30 million property with Mediterranean-inspired architecture and courtyards has 155 plush rooms with upscale amenities and the extra touches business travelers appreciate: dual-line speakerphones with voice mail and complimentary domestic and international newspapers. Some rooms have fireplaces and whirlpools; all have deluxe minibars. The Seafood Brasserie is the hotel's fine-dining establishment, focusing on French-inspired fresh seafood dishes (see the Restaurants chapter). You can get an in-room massage treatment too. Facials, massages, bodywork, and treatments of many types are offered, including a warmed river-rock massage.

The 21,000-square-foot conference center is the largest in the area, with a multitude of meeting rooms, big and small. All this, and it's a two-minute walk to Railroad Square's restaurants and antiques stores.

COURTYARD SANTA ROSA
BY MARRIOTT $$$$
175 Railroad Street, Santa Rosa
(707) 573-9000, (800) 321-2211
www.marriott.com
Right on the edge of historic Railroad Square, this Marriott hotel has close access to enough antiques shops to delight any collector looking for bargains or the unusual. All the standard amenities are available in this 138-room inn. Kids will love the swimming pool, spa, and in-room movies; adults can explore any of the interesting restaurants located within walking distance.

HOTEL LA ROSE $$$$

308 Wilson Street, Santa Rosa
(707) 579-3200, (800) 527-6738
www.hotellarose.com

A quaint and romantic hotel in Santa Rosa's historic Railroad Square, Hotel La Rose was reconstructed in 1985 and designated a National Historic Landmark. The hotel is graced with a charming English country interior decor that belies the fact that this is a very modern hotel. The four-story main hotel has elevator access to its 28 nonsmoking rooms, and the carriage house, added in 1985, has 20 additional guest rooms built around a lovely courtyard. One of the hotel's great assets is its proximity to the restaurants in Railroad Square, including its own, Josef's.

FLAMINGO RESORT HOTEL
& FITNESS CENTER $$$

2777 Fourth Street, Santa Rosa
(707) 545-8530
www.flamingoresort.com

Lush landscaping makes this resort hotel very appealing both as a vacation spot and as a business center offering conference facilities for 600 people. This property was extensively freshened up in 2004, with approximately $1 million spent on remodeling and renovations. For the harried executive or the tourist, there's plenty of physical activity available on-site, including a heated pool, Jacuzzi, tennis courts, lighted jogging path, basketball and volleyball courts, and table tennis. Available for a modest fee is the Montecito Heights Health & Racquet Club. The 170 rooms are luxuriously appointed with elegant furnishings—some rooms also have copy machines and refrigerators. This is a favorite base camp for Hollywood moviemakers when they come to town. In fact, portions of the film *Bandits* were filmed at the Flamingo.

FOUNTAIN GROVE INN $$$$

101 Fountaingrove Parkway, Santa Rosa
(707) 578-6101, (800) 222-6101
www.fountaingroveinn.com

In harmony with the natural environment, the Fountain Grove Inn's design is all redwood and

i For a room like no other, book one of the luxurious tent cabins at Safari West, an African-style wildlife preserve located between Santa Rosa and Calistoga. You'll get a king-size bed and private bath, plus the sounds of exotic animals nearby. See the Attractions chapter for more details.

stone, sweeping low across historic Fountaingrove Ranch. The lobby too is far from ordinary, dominated by a large redwood sculpture of the legendary horse Equus. Utmost restraint and understated elegance mark the inn's 125 rooms, which all have separate dressing alcoves, double closets, and work spaces with wireless Internet. The rooms underwent redecorating in 2007. The inn's pool, waterfall, and spa offer a view of the historic Round Barn, which sits atop a small nearby hill. The inn's restaurant, not surprisingly called Equus, carries out the theme, with the legendary horse etched in glass and redwood carvings.

HILTON SONOMA WINE COUNTRY $$$$

3555 Round Barn Boulevard, Santa Rosa
(707) 523-7555, (800) 445-8667
www.winecountryhilton.com

Just off US 101 north of downtown Santa Rosa on 13 acres of Fountaingrove Ranch, this hotel has let stand the historic landmark known as the Round Barn to mark its entrance. New in 2004 was a $6 million makeover of much of the facility. This chalet-style hotel has 246 rooms and suites and boasts many amenities, including a state-of-the-art in-room phone system, business center, an on-site restaurant called Nectar, an outdoor patio with a panoramic view of the Santa Rosa valley, a Junior Olympic–size swimming pool, and an on-site workout facility.

VINTNERS INN $$$$$

4350 Barnes Road, Santa Rosa
(707) 575-7350, (800) 421-2584
www.vintnersinn.com

Your first vision of Vintners Inn may make you feel

as if you've dropped into a charming European village. From the French country decor to the arched windows and wrought-iron railings, the hotel exudes old-world atmosphere—a group of three red-roofed buildings is arranged around a plaza and fountain, surrounded by acres of vineyards. Many of the 44 oversize rooms in this Provence-inspired inn have fireplaces, exposed-beam ceilings, and pine furniture, some of which dates from the turn of the 20th century. Ground-floor rooms have patios; second-floor suites have balconies with vineyard or courtyard views. In-room spa services can be arranged. A conference center with a lounge called the Front Room was added in 2005. On the premises is John Ash & Co., a nationally acclaimed restaurant serving some of the best cuisine in Sonoma County (see the Restaurants chapter).

Northern Sonoma

HOLIDAY INN EXPRESS $$$$
8865 Conde Lane, Windsor
(707) 837-0808, (877) 676-6662
www.sonomahi.com
The proven reputation of Holiday Inn Express doesn't disappoint at this location between Santa Rosa and Healdsburg, just off US 101. There are 75 rooms and 5 suites with either queen- or king-size beds, microwaves and refrigerators, and work desks with high-speed Internet access. A complimentary buffet breakfast is included.

HOTEL HEALDSBURG $$$$$
25 Matheson Street, Healdsburg
(707) 431-2800, (800) 889-7188
www.hotelhealdsburg.com
The biggest thing to pop up in Healdsburg in the past few years was this three-story, 55-room, $21 million luxury hotel that overlooks the quaint plaza in central Healdsburg. It's been extremely popular with visitors and made the list of the best 500 hotels in the world for 2008 compiled by *Travel & Leisure* magazine. The rooms all feature oversize bathrooms with walk-in showers and soaking tubs, French doors opening to private balconies, wood floors with Tibetan rugs,

bathrobes and fine linens, and the usual modern amenities for business travelers. Even more luxurious suites are available (there are six of them), if that's your pleasure. Room service is offered from the Dry Creek Kitchen (see the Restaurants chapter) and breakfast is delivered to your door. The lobby features a grappa bar, the garden has a 60-foot pool, and there's a cardio-fitness room for a quick workout. All this and a spa too! You can get pampered to your heart's content, from massages to facials to a couples room with a soaking tub for two. Thai massage and healing techniques are a specialty. Across Matheson Street on the south side of the hotel is its new 6,500-square-foot conference center.

LES MARS HOTEL $$$$$
27 North Street, Healdsburg
(877) 431-1700
www.lesmarshotel.com
In 2005, Healdsburg raised its profile even higher with the opening of this small but luxurious European-style hotel. The rooms—only 16 of them—are furnished with 18th- and 19th-century antiques, and feature four-poster canopy beds inspired by French royalty and dressed in Italian linens. The bathrooms have oversize showers or BainUltra tubs. Everything about this place is first-class, including the restaurant at street level, called Cyrus (see the Restaurants chapter). *Condé Nast Traveler* added the Les Mars to its "Hot List" of best new hotels in 2006. Without a doubt, this is the priciest stay of its kind in Sonoma County, with a Grand Room on the third floor fetching $1,000 per night. The "cheaper" rooms start at $575.

DUCHAMP HOTEL $$$$$
421 Foss Street, Healdsburg
(707) 431-1300, (800) 431-9341
www.duchamphotel.com
This contemporary hotel is made up of six cottage suites that are all unique, with artist Marcel Duchamp as the inspiration and the namesake. Unlike any lodgings in Wine Country, the rooms are poolside and creekside "villas" that are nearly spartan in their luxurious opulence. All the rooms feature modern amenities, fireplaces, down

comforters on king-size beds, and fabulous bathrooms with spa showers. The complimentary breakfast will start your day off right, and the 50-foot pool and heated Jacuzzi beckon after wine tasting and sightseeing. *Condé Nast Traveler* magazine once proclaimed the Duchamp as "one of the world's top 25 new hot hotels." It's a great location, down a quiet side road off the main thoroughfare through Healdsburg, yet an easy 2-block walk to the shops and restaurants on the town's plaza. This is a nonsmoking property that is unsuitable for children. English, German, and French are spoken here.

BEST WESTERN DRY CREEK INN $$$
198 Dry Creek Road, Healdsburg
(707) 433-0300, (800) 222-5784
www.drycreekinn.com
The distinguishing factor here is this motel's outstanding location for wine touring in the beautiful Dry Creek Valley. The 103 Vintage rooms are pleasant, redecorated in 2006 in an updated but standard motel style. An additional 60 Tuscan rooms are in a new courtyard building, and these are a bit more luxurious with extra amenities and comforts. A continental breakfast is included no matter which room you stay in. There's a pool, whirlpool, and exercise room. A new conference center opened in 2007 with meeting space for up to 150 people. Pets are permitted in the Vintage rooms.

GEYSERVILLE INN $$$
21714 Geyserville Avenue, Geyserville
(707) 857-4343, (877) 857-4343
www.geyservilleinn.com
Situated at the north end of the town of Geyserville and surrounded by vineyards, this hotel is ideal for visiting Dry Creek and Alexander Valley wineries as well as hitting the bike trails that crisscross this rural countryside. It's also close to Lake Sonoma (see the Parks and Recreation chapter). The 36 rooms have a Wine Country feel, decorated in shades of vineyard green and the russet colors of autumn. There are also two new suites. Rooms are graced with various amenities—for example, patios or balconies and fireplaces—and

there is also a swimming pool and spa. The views are lovely, and the rural atmosphere is very relaxing. A continental breakfast is served each morning. The Hoffman House restaurant is just steps away.

SUPER 8 $$
1147 South Cloverdale Boulevard, Cloverdale
(707) 894-9288, (800) 800-8000
www.super8.com
If it's a basic, clean motel you seek, Super 8 will satisfy. Located on the south edge of town, it's a short drive to the historic downtown. There's a pool, whirlpool, and exercise room, and a complimentary breakfast. This 43-room motel is ideally suited for exploring Alexander Valley's many wineries.

BEST WESTERN CLOVERDALE INN $$
324 South Cloverdale Road, Cloverdale
(707) 894-7500, (800) 995-9780
www.bestwestern.com
At the Citrus Fair exit of US 101 is this attractive, clean motel with 59 standard rooms and 3 suites. You can expect the amenities Best Western is known for, along with a fitness room and generous continental breakfast. The fairgrounds and historic downtown are just a short walk away.

Sonoma Coast
BODEGA BAY LODGE & SPA $$$$$
103 Coast Highway 1, Bodega Bay
(707) 875-3525, (800) 368-2468
www.bodegabaylodge.com
Luxurious and intimate on eight landscaped acres, the lodge overlooks wildflower-covered dunes, protected marshlands, the Pacific Ocean, and the gentle surf of Doran Beach. Though it's close enough to enjoy the sound of the surf, the wood-shingled lodge is sheltered from coastal winds. All 84 spacious guest rooms have fireplaces, private balconies, and original artwork. Many feature vaulted ceilings, spa baths, refrigerators, wet bars, and coffeemakers. The 5,000-square-foot conference center is impressive, with high, arched ceilings supported by thick beams of polished

oak. The Duck Club Restaurant can be counted on for imaginative cuisine. Complimentary wine is served in the late afternoon. An assortment of massages, body treatments, and facials are available in the on-site spa. The 18-hole Robert Trent Jones Jr.–designed Links at Bodega Harbour is next door (see the Parks and Recreation chapter).

INN AT THE TIDES $$$$
800 Coast Highway 1, Bodega Bay
(707) 875-2751, (800) 541-7788
www.innatthetides.com

Six coastal acres with natural landscaping surround this inn, which is actually an enclave of 12 separate lodges that appear to be part of the rumpled hills and tawny headlands. Each of the 86 guest quarters overlooks Bodega Bay. Most rooms have king beds and wood-burning fireplaces. Amenities include a heated indoor-outdoor pool, spacious spa, soothing sauna, and luxurious logo bathrobes. (One night under a starry sky I had the pool all to myself.) In-room massage can be arranged, too. A continental breakfast is served, and gourmet cuisine is featured in the Bay View Restaurant (see the Restaurants chapter).

FORT ROSS LODGE $$$
20705 Coast Highway 1, Jenner
(707) 847-3333
www.fortrosslodge.com

Just north of historic Fort Ross State Historic Park (see the Attractions chapter), the lodge is situated above a sheltered cove where seals lounge on rocky outcroppings. There's plenty of space in the guest rooms to stretch out and relax, or you can unwind in the hot tub and sauna. The 22 rooms are decorated in natural tones and hues. There's a barbecue on each deck and a country store across the highway. Children younger than 12 stay free. Intimate, secluded suites are available for adults only.

SALT POINT LODGE $$
23255 Coast Highway 1, Timber Cove
(707) 847-3234, (800) 956-3437
www.saltpointlodgebarandgrill.com

This is a well-maintained, older motor lodge, with 16 rooms. Situated on a knoll overlooking the ocean, Salt Point Lodge includes a restaurant with a full bar, serving breakfast, lunch, and dinner. Lovely gardens surround the place, and it's open year-round. There are TVs and VCRs in the rooms, but no phones. Besides the nearby beaches, there are miles of hiking trails to explore.

SEA RANCH LODGE $$$$$
60 Sea Walk Drive, Sea Ranch
(707) 785-2371, (800) 732-7262
www.searanchlodge.com

On bluffs above the Pacific Ocean, this lodge features one of the best vistas in Wine Country. All but one of its 20 rooms face the sea, and cozy window seats offer front-row viewing for spectacular sunsets. If you're in need of a peaceful getaway, this is the place. Rooms are walled in knotty pine, and the aura is rustic. Some units have fireplaces, and family units are available. All are luxuriously appointed. TVs are missing from most rooms. All rooms are nonsmoking. Hiking trails along the bluffs are well marked, and you can follow them down to the beach. A challenging 18-hole golf course is available, and there's also a restaurant.

West County/Russian River

SEBASTOPOL INN $$$$
6751 Sebastopol Avenue, Sebastopol
(707) 829-2500, (800) 653-1082
www.sebastopolinn.com

Conveniently located near downtown Sebastopol's quaint shops and eateries, this inn features comfortable rooms equipped with coffeemakers, microwaves, and hair dryers. On-site is a full-service day spa, a pool and Jacuzzi spa, and a coffeehouse with frequent live entertainment. Fireplace and spa tub suites are also available.

DAWN RANCH LODGE $$$
16467 Highway 116 E. (River Road),
Guerneville
(707) 869-0656
www.dawnranch.com

Dawn Ranch is the newest incarnation of this 100-year-old property, last known as Fife's. It features 15 forested acres of towering coast redwood and private gardens. The 51 cottages and cabins range from the basic one-room variety to an elegant two-bedroom, two-bath deluxe version with fireplace and hot tub. The rooms are not equipped with TVs or phones. The Roadhouse Restaurant includes a fine selection of pub food and grill specials. There is private access to the banks of the Russian River, and the resort is also walking distance to downtown Guerneville, where you can peruse the antiques shops and have coffee at a local cafe. The resort is closed in winter.

WEST SONOMA INN & SPA $$$
14100 Brookside Lane, Guerneville
(707) 869-2470, (800) 551-1881
www.westsonomainn.com
A charming family resort located at the edge of Guerneville's Korbel vineyards and bordered by Fife's Creek, West Sonoma Inn offers 36 spacious rooms, some with their own patio and kitchen. There are also 4 suites. Amenities include a pool and on-site spa facility with three treatment rooms. A new sundeck with a wine bar and large Jacuzzi tub were added in 2008. This property, under new ownership, has been significantly renovated.

NORTHWOOD LODGE & RESORT $$$
19455 Highway 116, Monte Rio
(707) 865-1655, (877) 865-1655
www.northwood-lodge.com
If you like to golf amidst towering redwoods, you can't find a better place to stash your golf bag. Northwood is an older but suitable motel for golf enthusiasts, with an assortment of room sizes, including cottages with full kitchens. Most rooms have microwaves and refrigerators; all have satellite TV and air-conditioning. Children—and adults—will like the pool on those hot August days. Golf packages are available for the links next door at Northwood Golf Course (see the Parks and Recreation chapter).

VACATION RENTALS

Sonoma County

RUSSIAN RIVER VACATION HOMES
14080 Mill Street, Guerneville
(707) 869-9030, (800) 997-3312
www.riverhomes.com
Since 1975 this firm has provided a large selection of vacation rental homes throughout western Sonoma County at two-night rates ranging from $380 to $1,500; weekly rates from $925 to $4,000. Many homes are suitable for two or more families vacationing together, and will accommodate from 4 to 14 people. The Summit Ridge Estate sleeps 24 in two separate houses on 60 private acres.

RUSSIAN RIVER GETAWAYS
14075 Mill Street, Guerneville
(707) 869-4560, (800) 433-6673
www.rrgetaways.com
All the homes this company offers are first-class and most are dog-friendly, with many choices in size, location, and amenities. Picture yourself in a cozy hideaway for two in the redwoods or an elegant lodge with a dramatic river view in the wine-tasting region. Prices range from $160 to $750 per night, $960 to $6,600 per week. Ask about the Palazzo Sergianni, a custom Italian-style villa with fabulous views.

RAMS HEAD RENTALS
1000 Annapolis Road, Sea Ranch
(707) 785-2427, (800) 785-3455
www.ramshead-realty.com
More than 120 vacation rentals are offered, from two-night stays to multiple weeks. Sites are available in the meadows, in the forest, or on the oceanfront. The most desirable oceanfront sites offer grand vistas and the dramatic crashing of the waves. Expect a two-night stay to range from $338 to $1,425, and weekly rates from $845 to $3,800.

BED-AND-BREAKFAST INNS

Around here, the definition of bed-and-breakfast is changing. Many lodgings in Wine Country are now blurring the lines between B&B and luxury inn. B&Bs are a throwback to a time when accommodations were small and homespun, offering travelers not just an affordable bed (and typically a shared bath) but a social experience as well. That basic premise still holds here, but the B&Bs themselves and the amenities they offer are nothing like what travelers of yesteryear could have imagined.

In this chapter I've included properties that remain true to the original intent of a bed-and-breakfast inn. A small number of rooms—and the owner more likely than not living on-site—adds to the personal feel of staying in someone's home, not a hotel. Most of these lodgings did indeed begin life as large houses or public buildings, now oozing with history, before being converted to B&Bs. Though many carry through with the antiques-and–country prints theme, others have tossed out the doilies and ruffles in favor of less cluttered, more contemporary decor. Modern touches include spa tubs and high-speed Internet access, now common at many B&Bs. Another plus: Quite a few of these lodgings can arrange in-room massages or spa treatments in garden settings. But one thing is certain: You can count on a lavish breakfast, and late afternoon wine and cheese or hors d'oeuvres are usually offered.

OVERVIEW

Nearly all innkeepers prohibit smoking in the rooms—and sometimes even on the grounds—and do not allow pets. Many establishments also have a two-night minimum on weekends, so always inquire when booking. What about kids? B&Bs usually do not forbid children, but innkeepers acknowledge that many of their guests are attempting to get away from children for a few days. In general, assume that bringing the little ones along is not a good idea. The few exceptions to this are noted in the descriptions.

Price Code

The following price ratings are based on the cost of one night's lodging for double occupancy on a weekend in high season (generally May through October). Most inns offer significant discounts for off-season or midweek stays. Note that prices do not include taxes, gratuities, or services that are considered extra.

$	Less than $130
$$	$131 to $160
$$$	$161 to $200
$$$$	More than $200

NAPA COUNTY

CHURCHILL MANOR BED & BREAKFAST INN $$$$
485 Brown Street, Napa
(707) 253-7733, (800) 799-7733
www.churchillmanor.com

In the heart of the Fuller Park Historic District is a grandiose, three-story Second Empire mansion built in 1889 for local banker Edward Churchill. With close to 10,000 square feet of space (and that doesn't include the full basement or the pillar-supported, three-sided veranda), it was said to be the largest domicile in Napa Valley for decades. The interior is essentially unaltered. There are four grand parlor rooms with beveled and leaded glass and redwood moldings and fireplace frames. You get a full breakfast in the dining room, plus complimentary wine and cheese (and fresh-baked cookies) in the afternoon. Play croquet in the side garden, borrow a tandem bicycle, or just stroll around the acre of grounds and toast the fat wallet of Edward Churchill. In-room spa services can be arranged, too.

CEDAR GABLES INN $$$$
486 Coombs Street, Napa
(707) 224-7969, (800) 309-7969
www.cedargablesinn.com
Chances are, you've never seen a house like this one. Designed by British architect Ernest Coxhead in 1892, it's an immense, brown-shingled home that you might expect to find on an estate in England's Cotswolds. In fact, the feeling here is decidedly masculine, making it a logical choice for people who begin whining when they hear the expression "bed-and-breakfast." Cedar Gables' nine guest rooms are sizable and brimming with period antiques. The Churchill Chamber, originally the master bedroom used by Edward and Alice Churchill, has a walnut-encased whirlpool tub to match the fireplace. Several of the rooms have old coal-burning fireplaces, converted to gas. Breakfast is served either at the long, formal dining room table or cafe-style in the adjacent sun room.

INN ON RANDOLPH $$$
411 Randolph Street, Napa
(707) 257-2886, (800) 670-6886
www.innonrandolph.com
This modest, tasteful inn is on a quiet street in a neighborhood of historic homes. The main house, an 1860 Gothic revival Victorian, has five rooms with seasonal themes (the fifth is called Equinox). Spring, for example, boasts intricate flowers painted on the walls and ceiling, and Autumn features a handcrafted bent-willow canopy bed. Five more expensive rooms are in cottages dating from the 1930s. All of the cottages and some of the main-house rooms have gas fireplaces and two-person whirlpool tubs; some have private decks. Roses line the front walk, and the gardens are flanked by a common deck, a gazebo, and

hammocks. The Inn on Randolph serves a full breakfast, and in-room massage can be arranged.

BEAZLEY HOUSE $$$
1910 First Street, Napa
(707) 257-1649, (800) 559-1649
www.beazleyhouse.com
On a row of rambling turn-of-the-20th-century mansions, this house was originally built for local surgeon and politician Adolph Kahn in 1902, but he and his wife divorced and left the area seven years later. Subsequent owners included the Hanna Boys Center and San Francisco jet-setter Joan Hitchcock, who reputedly had an affair with JFK and for a fact had seven husbands. The Beazley, the first B&B in the city of Napa, now has 11 rooms, 6 in the main house and 5 in the carriage house. The latter are large units, each with a fireplace and two-person spa tub. Ask for the Sun Room, a bright and nostalgic corner with a two-sided balcony and a 6-foot soaking tub. Flat-screen TVs recently were added to the rooms, as well as other upgrades. Full breakfast is served in the formal dining room. Children are permitted, and even your dog is treated like your best friend.

CANDLELIGHT INN $$$
1045 Easum Drive, Napa
(707) 257-3717, (800) 624-0395
www.candlelightinn.com
In the tradition of all good bed-and-breakfast inns, this English Tudor–style mansion with 10 guest rooms will pamper you with four-poster beds, French doors, private balconies, and a three-course breakfast. The Garden View room has a private entrance and deck, with—you guessed it—views of the garden and 30-by-60-foot swimming pool. Other rooms look out on the surrounding hills, and several rooms have Jacuzzi tubs for two and marble fireplaces. All rooms have TVs and phones.

HENNESSEY HOUSE $$$$
1727 Main Street, Napa
(707) 226-3774
www.hennesseyhouse.com

Adjacent to the Jarvis Conservatory on the fringe of Napa's turn-of-the-20th-century downtown, Hennessey House is an Eastlake-style Queen Anne built in 1889 for Dr. Edwin Hennessey, one-time mayor of the town. The 10 rooms (6 in the main residence, 4 in the carriage house) are air-conditioned, and most have canopy, brass, or feather beds. Some have claw-foot or two-person whirlpool tubs in the bathroom, and the carriage-house rooms have fireplaces. Breakfast has been known to feature delights such as blueberry-stuffed French toast or basil-cheese strata. A hand-painted, stamped-tin ceiling shelters the dining room. In the evening you can enjoy wine and cheese by the garden fountain.

ARBOR GUEST HOUSE $$$
1436 G Street, Napa
(707) 252-8144, (866) 627-2262
www.arborguesthouse.com

In the Napa neighborhood appropriately known as Old Town, the Arbor Guest House is a pretty, whitewashed colonial with a porch swing in front and a shady garden in back. The house is compact, but the rooms—three units upstairs, two more in the original carriage house—manage to be ample, and all have queen beds. Two of them have spa tubs, three have fireplaces, and the main-house rooms are cooled by a reliable cross-breeze (and air-conditioning, if the temperature spikes). Breakfast is served in the dining room or the garden or, if you're staying in the carriage house, it is brought to your door with prior notice.

LA BELLE EPOQUE $$$$
1386 Calistoga Avenue, Napa
(707) 257-2161, (800) 238-8070
www.labelleepoque.com

In 1893 Napa's leading hardware dealer built this splendid Queen Anne for his infant daughter, who died shortly thereafter. Tragic origins aside, La Belle Epoque beams with class: multigabled dormers, Oriental carpets, divans, marble-topped dressers, and radiant stained glass, much of it transplanted from an old church. There are a total of nine rooms (two are deluxe suites in a property

across the street from the main house). You get your full breakfast in the formal dining room, on the garden patio, or delivered directly to your suite. The inn also has its own wine cellar and, therefore, an evening wine reception with tastes of vino from small boutique producers.

THE OLD WORLD INN $$$
1301 Jefferson Street, Napa
(707) 257-0112, (800) 966-6624
www.oldworldinn.com

This 1906 Victorian isn't as noisy as you might think, despite being situated on busy Jefferson Street (where it meets Calistoga Avenue). The inn is touched up in mellow pastel blue, rose, peach, and mint—and the nine guest rooms are a mix of contemporary and quaint, with romantic names such as Starry Night and Chocolat. Five of the rooms have spa tubs, and all have large hi-def TVs/home theater. The most private unit is Walden Cottage, in a separate building on the property, and it's a good choice if you're traveling with small children. You'll receive cookies upon arrival, evening hors d'oeuvres such as smoked salmon or Moroccan eggplant on sourdough bread, and a late-night buffet of chocolate treats. Of course, you get a full, hot breakfast in the dining room.

BROOKSIDE VINEYARD
BED & BREAKFAST $$
3194 Redwood Road, Napa
(707) 252-6690
www.sandtcellars.com

With seven acres of land, Brookside offers plenty of room for blending with nature. Tom and Susan Ridley's homey spot is full of images and relics true to the house's mission style. The three ground-floor guest rooms are off a long hallway, and each opens onto the garden. About half the acreage is devoted to vineyard, and visitors have been known to join the autumn crush. Elsewhere, fruit trees, California poppies, and Douglas fir trees abound, and a path descends to a creekside clearing. (At least it's creekside when Redwood Creek is flowing.) Brookside has a swimming pool, and the largest bedroom has a dry sauna.

LA RÉSIDENCE $$$$
4066 Howard Lane, Napa
(707) 253-0337, (800) 253-9203
www.laresidence.com

Is La Résidence a hotel disguised as a bed-and-breakfast inn or a B&B masquerading as a hotel? Does it matter when you're sitting in the elegant, sun-infused dining room at a table for two, eating a three-course breakfast from the fixed but ever-changing menu? La Res, as it is called, is a nice surprise within shouting distance of Highway 29. The 16 rooms and 4 suites are divided between the 1870 Gothic revival mansion and the newer French Barn. Most include working fireplaces and patios or verandas, and all the modern amenities are here: flat-screen TVs, wireless Internet, and DVD players. The inn sits on two and a half acres of heritage oaks, pines, and vines. There is a swimming pool, a separate Jacuzzi, and a small meeting room for up to 15 people. New owners of this property, Craig and Kathryn Hall of Hall Winery fame, are planning improvements and changes to make the inn even more luxurious. King beds, significantly renovated bathrooms, and more services and amenities are part of their plans. The Halls also own a couple of boutique hotels in Paris, so they know what they're doing.

OAK KNOLL INN $$$$
2200 East Oak Knoll Avenue, Napa
(707) 255-2200
www.oakknollinn.com

The land around Oak Knoll Inn is part of Napa County's agricultural preserve, but businesses such as this were allowed to operate before the zoning regulations changed. It has a virtual monopoly on 360-degree vineyard views. There is a big wooden deck outside the rooms, so you can spend all day looking at the grapes and the mountains. Oak Knoll Inn has four units, each with a fireplace and private entrance. A heated pool and spa are available for common use. The place is known for its breakfasts; on a typical day the morning meal may include baked pears in cognac sauce, baked herbed eggs, and fresh muffins. But mostly the inn is renowned for the detailed itineraries that owner Barbara Passino customizes for guests. This is not a good option for couples with young children.

MAISON FLEURIE $$$
6529 Yount Street, Yountville
(707) 944-2056, (800) 788-0369
www.foursisters.com
www.maisonfleurienapa.com

In the middle of Yountville (but a block away from most of the traffic) is this French-style country inn. The 100-year-old main building has 2-foot-thick stone walls, terra-cotta tile, and a gas fireplace in the brick parlor. Two other structures—the Old Bakery (a working bakery in the 1970s) and the carriage house—bring the total number of rooms to 13. You get a gourmet breakfast (or breakfast in bed if you'd rather) and a jar of home-made cookies in the lobby. A swimming pool, spa tub, and mountain bikes are available for guest use. Maison Fleurie is part of Four Sisters Inns, a group of nine bed-and-breakfast establishments, most of them on the California coast.

> **i** California's gold rush brought an influx of new residents to the state, and with them came a variety of eastern U.S. architectural styles. For example, many of San Francisco's new Victorian homes were constructed in the Italianate style. An exceptional example can be found in St. Helena's Ink House, built in 1884.

BORDEAUX HOUSE $$$$
6600 Washington Street, Yountville
(707) 944-2855, (800) 677-6370
www.bordeauxhouse.com

A mixture of newer (1980) and older (1895) structures, Bordeaux House is in the heart of Yountville, surrounded by lovely trees and gardens, and with world-class restaurants and shops within easy walking distance. (The French Laundry is just steps away, in fact.) The inn's newer, main building has five guest rooms with fireplaces and private patios or decks. Modern amenities are provided in each room; all have private exterior entrances. The Old Water Tower, overlooking the garden, is about 15 steps up and down. The inn's reception area is where you can enjoy your morning buffet breakfast and late afternoon port and munchies.

THE INK HOUSE $$$
1575 St. Helena Highway S., St. Helena
(707) 963-3890
www.inkhouse.com

This remarkable house is a wedding-cake Italianate Victorian with a wraparound porch and a third-floor crow's nest. Built by Theron H. Ink in 1884, it's now a seven-room bed-and-breakfast inn where the highway meets Whitehall Lane. The Ink House has a formal parlor and dining room for guests. You get a full breakfast in the morning, appetizers and wine, usually poured by a local winery, in the afternoon. The rooms are lovely but not huge—five have private baths; two share a bath. The observatory serves as the TV room. While taking advantage of the 360-degree panorama, you might pop in a video of *Wild in the Country*, an Elvis Presley romp filmed at the Ink House in 1960. The inn also offers an antique pool table in the basement, and horseshoes and croquet outside. A steep staircase makes this an unsuitable choice for families with kids.

SHADY OAKS COUNTRY INN $$$$
399 Zinfandel Lane, St. Helena
(707) 963-1190
www.shadyoakscountryinn.com

The buildings are full of history at Shady Oaks, but it's the two acres of outdoor space that really sell the inn. On one side of the house is a working walnut orchard; on the other are grapevines. And in back, a twisted 100-year-old wisteria vine protects the patio. Shady Oaks offers two suites (each with private entrance) in a two-story stone structure that operated as a winery in the 1880s. Three more rooms are found inside the 1920s Craftsman-style home. Each unit features its own small collection of antiques; particularly lovely are the beds, such as the brass and ivory king in

the Winery Retreat. Three of the rooms have fireplaces, and the Sunny Hideaway has an adjoining second bedroom. Afternoon wine is served on the patio. Champagne breakfast, meanwhile, is a splendid affair likely to entail eggs Benedict or Belgian waffles served in elegant style.

GLASS MOUNTAIN INN $$$$
3100 Silverado Trail, St. Helena
(707) 968-9400, (877) 968-9400
www.glassmountaininn.com

Glass Mountain was named for its large deposits of obsidian, or black glass. That obsidian is evident in the dining room of the Glass Mountain Inn, where guests can peer into a wine cave dug by Chinese laborers (originally for perishables, not Pinots) in the late 1800s. The house, with its wood shingles and steepled roof, isn't nearly as old as the cave. The inn has five large rooms with private baths, most with private balconies and sitting areas. In addition to four-poster king beds (in four of the rooms), there are iPod docking stations, sound machines, and DVD players. Guests are greeted with a full breakfast each morning that might include egg and vegetable frittata or fresh blueberry pancakes. Children 12 and older are welcome in the cottage.

THE AMBROSE BIERCE HOUSE $$$$
1515 Main Street, St. Helena
(707) 963-3003
www.ambrosebiercehouse.com

Ambrose Bierce was a novelist, a poet, an essayist, a cartoonist, and a noted misanthrope. He wrote *The Devil's Dictionary* before disappearing in Mexico in 1913. The 1872 Victorian home he left behind in St. Helena bears his name and offers visitors three lovely rooms and a covered balcony tucked next to a grand redwood tree. The Ambrose Bierce Suite, secluded on the second floor, has a private sitting room (with a television) that can be converted into a second bedroom. All rooms have plush, raised beds; stools are provided to help you make your way up under the covers. A full champagne breakfast is served in the morning, premium wine and cheese in the evening. Each guest room is equipped with a crystal decanter of port. Relax to classical music in the parlor, or soak in the home's hot tub. Parents, please note that children are not recommended here.

SCARLETT'S COUNTRY INN $$$
3918 Silverado Trail, Calistoga
(707) 942-6669
www.scarlettscountryinn.com

A "country inn" can sometimes mean a suburban cul-de-sac and a large rose garden. But Scarlett's is the real thing, a bucolic acre midway between Calistoga and St. Helena, where guests share space with friendly dogs and chickens. The early-20th-century farmhouse now holds two of the three guest units—the Gamay Suite and the Camellia Suite, which actually can be opened into a full house for larger parties. Each room boasts a separate entrance, queen-size bed, TV, microwave, and fridge. But the outdoor space is the big selling point here: a hammock, a tree swing, an aviary with finches and canaries, a lush fig tree, a pine-protected swimming pool, and a spa. Full breakfast is served.

CHRISTOPHER'S INN $$$$
1010 Foothill Boulevard, Calistoga
(707) 942-5755, (866) 876-5755
www.christophersinn.com

Crafted by an architect who combined a house with two cottages to make one large building, this inn is nice enough from the outside, but that doesn't hint at the luxury held within the 21 rooms. Delicate prints, exquisite antique desks, fresh flowers, and high, open ceilings—it's a tasteful experience. Some rooms have private Jacuzzis. Breakfast—yogurt, baked cobbler, etc.—is delivered to your door. There's also complimentary espresso, cappuccino, and port. In-room massage can be arranged. Christopher's also has two voluminous flats in back, facing onto Myrtle Street, that sleep as many as five people. Children are allowed at the inn.

WINE WAY INN $$
1019 Foothill Boulevard, Calistoga
(707) 942-0680, (800) 572-0679
www.winewayinn.com

This bed-and-breakfast inn, opened in 1979, was the first in Calistoga. It's near Calistoga's busiest intersection, and the owners want you to know up front that there is some street noise. Nonetheless, from the solid oak front door with etched glass to the soft colors of the decor in each second-story room, the owners have managed to create a pleasant environment in their circa-1915 home. In addition to the five interior rooms, the Calistoga Room is a detached unit—it's out by the multitiered deck that backs up to a wooded hillside. The breakfasts alternate daily between sweet and savory, with specialties such as frittata and tomato omelets. They serve their own blend of coffee here, made by Calistoga Roastery and served French-press style.

CHELSEA GARDEN INN $$$$
1443 Second Street, Calistoga
(707) 942-0948, (800) 942-1515
www.chelseagardeninn.com

This small, five-suite bed-and-breakfast on the corner of Fair Way and Second Street tries for neither Victorian splendor nor designer finery but emphasizes comfort. Each unit has a sitting room, bedroom, and private bath; some have kitchen facilities. Air-conditioning is provided in all rooms. There is a latticed courtyard, pool, and hot tub. A full breakfast is served.

HIDEAWAY COTTAGES $$$
1412 Fair Way, Calistoga
(707) 942-4108
www.hideawaycottages.com

Look for the hedges and palm trees in front of a two-story gingerbread house on peaceful Fair Way. In back are 17 cottages facing onto a landscaped courtyard. The two-acre site is just 2 blocks from Lincoln Avenue. Many of the rooms have full kitchens, CD players, VCRs, and wireless Internet access. Hideaway, an affiliate of Dr.

Wilkinson's Hot Springs (see the Spas and Resorts chapter), has a large mineral pool and spa tub. Breakfast is made up of baked goods from the Model Bakery in St. Helena and coffee roasted right in town at Calistoga Roastery.

BRANNAN COTTAGE INN $$$
109 Wapoo Avenue, Calistoga
(707) 942-4200
www.brannancottageinn.com
Nearly 150 years ago, this spot had row upon row of one-story white bungalows, all with five-arch fronts, intricate gingerbread gable boards, wraparound porches, and scalloped cresting. Now only one of them remains on its original site, and it's a six-room inn. (Two of the rooms are out back in the carriage house.) The look of the place—the 11-foot ceilings, oak floors, and ceiling fans—whisks you right back to the days of Sam Brannan (see the History chapter). Each unit has a queen bed and a refrigerator. Full buffet breakfast is served in the dining room or on the patio. Children 12 and older are accepted, and dogs are allowed with prior approval.

COTTAGE GROVE INN $$$$
1711 Lincoln Avenue, Calistoga
(707) 942-8400, (800) 799-2284
www.cottagegrove.com
This location was once the promenade area of Brannan's Hot Springs Resort, the spa that gave birth to Calistoga (see the History chapter). The grove of Siberian elms was planted by Brannan in the 1850s, and today they form an effective visual barrier to the traffic of Lincoln Avenue. Each of Cottage Grove's 16 private cottages has a wood-burning fireplace (and a basket of wood on the porch), a CD stereo system, TV and VCR, air conditioner, private bath with two-person Jacuzzi tub, Egyptian cotton towels, and an ironing board. Each has a theme too, like the Music Cottage, the Audubon Cottage, and the Fly Fishing Cottage. Continental breakfast and evening wine and appetizers are served in the common room. The owners allow children age 12 and older. Smoking is not allowed.

CRAFTSMAN INN $$$
1213 Foothill Boulevard, Calistoga
(707) 341-3035
www.thecraftsmaninn.com
Appropriately named after its style of architecture, the Craftsman Inn has five rooms dubbed for local mountains and cliffs. All are elegant and classy, with 600-thread-count sheets, jetted tubs, flat-screen TVs, and a decanter of Madeira. The champagne breakfast is a treat; owner Gillian Kite is a chef, so the morning meal will make your day. It could be spinach and smoked salmon quiche, or sweet corn fritters with bacon. One of the perks at this inn is a package deal for a room and cooking classes, taught by Gillian. In-room spa services can also be arranged.

THE PINK MANSION $$$$
1415 Foothill Boulevard, Calistoga
(707) 942-0558, (800) 238-7465
www.pinkmansion.com
Alma Simic was a colorful character. She was the previous owner and longest resident to live in this stately home, and she had eclectic tastes in decorating, with a mixture of Victorian and Oriental influences. Fortunately for visitors, the current owners have made certain that Alma's sense of style remains intact. The six guest rooms are elegant and tasteful, and most have views. The Master and Honeymoon Suites are large—900 and 800 square feet, respectively—and feature king-size beds, two-person spa tubs, and private decks and sitting rooms. There's also an indoor heated pool and spa. A full breakfast is included, along with afternoon wine tasting. By the way, the mansion has been pink since the 1930s.

CALISTOGA WAYSIDE INN $$$$
1523 Foothill Boulevard, Calistoga
(707) 942-0645, (800) 845-3632
www.calistogawaysideinn.com
This split-level, Spanish-style home, built in the 1920s, is more like something you would expect to see in an older Los Angeles neighborhood, but it seems right at home in Napa Valley. The living room has rough beams and a wood fireplace.

The backyard is densely shaded by trees—a dogwood, English walnut, loquat, and at least a dozen others. The three guest rooms are comfortably furnished and cooled by ceiling fans. One of them, the Camellia Room, has sole use of the home's original master bathroom.

CHANRIC INN $$$$
1805 Foothill Boulevard, Calistoga
(707) 942-4535, (877) 281-3671
www.thechanricinn.com

This circa-1875 Victorian mansion was renamed by the new owners and given a freshening-up. The six guest rooms are nicely furnished with contemporary furniture and muted colors, and the wi-fi is property-wide. There's a private pool, spa, and sauna out back, and a full breakfast is included in the tariff (think parmesan polenta with sautéed spinach and tomato eggs). The views from the veranda of the Palisades to the east are worth toasting to.

AURORA PARK COTTAGES $$$
1807 Foothill Boulevard, Calistoga
(707) 942-6733, (877) 942-7700
www.aurorapark.com

Stair-stepping up the hill from Foothill Boulevard are six private cottages in refreshing yellow and white. Four of the cottages have queen beds, and two are kings. A large deck is attached to each cottage, perfect for sitting and contemplating the distant mountains and Calistoga's beautiful Palisades cliffs. The cabins have welcoming easy chairs, breakfast nooks, refrigerators, TVs, and baskets of pastries and fresh fruit delivered each morning. This is a country setting, but it's only a short walk to the action in downtown Calistoga. Ask the owners about their "semifamous" wine tasting notes.

BEAR FLAG INN $$$$
2653 Foothill Boulevard, Calistoga
(707) 942-5534, (800) 670-2860
www.bearflaginn.com

Just northwest of the intersection of Highway 128 and Petrified Forest Road, this five-room bed-and-breakfast is a renovated farmhouse built in the 1930s. Purportedly it was on this very site that Peter Storm constructed one of the flags used for the Bear Flag Revolt in 1846. The Bear Flag Inn sits on three acres, surrounded by vineyard and meadowed hillside. Four rooms are in the two-story house; the cottage is a detached unit with a sitting room. All guest rooms have private baths, queen-size beds, robes, cable TV and VCRs, and air-conditioning. There is a swimming pool and an outdoor hot tub for guests, and a bocce ball court, too. A full breakfast is served, with wine and appetizers in the afternoon.

FOOTHILL HOUSE $$$$
3037 Foothill Boulevard, Calistoga
(707) 942-6933, (800) 942-6933
www.foothillhouse.com

One of Calistoga's most renowned B&Bs sits in a woodsy setting on the northwest outskirts of town. Fountains and cascades lend a soothing air, and views to Mount St. Helena help to keep you oriented as you sit in the arbor or Jacuzzi. Each room includes TV and VCR, CD player, refrigerator, and fireplace or woodstove. Three of the four have whirlpool tubs. Each has its strengths, but the Quails Roost, a detached cottage just up the hillside, is clearly the palatial unit. Quiet and private, the Quails Roost has a full kitchen and a washer/dryer setup; guests have been known to rent it for a week and go into hiding.

SONOMA COUNTY

Southern Sonoma

THISTLE DEW INN $$$
171 West Spain Street, Sonoma
(707) 938-2909, (800) 382-7895
www.thistledew.com

This is a prime location for Wine Country visitors. Just a half block off the Sonoma Plaza, the Thistle Dew puts guests within short walking distance (or biking distance, if you want to borrow from the inn's stable) of fine restaurants, shops, wineries, and historic sites. The six guest rooms manage to provide a feeling of seclusion and privacy in spite of the fact that the inn is on a busy street on the edge of downtown. Breakfast is served in the dining room looking out on Spain Street. All rooms have private baths, and some have whirlpool baths (a shared hot tub is outside).

VICTORIAN GARDEN INN $$
316 East Napa Street, Sonoma
(707) 996-5339, (800) 543-5339
www.victoriangardeninn.com

It's a farmhouse built in 1870, but it's only blocks from the downtown plaza. The wraparound porch with wicker chairs harks back to a simpler time. But it's the gardens that make this inn unique. Lawns and paths wind through the trees and along the creek, with occasional spots to sit and contemplate. The four guest rooms—one in the main house and the rest in a century-old water tower—have private baths and are elegantly decorated. Woodcutter's Cottage is a private retreat with a fireplace, claw-foot tub, and garden view. Breakfast is served in the dining room, on the patio, or in your room. The inn also offers professional massage services in your room or on the patio. A pool and spa are available, too.

TROJAN HORSE INN $$$
19455 Highway 12, Sonoma
(707) 996-2430, (800) 899-1925
www.trojanhorseinn.com

A change in ownership resulted in a complete change in the theme and feel of this inn. Each of its six rooms is named for a music legend, and all are richly dressed in luxury linens. Check out the Sarah Vaughan room, for instance. There's also the Ellington room (for Duke), and Ms. Holiday's room (a tribute to Billie). A full breakfast is served along with fresh fruit and gourmet coffee. Friday and Saturday early evenings are for gathering in the parlor for wine and munchies.

ABOVE THE CLOUDS $$$
3250 Trinity Road, Glen Ellen
(707) 996-7371, (800) 736-7894
www.abovethecloudsbb.com

The mountain road called Oakville Grade (up Trinity Road on the Sonoma side) straddles the Mayacmas Mountains that rise between the Sonoma and Napa Valleys. Trinity Road sprouts from Highway 12 about 8 miles north of the Sonoma Plaza and winds through thickets of manzanita and scrub oaks for 3 miles before reaching Above the Clouds bed-and-breakfast inn. When the fog rolls through the Sonoma Valley, this inn lives up to its name. It's a secluded mountain retreat that surveys forests and catches the sunset. Three guest rooms are furnished with antique iron or brass beds, and each has a private bath, queen-size bed, down comforters, and lots of pillows. Robes are provided for those who want to take advantage of the swimming pool and spa tub. A gourmet breakfast is served.

BELTANE RANCH $$$
11775 Highway 12 (Sonoma Highway),
Glen Ellen
(707) 996-6501
www.beltaneranch.com

The place has an exotic—even romantic—past. The land was first settled in 1882 by Mary Ann "Mammy" Pleasant, whose exploits as a madam to San Francisco's upper crust (plus suspicions of a possible homicide in her posh establishment) led to alarming headlines. It was said she conducted black magic sessions too. But Mammy had another side: She became known as the western terminus of the Underground Railroad, making frequent trips to the South to secretly help thousands of blacks escape to Canada. Beltane Ranch's architectural style suggests Deep South, with a stylish veranda set off with an elaborate gingerbread railing. But the ranch's recent past is more mundane. In the 1920s it was the bunkhouse for a turkey ranch. Inside are five guest rooms (and one cottage), each with an individual outdoor entrance. The rooms are rustic but cozy, furnished with antiques. The 1,600 acres include a working vineyard, and the owner is happy to tour the grounds with you and explain what viticulture is all about. This is a popular lodging place, and reservations are definitely recommended during the harvest season of August through October.

GLENELLY INN $$$

5131 Warm Springs Road, Glen Ellen
(707) 996-6720
www.glenelly.com

This is one of the few Wine Country bed-and-breakfast inns that was actually built as an inn. Visitors of the 1920s and '30s came by railroad and basked in the sun on the inn's long verandas. Each of the eight rooms has a private entrance and is furnished in a country motif, with antique furniture and down comforters. The Jack London Room has a sleigh bed and wood-burning stove. An outdoor spa is set amid native landscaping. (Changes and improvements were planned at this inn at press time; check the Web site for updated information.) In the morning, a full breakfast is served by a large cobblestone fireplace in the common room. This is a child-friendly inn.

THE GABLES INN $$$

4257 Petaluma Hill Road, Santa Rosa
(707) 585-7777, (800) 422-5376
www.thegablesinn.com

Built in 1877 at the height of Victorian Gothic revival architecture, this home was constructed with 15 gables rising above some unique keyhole-shaped windows. There are seven rooms in the main house—five up a mahogany staircase, and two accessible to disabled guests—some of which include fireplaces, and all of which share central air-conditioning. Each room is furnished in unique decor that displays its history and character. An adjacent cottage is furnished with a kitchenette, TV with video library, stereo, woodstove, and two-person whirlpool tub. A lavish country breakfast is served.

MELITTA STATION INN $$

5850 Melita Road, Santa Rosa
(707) 538-7712, (800) 504-3099
www.melittastationinn.com

Once this was a busy railroad station; before that it was a general store and post office. Today it's a warm inn with six guest rooms (five if the two-room suite is occupied) furnished with antiques and folk art. The inn's former life is evident in its unique plank flooring and hand-sawed fir

boards with the sawyer's strokes still well marked. The style here is American antique, with lots of collectibles to admire. The setting is part of the charm: The inn is surrounded by state parks, hiking trails, and biking opportunities. A full buffet breakfast is served by the wood-burning stove in the large sitting room on the balcony. It's in a good location for exploring both the Sonoma Valley and the city of Santa Rosa.

Northern Sonoma

CAMELLIA INN $$$

211 North Street, Healdsburg
(707) 433-8182, (800) 727-8182
www.camelliainn.com

From November to May the inn is overtaken by blooming camellias, hence the name. Built in 1869, the house served at one time as Healdsburg's first hospital, and in fact the room you rent might have been the lab. As a plus, the Camellia Inn is just two blocks from historic Healdsburg Plaza and its chic shops and restaurants. When you return to your room from your excursions, you might recuperate from the rigors of shopping in your whirlpool tub for two, light up the gas fireplace if you're chilly, and have a lovely night's sleep in your four-poster bed. The Camellia Inn includes a family suite—unusual in an industry largely geared toward couples. Breakfast is served buffet style, and evening wine and cheese is included. The family that owns this inn also operates Camellia Cellars—visit its tasting room at 57 Front Street in Healdsburg.

GRAPE LEAF INN $$$$

539 Johnson Street, Healdsburg
(707) 433-8140
www.grapeleafinn.com

Pssst! Don't look now, but there's a secret room behind that bookcase in the corner. Yes, this inn takes the B&B experience a step further with a hidden speakeasy just for guests. A gentle push on the bookcase and it swings open to reveal a secret wine cellar and gathering spot. Here you will find many local small-production wines available for tasting, sometimes poured by the winemakers themselves. Elsewhere around the 1900 Queen Anne Victorian are 12 guest rooms ranging from masculine to feminine—there's a room for just about any taste. Some feature fireplaces and spa tubs. The award-winning gardens add to the charm. Expect a full gourmet breakfast that might include Grand Marnier croissant French toast with mango-papaya salsa. The inn is just a five-minute walk from the town plaza.

i The Grape Leaf Inn in Healdsburg has a special "speakeasy" hidden behind a bookcase. Each evening, guests at the inn are treated to a generous pouring of Sonoma County wines in the secret hideaway.

HAYDON STREET INN $$$
321 Haydon Street, Healdsburg
(707) 433-5228, (800) 528-3703
www.haydon.com
In a quiet residential area within walking distance of Healdsburg's historic plaza, this Victorian inn has nine charming guest rooms. One of the most popular is the Turret Room, tucked into the slope of the roof, with a step-down entrance to the sleeping level. Each of the other rooms is distinctively different in decor, from iron bedsteads and handmade rugs to French antique furnishings. Six of the guest rooms are in the main house, a 1912 Queen Anne structure, and three are in the adjoining two-story Victorian cottage. All rooms have private baths; those in the cottage also have double whirlpool tubs.

HEALDSBURG INN ON THE PLAZA $$$$
110 Matheson Street, Healdsburg
(707) 433-6991, (800) 431-8663
www.healdsburginn.com
Once a Wells Fargo building, the inn now rates high on the luxury scale. Two rooms are downstairs, and a staircase leads to the 10 light-filled rooms upstairs—most with fireplaces, all with private baths, in-room phones, and TVs, and some with whirlpool tubs for two. Room 3 is spacious, with a bay window view of the plaza;

room 7 has its own deck on the south side of the inn. A solarium on the second floor is the common area where guests meet for breakfast and afternoon refreshments. Susan, the chef, offers a main egg dish, fresh baked scones or muffins, house-made granola, French toast, fresh fruit, and more. The afternoon goodies usually consist of an artisan cheese platter and hors d'oeuvres with wine tasting.

BELLE DE JOUR INN $$$$
16276 Healdsburg Avenue, Healdsburg
(707) 431-9777
www.belledejourinn.com
This inn's hilltop setting is on six acres and looks out on rolling hills. The farmhouse, a single-story Italianate built around 1873, is the residence of the innkeepers, and it is here guests enjoy a hearty breakfast. Guests are quartered in five white cottages, all with fireplaces and some with decks. Each cottage is its own country experience. The Caretaker's Suite, for instance, has a king-size canopy bed and a fireplace in the sitting room. There's a sunny studio atelier room with a high, vaulted ceiling, and the grand Carriage House has everything, including views and a tub for two.

MADRONA MANOR $$$$
1001 Westside Road, Healdsburg
(707) 433-4231, (800) 258-4003
www.madronamanor.com
Tucked away in the lush Dry Creek Valley, Madrona Manor is an estate for which adjectives like *elegant* and *majestic* were invented. As you ascend the driveway and the house reveals itself, a soft "wow" may exit your lips. Originally built in 1880 by business tycoon John Paxton, Madrona Knoll Rancho, as it was then called, became one of the grandest showplaces in all the valley. Today it stands as a wonderful exponent of a bygone era of grandeur and refined taste. Of only a handful of Wine Country inns and resorts that made *Travel & Leisure* magazine's "Best 500 Hotels in the World" list in 2008, Madrona Manor came out on top. The manor's accommodations include 21

rooms in four buildings on eight acres of wooded and manicured grounds. Eighteen of the rooms have fireplaces, and eight have a balcony or deck. Probably the most luxurious suites are the two found in the "schoolhouse," with king beds, large sitting rooms, and big bathrooms. (This is a no-TV environment.) A buffet-style breakfast is included. Need more elegance? World-class gourmet dining can be enjoyed Wednesday through Sunday in a romantic candlelight setting (see the Restaurants chapter). And you've been warned: If you stay in the main house, the aromas coming from the kitchen at dinnertime will drive you mad.

RAFORD INN $$$
10630 Wohler Road, Healdsburg
(707) 887-9573, (800) 887-9503
www.rafordinn.com

Here's a Victorian inn with an expansive porch ideal for sipping wine. Raford Inn sits on a knoll surrounded by vineyards and palm trees, and the view from the porch is worth the price. The structure dates from the 1880s and is listed as a Sonoma County historical landmark. The six guest rooms are furnished with queen-size beds, and each has a private bath. A hearty breakfast is dished up every morning. Smoking is prohibited property-wide.

VILLA MESSINA $$$
316 Burgundy Road, Healdsburg
(707) 433-6655
www.villamessina.com

The setting is unbelievable, with a 360-degree view of three exquisite valleys—Alexander, Dry Creek, and Russian River. The Italian villa–style inn was built in 1986 on top of the foundation of a former water tower. The inn's five guest rooms are furnished with antiques, and the floors are carpeted with Oriental rugs. All rooms have private baths, plus TVs, VCRs, and phones. Some have Jacuzzis or fireplaces. For breakfast the chef prepares such treats as fresh-squeezed orange juice and blueberry pancakes with bacon. There is a swimming pool and hot tub.

HOPE-BOSWORTH HOUSE $$
21238 Geyserville Avenue, Geyserville
(707) 857-3356, (800) 825-4233
www.hope-inns.com

Driving down Geyserville Avenue, you'll have no trouble recognizing the Hope-Bosworth House—it's the Queen Anne with the picket fence covered with "roses of yesteryear" varieties that were popular when the house was built in 1904.

All four of the guest rooms are a step into the past. The original oak-grained woodwork is evident everywhere, from the sliding doors in the hallway to the upstairs bedrooms. Polished fir floors and antique light fixtures enhance the period furnishings. A country breakfast is served in the formal dining room and includes fresh fruit, egg dishes, homemade breads and pastries, and coffee or tea.

HOPE-MERRILL HOUSE $$$
21253 Geyserville Avenue, Geyserville
(707) 857-3356, (800) 825-4233
www.hope-inns.com

In its former life, it was a stagecoach stop of the 1870s. Now it's an enchanting inn, listed on the Sonoma County landmarks register. Anyone interested in architecture will recognize the squared-off look of Eastlake Stick style, popular between 1870 and 1885. J. P. Merrill, who was a land developer, saw to it that he had the best of everything for his house, and he built it entirely of redwood. The inn has eight rooms, all with queen-size beds and private baths. Four rooms have fireplaces, two have whirlpool baths, and one has a sitting room. There's also a swimming pool. Breakfast is superb, served in the dining room.

OLD CROCKER INN $$$
1126 Old Crocker Inn Road, Cloverdale
(707) 894-4000, (800) 716-2007
www.oldcrockerinn.com

Dripping with history, this fine old Victorian was recently converted into a comfortable B&B with rooms in the main house and several outdoor cottages. Up a winding road in a secluded setting on five acres southeast of the town of Cloverdale, the inn was once the home of railroad tycoon Charles Crocker of the Central Pacific Railroad, who used the property as his summer hunting grounds. He occasionally brought along other railroad barons to enjoy a bit of the sport, as well as President Ulysses S. Grant. From the main house are wonderful views of the Russian River, vineyards, and surrounding hills. Each lodge room has a door that opens onto the main deck, which in itself is a relaxing environment. The rooms are equipped with private baths, gas fireplaces, ceiling fans, DVD/VCRs, and high-speed Internet access. The Crocker room has a magnificent carved king poster bed. My favorite is the cottage set away from the main lodge, the Canton, furnished by the owners with Chinese treasures from their travels in the Orient.

VINTAGE TOWERS INN $$
302 North Main Street, Cloverdale
(707) 894-4535, (888) 886-9377
www.vintagetowers.com
Mining executive Simon Pinchower had an unusual idea when he asked an architect to design a Queen Anne house in 1901. He wanted three towers, all built in different shapes—one round, one square, and one octagonal—so his house would be different from its neighbors. Pinchower is long gone, but his legacy has given travelers a fine way to spot the seven-guest room Vintage Towers Inn. Each of the three tower suites has its own sitting area, sleeping quarters, and private bath. There's even a telescope in the Vintage Tower suite. The wide front veranda's porch swing is a pleasant place to relax after a day of touring the countryside. A hearty breakfast can be expected, such as basil and artichoke frittata.

West County/Russian River
THE INN AT OCCIDENTAL $$$$
3657 Church Street, Occidental
(707) 874-1047, (800) 522-6324
www.innatoccidental.com
This is the type of romantic getaway where you can be together surrounded by the forested hills of western Sonoma County. Each of the 16 rooms

is decorated with meticulous care. All rooms have a private bath and fireplace, and most have decks. Several units have double spa tubs and views of the courtyard, and a two-bedroom cottage is also available. TVs are optional. For eye-popping yellow walls, ask for the Cirque de Sonoma room. A full breakfast is included.

THE FARMHOUSE INN & RESTAURANT $$$$
7871 River Road, Forestville
(707) 887-3300, (800) 464-6642
www.farmhouseinn.com
It's one of those places that's difficult to categorize because it does it all: an inn with breakfast included in the tariff, an award-winning restaurant, and a full-service spa with a Pilates and yoga studio. In 1878 it really was a working farm, with a row of cottages off to the side for the workers. Those cottages are now charming private guest rooms with luxurious amenities such as jetted spa or soaking tubs, CD players, flat-panel TVs, DVD players, refrigerators, feather beds, rich linens, and European-style rain showerheads. Many of the rooms also have fireplaces and personal saunas. Full concierge services are offered, too. What really put this inn on the map is its restaurant, which has been collecting major accolades over the past few years (see the Restaurants chapter).

SONOMA ORCHID INN $$
12850 River Road, Guerneville
(707) 887-1033, (888) 877-4466
www.sonomaorchidinn.com
This property was formerly known as Ridenhour Inn, after Louis Ridenhour, who came to this land in 1850 and began farming 940 acres along the Russian River. The house, however, was not built until 1906. What guests find today is a large living room overlooking redwoods, and six guest rooms in the main house, each with a private bath, and four rooms in a nearby cottage. One of them, Hawthorn Cottage, has a fireplace and cozy window seat. New owners have significantly upgraded and redecorated the rooms. Korbel Champagne Cellars is within walking distance (see the Wineries chapter), and the Russian River

is five minutes away by foot. The eggs in your breakfast are courtesy of the inn's own chickens, and the fresh produce is grown on-site. A down-home touch: The kitchen is available to guests 24 hours a day.

APPLEWOOD INN & RESTAURANT $$$$
13555 Highway 116, Guerneville
(707) 869-9093, (800) 555-8509
www.applewoodinn.com

Nineteen stylish rooms and suites fill three multi-story Mediterranean-style villas set among apple orchards and redwood trees. Each is individually decorated, romantic, and formal, yet familiar—like the home of a wealthy great-aunt. The newer rooms have fireplaces, sitting areas, private verandas or decks, and either couples showers or spa tubs for two. The common area is centered on a huge stone fireplace. The restaurant seats 50 (see the Restaurants chapter). The kitchen, once reserved for breakfast, now offers dinner Tuesday through Saturday. A full breakfast is served. A spa suite on the property is where you can get rubbed and scrubbed. No smoking is permitted anywhere on the grounds, and guests must be 21 or older.

FERN GROVE COTTAGES $
16650 Highway 116, Guerneville
(707) 869-8105, (888) 243-2674
www.ferngrove.com

A small, quaint village of 22 cottages, Fern Grove provides a stylish country atmosphere and a base for exploring the back roads of the West County. Cottages range from spacious one-bedroom suites to intimate guest rooms with sitting areas, most with knotty pine walls. All have a refrigerator; some have fireplaces, spas, or TVs. Stroll the gardens, swim in the pool, enjoy the general ambience. The buffet breakfast features homemade pastries. The shops of downtown Guerneville are within walking distance.

SPAS AND RESORTS

Our mud is world famous. I'm not kidding. In addition to ultrapremium wine grapes, the region known as Wine Country has unlimited quantities of rich volcanic ash just below the surface, thanks to prehistoric eruptions of our resident inactive volcano, Mount St. Helena (pronounced Hel-LAY-nah). The ash and the hot water that naturally percolates way down in the earth's strata constitute the main ingredients of our legendary mud baths that attract visitors by the hundreds of thousands. Some of the nation's finest and famous full-service resort spas are here, and most of them revolve around mud, steam, massaging fingers, and the like. Treatments invented to make use of the antioxidant benefits of wine grapes—who knew?—are now found on most spa menus. You won't literally be stomping the grapes, but you can pay to sit up to your neck in a "red wine bath," and that's not too far removed.

OVERVIEW

These resorts offer amenities and services above and beyond a standard lodging—places that will rub you, wrap you, soak you, feed you, and give you a bed in which to drop your newly detoxified body. Make no mistake: Most of these are pricey, luxurious accommodations, as the price code below reflects. ("Bargains" can still be found in Calistoga.) Even if you can't afford to rent a room, cottage, or lodge at one of these places, it's fun to read about them and dream. But they aren't as out of reach as you might think: Most offer day-spa services—the same treatments available to the resort's guests— so you needn't miss out on the body pampering. You can also get exceptional services at one of the day spas listed at the end of this chapter.

Price Code

The following price ratings are based on double occupancy for the least expensive room on a weekend night in high season (generally May through October). Most resorts require a minimum two-night stay on weekends, but many offer significant discounts for off-season or mid-week visits. Special package deals—room, spa treatments, and possibly dinner—might also be available. The tariff usually includes use of facilities such as tennis courts and gyms, but you will pay separately for spa services and golf (where applicable). The prices do not include taxes and tips.

$	Less than $250
$$	$251 to $350
$$$	$351 to $500
$$$$	$501 to $700
$$$$$	More than $701

RESORTS

Napa County

THE CARNEROS INN　　　　　　**$$$$**
4048 Sonoma Highway, Napa
(707) 299-4900, (888) 400-9000
www.thecarnerosinn.com

What happens when you take a 27-acre former trailer park and spend $57 million to transform it into a world-class spa resort? You get the Carneros Inn, one of Napa Valley's premier getaway destinations. The property is southwest of the city of Napa by a few miles in the Carneros grape-growing appellation and is surrounded by vineyard landscapes and sprinkled with fruit orchards and flower gardens. Many celebrities have already partaken of this inn's rural luxuries, and you can too.

A $30 million expansion in the past couple years created a "plaza," a new restaurant, a post office and general store, bocce courts, and an outdoor pavilion. A 5,000-square-foot conference center was also added in 2007. Each of the 86 guest cottages and 10 suites has its own private patio and garden space, accessed through French doors. The cottages provide all the comforts of home—and then some: wood-burning fireplaces, cherrywood floors, spacious bathrooms with heated slate floors (and a choice between showering inside or outside), high-speed Internet access, flat-panel TVs, DVD players, and more. The cottages range in size from 975 to 1,800 square feet of private indoor and outside living space.

Spa treatments borrow from the natural rural setting and incorporate mixtures of herbs, fruits, and flowers. Take the Huichica Creek Bath treatment overlooking the creek of the same name, where your weary muscles will be soothed by jets of warm water. And expect some massaging with gooseberries and goat butter, too. There's also croquet when you're ready for some spirited competition, and full concierge services when you wish to investigate the area's many attractions.

The inn's restaurant, for guests only, is located in the Hilltop reception building. Meals can be delivered to your cottage for private dining. A more casual eatery and wine bar, Boon Fly Cafe, is open to the public. Another restaurant for everyone, called Farm, was added in the 2007 expansion. Among the many accolades the inn has amassed since opening is this one from *Travel & Leisure* magazine: "Carneros Inn is one of the top 25 romantic getaways in the world."

i Sparkling wine is both fun to sip and to rub on your body: The ingredients of white wine yeast extract and the skins of the grapes (with antioxidant-rich properties) can promote skin regeneration. Several spas in Wine Country offer body treatments using these grapes.

SILVERADO RESORT $$
1600 Atlas Peak Road, Napa
(707) 257-0200, (800) 532-0500
www.silveradoresort.com

It is hard not to be impressed by this megaresort at the base of Atlas Peak. For one thing, it's big. Silverado includes 1,200 acres and more than 400 rooms—every one of them a deluxe accommodation with living room, wood-burning fireplace, full kitchen, and a private patio or terrace. Most of the hubbub is centered on the two 18-hole, Robert Trent Jones Jr.–designed golf courses. But there is a slew of additional activity, including mountain-bike rentals, 9 swimming pools, jogging trails, 17 plexi-paved tennis courts, and a 16,000-square-foot spa and gym. Check-in and concierge service are in the circa-1870s colonial mansion, originally owned by Civil War Gen. John F. Miller. There you'll also find a conference center with 15,000 square feet of flexible meeting space (including a 5,200-square-foot grand ballroom) and a fully staffed catering and conventions department. Dining options include the Grill for breakfast and lunch and the Royal Oak for dinner.

VILLAGIO INN & SPA $$$
6481 Washington Street, Yountville
(707) 944-8877, (800) 351-1133
www.villagio.com

Here's an inn inspired by the colors and architecture of Rome and Tuscany. The images of nine Roman goddesses give this property a mythical atmosphere, complete with fountains, vineyards, and gardens galore. The inn has 112 rooms in two-story clusters of buildings; 26 of these are minisuites. Each room comes equipped with fireplace, refrigerator, welcoming wine, TV, terry robes, and the usual modern amenities. Daily continental champagne breakfast is included; afternoon tea, coffee, and cookies are also served. Outside are two heated pools and two tennis courts.

The new 13,000-square-foot Spa Villagio, which opened in spring 2008, features male and female treatment rooms where your epidermis will be delightfully recharged. An additional five new spa suites offer a three-and-a-half-hour experience for individuals or couples. The suites include soaking tubs, wet bars, flat-screen TVs, and saunas for a luxurious pampering. Villagio does all the usual treatments: facials, massage, a Mediterranean salt scrub, and herbal- and oil-infused rubs and wraps. Body treatments include the green coffee wrap ($210) and the elemental body polish using oatmeal, raw sugar, or crushed Carneros grape seeds ($120).

AUBERGE DU SOLEIL $$$$$
180 Rutherford Hill Road, Rutherford
(707) 963-1211, (800) 348-5406
www.aubergedusoleil.com

It began as a restaurant more than 25 years ago but has blossomed into one of Wine Country's most exclusive resorts, nestled among 33 acres of olive trees and chaparral. The whole operation exudes brightness and health, with terra-cotta tile floors, fresh bouquets, natural wood and leather furnishings, and Mediterranean color schemes. The 31 guest rooms and 19 suites all have private terraces, fireplaces, down comforters, stereo CD systems, DVD players, and wireless Internet access. The sizable bathrooms have double sinks and huge tubs under skylights. All of the lodgings have recently undergone remodeling, with fresh new furnishings and Italian linens.

The recreational opportunities include three tournament-surface tennis courts, a swimming pool, a whirlpool tub, and an exercise room. There is a sculpture garden and three separate facilities for meetings, receptions, or special occasions. The spa services are an attraction in their own right. You can get a facial, body wrap, or scalp treatment and choose from a variety of massage styles. The spa also delves into ayurvedic treatments (a holistic approach developed in India some 5,000 years ago), yoga, and somatics, based on "neuromuscular retraining principles." There are also several grapeseed-based massages and exfoliation treatments. Auberge du Soleil is not appropriate for children younger than 16.

MEADOWOOD NAPA VALLEY $$$$$
900 Meadowood Lane, St. Helena
(707) 963-3646, (800) 458-8080
www.meadowood.com

In the 1800s Chinese laborers harvested rice in the small valley known as Meadowood. The full-service Relais & Châteaux estate that now graces the area would have been beyond the wildest dreams of those immigrants. There are 85 suites, lodges, and cottages spread among 250 acres and often tucked into the hillside scenery. All accommodations feature high-beamed ceilings, heated bathroom floors, private porches, and down comforters. If you're feeling active, choose among two pools, a whirlpool, saunas, seven tennis courts, two championship croquet lawns, a nine-hole golf course, and a 3-mile hiking trail. The Health Spa features a dizzying array of fitness classes, personal training, yoga, skin-care treatments, salt treatments, and body wraps (try the Cabernet Crush exfoliation for $135). Be sure to have a romantic dinner in the restaurant to round out the resort experience (see the Restaurants chapter). Meadowood's staff of resident experts includes a wine director who leads Friday-night wine receptions and a croquet pro—one of only two in America. The resort also has five private conference and event rooms with a total reception capacity of 200. Accommodations start at $700 and go up to many times that: The lodges top out at more than $7,000.

CALISTOGA RANCH $$$$$
580 Lommel Road, Calistoga
(707) 254-2800, (800) 942-4220
www.calistogaranch.com

Continuing a trend in Wine Country toward pricey, upscale lodgings that offer it all is Calistoga Ranch, a resort spa that opened in 2004 outside the town of Calistoga. This exclusive enclave of 46 guest lodges, the Bathhouse spa, and for-guests-only Lakehouse restaurant means you can disconnect from the world for a few days of quiet bliss. Of course your room comes with high-speed Internet access when it's time to see how the planet is getting along without you.

The lodges—available in three sizes and tastefully furnished—are equipped with minibars; entertainment centers with TV and DVD and CD players; and down duvets. Prices range from $650 to $845 per night for the deluxe lodges (approximately 600 square feet). The estate lodge on the property is a two-bedroom, two-bath suite with 2,400 square feet of living space. This unit includes a full kitchen, private drive-up entry, and outdoor fireplace (an indulgence at $2,850 to $3,850 per night, depending on the season). Calistoga Ranch provides its guests with a full-service fitness center, bocce courts, valet service, a wine cave for private events, wine seminars and classes, 24-hour concierge service, and 24-hour in-lodge dining. There's even a poolside menu, and picnic baskets may be arranged for day trips. The spa features a natural, spring-fed mineral pool, outdoor treatment tents, and a yoga deck. Because of the resort's setting in a secluded canyon, there are also 157 acres of hiking options.

SOLAGE CALISTOGA $$$
755 Silverado Trail, Calistoga
(866) 942-7442
www.solagecalistoga.com

Combine 89 studio-style rooms and a spa treatment called a Mud Slide and you've got Solage, the newest resort spa to open in northern Napa Valley, just outside the town of Calistoga. In a unique twist, there are two swimming pools (one for adults, and one especially for kids and families). Yes, this is a child-friendly and dog-friendly resort. It's casual, upscale lodging aimed at the younger generation. Rooms range from the Vega studio to the Capella suite. All the latest high-tech gadgetry come with each room (including a docking station for your iPod), along with Italian linens and down bedding. Another plus: Each room gets two bicycles for the short pedal into town for shopping and dining. Calistoga is Mud City, so the signature spa treatment is the aforementioned Mud Slide, where you are greased up with a special mud cocktail and left to bake a bit while your skin is reenergized. After soaking in a tub of geothermal spring water to remove the mud, you cap off the whole experience in a sound chair. The spa and restaurant, Solbar, are open to the public.

DR. WILKINSON'S HOT SPRINGS $
1507 Lincoln Avenue, Calistoga
(707) 942-4102
www.drwilkinson.com

This has been a Calistoga institution since the late John Wilkinson opened his spa in 1952, and it celebrated its 50th anniversary in a big way in 2002. More than a million people have passed through the doc's treatment rooms, and the facility has been profiled on *Good Morning America* and cable travel programs and in the *Los Angeles Times* and *GQ* magazine. A perennial favorite for five decades, "the works"—mud bath, facial mask, mineral whirlpool bath, steam room, blanket wrap, and half-hour massage—is still the most popular package. But expect to pay about $129.00 rather than the original $4.50. Individual spa services start at $59.00 for a half-hour massage. Children must be 14 or older to take a mud bath. Doc also offers an on-site salon where you can get facial and skin-care treatments or select from a wide range of related products.

Doc was a local legend who once served as the town's mayor. As often as not, the fit octogenarian could be found prowling the town's streets, serving as a walking billboard for his health treatments. His two children, Mark and Carolynne, now run the business.

Dr. Wilkinson's has 43 rooms, some with kitchens, all with refrigerators and private baths. Rooms in the adjacent five-unit Victorian—which underwent upgrading and renovation in 2008—are slightly more expensive.

i **President George W. Bush visited Wine Country briefly in 2006, staying overnight at Meadowood resort. The next day he went mountain biking nearby under heavy security. In case the prez crossed paths with a viper, St. Helena Hospital was asked by the White House to have rattlesnake antivenom on hand.**

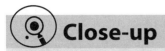

Close-up

Rub-a-dub-dub . . . the Spa Experience

No matter which town or city you're visiting in Wine Country, there's a spa not far from you. Many of our visitors come here especially for the spa treatments, and the spa industry has boomed to make certain they will have a memorable experience. So take the plunge and get ready for a vacation within your vacation as you surrender to a luxurious pampering that redefines "relaxation." Here's a brief sampling of the many body treatments and techniques you will find at our spas.

Mud baths: This is the signature body treatment in Wine Country, and Calistoga is one of the best places to get down in the muck. Typically a mixture of volcanic ash, white clay, peat moss, hot mineral water, and maybe some lavender thrown in for good measure, the magical mud is warmed to a temperature of about 106 degrees. The one-hour mud-bath procedure varies among spas but in general goes something like this: You are immersed and swathed in the gooey mixture up to your neck for 10 to 12 minutes. Attendants watch closely and supply you with cold water and cloths soaked in soothing oils. The hot mud detoxifies your system as it raises your body temperature and increases circulation. When your time is up, you pull yourself out of the ooze and thoroughly rinse off. Follow that with a mineral Jacuzzi bath or five minutes in a eucalyptus steam cabinet. After steaming, you might retreat to a private room and be covered with light sheets for a brief nap. Relaxed yet?

Wraps: Indulge your skin with this ancient Egyptian spa technique. Many different mixtures may be used, from mineral-rich mud to seaweed to herbal concoctions. Also used in some spas are grape seeds and grapeseed oil. Rich in antioxidants, grapes make a great exfoliant. These mixtures are generously smoothed over your body to purify and tone the skin.

Salt or sugar rubs: These ingredients don't come out of a Morton's box or C&H bag. It could be ancient sea salts from Austria or native Amazon sugar, combined with scented oils and massaged over the skin for a radiant and aromatic finish. You may also find rubs of organic olive oil, used over the entire body to add moisture to skin and hair.

Massage: Swedish massage is the most common type offered in Wine Country, but some spas also provide massage methods such as Esalen, shiatsu, Thai, cranio-sacral, Jin Shin—and even underwater techniques. Facials, foot reflexology, and scalp treatments are also on the menu at most spas. Don't be afraid to ask for massage on specific body parts, such as the neck and shoulders, where many of us feel most tense.

Hot rock massage: Heated stones are placed on strategic areas of your body to warm and relax muscles and joints. A light massage with lava rocks may follow.

Don't forget to keep yourself hydrated. Drink lots of water before, during, and after your treatments to help flush the toxins from your body. If you don't, you may feel worse the next day instead of feeling better.

INDIAN SPRINGS $$

1712 Lincoln Avenue, Calistoga

(707) 942-4913

www.indianspringscalistoga.com

If this collection of teal and white buildings evokes the heyday of the recuperative spa, it's appropriate. Indian Springs is on land that was once part of Sam Brannan's inspired attempt to make this town the Saratoga of the West. The bathhouse and Olympic-size swimming pool date to 1913, and most of the bungalows were built in the 1930s. The property has a scattering of squat buildings (most units are duplexes) and open vistas. In addition to the 17 studio and one-room units, Indian Springs offers the Merchant Bungalow, a three-bedroom, two-bath suite that sleeps six. Indian Springs added 24 rooms when it renovated the former Nance's Hotel, now called the Lodge. The spa services include 100 percent volcanic-ash mud baths starting at $75, mineral baths for $65, facial or body polish treatments, and combinations thereof.

> **i** The Olympic-size swimming pool at Indian Springs spa in Calistoga is one of the oldest and largest in California. Built in 1913, it is naturally heated by mineral water from nearby geysers.

CALISTOGA SPA HOT SPRINGS $
1006 Washington Street, Calistoga
(707) 942-6269, (866) 822-5772
www.calistogaspa.com
Considering Calistoga Spa's services, excellent in both quality and quantity, this has to be considered something of a bargain. The spa is a block off Lincoln Avenue, behind the depot and a hardware store. All 57 rooms come with kitchenettes (all the basics provided except an oven), air-conditioning, and cable TV; two suites have full kitchens. Guests are free to use the small but well-maintained gym and four naturally heated mineral pools that range from 80 to 104 degrees. And then there is the typical lineup of spa services: mud baths, mineral baths, massage, and steam-and-blanket combos. Prices start at $40 for a basic whirlpool, steam bath, and blanket wrap; a mud dunk, mineral bath, blanket wrap, and one-hour massage go for $129. (I can weigh in only about the women's side of the spa, but the massages I've received here have been exceptional.) Calistoga Spa also has a conference room that accommodates as many as 40 people.

ROMAN SPA HOT SPRINGS RESORT $
1300 Washington Street, Calistoga
(707) 942-4441, (800) 914-8957
www.romanspahotsprings.com
The Roman Spa is a straight-up motel, but you can get pampered next door at the Oasis Spa. Roman Spa, just a block from downtown

Calistoga, has water-lily ponds; a large, heated outdoor pool; an indoor, hydro-jet therapy pool; and outdoor hydro-jet and Finnish-style saunas. The 60 rooms include everything from a single with a queen-size bed to a family suite with two full rooms. About a third of the rooms have kitchen facilities.

GOLDEN HAVEN HOT SPRINGS $
1713 Lake Street, Calistoga
(707) 942-8000
www.goldenhaven.com
This is a comparatively affordable spa in a quiet section of Calistoga. The exterior is nothing special, but the 28 rooms are clean and full of conveniences, including air-conditioning, cable TV, and refrigerators. All the soothing spa treatments are there if you want them. The lineup features mud baths (including private rooms for couples), herbal mineral baths, herbal facials, and massage. Those fees range from $78 for a half-hour massage to $179 for a full body wrap. Guests use the swimming pool and hot mineral pool free.

Sonoma County
THE FAIRMONT SONOMA MISSION INN & SPA $$$
100 Boyes Boulevard, Sonoma
(707) 938-9000, (800) 257-7544
www.fairmont.com/sonoma
The style is Spanish-influenced early California, a sprawling pink building with red tile roof, arcade, and bell tower. Lobby decor features heavy Spanish furnishings grouped around a massive fireplace. It would be no surprise to see a film star or world leader—Mikhail Gorbachev, Elizabeth Taylor, and Billy Crystal have stayed here, among many other celebrities. The health and fitness program covers all bases—aerobics, aromatherapy, body sculpting, yoga, herbal wrap, seaweed sauna, and steam room—in a huge 40,000 square-foot facility. For total indulgence, ask for the 90-minute Sonoma Stone treatment ($245) or a couples Sonoma Lavender Kur (100 minutes for $495). To refuel after all this activity, two great restaurants—Sante, in the main building, and the

nearby Big 3 Diner—offer low-calorie cuisine (see the Restaurants chapter). Guests at the resort also have privileges at the inn's private golf course when they feel like knocking around little white balls (with a green fee of $185, including cart). It's less than a mile away on Arnold Drive.

The inn itself has a colorful history. The first spa was built in 1860 by an eccentric doctor who burned it down after a tiff with his wife. But it was rebuilt, and by the 1890s San Francisco society was journeying north by rail and auto to "take the waters." The present inn dates to 1927, when it took shape in the style of a California mission. In 1985 a total renovation added 70 rooms and a conference center. The hot springs, however, lay dormant, lost in the earth until 1993, when the legendary waters were brought back to the surface from 1,100 feet below the inn. And today this spring water is the elixir that fills the two pools and whirlpools. Further expansion totaling $36 million took place, culminating in the inn's affiliation with Fairmont Hotels & Resorts corporation. An additional $12 million restoration was completed in 2004.

THE LODGE AT SONOMA $$$
1325 Broadway Avenue, Sonoma
(707) 935-6600 (lodge), (707) 931-2034 (spa)
www.thelodgeatsonoma.com
www.raindancespa.com

Sonoma is a spa town, and this world-class facility helps keep the town's reputation for hot water and luxurious body scrubs intact. The 182 spacious guest rooms are nicely appointed with fireplaces, balcony or patio, two-line phones, cable TV, and complimentary breakfast in the restaurant, Carneros Bistro (see the Restaurants chapter), or in room. The rooms were recently freshened up, to the tune of $2 million, with new carpets and paint, as well as bigger LCD TVs. A wellness center was also added to the property. Hot mineral waters flow right beneath the property, so the Raindance Spa is the perfect source for therapeutic bathing treatments. There are outdoor soaking and watsu therapy pools, and underwater massage is offered. The full-service spa has a full menu of massages, skin-care treatments, body wraps, and facials, including the clarifying mustard bath ($65) to detoxify and rejuvenate your overstressed bod. Prices range from about $120 for a grapeseed facial to $255 for the Encapsulated Wrapsody (sounds divine!).

MACARTHUR PLACE $$$
29 East MacArthur Street, Sonoma
(707) 938-2929, (800) 722-1866
www.macarthurplace.com

MacArthur Place began its life as a 300-acre horse and cattle ranch with vineyards. The two-story Victorian house dominating the former Burris-Good ranch was built in the 1850s. Constructed with wooden pegs and square nails, the house was home to David Burris and his family of nine children. Burris was also a banker; he founded Sonoma Valley Bank, still in business today, in the corner library on the home's first floor. The site became a luxury destination in 1997, when it was transformed into a 64-room hotel with full-service spa and a steakhouse restaurant called Saddles (see the Restaurants chapter). Ten of the rooms are in the original stately home; 29 other suites are luxuriously appointed with fireplaces, wet bars, flat-panel TVs with DVD players, and king beds. More recent additions are two garden spa suites, guaranteed to satisfy your primal craving for water. These suites have their own tearoom with a teak soaking tub and private garden with waterfall (really). When you've had enough bubbling tranquility, fire up the 37-inch LCD TV with six-speaker surround sound. On the lush grounds, with its many private corners and sculptures, the giant outdoor chess set could keep you occupied for hours. The Garden Spa lives up to its name, using the herbs, flowers, and fruits grown on the property in its treatments. Most of the massages, facials, body polishes, and mud wraps (with grape seeds) run about $120; a citrus-based bath and body scrub will set you back about $225. Several signature treatments, also about $225 each, utilize rose petals, lavender, eucalyptus, and essential oils.

THE KENWOOD INN & SPA　　　$$$
10400 Highway 12 (Sonoma Highway),
Kenwood
(707) 833-1293, (800) 353-6966
www.kenwoodinn.com

This place just feels *right* to me. Intimate in scale with a peaceful, old-world charm, the Kenwood Inn offers the ambience of an Italian country villa nestled in the heart of Sonoma Valley. The inn is situated on a secluded hillside facing more than 1,000 acres of sloping estate vineyards. A recent expansion brought the number of rooms to 30, with two additional courtyards. The suites contain feather beds, down comforters, European antiques and lush fabrics, private baths, and fireplaces. Breakfast is served either in the dining room or at outdoor tables in good weather. In the evening, light appetizers, salads, and entrees are offered a la carte at the private wine bar. A full-service spa pampers guests and day visitors alike. This inn is the first in the United States to offer Caudalie Vinotherapie treatments that use grapevine-derived extracts. The many spa offerings—baths, scrubs, massages, wraps, and facials—are given using Vinotherapie products created in Bordeaux. Give yourself over to a wine barrel bath ($65), a crushed Cabernet scrub ($115), or the Tia Amo Togetherness massage for two ($390 per couple).

i Kenwood Inn & Spa was recently named one of the best Wine Country retreats in all of California and one of the 10 best in the world by *Food & Wine* magazine.

DAY SPAS

Along with the destination spa resorts, you also have the option of getting wet and muddy at one of several day spas. Spend a few rejuvenating hours sunk neck deep in mud, or enveloped in a stress-relieving hydro wrap, or soothed by the skilled hands of a masseuse, and then be on your way (reservations are strongly recommended, but walk-ins can sometimes be accommodated). Here are just a few of the many possibilities.

Napa County
MOUNT VIEW SPA
1457 Lincoln Avenue, Calistoga
(707) 942-5789, (800) 816-6877
www.mountviewspa.com

In the Mount View Hotel building (see the Hotels, Motels, and Inns chapter), but run separately, this spa is the ultimate in luxury. The tasteful furnishings, personalized service, and waffle-weave cotton robes in the dressing rooms all combine to set a mood of elegant decadence. They can do it all here, including the herbal linen wrap, the stress-relief hydro wrap (a warm, aloe vera–based gel), and the Enzymatic Sea mud wrap, which is painted over your entire body like a dusky leotard. All of it is performed in private rooms. The massages cost $65 (for 25 minutes) to $140 (for 80 minutes). A bath treatment followed by a 50-minute massage runs $130.

i When booking a massage, don't hesitate to specify your preference for a female masseuse or a male masseur. Sometimes the spa will ask, but not always. If it's important to you, please make your wishes known ahead of time.

LINCOLN AVENUE SPA
1339 Lincoln Avenue, Calistoga
(707) 942-2950
www.lincolnavenuespa.com

Set in an old stone building in the heart of town, Lincoln Avenue specializes in the easygoing Swedish/Esalen style of massage, with rates ranging from $60 for back, neck, and shoulder work to $90 for a full-body massage. The mud treatments are longtime favorites too. Packages are available, of course, such as the Luxury Pamper Package, a four-hour-plus slice of heaven that costs $410.

LAVENDER HILL SPA
1015 Foothill Boulevard, Calistoga
(707) 942-4495, (800) 528-4772
www.lavenderhillspa.com

This intimate retreat bills itself as "A Garden Spa

for Couples," and indeed, the verdant grounds in back of the bathhouses are a suitably romantic spot for postmassage reverie and sweet talk. Choose from four basic bath treatments: volcanic mud bath, seaweed bath, herbal blanket wrap, or aromatherapy mineral salt bath, all of which come with a facial mask and a foot massage. Prices range from $65 for a basic half-hour massage to $145 for a bath treatment with one-hour massage.

CALISTOGA MASSAGE CENTER
1219 Washington Street, Calistoga
(707) 942-6193
www.calistogamassage.com
The Massage Center is for connoisseurs of massage. The staff offers deep-tissue and sports massage, shiatsu, reiki, aromatherapy, and hot-stone too. Select a mode and a duration—it's $85 for an hour, or $125 for 90 minutes. Foot reflexology is $45 for a half-hour. The center also offers a parafango wrap for $125 and a champagne facial for $75.

Sonoma County
SONOMA SPA ON THE PLAZA
457 First Street W., Sonoma
(707) 939-8770
www.sonomaspaontheplaza.com
When you've worked yourself into a tizzy shopping and dining in Sonoma, slip into this conveniently located spa for a relaxing tune-up. You'll find everything from specialty massages to body treatments and herbal facials, in package form or a la carte. Deluxe packages, lasting from two to five hours, run from $159 to $370. Three types of one-hour, mud-based body treatments are offered at $75 each. I can personally vouch for this place; ask for massage therapist Sunset.

OSMOSIS DAY SPA SANCTUARY
209 Bohemian Highway, Freestone
(707) 823-8231
www.osmosis.com
You've heard about our mud, sure, but you won't believe what our enzymes can do. Named the best day spa in America by *Travel & Leisure* magazine, Osmosis features a Japanese enzyme bath of fragrant cedar fiber, rice bran, and more than 600 enzymes. The action of the enzymes produces a special quality of heat that improves circulation and metabolism, cleanses skin pores, and beautifies the skin. Massage treatments include the Swedish/Esalen method and many others. If you like, you can have your massage outdoors under a pagoda near Salmon Creek. The enzyme bath is $80/$85, with massage $170/$185. Osmosis is located off Highway 12 in the small town of Freestone, about halfway between Sebastopol and Bodega.

A SIMPLE TOUCH SPA
239 Center Street, Healdsburg
(707) 433-6856
www.asimpletouchspa.com
This lovely little spa down a short walkway in downtown Healdsburg offers aromatherapy baths, massage, facials, and body treatments. One of the specialty baths features detoxifying fango mud made from dehydrated volcanic ash. Several special packages are available that range from $90 for a bath and half-hour massage to the deluxe package for $350, a four-hour experience that includes a bath, salt scrub, one-hour massage, one-hour wrap, and one-hour facial.

CAMPING

If you're on a budget or desire more in the way of outdoor adventure, many campgrounds in Wine Country afford ample opportunities for backpacking, hiking, and fishing. Unless I say otherwise, assume that each campground has piped, potable water, a desirable part of any outdoor experience. If it doesn't, arrange to bring or pump your own. And note that some of the listed sites are part of the region's state parks. In those cases you'll find the basic camping information here, but for a more thorough description of each park, you should turn to the Parks and Recreation chapter. To pitch your tent or park your RV, expect to pay from $12 to $25 nightly, depending on the location and the degree of development. Most state park campsites cost from $11 to $25 per night, and even higher for coveted coastal sites. Senior rates are offered in many places, while some of the more primitive campgrounds are free.

NAPA COUNTY

NAPA TOWN & COUNTRY FAIRGROUNDS
575 Third Street, Napa
(707) 253-4900
www.napavalleyexpo.com
The fairgrounds are just off Third Street in Napa as it approaches the Silverado Trail. There are about 75 motor-home spaces in this recently renovated facility, and restrooms and showers are on-site. A laundry and a market are close by. Pets are permitted on leashes. Note that Town & Country is closed to campers for the latter half of July and most of August.

SPANISH FLAT RESORT
4290 Knoxville Road, off Highway 128,
Lake Berryessa
(707) 966-7700
www.spanishflatresort.com
Spanish Flat has 120 campsites for tents or motor homes, a few of them with partial hookups. Rustic lakefront cabins have been added, as well as several yurts. Picnic tables, fire pits, flush toilets, and showers are provided. The hosts also have complete marina facilities, a boat launch, and rentals. A laundry and a restaurant are a short drive away.

BOTHE–NAPA VALLEY STATE PARK
Highway 29, south of Calistoga
(707) 942-4575 (info),
(800) 444-PARK (reservations)
www.parks.ca.gov/default.asp?page_id=477
While a million or so industrious tourists whiz by on Highway 29, you can recline next to your tent and look up at the boughs of oaks and pines or at the stars of the Milky Way. The park has a first-rate campground along Redwood Creek, with 9 tent-only sites and 50 for tents or RVs up to 31 feet long. You get picnic tables and fire pits, toilets, and showers. Wheelchairs can be used here, and pets are allowed (campground only). There is a spring-fed swimming pool, where you can take the plunge for $1 (free for children).

NAPA COUNTY FAIRGROUNDS
1435 North Oak Street, Calistoga
(707) 942-5111
www.napacountyfairgrounds.com
If you're going to pick a municipal campground, you could do a lot worse than Calistoga's. The scenery is great, it's just a short walk to restaurants and spas, and next door is Mount St. Helena Golf Course (see the Parks and Recreation chapter). There is a 70-space RV park with electrical hookups, another area that can accommodate up to

300 RVs (some with hookups), plus a small grassy area for tents. Restrooms, showers, and propane are available, but campfires are not permitted. Pets are allowed on leashes. The campground is closed from mid-June through mid-July as the grounds are prepared for and cleaned up after the Napa County Fair (see the Festivals and Annual Events chapter).

HUNTING CREEK CAMP
Knoxville-Devilshead Road, Knoxville
(707) 468-4000
**www.blm.gov/ca/st/en/fo/ukiah/knoxville
.html**
This is one of Wine Country's least-known campgrounds and, because of its isolation in the uppermost northern tip of Napa County, that isn't likely to change anytime soon. Located about 17 miles north of Lake Berryessa near the small community of Knoxville, Hunting Creek has only five sites for tents or RVs, but it does have picnic tables, fireplaces, and vault toilets. Pets are permitted on leashes. Be forewarned that the campground is popular with off-road enthusiasts and hunters. Take Lake Berryessa Road to Devilshead Road. A map of the area is available from the Bureau of Land Management at the number listed. There is no charge for camping here.

i To reserve a campsite in one of California's state parks, you must book through the Reserve America service at (800) 444-PARK. Reserve America will add a one-time $7.50 surcharge to any reservation; get more details at www.reserveamerica.com.

SONOMA COUNTY
Southern Sonoma

SUGARLOAF RIDGE STATE PARK
2605 Adobe Canyon Road, Kenwood
(707) 833-5712,
(800) 444-PARK (reservations)
www.parks.sonoma.net/sugarlf.html
www.parks.ca.gov/default.asp?page_id=481
This locale in the Mayacmas Mountains has 50

campsites for tents or motor homes up to 24 feet long. Piped-in water and restrooms are available. In 1996 Sugarloaf Ridge State Park became the home of the largest observatory in the western United States that is completely dedicated to public viewing and education. Hiking is the main recreation at this popular state park (see the Parks and Recreation chapter). Pets are OK.

PETALUMA KOA
20 Rainsville Road, Petaluma
(707) 763-1492, (800) 562-1233
www.petalumakoa.com
There are advantages to camping so close to San Francisco: guided bus tours to "the City" leave from this KOA during the summer (it's approximately 35 miles to the City by the Bay). The facility has 312 campsites, plus a swimming pool. Six new lodges were planned for 2008, all with bathrooms, kitchens, and a kids' loft. Located on the north edge of Petaluma, there is convenient access to U.S. Highway 101 and the restaurants of Petaluma. Free wi-fi, too.

SONOMA COUNTY FAIRGROUNDS RV PARK
1350 Bennett Valley Road, Santa Rosa
(707) 293-8410, (707) 545-4200
www.sonomacountyfair.com
If you want to hook up your RV in the middle of the city of Santa Rosa, this is the place. The park itself is behind the main fairgrounds, surrounded on three sides by residential neighborhoods. You can't brag about the ambience here, but the price is right: $20 per night, with a seven-night maximum (discounts may apply). There are full hookups for 164 RVs of any size, and a laundry room and wi-fi are available. It's a short drive to shopping and restaurants.

SPRING LAKE REGIONAL PARK
5585 Newanga Avenue, Santa Rosa
(707) 539-8092, (707) 565-2267
www.sonoma-county.org
A group camping area and 30 family campsites (4 for tents only) at Spring Lake Park have centrally located restrooms and shower facilities. Also

available are 200 picnic sites, barbecue pits, a bikeway, a hiking trail, and equestrian trails. No electricity is available at this campground, which is open daily from the week before Memorial Day until the week after Labor Day and open weekends only during the winter. Please reserve at least 10 days in advance during high season.

Northern Sonoma

WINDSORLAND RV TRAILER PARK
9290 Old Redwood Highway, Windsor
(707) 838-4882
There are 66 sites here, with 56 full-hookup, pull-through sites. Windsorland also features a laundry, playground, a small store, showers, and restrooms. A pool is open seasonally. The park is open all year, and night registration is available.

CLOVERDALE KOA
26460 River Road, Cloverdale
(707) 894-3337, (800) 368-4558
www.winecountrykoa.com
www.koa.com
This 60-acre campground has 152 campsites (50 for tents), plus a swimming pool, recreation hall, store, minigolf course, stocked fishing pond, ball courts, and horseshoe pits. Located 1 mile from the Russian River on a hill overlooking the Alexander Valley, the Cloverdale KOA is open all year. There are also 14 Kamping Kabins for two (with no water or electricity). A bit pricier than most KOAs, but the location is stunning.

LAKE SONOMA–LIBERTY GLEN
3333 Skaggs Springs Road, Lake Sonoma
(707) 433-9483
www.parks.sonoma.net/laktrls.html
Eleven miles northwest of Healdsburg, off Dry Creek Road, this Lake Sonoma park offers more than 17,000 land and water acres. Lake Sonoma facilities include a visitor center and fish hatchery (see the Kidstuff chapter), with 113 campsites available for tents or RVs up to 50 feet. There are two group sites for up to 50 campers (advance reservations required). In addition, there are 8

boat-in/hike-in primitive campgrounds around the lake and a privately operated marina that offers boat rentals and a launch ramp. Piped water, flush toilets, solar-heated showers, and a sanitary disposal station are available in the developed area.

Sonoma Coast

DORAN REGIONAL PARK AND WESTSIDE REGIONAL PARK
Highway 1, south and west of Bodega Bay
(707) 875-3540, (707) 565-2267
www.sonoma-county.org
Doran's facilities include 113 sites for RVs or tents, 19 first-come, first-served sites, 1 hiker/biker site, and a reservable group site. Westside has 47 campsites. There are tables, fire rings, and a trailer disposal site. For extra comfort, showers and flush toilets are available too. Parking is $5 in summer, $4 the rest of the year. What to do? Try fishing, beachcombing, clamming, boating, and picnicking. A boat ramp and fish-cleaning station are available. There's an extra charge of $5 per vehicle and $1 per dog.

i Be aware that some seaside camping locations can be breezy and cold any time of the year. Come prepared with plenty of warm clothing.

BODEGA BAY RV PARK
2001 Highway 1, Bodega Bay
(707) 875-3701
www.bodegabayrvpark.com
Accommodations include 72 RV sites, most with full hookups and complimentary cable TV and wireless Internet too. The maximum RV length in this park is 55 feet. There's a laundry on-site, and fishing and golf are close by.

STILLWATER COVE REGIONAL PARK
22455 Highway 1,
approx. 15 miles north of Jenner
(707) 847-3245, (707) 565-2267
www.sonoma-county.org
This 210-acre park comprises open meadow and coastal forest with spectacular ocean views from Stillwater Cove. A half-mile trail leads to the historic one-room Fort Ross Schoolhouse. Twenty-three campsites serve most campers (drivers of large RVs and trailer campers should contact the park office to ensure that their vehicle will fit) and there is a hike-in/bike-in area. Facilities include pay showers, flush restrooms, and day-use parking.

SALT POINT STATE PARK
25050 Highway 1,
approx. 20 miles north of Jenner
(707) 847-3221,
(800) 444-PARK (reservations)
www.parks.sonoma.net/coast.html
www.parks.ca.gov/default.asp?page_id=453
This campground offers picnic areas, hiking trails, diving, horseback trails, and the beautiful adjacent Kruse Rhododendron State Reserve (see the Parks and Recreation chapter). It's open all year, but there are no RV hookups. There are 107 campsites in summer but only 28 in winter. Piped water and flush toilets are available. In early winter this is headquarters for local abalone divers.

GUALALA POINT REGIONAL PARK
Highway 1, 1 mile south of Gualala
(707) 785-2377, (707) 565-2267
www.sonoma-county.org
The 195-acre park is located near the coast, adjacent to the Gualala River. The overnight camping area is across the highway from the park's day-use facilities, and it contains tables and stoves. Water and restroom facilities are nearby. Recreation options for day-use or overnight campers include fishing, bike trails, hiking (one trail beside the bluff is especially good for bird-watching), and picnic areas. It's open all year and offers 19 family campsites for tents and motor homes up to 28 feet, 7 hike-in/bike-in campsites, and a trailer sanitary station.

West County/Russian River
VILLAGE PARK CAMPGROUND
6665 Highway 12, Sebastopol
(707) 823-6348
Village Park is open from May 1 to October 31 for overnight or weekly stays. Laundry facilities and restrooms with showers and hot water are offered, and children and pets are welcome.

RIVER BEND CAMPGROUND
11820 River Road, Forestville
(707) 887-7662, (800) 877-0816
Eleven miles from US 101, off the River Road exit, this campground has 65 sites, 35 with full hookups. Canoe rentals, volleyball, barbecue pits, and basketball courts are among the amenities. Other features include flush restrooms, hot showers, groceries, tepees for rent, and a huge Paul Bunyan statue. It's open all year.

Every summer, forest fires rage in various parts of California, many of them caused by careless smokers and campers. Please be cautious when using fire in our wilderness areas—which are tinder-dry by midsummer—and always make certain campfires are extinguished thoroughly.

SCHOOLHOUSE CANYON CAMPGROUND
12600 River Road, Guerneville
(707) 869-2311
This camping option lies adjacent to a 200-acre wildlife sanctuary, with tent and RV sites set in the redwoods. Hot showers, fishing and swimming along the nearby Russian River, hiking, and nature trails are among the attractions. It's open April through October.

RESTAURANTS

"Food and Wine Country" could be the title of this book, based on this chapter, because some visitors are not here only for the wine. They come for the experience of dining in world-class establishments, and the wine is a great bonus. Some of the region's restaurants consistently are named to the "top" lists published in gourmet, wine, and travel magazines. These restaurants achieve accolades by inventing some of the most delectable dishes imaginable. Just a quick read through this chapter will have your mouth watering. I make no attempt to include every great eatery in this huge area, but I have listed restaurants that are well established and highly regarded for their food, service, and overall reputation. Some are tried-and-true favorites. Others are newer places helmed by prestigious chefs who made names for themselves in cities like Los Angeles, San Francisco, New York City, and Paris before deciding to ply their trade in a more laid-back environment. Remember, menus change frequently, depending on the season and the availability of fresh, local ingredients. Wine Country chefs enjoy concocting new dishes and making the best use of the region's bounty, so they can—and do—transform menus often to suit their fancy. Take the tasty descriptions in these listings as a guide to what you might find on a particular restaurant's menu during your visit. Also keep in mind that days and hours of operation are subject to change, and it helps to call ahead to avoid disappointment.

OVERVIEW

NOTE: This chapter is organized a bit differently from the rest. It still follows the geographical method of listing Napa County first, followed by Sonoma County. But to make it easier to locate that famous bistro you read about in *Food & Wine* magazine, restaurants are listed alphabetically within their respective regions and cities.

As you read these entries, remember that unless a listing says otherwise, you can count on certain things: The restaurant serves beer and wine but does not have a full bar, it accepts major credit cards, it is wheelchair accessible, and it takes reservations. Most of the upscale restaurants do not have children's menus, but the down-home places do.

Many of the high-end restaurants (the French Laundry, Dry Creek Kitchen, Madrona Manor, and others) present a fixed-price "chef's" menu or "tasting" menu, meaning you'll receive multiple courses for one price (typically starting at $75 per person and going up, not including wine).

Price Code

Each price code refers to the average price of two entrees only—no appetizers, no dessert, no drinks, no tax or gratuity. I don't actually expect you to eat that way—or forgo the tip!—I just wanted to keep the calculations simple.

$	Less than $25
$$	$26 to $35
$$$	$36 to $50
$$$$	More than $50

NAPA COUNTY

City of Napa

ANGÈLE $$$
540 Main Street, Napa
(707) 252-8115
www.angelerestaurant.com
Adding to the revitalization of the Hatt Building complex is this restaurant serving French brasserie cuisine. The building was once a boathouse along the first bend of the Napa River. In addition

to the large indoor dining area, there is also a pleasant patio that seats 80. Some examples of the entrees you can expect are roasted striped bass on bean stew; petrale sole with baby spinach, capers, and raspberry vinegar; chicken with morels and asparagus; and duck breast with roasted fingerling potatoes. Dessert options include gratin of banana with almond crust or vanilla ice cream with candied chestnuts. There is a full bar, and reservations are accepted for daily lunch and dinner.

BARBERSQ $$
3900 Bel Aire Plaza, Suite D, Napa
(707) 224-6600
www.barbersq.com

As the name suggests, the fare here is barbecue, Memphis style: baby back ribs, pulled-pork sandwiches, short-rib sandwiches, lamb burgers, and all the fixins. The whole roasted vinegar chicken is worth the cost and the wait (45 minutes), but it's enough for two to four. For a barbecue joint, the wine list is well developed. It's a fun atmosphere suitable for families, and it's open daily for lunch and dinner.

BAYLEAF $$$$
2025 Monticello Road, Napa
(707) 257-9720
www.bayleafnapa.com

If you need a special place for a big party or wedding reception, Bayleaf may be the answer. It's spacious, with four separate dining rooms and a 150-seat patio. Each dining room has its own distinct feel—huge skylights in one, a large wood bar and fireplace in another. The food portions are generous, and menu items might include seared scallops, garlic mint chicken breast, and several pizza selections. For your sweet tooth there's mango-apple cobbler. Lunch and dinner are served daily except Tuesday.

BISTRO DON GIOVANNI $$$
4110 Howard Lane (at St. Helena Highway S.), Napa
(707) 224-3300
www.bistrodongiovanni.com

This place is romantic, with subdued earth tones, unpolished wood, vineyard views, high ceilings, and fireplaces in and out. Just make sure you can still concentrate on the food, which favors regional Italian dishes while tossing in a bit of Provence. The pan-seared salmon fillet with buttermilk mashed potatoes is excellent, as is the grilled portobello mushroom appetizer. Side dishes not to be missed are the sautéed spinach with garlic or the house-marinated Mediterranean olives. The restaurant is also noted for its risottos and pastas. Don Giovanni is open seven days a week for lunch and dinner. The menu changes daily, and there is a full bar.

BLEAUX MAGNOLIA $$$$
1408 Clay Street, Napa
(707) 252-2230
www.bleauxmagnolia.com

Cajun food in Napa Valley has been hard to come by before now. This restaurant (the Bleaux is pronounced "blue") set out to turn French cuisine on its ear with contemporary Creole cooking by way of Louisiana. The cornbread-crusted catfish is drizzled with huckleberry sauce, and the seafood gumbo is cooked to order. Huckleberries appear again in the bread pudding at meal's end, unless you choose to indulge in a house-made root beer float. Lunch and dinner are served Tuesday through Saturday; brunch and dinner are served on Sunday.

CELADON $$$
500 Main Street, Napa
(707) 254-9690
www.celadonnapa.com

Global comfort food is the emphasis of this fine eatery housed in the historic Napa Mill and Hatt Marketplace along the Napa River. In addition to the main dining room, there's a spacious patio and all-day dining in the bar. The flavors are inspired by Asia, the Mediterranean, and the Americas. The chef might tempt you with crab cakes or flash-fried calamari, followed by a truffle-and-honey-glazed pork chop or braised Algerian-style lamb shank. Celadon is open daily for lunch and dinner, and reservations are accepted.

COLE'S CHOP HOUSE $$$$
1122 Main Street, Napa
(707) 224-6328
www.coleschophouse.com

As its name implies, this is where one goes to get red meat—in huge portions. The menu's pricier steaks include the 21-day Chicago dry-aged New York strip or porterhouse, and a 2-inch-thick Black Angus filet mignon. For noncarnivores, there's plenty of fish and even a short stack of rosemary-scented portobello mushroom caps. Housed in a restored historic building dating from 1886, the restaurant, with dining rooms on two levels, features stone walls and a wood-beamed ceiling. It's elegant and masculine at the same time. Another draw here is the great old bar, where you can belly up for a classic Manhattan, martini, or cosmopolitan. Not surprising is the varied assortment of bold Napa Valley Cabernets on the wine list. Dinner is served Tuesday through Sunday, accompanied by live jazz on weekends.

CUVÉE $$$
1650 Soscol Avenue, Napa
(707) 224-2330
www.cuveenapa.com

You might want to time your visit to Napa to take advantage of the outdoor patio at this restaurant. It's a lovely and inviting place to enjoy potato-wrapped salmon, rock shrimp and salmon potpie, or spice-rubbed skirt steak. Combine one of those entrees with a succotash of fava beans, peas, and grilled corn on the side. For dessert there might be strawberry peach crisp or flourless chocolate cake. Cuvée is open for lunch and dinner Monday through Friday; a late-night menu is offered until midnight Friday and Saturday in the bar.

HIGHWAY 29 CAFE $
101 Cafe Court (off South Kelly Road at Highway 29), American Canyon
(707) 224-6303

Remember that old TV commercial ditty about the "Old Home Fill 'Er Up and Keep on Truckin' Cafe"? Well, it might have been written about this place, the antithesis of the typical Wine Country restaurant. But I'm so grateful it's still around, after more than 50 years, to dish out huge platters of eggs, hash browns, and bacon for the breakfast and lunch crowds (the morning meal is served until a half-hour before closing time, 2:30 p.m.). The outside of the building is barn red, and inside it feels like the all-American diner: red stools and chairs, friendly waitresses, and a bottomless cup of java.

LA TOQUE $$$$
1314 McKinstry Street, Napa
(707) 257-5157
www.latoque.com

French-inspired with occasional Asian influences—that's one way to describe this elegant restaurant once listed among the top 20 in America by *Wine Spectator* magazine. The decadent five-course prix fixe menu changes with the seasonal ingredients available locally, and it can include pan-roasted squab, a Niman Ranch beef or pork selection, and duck and mushroom consommé. But La Toque goes one step further in its pursuit of excellence with its annual truffle menus, offered for a few months in the fall when fresh white truffles come into season. When white truffle season slows down, out come the first black truffles. Season permitting, the black truffle menu options are available from January through Valentine's Day.

Dining at La Toque is an excuse to dress up a bit, so blue jeans should be left back at your hotel. Cocktail dresses and sport coats are more in line here, a place many diners choose for celebrating a special occasion or popping the question.

PEARL $$
1339 Pearl Street, Suite 104, Napa
(707) 224-9161
www.therestaurantpearl.com

Proprietors Nickie and Pete Zeller have created a comfortable bistro with soaring ceilings and lots of artwork to ponder as you enjoy fresh oysters served in a multitude of ways. There are soups, pizzas, sandwiches, and chicken and beef dishes with Mexican, Italian, and even Asian influences.

Try the triple-double pork chop with an apple-Dijon brine, or a New York steak with blue cheese and roasted garlic butter. The wine list includes several obscure Napa Valley labels. Open Tuesday through Saturday for lunch and dinner; closed Sunday and Monday.

PICCOLINO'S ITALIAN CAFE $$
1385 Napa Town Center, Napa
(707) 251-0100
www.piccolinoscafe.com
Food has always meant comfort to Joe Salerno, who grew up stirring pots and making sausage with his extended Italian family in upstate New York. Salerno now does his best to create fond memories at Piccolino's, his unpretentious, child-friendly restaurant in downtown Napa. The cafe offers fresh fish dishes, house-made sausage, and four types of pizza. The pasta entrees are highlighted by the colorful fettuccine Calabrese, with its multitude of simple ingredients, and the lasagna, a family recipe that employs a light ricotta shipped in from the East Coast. Lasagna and spaghetti are available in immense family-style portions. The wine list is primarily Napan, though it does include a small line of Italians. Piccolino's is open daily for lunch and dinner, plus brunch on weekends.

TUSCANY $$$
1005 First Street, Napa
(707) 258-1000
www.restaurant.com/tuscany
Guess the specialty: the cooking of northern Italy. Start with a traditional minestrone with a bevy of vegetables and pancetta. Follow that with risotto *con quaglia,* featuring walnuts and a touch of Gorgonzola cheese topped with two roasted quail. Classic cannoli is the perfect finishing touch. The menu also includes pizzas from the wood-fired oven and rotisseried rabbit, veal, pork, and chicken. There's a counter with stools where you can watch the chefs preparing such fare as a halibut steak with roasted red and golden beets on the side. Open daily for dinner; lunch is served Monday through Friday.

UBUNTU $$$
1140 Main Street, Napa
(707) 251-5656
www.ubuntunapa.com
Focused on a philosophy of "humanity toward others," Ubuntu (a Zulu word pronounced "oo-boon-too") is without a doubt the most unique eatery to open in Napa Valley in quite some time. It's a combination vegetarian restaurant and yoga studio, with some sculpture added for atmosphere. Sounds odd, but it works. Works so well, in fact, that the revered food critic for the *New York Times,* Frank Bruni, placed Ubuntu at No. 2 on that newspaper's list of "Most Intriguing New Restaurants Outside of New York City" in early 2008. Bruni called Ubuntu "the Angelina Jolie of restaurants . . . where virtue meets naughty sensuality." Whatever. Forget about tofu and brown rice—the fresh garden bounty found all around Wine Country is the inspiration for some amazing dishes, minus those traditional vegetarian fillers. There are plenty of greens and fruits, and cauliflower done three ways. Try the seven-course tasting menu and see if you even notice there is no meat. I doubt it. What you *will* notice is the striking sculpture *Alternative View.* Meanwhile, a bona fide, full-service yoga studio is upstairs, teaching more than 50 classes a week.

Yountville

AD HOC $$$$
6476 Washington Street, Yountville
(707) 944-2487
www.adhocrestaurant.com
Thomas Keller was *made* for Yountville—it's his muse. The renowned chef (the French Laundry, just down the street) opened Ad Hoc in 2006 as a "temporary" place to offer more casual dining than he is known for, where the average person could enjoy an affordable chef's menu—for a short time. Keller had planned to turn this building into a "burger and bottles joint" eventually. *Say what?* That all changed when Keller's fan club descended upon the restaurant, and he decided Ad Hoc was here to stay. It's rustic, family-style dining, for four short hours every night of the

week (and brunch on Sunday). The $48 four-course meal might include a remarkable salad or mezze plate, followed by a skirt steak with cauliflower florets, fingerling potatoes, bacon lardons, and buttermilk onion rings. That might be topped off with smoked chèvre with persimmon jam, and banana upside-down cake with peanuts and chocolate sauce. Keller isn't wearing the toque here every night (that honor goes to chef Dave Cruz) but his signature touch is all over the place. (In the meantime, Tom, some of us are still waiting for that burger joint.)

BISTRO JEANTY $$$
6510 Washington Street, Yountville
(707) 944-0103
www.bistrojeanty.com
Philippe Jeanty opened his comfortable, two-room bistro in 1998 and quickly occupied a niche that, Philippe explains, is part Paris, part French countryside. You won't find a single pasta on this small menu, no Caesar salad or hamburgers. Instead, be on the lookout for lamb tongue and potato salad, beef tournedos in black pepper cream sauce, cassoulet, and mussels steamed in red wine. The setting is just as authentic, with French furnishings and paintings by Guy Buffet. And the color of the walls? Dijon, of course. Bistro Jeanty is open for lunch and dinner seven days a week. It has a full bar; the staff calls the giant rooster that sits atop it "Philippe."

BOUCHON $$$$
6534 Washington Street, Yountville
(707) 944-8037
www.bouchonbistro.com
If you're looking for a place to have a late-night dinner, here's one of the few gourmet delights in Napa Valley, owned by chef Thomas Keller of the French Laundry, that will serve you late—until about 12:30 a.m. The fare is classic French bistro ("bouchon" is the local term for "bistro" in Lyon, France). But it's typically not the trendy stuff; instead, it's classics like mussels marinières and leg of lamb with flageolet beans. The appetizers include an extensive raw seafood bar. The sweets run to crème caramel or tarte tatin. The

atmosphere is lively and loud, but that's part of the charm. Because it keeps late hours, Bouchon is a favorite with local winemakers and staff from other restaurants. Open for lunch and dinner daily. Bouchon Bakery is next door, creating the breads served at this restaurant, the French Laundry, and Ad Hoc (see previous listing).

BRIX $$$$
7377 St. Helena Highway, Yountville
(707) 944-2749
www.brix.com
Seared dayboat scallops with broccoli, walnuts, golden raisins, and Gruyère cheese? Grilled salmon with polenta, brussels leaves, and Meyer lemon gastrique? Rack of lamb with spinach, garlic potato puree, and black olive jus? This is the food of Brix, the restaurant just north of Yountville. It's surrounded by several acres of vineyard and a couple acres of olive trees, making the outdoor seating especially fun. There's a full bar, including what the *San Francisco Chronicle* called an "Academy Award–winning wine list." Brix is open for lunch and dinner seven days a week.

ÉTOILE AT DOMAINE CHANDON $$$$
1 California Drive, Yountville
(707) 204-7529, (800) 736-2892
www.chandon.com
Parked against the hills west of Yountville, Étoile at Domaine Chandon sits amid century-old oaks and the winery's own vineyards. The atmosphere is elegant, immaculate, and très français (*étoile* means "star" in French)—more precisely, it's regional California cuisine with a French influence. The fixed-price menu changes frequently, but expect such dishes as Madeira-braised veal, venison loin, Japanese beef, and striped bass with foie gras risotto. Étoile at Domaine Chandon is open daily for lunch and dinner. Reservations should be booked well in advance.

THE FRENCH LAUNDRY $$$$
6640 Washington Street, Yountville
(707) 944-2380
www.frenchlaundry.com
The French Laundry has been elevated to almost

mythical status among foodies, many of whom have never come close to eating here, possibly because it's so difficult to procure a reservation. (See the close-up in this chapter for more about the French Laundry.) Chef Thomas Keller, though a devotee of traditional French principles, is also known for his whimsical takes on common meals, like "macaroni and cheese" that turns out to be butter-poached Maine lobster with creamy lobster broth and mascarpone-enriched orzo, or "coffee and doughnuts" that are in fact fresh-baked cinnamon-sugared doughnuts with cappuccino semifreddo. The French Laundry is open for dinner seven days a week and lunch Friday through Sunday.

HURLEY'S $$$$
6518 Washington Street, Yountville
(707) 944-2345
www.hurleysrestaurant.com
Bob Hurley has a long history in Napa Valley as a chef at Domaine Chandon for many years before helming the kitchen at Napa Valley Grille. In 2002 he opened his namesake restaurant, where he specializes in lighter preparations of California cuisine with Mediterranean influences. The food here has been designed with Merlot in mind, and the sea bass with Merlot sauce is one of the most popular dishes. You will also find grilled rib-eye steak with buttermilk mashed potatoes, roast chicken with onions and peas, and a spicy Moroccan eggplant.

MUSTARDS GRILL $$$
7399 St. Helena Highway, Yountville
(707) 944-2424
www.mustardsgrill.com
Roadhouse meets fine dining at Mustards Grill. The restaurant is situated on Highway 29 (aka St. Helena Highway), and the casual dining room looks onto a beautiful swath of the Napa countryside. But the real action here is in the kitchen. The menu changes seasonally, but classics like Mongolian pork chops (marinated, grilled chops with braised cabbage and garlic mashers) and hanger steak with sweet onion jam are available

year-round. Everything is made from scratch—don't miss the house-made ketchup served with paper-thin onion rings. The menu tends toward creatively reinvented American classics, with daily fish specials providing the haute end of the cuisine. Mustards has a full bar with a huge wine list and is open for lunch and dinner seven days a week.

NAPA VALLEY GRILLE $$$$
Highway 29 at Madison Street, Yountville
(707) 944-8686
www.napavalleygrille.com
Like those at most restaurants in Wine Country, the chefs here dish up a changing menu that uses seasonal ingredients produced locally, described as California cuisine with Italian and French influences. A past award-winning dish here was the wild mushroom and pine nut raviolini, voted recipient of the People's Choice award in the 2002 Napa Valley Mustard Festival. The wine list is extensive and includes rare and older vintages. The dining room looks out onto vineyards, and the exhibition kitchen adds interest. Lunch and dinner are served daily, with brunch on Sunday.

REDD $$$$
6480 Washington Street, Yountville
(707) 944-2222
www.reddnapavalley.com
Chef Richard Reddington garnered fame and accolades when he was at Auberge du Soleil. Now the restaurant that bears an abbreviated version of his name draws from many influences. This French-trained chef also infuses dishes with touches of Italy, Germany, and Asia. One night there might be braised short ribs with a horseradish crust, or a pork chop with mustard spaetzle, Swiss chard, and cippolini onions. At another time it could be al dente risotto over chunks of lobster, lemon confit, and white truffle oil. Dinner is served daily; lunch Monday through Saturday; and brunch on Sunday. A late-night bar menu is also available.

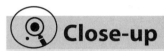 **Close-up**

"Best Restaurant in the World" is on a Quiet Street in Napa Valley

It's easy to find as you wind slowly through the small town of Yountville. There will be a curious tourist—maybe two—with camera in hand, dodging cars to stand smack in the middle of Washington Street, trying from all angles to capture the best photograph of the oddly shaped historic building. For most visitors, snapping a picture of the French Laundry is as close as they will get to a sit-down meal in the much-acclaimed restaurant.

Millions of words have been written about the French Laundry since Chef Thomas Keller took the helm in 1994. As its fame—and his—gained momentum over the years, the food raised to legendary status, folks with deep pockets have beaten a path to the restaurant's rustic door.

Reviewers can't say enough about the French Laundry, most of it breathless expressions of glee. *New York Times* food critic Ruth Reichl called the restaurant "the most exciting place to eat in the United States." Big-time celebrity chefs like the bad boy of the Travel Channel, Anthony Bourdain, have gone on record to say the French Laundry is the best restaurant in the world, hands down, and Keller is the planet's best chef. As Bourdain wrote about his dinner there in the book "A Cook's Tour": "It was, far and away, the most impressive restaurant meal I'd ever had . . . absolutely awe-inspiring."

Keller's star is so bright, he was asked to consult on French cooking and the idiosyncrasies of the restaurant kitchen for the 2007 Academy Award–winning animated film *Ratatouille*. Working at Pixar Animation Studios in the Bay Area, Keller whipped together the dishes that would be prepared in the movie. This was so the animators could accurately draw the food and show with authenticity how it was created. He also had a small voice part in the film.

I've been wowed by one of Keller's signature creations, the salmon tartare cornet, at Napa Valley wine functions. (More precisely, the cornet is an *amuse-bouche*, or "mouth amuser," in French cuisine vernacular.) Each time, Keller himself graciously handed the tiny cone to me, wrapped in a mini-napkin, and with his other hand slipped an old-fashioned wooden clothespin onto my lapel. (The clothespin, with the restaurant's logo stamped in blue, is an integral part of French Laundry's branding.)

Keller says a visit to Baskin-Robbins many years ago was his inspiration for the cornet. It is created by first placing sweet red onion crème fraîche inside a savory cone dotted with black sesame seeds. A dollop of the salmon tartare is then gently pushed ice cream–style onto the cone. Two or three slow, satisfying bites and it's gone.

Booking a table at the French Laundry has been called everything from "antiquated" to "ingenious," depending on whom you ask. It does require persistence and patience. *Exactly* two months to the day before you wish to dine there, call (707) 944-2380. Let's say you want

---

Rutherford

AUBERGE DU SOLEIL $$$$

180 Rutherford Hill Road, Rutherford
(707) 963-1211, (800) 348-5406
www.aubergedusoleil.com

Before Auberge du Soleil the inn, there was Auberge du Soleil the restaurant. It's known as one of Napa Valley's premier eateries, not just for the food but for the remarkable vistas from the dining terrace. The cuisine has included marinated raw yellowfin tuna with baby beets, radish slices, and Meyer lemon oil; and slow-cooked wild salmon with calamari, cranberry beans, and arugula. The sweeter stuff runs to phyllo-wrapped chocolate dumplings with tarragon ice cream or vanilla-bean gratin with fresh Oregon huckleberries. The prix fixe, four-course dinner without wine is $98 per person (a la carte

The French Laundry in Yountville is the most famous of Chef Thomas Keller's restaurants.
JEAN SAYLOR DOPPENBERG

to have dinner on June 1 (a wedding anniversary or other special occasion?). Plan to spend the morning—and possibly longer—of April 1 on the phone, punching Redial over and over again. The line, you see, is always busy. There are hundreds of others like you wanting to get one of the 16 coveted tables at the French Laundry on that same day.

If you get through and make a reservation, congratulations. Now begin saving your money. The fixed-price meal, at press time, was $240 per person. That doesn't include wine, which, of course, is de rigueur and can add many, many more dollars to the total bill. But forget about the cost—enjoy yourself when you finally sit down for the multicourse meal, which will last three to four hours.

On the strength of the popularity of the book *1,000 Places to See Before You Die,* someone should pen another book called *100 Places to Eat Before You Die.* The French Laundry would likely be No. 1 on the list.

ordering is also offered). The restaurant is open for lunch and dinner seven days a week, and it has a full bar.

RUTHERFORD GRILL $$$
1180 Rutherford Road, Rutherford
(707) 963-1792
www.hillstone.com
This restaurant is easy to spot by the large Phoenix date palm trees swaying in front. It's a casual "neighborhood" roadhouse that offers American comfort food in big portions. The mashed potatoes are legendary and make a yummy accompaniment to the rotisserie chicken, steaks, burgers, and prime-rib offerings. (Start your meal with the deviled eggs or grilled jumbo artichoke.) The decor is warm, with redwood walls made from old wine barrels. The huge outside patio is a great

place to watch Wine Country visitors hurrying by on the highway. More than 100 Napa Valley wines are offered, with at least 30 available by the glass. Open daily for lunch and dinner.

St. Helena

CINDY'S BACKSTREET KITCHEN $$$
1327 Railroad Avenue, St. Helena
(707) 963-1200
www.cindysbackstreetkitchen.com
At this local favorite, Cindy Pawlcyn, renowned for her Mustards Grill farther down Highway 29 in Napa Valley (and the newer Go Fish on the south edge of St. Helena—see the listing in this chapter), serves the more traditional comfort food for which she is revered. The menu ranges from innovative salads (the curry chicken salad is great) to small plates such as shiitake mushrooms and asparagus, to the popular rabbit tostada, spice-crusted lemon chicken, spice-rubbed quail, or wild mushroom tamales. This is a friendly place on two floors, with an inviting and comfortable bar and a patio when the weather is agreeable. The wine list is equal opportunity, not devoted entirely to Napa Valley, and spirits are served too.

GILLWOODS RESTAURANT $$
1313 Main Street, St. Helena
(707) 963-1788

1320 Napa Town Center, Napa
(707) 253-0409
www.gillwoodscafe.com
You have to get up pretty early in the morning to beat the locals to Gillwoods, St. Helena's favorite breakfast joint. (You'll recognize it by the people milling about outside for the short wait for a table.) It's casual, intimate, and filled with good cheer and caffeine. The big draw always has been the scrambles—eggs and cheese mixed with various ingredients. The restaurant is open for breakfast and lunch seven days a week and does not take reservations. Gillwoods has a second location in Napa Town Center. The menu is the same there, and kids get their own menu at both places.

GO FISH $$$$
641 Main Street, St. Helena
(707) 963-0700
www.gofishrestaurant.net
Like Thomas Keller, Cindy Pawlcyn is a big presence in Napa Valley's restaurant scene. Go Fish is her third eaterie in this valley, all of them successful and popular with locals and visitors. The focus here is on the raw bar, but you can also get fish prepared "Your Way"—whatever the day's catch might be—sautéed, wood grilled, or poached. The kitchen also offers "Fish Our Way," when the chefs decide what goes with what. The "No Fish" menu includes chicken, beef, and risotto. The desserts range from crepes to panna cotta to a chocolate bombé. Lately, Go Fish has been featuring the Tuesday-night Crustacean Crawl, a three-course, $40 dinner feast. The restaurant is open daily for lunch and dinner.

MARKET $$$
1347 Main Street, St. Helena
(707) 963-3799
www.marketsthelena.com
Ready for some comfort food? It's hard to beat the offerings here. This restaurant bustles with locals and visitors, who come for the exceptional buttermilk fried chicken with mashed potatoes and corn bread, the chicken potpie, and the glazed meatloaf. Start your meal with the chopped Market salad with blue cheese and bacon. End the experience with home-style goodies such as a waffle cone sundae, a root beer float, or a plate of freshly baked cookies. Market is a homey eatery with an interesting bar, fieldstone walls, and friendly and efficient service. It's open daily for lunch and dinner.

MARTINI HOUSE $$$$
1245 Spring Street, St. Helena
(707) 963-2233
www.martinihouse.com
Housed in a vintage California Craftsman bungalow originally built by an opera singer named Walter Martini, this restaurant has garnered fabulous reviews since opening in 2001. Famed

restaurant designer Pat Kuleto teamed with chef Todd Humphries (formerly of the Wine Spectator Greystone Restaurant) to create a beautiful setting as well as a unique dining experience. Martini House excels in rare wines, with the Wine Cellar bar that includes a 600-bottle list. The menu changes with the seasons and the availability of local produce, but just about anything made with mushrooms (the cream of mushroom soup is excellent) is sure to be delicious. Among the other options may be seared Maine sea scallops, sautéed squab breast and leg confit, grilled prime beef tenderloin, or Atlantic striped bass. Save room for persimmon pudding with ice cream, maple cheesecake tart with pomegranate glaze, or a chocolate crepe soufflé.

THE RESTAURANT AT MEADOWOOD $$$$
900 Meadowood Lane, St. Helena
(707) 967-1205, (800) 458-8080
www.meadowood.com

A new chef, Christopher Kostow, came aboard early in 2008, which will no doubt change the culinary direction here a bit. What's likely to remain unchanged is the source of their fresh produce for the meals, much of it grown on the property or nearby. You can also count on the "Wine Country cuisine" theme to continue. The fixed-price menu has a la carte selections, and guests also get the Chef's Tasting Menu to choose from, a seven-course meal that might include lobster and squab with spinach, mushrooms, and Zinfandel onion marmalade. The Restaurant at Meadowood is open for dinner Tuesday through Saturday.

MODEL BAKERY $
1357 Main Street, St. Helena
(707) 963-8192

644 First Street (Oxbow Public Market), Napa
(707) 259-1128
www.themodelbakery.com

You'd think it was a film set if those whiffs of fresh-baked bread didn't call you from the kitchen. The look is perfect for a small-town bakery, with ceiling fans and a black-and-white checkerboard

i Most Wine Country restaurants are not picky about how you dress for dinner. Blue jeans are almost always acceptable, and "casual" is the byword, as long as you're well groomed.

floor. The Model Bakery makes scones, croissants, danishes, bagels, and at least a half-dozen types of muffins. The repertoire includes six or so daily breads, plus regular daily specials. The bakery also sells juices, soups, fresh salads and sandwiches, brick-oven pizza, and, as you would guess, coffee and espresso drinks. It's open every day but Monday. A second location can be found at Napa's new Oxbow Public Market.

TAYLOR'S AUTOMATIC REFRESHER $
933 Main Street, St. Helena
(707) 963-3486

644 First Street (Oxbow Public Market), Napa
(707) 224-6900
www.taylorsrefresher.com

Retired traveling salesman and pharmacist Lloyd Taylor opened the Refresher for business in 1949. In the 1990s it went out of business for a time, and now it's owned by the Gott family, who spruced it up—but managed to retain the quaint atmosphere—in 1999. Taylor's cooks up lunch and early dinner seven days a week. The menu includes burgers, a very popular ahi burger, hot dogs, tacos, salads, and fountain treats. There are nice picnic grounds behind the eatery. The city of Napa was thrilled when Taylor's opened a location at the Oxbow Public Market in 2008; now they don't have to drive upvalley to get their favorite burgers and fries. (Another Taylor's is located in San Francisco's Ferry Plaza Marketplace.)

TERRA $$$$
1345 Railroad Avenue, St. Helena
(707) 963-8931
www.terrarestaurant.com

Terra sits one block away from Main Street in a historic landmark, a hardy fieldstone foundry constructed in 1884. The open redwood-beamed ceilings in the two dining rooms give you the feel of a Tuscan villa. Chef Hiro Sone's one-page menu aims for southern France and northern Italy, though he admittedly takes a few geographic twists and turns. The most popular main course might be the broiled, sake-marinated sea bass with shrimp dumplings in shiso broth. Terra is open for dinner every night except Tuesday.

TRA VIGNE $$$
1050 Charter Oak Avenue, St. Helena
(707) 963-4444
www.travignerestaurant.com
Chef Michael Chiarello made it to the top of the Napa Valley dining hall of fame on the strength of this cozy trattoria in St. Helena. The stone building is an old landmark, and Tra Vigne has become a contemporary one. The regional Italian menu encourages grazing, with a host of interesting small plates, pastas, and pizzas to complement the meats and fish. The restaurant is open for lunch and dinner seven days a week. The full bar and wine cellar are stocked with Italian reds and whites, plus a good selection of Californians.

WINE SPECTATOR GREYSTONE
RESTAURANT $$$$
2555 Main Street, St. Helena
(707) 967-1010
www.ciachef.edu
Don't worry, eating at the Culinary Institute of America's restaurant doesn't make you a guinea pig for fresh-faced chefs-in-training. This branch of the CIA is for the continuing education of chefs. Dishes here might include mussels steamed in Fritz Winery Melon, torchon of foie gras, or oxtail roulade. Second-course selections could be wild mushroom lasagna or a grilled pork chop with sage spaetzle, apples, braised escarole, and whiskey sauce. Try not to dribble while craning your head around the dining room, with its cement floor and stone walls lightened by blues and yellows. Greystone has a full bar and is open seven days a week for lunch and dinner.

Calistoga

ALL SEASONS CAFE $$$$
1400 Lincoln Avenue, Calistoga
(707) 942-9111
www.allseasonsnapavalley.com
If you read the food-and-wine magazines, you've probably been introduced to All Seasons. It has been profiled in *Gourmet* and *Wine Spectator*, among others, and its high standards haven't faltered in nearly two decades. Mixing the quaint and the luxurious, the cafe has a wine bar that makes use of a truly exceptional wine list—it ranges far beyond the valley and is especially deep in Pinots and Zinfandels. The menu changes often, but you can expect "seasonal California" dishes along the lines of grilled rib-eye steak with Cabernet glaze and creamy horseradish sauce; or English pea risotto with asparagus, spring garlic, tomato, and mushrooms. All Seasons is open for lunch and dinner daily.

BARVINO $$$
1457 Lincoln Avenue, Calistoga
(707) 942-9900
www.bar-vino.com
"Big wines—small plates" is the focus of this tasting bar. The wine list changes frequently, but you can count on it to emphasize Napa Valley vintages. Many reds and whites are available four ways: in three-ounce tastes, six-ounce glasses, half-bottles, and full bottles. Combine the wine with a series of small plates of food at reasonable prices, such as a crock of crab (thermidor style), oysters with slaw, an artisan cheese plate, seared scallops with foie gras potato puree, and many others. Most of the same dishes are offered in larger portions at larger prices. BarVino is open for dinner only.

BRANNAN'S GRILL $$$$
1374 Lincoln Avenue, Calistoga
(707) 942-2233
www.brannansgrill.com
Brannan's is physically arresting both inside and out, with refinished trusses and ironworks (all original to the 1911 building, long used as a

motor garage) and windows that open onto Lincoln in warm weather. Most notable is the bar, a mahogany Brunswick design that was shipped around Cape Horn in the late 1800s. The food is regional American, decidedly carnivore. Try the grilled hanger steak with potato-leek gratin and roasted portobello mushrooms or the blue cheese and walnut–crusted filet mignon. Brannan's has a full bar. It's open seven days a week for lunch and dinner in high season, but lunch is Friday through Sunday in the winter.

CAFE SARAFORNIA $$
1413 Lincoln Avenue, Calistoga
(707) 942-0555
Calistoga's most popular breakfast spot playfully incorporates the other half of Sam Brannan's legendary malapropism: "I'll make this the Calistoga of Sarafornia." The busy, sun-infused dining room has a central counter and sidewalk booths. Regulars swear by the cheese blintzes, the Brannan Benedict (two poached eggs with guacamole, bacon, and Cajun cream on toast), the chicken-apple sausage, and the Wildcat Scrambler (three eggs scrambled with mushrooms, Italian sausage, spinach, and choice of cheese). The burgers are good at lunchtime. The cafe does not take reservations, which makes it easy to spot on Sunday morning— it's the place with the line out the door.

CALISTOGA INN & RESTAURANT $$$
1250 Lincoln Avenue, Calistoga
(707) 942-4101
www.calistogainn.com
Popular any time of year, this restaurant really booms in the summer, when dining moves to the delightful creekside patio. (The meat is even grilled outside, over hardwood.) Regional American cuisine is served. The marinated Australian lamb sirloin, the Jamaican jerk half chicken, and the tri-tip sirloin finished with blue-cheese butter are all winners. There are fish specials too. The inn is open for lunch and dinner every day of the year but Christmas. The restaurant has a full bar, including an extensive wine list and its own line of beers (see the close-up in the Nightlife chapter for more on that).

CALISTOGA ROASTERY $
1426 Lincoln Avenue, Calistoga
(707) 942-5757
www.calistogaroastery.com
This place must be doing something right: Half the inns and restaurants in the vicinity boast about serving Roastery coffee. The owners roast almost 20 varieties of beans—sometimes right on the spot in a preserved 1919 Probat roaster, the oldest of its kind in the nation. If the regular house coffee isn't exciting enough for you, there is a selection of espresso drinks, frappes, and ice-cream mochas, not to mention iced teas, Rocket Juices, and Italian sodas. Yes, there are fresh-made baked goods too: bagels, croissants, scones of various stripes, banana bread, granola, and more. The Roastery opens at 6:30 a.m. every day and doesn't close its doors until 6:00 p.m. It's an atmosphere designed for lounging, so bring a newspaper. Better yet, get a seat at the window and people-watch. If you wait long enough you might see a famous face walk by. A St. Helena location of the Roastery can be found at 617 St. Helena Highway, near Dean & Deluca; call (707) 967-0820.

ENGLISH GARDEN TEA ROOMS $$
1107 Cedar Street, Calistoga
(707) 942-4262
www.englishgardentearooms.com
Park your wineglass for a few hours and lift a teacup instead. This genuine English tearoom, whose owners are all originally from the United Kingdom, opened in 2007 along Lincoln Avenue at the corner of Cedar Street. This may be just the palate cleanser you seek for a break from the pervasive wine culture of Napa Valley. Step into this lovely restaurant and gift shop and tuck into a sweet scone with clotted cream as you sip Earl Grey. The hospitality can't be beat—proprietors Jane and Jim Mitchell offer you a warm welcome and six types of tea service, priced from $12.99 to $31.99 per person. The tearoom is open Thursday through Monday from 10:00 a.m. to 7:00 p.m.

FLATIRON GRILL $$
1440 Lincoln Avenue, Calistoga
(707) 942-1220
www.flatirongrill.com

Hungry for steak? Slip on in to the Flatiron Grill, which beckons with a bovine-inspired sign outside. The stylish cow theme continues inside in the artwork. You can usually count on the house specialty, the Flatiron steak (boneless shoulder steak), roast chicken, grilled salmon, pork chop, seafood pasta, and maybe stuffed roast quail and beef brisket. Open daily for dinner.

HYDRO BAR & GRILL $$
1403 Lincoln Avenue, Calistoga
(707) 942-9777

In a town where the sidewalks sometimes roll up at dusk, the Hydro is the restaurant that doesn't sleep. It offers dinner until 11:00 p.m. on weekdays and midnight on weekends, then greets you for breakfast the next morning. (It's closed only for lunch on Thursday.) It does daily fish specials and top-notch hamburgers, and the crispy-skin boneless chicken with warm white Tuscan beans, grilled red onions, arugula salad, and herbed pan jus might be just the ticket after a relaxing mud bath. The full bar has 20 carefully selected microbrews.

PACIFICO RESTAURANTE MEXICANO $$
1237 Lincoln Avenue, Calistoga
(707) 942-4400

Calistoga isn't your typical small town, so why should Pacifico be your typical Mexican restaurant? Instead of mountain ranges of rice and beans, the kitchen cooks up traditional specialties from Jalisco, Veracruz, and Oaxaca. The restaurant is especially noted for its fish dishes, such as grilled fish tacos with avocado tomatillo salsa or *camarones a la diabla*—sautéed prawns with garlic, onion, arbol chilies, and lime. There is a full bar, and the margaritas won't let you down. Pacifico is open seven days a week for lunch and dinner. It's also popular for Saturday and Sunday brunch. (The morning favorites are huevos Benito and huevos Pacifico, Mexican eggs Benedict with

a mulato chili hollandaise.) The restaurant takes reservations for parties of seven or more.

SOLBAR AT SOLAGE $$$
755 Silverado Trail, Calistoga
(707) 226-0800
www.solagecalistoga.com

One would expect the cuisine at a spa resort to be of the healthful, light variety. Half of the food at Solbar, the restaurant within Solage Calistoga, matches that description. The other side of the menu (the comfort-food side) offers meatier, more decadent options. So the person at your table who is watching his or her weight can dive into Columbia River steelhead, while you (presumably the person *not* watching the scales) can indulge in a flatiron steak or beef short ribs. The pizza is excellent, as are the spicy chicken lettuce wraps. The dining room spills outside onto a large patio, where the views are lovely. Breakfast and lunch are served daily from 7:00 a.m. to 3:00 p.m.; dinner is 5:00 to 11:00 p.m. daily.

WAPPO BAR & BISTRO $$$
1226 Washington Street, Calistoga
(707) 942-4712
www.wappobar.com

One of the few Calistoga restaurants not found on Lincoln Avenue, the compact Wappo Bar is easy to miss—and that would be a big mistake. The scene is fairly informal and always gratifying, especially in the summer when the arbor-protected brick patio takes center stage. The inside features copper-topped tables and a wine bar with redwood interior; in the warmer months, ask for a table next to the fountain outside. The smoked chicken salad at lunch is great, and the daily specials can be inventive.

Signature dishes include the chili relleno with walnut pomegranate sauce; a paella of chorizo, rabbit, prawns, clams, and mussels; and the Chilean sea bass with Indian spices. The Wappo Bar is open for lunch and dinner six days a week (closed Tuesday).

SONOMA COUNTY

Sonoma

THE BIG 3 DINER AT THE FAIRMONT SONOMA MISSION INN $$$
18140 Highway 12 (Sonoma Highway), Sonoma
(707) 939-2410, (800) 862-4945
www.fairmont.com/sonoma

This is a great place for breakfast—the eggs Benedict with rosemary potatoes are very good, and the meal is served until 3:00 p.m. Because this is part of the Fairmont Sonoma Mission Inn Spa (see the Spas and Resorts chapter), the menu also includes dishes for the calorie watcher that are equally tasty—especially apple oatcakes with walnuts and crème fraîche. The salads are excellent too; the delectable Cobb keeps me coming back again and again. Lunch and dinner are served each day, with a fine wine list and full bar.

CAFE LA HAYE $$$
140 East Napa Street, Sonoma
(707) 935-5994
www.cafelahaye.com

The small, two-level dining room is highlighted by artwork that changes periodically. The risotto is different every day, as is the fish special. Dig into the oven-roasted quail with almond sauce, preceded by house-smoked trout. A double chocolate parfait makes the perfect end to the meal. Cafe La Haye has been around for nearly 14 years and has many loyal fans in the Bay Area who come to Sonoma especially to dine here. With only 32 seats, it's intimate but fun. Open for dinner Tuesday through Saturday.

CARNEROS BISTRO AT THE LODGE AT SONOMA $$$$
1325 Broadway, Sonoma
(707) 931-2042, (707) 935-6600
www.thelodgeatsonoma.com

It's within the hotel/spa complex the Lodge at Sonoma (see the Spas and Resorts chapter), but you needn't be a guest at the lodge to enjoy dining here. The interesting dishes change with the seasons. Here are a few examples of what you might find: wood oven–roasted whole fish with baby artichokes, horseradish *pappardelle* with short rib ragu, rotisserie rib eye with caramelized shallots, and Sonoma lamb offered with braised fennel or slow-roasted with tomatoes and lemon thyme. The atmosphere is relaxed and casual. It's open for breakfast, lunch, and dinner daily.

DELLA SANTINA'S $$
133 East Napa Street, Sonoma
(707) 935-0576
www.dellasantinas.com

This intimate, no-frills Italian trattoria-pasticceria faces onto the main street, and the food is authentic Italian prepared from recipes inspired by owner Dan Santina's grandmother. All dishes are made from scratch, using a rotisserie to contain the flavors of all the herbs and spices used in such dishes as locally raised chicken, rabbit, and duck. The menu offers traditional northern Italian fare such as lasagna Bolognese, pressed squab, and all sorts of antipasti. One of the best entrees—maybe the best in all of Wine Country—is *pollo allo spiedo,* a traditional Italian roast chicken. Della Santina's serves lunch and dinner every day. Because the restaurant is small, reservations are advised.

DEPOT HOTEL CUCINA RUSTICA $$$
241 First Street W., Sonoma
(707) 938-2980
www.depothotel.com

Located in a historic stone building a block from the plaza, this was once a hotel but it is now a delightful restaurant serving northern Italian cuisine. The chef does wonders with such dishes as ravioli *al bosco* (shiitake mushrooms and herbs sautéed with white wine and shallots) and hand-stuffed tortellini. One of the real delights of the restaurant is its garden, with Roman fountain and poolside dining. Vegetarian dishes and heart-healthy choices are also offered. Lunch is available Wednesday through Friday and dinner is served

Wednesday through Sunday. Ask about the cooking classes offered by chef Michael Ghilarducci, typically on Monday or Tuesday evenings.

DEUCE $$$
691 Broadway, Sonoma
(707) 933-3823
www.dine-at-deuce.com
A popular eatery for more than 13 years, the cuisine at Deuce reflects mostly French and Italian influences. You can expect such dishes as a braised pork shoulder with chive mashed potatoes, bucatini pasta with toasted walnuts, and Dungeness crab gratin. Sweeten your experience by ending with peanut butter pie or spiced apple crisp. Deuce serves lunch and dinner daily.

THE GIRL & THE FIG $$$$
110 West Spain Street, Sonoma
(707) 938-3634
www.thegirlandthefig.com
The name conjures up a sensual experience that's slightly naughty. Perhaps it's because the food is sinful, the service attentive, and the decor awash in pastels. On the ground floor of the Sonoma Hotel on the plaza, the Girl & the Fig promises and delivers country-style Provençal-inspired cuisine. Figs figure prominently in some of the dishes, especially the signature fig salad with goat cheese, pancetta, pecans, and arugula. Several cheese cart and charcuterie selections are offered (a goat cheese sampler, for instance), spring vegetable risotto, free-range chicken, and sea scallops with bean and lobster ragout. The owner, Sondra Bernstein, emphasizes local seasonal produce, so the menu selections will vary. Also, a welcome touch in a town that closes early: a late dinner menu from 9:30 to 11:00 p.m. on Friday and Saturday. The owner also operates the Fig Pantry, a great gift shop with wine, food, coffee bar, and more, at 1190 East Napa Street in Sonoma.

LA CASA RESTAURANT $$$
121 East Spain Street, Sonoma
(707) 996-3406
www.lacasarestaurant.com
In a town dedicated to Italian cuisine, La Casa's smashing Mexican food is as welcome as a breeze in the heat of summer, and it's been that way for more than 40 years. The ambience is as close to authentic as you can get north of the border, with Mexican woven leather chairs and a tiled bar. The nachos are sensational, the salsa and chips addictive. For a view of the Sonoma Mission and Barracks (see the Attractions chapter), ask for a window seat. Or choose to eat outdoors on the patio facing onto El Paseo de Sonoma courtyard. Fiesta hour (from 4:00 to 6:00 p.m. Monday through Friday) is popular among the locals, thanks to the ambience and the great margaritas.

THE RED GRAPE $$
529 First Street W., Sonoma
(707) 996-4103
www.theredgrape.com
Just off the Sonoma Plaza is this fun pizza joint that puts the pie on a pedestal. Try 30 kinds of pizza (olive oil– or pesto-based, or plum tomato sauce–based) and a couple of calzones, too. There's a huge selection of toppings, if you want to build your own pie. If you're not in the mood for pizza, try one of the pasta dishes combined with a Gorgonzola salad. The Red Grape has an extensive wine list, too. Open daily for lunch and dinner.

SADDLES $$$$
29 East MacArthur Street, Sonoma
(707) 933-3191
www.macarthurplace.com
Within the classy MacArthur Place hotel and spa (see the Spas and Resorts chapter), this restaurant exudes a rustic, bunkhouse feel, because it's in the original barn on the property. It has a cowboy motif—with real saddles made into chairs in the lobby and the wait staff in denim—but don't expect beans and boiled coffee here. What you will find is plenty of red meat and fixins, primarily midwestern corn-fed, mesquite-grilled USDA prime beef. For lighter appetites, there's salmon, mahimahi, and chicken entrees. Start your meal with the cornmeal onion rings—a crunchy, tasty bit of heaven. The wine list runs about 70 labels

strong and there's a martini bar that offers 14 oversize libations. Saddles is open daily for lunch and dinner, with a weekend brunch to boot.

SANTE AT THE FAIRMONT
SONOMA MISSION INN $$$$
18140 Sonoma Highway, Sonoma
(707) 938-9000, (800) 862-4945
www.fairmont.com/sonoma

If you're ready to go upscale, walk to the main building of the inn for a Sunday brunch overlooking the pool, or have lunch or dinner in an ambience that has country-club class—elegant but not stuffy. This is a spa, after all (see the Spas and Resorts chapter), so the cuisine leans toward healthful preparations using lighter sauces, lots of vegetables, and delicate fish and chicken dishes. But have no fear—you can still order a bit of decadence by topping off your meal with crème brûlée. The award-winning wine list features 500 selections from Napa and Sonoma vineyards. Reservations are recommended for dinner. Sante is open daily.

THE SWISS HOTEL $$$
18 West Spain Street, Sonoma
(707) 938-2884
www.swisshotelsonoma.com

It's a wonderful old building—a remarkably preserved adobe that was once the home of Gen. Mariano Vallejo's brother, Salvador, who built it in the late 1830s. It became "the Swiss" when a stagecoach operator bought it and changed the name. Today it is easily recognizable by the Swiss flag flying over the door. For decades the restaurant was patronized largely by local families who came for the generous family-style Italian dinners. The barroom was a hangout for locals as well, who came to meet and greet friends, and it hasn't changed much over the past 100 years. The menu is a bit upscale from the days of the massive Italian feasts, but the pastas are still served al dente, and the pizzas are turned out of wood-burning brick ovens. It's open daily for lunch and dinner.

i Popular at many French-inspired restaurants is the serving of an *amuse-bouche* a couple of times throughout a multicourse meal. Roughly translated as "mouth amuser," these tiny tastes are delivered between courses to keep you entertained.

Glen Ellen

THE FIG CAFE AND WINE BAR $$
13690 Arnold Drive, Glen Ellen
(707) 938-2130
www.thegirlandthefig.com

Sondra Bernstein owns two restaurants in the Sonoma Valley: the one described in the Sonoma listings, and this one, a bright and airy place that serves American comfort food with French accents. Figs are featured in some dishes, but you can also expect several pizzas and sandwiches, duck confit, braised pot roast, chicken stew, and such satisfying desserts as a mixed nut tart with caramel sauce. Prices are reasonable, kids are welcome, and the blues can be heard on the sound system. Open for dinner every night, and brunch on Saturday and Sunday (the cafe eggs Florentine is scrumptious).

GARDEN COURT CAFE & BAKERY $
13647 Arnold Drive, Glen Ellen
(707) 935-1565
www.gardencourtcafe.com

Look for this popular cafe's bright green awning. Breakfast is the big draw, with eggs Benedict in several varieties and sizes (one, two, or three eggs) leading the popularity list and omelets and scrambles following close behind. Dogs are welcome under certain circumstances. The cafe is open for breakfast and lunch six days a week (closed Tuesday).

GLEN ELLEN INN OYSTER GRILL &
MARTINI BAR $$$$
13670 Arnold Drive, Glen Ellen
(707) 996-6409
www.glenelleninn.com

Set inside a Cape Cod–style cottage, this tiny restaurant delivers one delight after another. You have three choices of where to eat—the indoor dining room, the sun porch, or the patio. In addition to oysters done many ways, expect California fusion cuisine, such as artichoke and Stilton ravioli. The desserts are truly decadent. If you can manage two, go for the warm pecan spice bread pudding and the French vanilla ice cream rolled in toasted coconut and drizzled with caramel sauce. The bar serves about 30 types of martinis.

Kenwood

KENWOOD RESTAURANT $$$$
9900 Highway 12 (Sonoma Highway), Kenwood
(707) 833-6326
www.kenwoodrestaurant.com
The parking lot is always full—which is a sure sign of the restaurant's well-deserved popularity. The chef concocts interesting fare such as crispy veal sweetbreads on mushroom ravioli, and duck spring roll with mango salad and ponzu sauce. *Gourmet* magazine once voted this one of the top 20 restaurants in the entire Bay Area. One of the real pleasures of dining here is the opportunity to drink in the exquisite view as the late-afternoon sun hits the peaks of Sugarloaf Ridge. The scene is particularly rewarding from the deck. The wine list is acclaimed for featuring the best wines produced in Kenwood (bar drinks are also available). Lunch and dinner are served Wednesday through Sunday.

Petaluma

CAFE ZAZZLE $
121 Kentucky Street, Petaluma
(707) 726-1700
www.zazzlecafe.com
The food has Asian influences, and the motto "Eat this!" is a welcome invitation to come on in and get comfortable. Start with miso soup, and follow with a grilled beef salad. At least seven wraps are offered, and fish tacos, too. Noodles in broth, and tossed noodles and pasta round out the savory portion of the menu. The sweets include key lime pie and a honey baked apple. The kids get their own menu. Open daily for lunch and dinner.

MCNEAR'S SALOON AND DINING HOUSE $$
23 North Petaluma Boulevard, Petaluma
(707) 765-2121
www.mcnears.com
It's friendly, funky, and great fun. Every square inch of the walls is covered with historic memorabilia and old photographs, including old sleds, skis, street signs, flags, and banners. The name McNear looms large in Petaluma history, stretching back to 1856 when John McNear came to town, creating a business empire and becoming the first owner of the McNear Building. The goal of the present-day owners is to provide a meeting, eating, and entertainment spot for locals and fun-loving visitors (see the Nightlife chapter for more about the entertainment at McNear's Mystic Theatre next door). Barbecue is the house specialty, with an extensive menu to back that up, and the saloon is well stocked. The dining room is large, but the sidewalk cafe in front is the popular place to sip espresso on Sunday morning. McNear's is open for lunch and dinner every day of the week, plus brunch on weekends. It's open late, too, with food served until midnight.

VOLPI'S RISTORANTE $$$
124 Washington Street, Petaluma
(707) 765-0695
There's a lot of old-world charm in this place run by the Volpi family; it's been on the local scene since 1925—in a building that was once a speakeasy. This is family-style dining in an unhurried atmosphere. The cuisine is Italian, created by chef Glen Petrucci, who specializes in homemade pastas, veal, and seafood. The fully stocked bar serves tavern and restaurant patrons. If you're up to it, you can listen to live accordion music Friday and Saturday evenings. Lunch is served Wednesday, Thursday, and Friday; dinner Wednesday through Sunday.

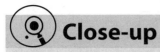 **Close-up**

Make a Meal of Dungeness Crab

Traveling in Wine Country between late autumn and early spring? Your visit won't be complete without sinking your teeth into a delicious Dungeness crab, a fine delicacy that's usually available from November through March. Fresh fish purveyors such as the Tides Wharf and Lucas Wharf in Bodega Bay—and most supermarkets inland—are well stocked with the crustacean during its special season. (If you visit San Francisco restaurants during the winter, you can expect Dungeness crab specials on menus, too.) The coastal markets also carry fresh bread, cheeses, bottles of wine, and many other goodies for assembling a daytime picnic or after-dark dinner in the privacy of your hotel room.

These delicious crabs are a favorite for holiday meals, with locals reserving a few in advance for Thanksgiving and Christmas feasts. Visitors to the area can easily score a couple around the holidays, too, if your timing is good.

One two-pound crab feeds two nicely as an appetizer; with two crabs, a side salad, and crusty bread you have a substantial meal for two. Ask the fish market to clean the crabs (a nasty job better left to the pros) and crack the shell lightly. Stock up on napkins or paper towels (mining the crabmeat can get messy, but that's part of the fun) and have your favorite cocktail sauce or other condiment nearby for dipping. Use the hard, pointy end from one of the legs to help extract the meat from the legs, claws, and body. Pour yourself a glass of Sauvignon Blanc (tastes great with crab), then dig, dip, and devour!

Santa Rosa

JOHN ASH & CO. $$$$
4330 Barnes Road, Santa Rosa
(707) 527-7687
www.vintnersinn.com

John Ash is no longer there, but the cuisine he created carries on, with each entree made a masterpiece of taste, texture, color, and design. Nothing here is ordinary. The fare is "Wine Country cuisine," i.e., California cuisine using only the freshest produce from local farmers and local goat cheeses—a signature dish is the Dungeness crab cakes. Large, arched windows give the dining room an open, airy feel. The wine list is one of the best, with a good selection sold by the glass. John Ash & Co. is adjacent to Vintners Inn, a Provençal-style hotel arranged around a central plaza and fountain, all set in a large vineyard (see the Hotels, Motels, and Inns chapter). The restaurant and bar are open for dinner seven days a week. Added recently to this property was the Front Room Bar & Lounge, which has become a favorite meeting place for locals.

FLAVOR $$$
96 Old Courthouse Square, Santa Rosa
(707) 573-9600
www.flavorbistro.com

You can't go wrong with the pastas at Flavor, located in the heart of downtown Santa Rosa at the corner of Mendocino Avenue and Fourth Street. I personally like the chicken fettuccine and the butternut ravioli, but you may find your own favorite on the list. There are plenty of other options: eggplant parmesan, pork chops, flatiron steak, chicken, and so forth. The best of both worlds is to sit at a table just inside from the patio, if you can arrange it. Flavor is open daily for lunch and dinner; breakfast is served Saturday and Sunday from 8:00 a.m. to 1:30 p.m.

LA GARE FRENCH RESTAURANT $$$
208 Wilson Street, Santa Rosa
(707) 528-4355
www.lagarerestaurant.com

La Gare has been voted "most romantic" and "best restaurant" by the *Press Democrat* newspaper. The *North Bay Bohemian* also has awarded

La Gare its "best restaurant" award for the past few years. Tucked away in Santa Rosa's historic Railroad Square, it's a favorite of the locals, who come for hearty, country-style, traditional French cooking. Romantic it is, with lace curtains, soft lighting, and stained glass. It is one of the few places in Wine Country where you are offered (gasp!) French wines. La Gare ("railway station") is open for dinner Wednesday through Sunday.

i Santa Rosa restaurateur Guy Fieri rocketed to fame in 2006 when he starred in a reality TV show on the Food Network, beating out other chefs from around the nation to win his own six-episode cooking show called *Guy's Big Bite.*

LATITUDE ISLAND GRILL $$$$
5000 Roberts Lake Road, Rohnert Park
(707) 588-1800
www.latitudegrill.com
Latitude is a large restaurant with both a dining room and a cafe area with full bar. For alfresco seating in warm weather, a patio overlooks pleasant Roberts Lake. The food here is called "new American," meaning it's inspired by many international flavors with a tropical bent and paired with Sonoma County's freshest products. For example, you can expect dishes such as grilled ahi tuna, braised short ribs in rosemary-mushroom juice, and miso glazed salmon. Meal starters might include spicy fried prawns and a pupu platter. The cafe/bar has its own menu that is served all day, and you can also order off the regular lunch and dinner menus. Latitude is located in Rohnert Park, just outside the Santa Rosa city limits.

OMELETTE EXPRESS $
112 Fourth Street, Santa Rosa
(707) 525-1690
www.omelette.com
If you happen to be walking around Santa Rosa's Railroad Square on a weekend morning, you'll see as many people on the sidewalk waiting to get into this restaurant as there are patrons inside. The menu lists more than 40 varieties of the humble omelet—both plain and fancy, including vegetarian and seafood. The choices for lunch include two dozen "Pullman Car" sandwiches. You might want to bite into the Hot Express Special—grilled onions, mushrooms, melted jack and cheddar cheese, served open face on dark rye. The restaurant is open for breakfast and lunch seven days a week and most holidays.

ROSSO $$
53 Montgomery Drive (in the Creekside Center), Santa Rosa
(707) 544-3221
www.rossopizzeria.com
Craving some good Italian food, and pizza in particular? This gem is worth seeking out in an otherwise ordinary strip center. Wood-burning ovens are used to make authentic Neapolitan-style pizza. I can recommend the Margherita or the Funghi without hesitation. Perhaps a *piadine* is more to your liking. It's a flatbread with yummy salad toppings that you fold up and eat; three types are offered. Walk in the door and have a glass of your favorite red at the wine bar while waiting for a table, and take in the colorful paintings. Open daily for lunch and dinner, until 10:00 p.m.

THE SEAFOOD BRASSERIE $$$$
170 Railroad Street, Santa Rosa
(707) 636-7388
www.vineyardcreek.hyatt.com
Housed in Santa Rosa's Vineyard Creek Hyatt Hotel, Seafood Brasserie leans toward seafood, and lots of it. There are dishes revolving around swordfish, scallops, Sacramento Delta crayfish, Dungeness crab, Alaskan halibut, and Hawaiian opah. The wine list is heavy on Sonoma County selections, with reasonable prices. The service in particular is very good.

STARK'S STEAKHOUSE $$$$
521 Adams Street (Railroad Square vicinity), Santa Rosa
(707) 546-5100
www.starkssteakhouse.com
Get your red meat here. A longtime Italian restaurant called Michele's was recently reincarnated

into this fabulous steakhouse, another success brought to you by the owners of the two Willi's restaurants in Sonoma County (see next listing and the Healdsburg section). Stark's does steaks with toppers (optional), such as foie gras, roasted bone marrow, or sweetbreads. Many sauces are offered, too. Duck, chicken, and lamb selections are available for the non-steak eater. The wine list is nearly 30 pages long, so there's sure to be a good red to go with your meaty main course. Stark's is open daily for dinner; lunch is served Monday through Friday.

WILLI'S WINE BAR $$$$
4404 Old Redwood Highway, Santa Rosa
(707) 526-3096
www.williswinebar.net
Willi's emphasis is on small plates that are meant to be shared. The flavors and the prices for each plate vary widely, but everything is tasty. There are more than 30 plates to choose from, plus desserts, and it's fun to mix and match many different items into a complete and satisfying meal. Some plates to try are the black truffle risotto with Parmesan, caramelized parsnips and leeks, skillet-roasted shrimp, and Hog Island oysters prepared two ways. Wine tastes come in two-ounce, five-ounce, and half-bottle pours. The restaurant is located in a house built in 1886, and there are plenty of nice old touches to the place, including a copper ceiling above the 14-seat wine bar. The owners of this restaurant also operate Stark's Steakhouse in Santa Rosa's Railroad Square and Willi's Seafood and Raw Bar in Healdsburg (see listings in this chapter).

ZAZU $$$
3535 Guerneville Road, Santa Rosa
(707) 523-4814
www.zazurestaurant.com
When it was the Willowside Cafe, loyal droves from as far away as San Francisco came to partake of the cuisine. Reincarnated in the same location, Zazu offers familiar food with a twist. Owners/chefs Duskie Estes and John Stewart have created a great place with a dedicated following. Everything here is incredibly fresh,

from the eggs collected from the couple's own chickens for creating the pasta, to the produce growing out back, picked at the peak of flavor. The menus change with the seasons, and there are small plates and big plates to choose from. Choices might include an antipasto plate brimming with Stewart's own hand-made salumi (under the Black Pig label); Hog Island oysters; butternut squash hash with quail eggs; wild salmon with corn griddle cakes; duck soup with white truffle oil; and venison, swordfish, and flatiron steak. Zazu is open for dinner Wednesday through Sunday. A recipe by these chefs is featured in a close-up in this chapter. (John and Duskie also own and operate Bovolo in Healdsburg; see the listing in this chapter.)

Healdsburg/Northern Sonoma County
BARNDIVA $$$$
231 Center Street, Healdsburg
(707) 431-0100
www.barndiva.com
It's sort of barnlike, but way cooler. On one side is a hip cocktail bar, and the rest of the room is for dining. Nearly everything served here comes from sources nearby, from the cheese to the produce to the fresh duck. You can select from light items such as a Dungeness crab tian, or something spicy like pork spring rolls. The comfort-food list might include chicken potpie. Barndiva serves dinner Wednesday through Sunday, and lunch Friday through Sunday.

BISTRO RALPH $$$$
109 Plaza Street, Healdsburg
(707) 433-1380
www.bistroralph.com
Bistro Ralph offers a somewhat formal but unstuffy atmosphere, featuring American country French cuisine. The white-linen-covered tables lined up along one wall are reminiscent of earlier San Francisco Italian restaurants. The food is prepared with an imaginative touch and fresh ingredients. Chef-owner Ralph Tingle can be seen at the farmers' market Saturday mornings, selecting from the seasonal bounty of vegetables that will be on his

Close-up

Chefs Reveal Favorite Recipe

Two of Wine Country's culinary shining stars are the husband-and-wife team of John Stewart and Duskie Estes, who have established a two-restaurant dynasty in Sonoma County that is thriving. The chefs' restaurants—Zazu in Santa Rosa and Bovolo in Healdsburg—are favorites with locals and visitors.

John is a salumist who makes the restaurants' bacon and salumi from antibiotic-free and hormone-free pork, boar, and lamb (under the Black Pig brand). Duskie worked in the kitchens at some of Seattle's most acclaimed restaurants before she and John tied the knot and moved to Sonoma County.

In 2007 the couple appeared on the cover of *Wine Spectator* magazine in front of Zazu, and they have recently been featured in a TV commercial for California tourism that spotlights widely known chefs working in the Golden State.

The husband-and-wife chef team of John Stewart and Duskie Estes operates two popular restaurants in Sonoma County. JOE BURULL

menu that night. The smoked salmon starter with an unusual focaccia pastry is a good choice. Enjoy a bottle of local wine or beer with your meal or the specialty of the house: a dry martini. Bistro Ralph is open for lunch and dinner six days a week (closed Sunday).

BOVOLO $$
106 Matheson Street (in Copperfield's Books), Healdsburg
(707) 431-2962
www.bovolorestaurant.com
I would eat breakfast here every day of the week if I could. In particular I'd devour the farfalline

The recipe featured here is delicious—great for home chefs who want to blend the freshness of homemade pasta with asparagus and bacon. "Because we make all of our own bacon from free-range heritage pork, we like to highlight it in everything," says Duskie. "Quality bacon makes or breaks this dish," she adds, noting that "carbonara" refers to the fresh black pepper in the dish.

BACON AND ASPARAGUS CARBONARA

Serves 4 to 6

For the pasta:

3 1/2 cups all purpose flour

5 eggs

2 tablespoons olive oil

In a bowl, combine flour, eggs, and oil. Knead, wrap in plastic, and let rest at least 1/2 hour. Roll out in pasta machine three times at each setting, folding it each time (this gives it the tooth). Bring to desired thickness (depends on machine, usually 2 notches above the thinnest setting). At the desired thickness, roll it through twice without any folding (that sets the thickness) and cut with tagliatelle cutter.

6 slices quality bacon, cut in lardons

1 bunch (pencil-thin) asparagus, cut into 3/4-inch lengths on the bias

4 eggs, whisked

1 cup fresh grated Parmesan cheese, plus more for garnish

kosher salt and fresh ground black pepper

Bring a large pot of salted water to a boil. In a sauté pan on medium-high heat, cook the bacon until crispy, about 4 minutes. Cook the pasta until done, about 4 minutes. Halfway through the cooking, add the asparagus. Meanwhile, in a bowl combine the eggs with the Parmesan, salt, and pepper.

Strain the pasta, reserving 1/2 cup of the pasta water for the sauce. Add the hot pasta and asparagus, some of its water, and the hot bacon and its rendered fat to the egg and cheese. With tongs toss and add pasta water to desired consistency. Season to taste with salt and pepper.

It is important that the pasta and the bacon be hot because they are cooking the egg and thickening the sauce. It's also important to work quickly so you don't overcook the eggs or they will scramble. Plate up into pasta bowls and garnish with more Parmesan cheese.

pasta carbonara, made with the chef's own Black Pig label bacon. Bovolo (it means "snail shell" in Italian) opens for the morning meal at 9:00 a.m. (enter through the back door), or wait for lunch or dinner and get a delicious pizza, a Bovolo burger (with house-made Italian sausage), or a salad from the large selection. (The aforementioned pasta is also available for lunch and dinner.) Chefs Duskie Estes and John Stewart also own Zazu Restaurant in Santa Rosa (see listing in this chapter). You can make one of their pasta carbonara recipes for yourself (see the close-up in this chapter).

i A national model for food recycling is taking place in some Wine Country vineyards. In a program called Four Course Compost, tons of food scraps from San Francisco restaurants are processed into high-grade compost that is spread among the vines. Giving back to the earth is good for the crops, reduces trash-hauling costs, and keeps food waste out of landfills.

CYRUS $$$$
29 North Street, Healdsburg
(707) 433-3311
www.cyrusrestaurant.com
If Sonoma County can lay claim to its own French Laundry, Cyrus is the likely candidate. From the day it opened in 2005, Cyrus began collecting high praise and eventually Michelin stars. The restaurant aims to make your meal an elegant experience. The menu is fixed price, ranging from $70 to more than $100 per person, with nine categories. Diners may choose a three-, four-, or five-course meal from such delectable delights as chestnut soup with sherry and duck confit, bacon-wrapped pork with braised cabbage, roasted porcini with arugula and crisp polenta, or quail. A jacket for the gent is a good idea, as the atmosphere is generally more formal than at most Wine Country restaurants. Cyrus is at the Les Mars Hotel, a block north of the town plaza.

DRY CREEK GENERAL STORE $
3495 Dry Creek Road, Healdsburg
(707) 433-4171
www.dcgstore.com
It's an old-time grocery store that looks as if it's been there forever. But if you've been cruising the Dry Creek vineyards for hours and your tummy says it's picnic time, you'll love the simple, delicious homemade sandwiches and salads, the wine selection, and the gourmet food section. Take your purchases to any one of the many wineries in the area, buy yourself a bottle of their best, and settle in for a beautiful picnic. The store is open Monday through Thursday from 6:00 a.m. to 6:00 p.m. and 6:00 a.m. to 7:00 p.m. Friday and Saturday.

DRY CREEK KITCHEN $$$$
317 Healdsburg Avenue, Healdsburg
(707) 431-0330
www.hotelhealdsburg.com
www.charliepalmer.com/dry_creek
Maybe you've heard of Charlie Palmer. He was named New York City's best chef in 1997. His restaurant ventures include Aureole, with locations in New York and Las Vegas; Alva American Bistro in Manhattan; and Charlie Palmer Steak at the Four Seasons Hotel in Las Vegas. A few years back he brought his award-winning way with cuisine to Wine Country, in the restaurant of the Hotel Healdsburg (see the Hotels, Motels, and Inns chapter). Charlie's approach is to present American cooking with European influences and do it spectacularly with a hearty heaping of locally grown organic produce. Expect fabulous flavors and presentations around duck, salmon, beef—to name a few—and appetizers and desserts to die for. There's also a fixed-price seven-course tasting menu. To accompany your meal, you're sure to find just the right vino among the eight-page wine list. The dining room is delightful, with soft lighting, fine art, and views of leafy Healdsburg Plaza. Lunch is served until 2:30 p.m. Friday to Sunday; dinner begins at 5:30 p.m. daily.

HEALDSBURG BAR AND GRILL $
245 Healdsburg Avenue, Healdsburg
(707) 433-3333
www.healdsburgbarandgrill.com
The owners of Cyrus restaurant just up the road in the Le Mars Hotel took over operation of this cafe in 2008 and by doing so upped the ante on the food. It's reasonably priced for this tourist town, with most entrees and sandwiches averaging 10 bucks. The most expensive item on the menu is seared tuna on a pita. Burgers built the way you want them, comfort food such as chicken pot pie and macaroni and cheese, and a good selection of salads are the stars of the menu. French fries are given extra attention here, available four ways. The big selling point is the large patio, delightful any time of day or night for people-watching. It even has a bocce ball court just

for fun. The restaurant is open Sunday through Thursday from 11:30 a.m. to 9:00 p.m., and one hour later on Fridays and Saturdays.

MADRONA MANOR $$$$
1001 Westside Road, Healdsburg
(707) 433-4231
www.madronamanor.com
Nestled on a wooded knoll surrounded by lush vineyards, Madrona Manor is a majestic sight, its mansard roof rising three stories into the tree-tops (see the Bed-and-Breakfast Inns chapter). The dining room is opulent, the atmosphere romantic. Chef Jesse Mallgren specializes in New California cuisine, using the freshest produce and ingredients available in Sonoma County. He might create an appetizer of crab with ruby red grapefruit, avocado, arugula, and pancetta vinaigrette; and an entree of roast venison loin with carrots, leek risotto, nectarine-rosemary bro-chettes, and vanilla sauce. A fixed-price chef's menu of seven to nine courses and an a la carte menu are offered daily. Madrona Manor is open Wednesday through Sunday for dinner, but prior to eating you might want to stroll through the delightful eight-acre gardens.

MANZANITA $$$$
336 Healdsburg Avenue, Healdsburg
(707) 433-8111
www.manzanita336.com
Manzanita has been around for several years serving standard Wine Country menu selections such as cassoulet and roast sea bass—California cuisine with European influences. The restau-rant offers food with flair, combined with ter-rific service in comfortable surroundings. The first-course options are exceptional—butternut squash bisque or roasted organic beets with fen-nel—and the entrees might include grilled white sea bass or wood oven–roasted duck breast. The pizza is also great. There's a small wine bar, and the wine list is impressive. Lunch and dinner are served Tuesday through Saturday.

PALETTE ART CAFE $$
235 Healdsburg Avenue, Suite 105,
Healdsburg
(707) 433-2788
www.palette-art.com
Is it a restaurant or an art gallery? It's both, dubbed by the owners as "a visual and culinary gallery." The art is for sale here, which is not uncommon in restaurants, but it's been elevated to greater importance, with frequent artists' receptions accompanied by light live jazz or acoustic soul. So it's a bona fide art gallery made more fun with food. There are no big surprises on the menu—count on soups, sandwiches, salads, a charcuterie platter, and an artisan cheese plat-ter to go with the small wine list. Or skip right to the fondues, both sweet and savory (including a s'mores fondue—melted chocolate and marsh-mallow with graham crackers). Palette Art Cafe serves breakfast, lunch, and dinner.

PICK'S DRIVE-IN $
117 South Cloverdale Boulevard, Cloverdale
(707) 894-2962
Pick's could have been a location in the movie *American Graffiti*. It serves straightforward burg-ers, fries, hot dogs, sodas, and milk shakes, at a small counter or on picnic tables out front. Set-ting their sandwiches apart from the rest is Pick's Famous Red Relish, which is "what makes our burgers taste *soooo* good." Yes, they *are* good. Pick's has been in business a long time—since 1923. You can't miss it along the boulevard; just look for the giant neon sign.

RAVENOUS $$$
420 Center Street, Healdsburg
(707) 431-1302
Once a tiny restaurant next to the Raven Film Center, with just a few tables and many people milling about outside waiting for those coveted tables, Ravenous has moved up in the world. It's now a full-size restaurant not far from the old place, and the food is better than ever. The gen-erous portions of amazing cuisine defy categoriz-ing. A typical menu selection might be Liberty

duck legs steamed and roasted, presented atop noodles, and accompanied by grilled white and black eggplant; or choose the beef brisket braised in red wine. It comes with potato fritters and tasty vegetables too. Lunch and dinner are served Wednesday through Sunday.

i If you're ready to open that special bottle of wine you purchased at the tasting room to enjoy with a special meal, corkage fees at many restaurants are waived on certain nights of the week. Always inquire when making a reservation.

ZIN $$$$
344 Center Street, Healdsburg
(707) 473-0946
www.zinrestaurant.com
Why name a restaurant after a wine varietal? Because Zin delivers great food and offers lots of great Zinfandels too. Much of the cuisine is created to be enjoyed with Zinfandel and features an all-American accent. You might find St. Louis–style ribs one night and roasted chicken with polenta on another night. Chefs Jeff Mall and Scott Silva call their cuisine "New American"—updating classic American dishes with more interesting flavors and imagination. The dining room is simple, with big bouquets of flowers and soothing paintings. You can get dinner here every night but Tuesday and lunch on weekdays (except Tuesday).

Sonoma Coast
BAY VIEW RESTAURANT $$$$
800 Coast Highway 1, Bodega Bay
(707) 875-2751, (800) 541-7788
www.innatthetides.com
Bay View is part of Inn at the Tides, one of the most relaxing hostelries at Bodega Bay (see the Hotels, Motels, and Inns chapter). The restaurant features a menu that changes weekly and goes well beyond the local catch. Look for grilled ahi tuna on the menu, bouillabaisse, grilled wild king salmon, and rack of lamb. Cocktails are served in the lounge, a romantic setting as the sun goes down over the Pacific. The restaurant is open for dinner Wednesday through Sunday.

LUCAS WHARF RESTAURANT & BAR $$$
595 Highway 1, Bodega Bay
(707) 875-3522
This is a cozy, romantic place, with a vaulted ceiling and a fireplace to warm you when the weather cools (as it often does on this coast). Seafood will never be fresher than it is here, for this is a commercial fishery that supplies grocers and the public with fresh Pacific catch. The chef's special of the day is based on the best of the day's catch—salmon, halibut, crab, calamari, and oysters. Bask in the glow of the setting sun while you enjoy your meal or watch sea birds cavort as fishermen deliver their bounty at the pier (ask for a window table). Lucas Wharf is a great place to pick up fresh cracked crab or custom-smoked fish. The restaurant is open for lunch and dinner seven days a week. Fresh crab season is mid-November through June, and fresh salmon season is mid-May through September.

RIVER'S END RESTAURANT $$$$
11048 Highway 1, Jenner
(707) 865-2484
www.ilovesunsets.com
From its position on a bluff where the Russian River flows into the Pacific, River's End has an extraordinary view. Menu offerings have left local seafood far behind and moved on to upscale comfort foods with a European flair. Here you can have crispy duck confit rolls for an appetizer, clam chowder for the soup course, and North American elk for the entree. The restaurant is open for lunch and dinner Thursday through Monday.

SANDPIPER $$
1410 Bay Flat Road, Bodega Bay
(707) 875-2278
www.sandpiperrestaurant.com
Did you ever know a good seafood restaurant that *didn't* claim its clam chowder to be the best you've ever tasted? The Sandpiper will even sell

you merchandise proclaiming its chowder is the best. The restaurant is off the main drag through Bodega Bay; you must turn at the sign for Bodega Head to reach Bay Flat Road. The vehicle parked next to yours might be a fisherman's; it's a casual place that's more comfortable for the locals than the other restaurants in town. Sandpiper serves breakfast, lunch, and dinner, and the menus for each are the traditional fare. In addition to prawns, snapper, calamari, and the like, burgers, steaks, and chicken dishes are also available.

THE TIDES WHARF & RESTAURANT $$$
835 Highway 1, Bodega Bay
(707) 875-3652
www.innatthetides.com
If the setting looks familiar, it's because you saw it in Alfred Hitchcock's film *The Birds*. If you didn't see the movie, you can get a taste of the action through a poster on the wall. Aside from the renown that has come from Tippi Hedren fending off birds, the restaurant has earned its own fame as the long-standing favorite of regulars who have been popping in since the place was small. There's both a snack bar and a full-service sit-down restaurant, as well as a fish market. Pick up some fresh Dungeness crab at the market when it's in season (see the close-up in this chapter), along with wine, bread, cheese, and many other deli items. The restaurant is open every day for breakfast, lunch, and dinner, and it offers full bar service.

West County/Russian River

ALICE'S RESTAURANT AT 101 MAIN $$$
101 South Main Street, Sebastopol
(707) 829-3212
www.alicesrestaurant.net
This small, cozy restaurant—with comfortable upholstered chairs and fresh flowers on every table—is friendly and inviting, and the food is among the best in town. The grilled chicken Caesar salad is excellent, as is the duck confit, which includes crispy fried organic baby spinach and garlic mashed potatoes. Alice's also serves delicious crab cakes, and there's a menu for kids

too. North Coast labels predominate on the wine list, many available by the glass. Alice also serves locally produced Ace Pear Cider, and her desserts are made on the premises with Ghirardelli chocolate. Open daily for breakfast, lunch, and dinner.

APPLEWOOD INN & RESTAURANT $$$$
13555 Highway 116, Guerneville
(707) 869-9093, (800) 555-8509
www.applewoodinn.com
Snuggled among the redwoods just south of Guerneville, Applewood Inn is famed for its sophisticated meals and comfortable lodgings (see the Bed-and-Breakfast Inns chapter). It's one of those special places you want to keep to yourself, but you can't stop talking about it. The fire-lit dining room serves 60 at individual candlelit tables with windows facing the redwoods on three sides. The restaurant does wonderful things with a crisp duck breast set off with corn and bing cherries, stuffed pork loin cured in spiced black tea and basmati rice, or roasted salmon with mushrooms and chive-caviar butter. Leave room for the blueberry and *fromage blanc* cheesecake in semolina cookie crust. Applewood is open for dinner Tuesday through Saturday.

> **i** Wine lists can be confusing if not intimidating at times, with many obscure labels from boutique wineries unfamiliar to the average diner. Don't hesitate to ask a restaurant's sommelier (pronounced suh-muhl-YAY) for help in making your selection. These wine experts can recommend a good, reasonably priced bottle to complement your meal.

CAPE FEAR CAFE $$
25191 Main Street, Duncans Mills
(707) 865-9246
If you can, try to visit this restaurant for one of its weekend brunches, when the chef's phenomenal menu of Benedicts is available. The cooking here is a mixture of California cuisine with a southern drawl, so expect such dinner entrees as Carolina

chicken (with bourbon and pecans) or pork tenderloin with mahogany ginger sauce. But it's those Benedicts that can make your weekend. Instead of English muffins, the poached eggs are served over peppered grits. Similar to polenta, the grits are cooked, cooled, mixed with cheese, and then grilled. Wow.

 Smoking is not permitted in California restaurants and nightclubs.

CORKS AT RUSSIAN RIVER VINEYARDS $$$
5700 Gravenstein Highway N., Forestville
(707) 887-3344
www.russianrivervineyards.com
Corks is where locals go to enjoy a revolving menu of creative delicacies, whipped up by chef-owner Greg Hallihan. Items such as the steamed half artichoke stuffed with a scoop of purple-black niçoise olive tapenade, the hearty lentil-carrot soup, the lamb kabob, or the pan-roasted chicken with truffled mashed potatoes—not to mention the mocha crème brûlée and other luscious desserts—keep this place packed on most nights. Open Wednesday through Monday for dinner, and lunch every day except Sunday. The restaurant is closed on Tuesday.

THE FARMHOUSE INN & RESTAURANT $$$$
7871 River Road, Forestville
(707) 887-3300
www.farmhouseinn.com
Though part of a bed-and-breakfast inn, the Farmhouse restaurant is open to the public as well as the inn's guests, which is a good thing because a riot would ensue otherwise. The restaurant has received accolades from high places, and a Michelin star, too. *Gourmet* magazine named it one of the "World's 36 Best Food Destinations." The menu changes frequently, but one dish that appears regularly is rabbit, prepared three ways. Count on braised pork shank, braised veal osso bucco, Merlot-and-mint-braised lamb shank, and petrale sole fillet crisped with couscous. For dessert you can choose baked Alaska or chocolate

soufflé. The romantic dining room seats no more than two dozen, with views through French doors onto the magnificent gardens. Open for dinner Thursday through Sunday (see the Bed-and-Breakfast Inns chapter).

K&L BISTRO $$$
119 South Main Street, Sebastopol
(707) 823-6614
Sebastopol has certainly come up in the restaurant world, with this restaurant awarded a Michelin star in 2007. K&L Bistro owners and chefs Lucas and Karen Martin brought impressive restaurant résumés with them when they opened their own place in Sebastopol. You can count on French onion soup, steak frites, vegetable risotto, and apple rhubarb crisp to round out the meal. Open for lunch and dinner Monday through Saturday; closed Sunday.

NEGRI'S $$
3700 Bohemian Highway, Occidental
(707) 823-5301
www.negrisrestaurant.com
It's a toss-up whether the hungry folks of Sonoma County head first for Union Hotel or Negri's—they're both terrific purveyors of great Italian meals. Negri's has been cooking pasta since 1940. A family-style meal starts out with a tureen of minestrone that's so popular people come in to buy it by the bucket. The pasta list is long, including vegetarian spaghetti, penne, and homemade ravioli. After that, if you choose, you can order some of their other specials, such as deep-fried calamari, grilled red snapper, and prawns—wash it down with a drink from the fully stocked bar. Open for lunch and dinner every day.

UNDERWOOD BAR & BISTRO $$$
9113 Graton Road, Graton
(707) 823-7023
www.underwoodgraton.com
North of Sebastopol just off Highway 116 in the tiny town of Graton is Underwood Bar & Bistro, housed in a refurbished building that still feels old and familiar. Here's where to get tapas and

small plates, such as a fresh asparagus appetizer with baguettes with tapenade. A regular dinner menu is served, too, with beef, chicken, and seafood options. Try the fish stew made with prawns, clams, calamari, and mussels; roasted duck breast on a bed of lentils; or lamb with Moroccan spices. There's also a cheese plate and several excellent salads and oysters to choose from.

UNION HOTEL RESTAURANT $$
3731 Main Street, Occidental
(707) 874-3555
www.unionhotel.com
It seems like the Union Hotel dining room has been there forever, housed in a building that dates from 1879. The restaurant has not been around quite that long, but the same family has run it since 1925. The great fame of the place comes from the huge portions of pasta that are served family-style—it's known far and wide for the heaping helpings. The establishment has its own bakery and makes great croissants and muffins to serve in its cafe. Union Hotel is open for lunch and dinner every day, serving family-style meals and drinks from the saloon. The restaurant also has two locations in Santa Rosa—one on the east side of town and one on the west side—but it's the Occidental location that has the charm and history.

NIGHTLIFE

Let me make this clear right from the start: When it comes to nighttime entertainment, Wine Country isn't Hollywood, or South Beach, or Manhattan. It's unlikely you'll find an after-hours club within this two-county area where you can dance till dawn and be chased by paparazzi as you dive headfirst into your limo. Generally speaking, "nightlife" around here means staying out late to take in a movie at the multiplex. Most towns start rolling up the sidewalks after sundown, but there are some popular music venues and dance hot spots to keep your toes tapping well into the night. Napa and St. Helena have some options, and the downtown areas of Petaluma and Santa Rosa can be relied upon for several shows on the weekend. And those willing to make a 75-minute drive to Lake County's Konocti Harbor Resort will be rewarded with big-time music acts—much of it country and "dinosaur" rock—combined with water sports. Still looking for more fun even after sipping wine all day? Here I list a few Wine Country music halls, bars, and clubs where you can look for after-hours entertainment. (A few of these places are also featured in the Restaurants chapter.) Some of the smaller establishments don't collect a cover charge, but many do. In general, expect to pay from $2 to $5 to watch local talent, more if someone of greater renown is taking the stage. Guidelines for pricier show tickets are given in the listings.

The bar and club listings are followed by movie theaters in the region. Check a local newspaper for more up-to-date information. I don't want to nag about this, but one thing bears repeating, especially in this chapter: Please observe the same common sense about drinking and driving that applies anywhere. California's legal blood-alcohol threshold is a stringent 0.08, so taking to the road after more than one drink can be expensive and embarrassing as well as extremely dangerous. If you need a taxi, consult the Getting Here, Getting Around chapter.

BARS, PUBS, AND CLUBS

Napa County

DOWNTOWN JOE'S
902 Main Street, Napa
(707) 258-2337
www.downtownjoes.com
This riverside microbrewery offers a variety of live entertainment Tuesday through Friday. Wednesday nights are for contemporary jazz; on Sunday evenings there might be a blues jam or comedy (second Sunday of each month). On other nights there are singer-songwriters.

TUSCANY
1005 First Street, Napa
(707) 258-1000
www.restaurant.com/tuscany
It's known more for its food, but on Friday and Saturday from 7:00 to 11:00 p.m. there's also live jazz or blues.

PICCOLINO'S ITALIAN CAFE
1385 Napa Town Center, Napa
(707) 251-0100
www.piccolinoscafe.com
Forget Jerry Vale's versions of those old Italian ballads. Catch them performed here by the duo of Steve Albini and Helen Mead, who also throw

in a few of today's tunes. Hours are generally 5:00 to 9:00 p.m.

ANA'S CANTINA
1205 Main Street, St. Helena
(707) 963-4921

This tropical-themed Mexican restaurant heats up from 9:30 p.m. to 1:30 a.m. most Fridays and Saturdays, with a stream of bands that run from Latin-Mediterranean to jazz to rock to reggae. Wednesday and Sunday are karaoke nights; Thursday is open-mic night.

CALISTOGA INN
1250 Lincoln Avenue, Calistoga
(707) 942-4101
www.calistogainn.com

The bartender here slings Napa Valley Brewing Company beers, and every Friday and Saturday from 9:00 p.m. to midnight, live music fills the small oblong bar. The material varies but tends toward world beat, blues, reggae, and jazz. Wednesday is open-mic night.

HYDRO BAR & GRILL
1403 Lincoln Avenue, Calistoga
(707) 942-9777

Calistoga's late-night eatery is a perfect spot for everything from swing music to rock 'n' roll, generally from 9:00 p.m. to 1:30 a.m. Saturday.

Sonoma County

MURPHY'S IRISH PUB
464 First Street E., Sonoma
(707) 935-0660
www.sonomapub.com

This pub keeps sleepy Sonoma awake, usually every Thursday through Sunday night. The genre is hard to predict. It could be blues one night, traditional Celtic the next. Or it might be folk ballads followed by a melodious string ensemble. There is no cover, but expect a two-pint minimum.

KODIAK JACK'S (AKA KJ'S)
256 North Petaluma Boulevard, Petaluma
(707) 765-5760
www.kodiakjacks.com

On different nights, there is West Coast swing dancing, two-step, line dancing, "beginner couples," power country, and honky-tonk. You can take lessons every night. On Thursday, Friday, and Saturday they offer karaoke (usually with a live band). There's also a restaurant serving burgers and pasta.

MYSTIC THEATRE & MUSIC HALL
23 North Petaluma Boulevard, Petaluma
(707) 765-2121
www.mystictheatre.com

The Mystic Theatre might be Wine Country's coolest venue. Built in 1911 in the historic McNear Building, it's a vaulted, double-decker palace that wouldn't be out of place on the Sunset Strip. Much of the music is rock of all shades and tones, from the Dave Alvin Band to Tower of Power, Richard Thompson to Tommy Castro, Emmylou Harris to Todd Rundgren, the Marshall Tucker Band to the Johnny Winter Band. Van Morrison even recorded some tracks here for one of his live albums. Stand-up comedy passes through from time to time, featuring jokers like Will Durst. Tickets generally range from $15 to $30.

SPANCKY'S
8201 Old Redwood Highway, Cotati
(707) 664-0169

In downtown Cotati, two clubs rule. Spancky's is one of them. It's been in that spot for decades and has a colorful past. But the place has been freshened up, and the rough customers who once held court are long gone. Live rock 'n' roll is the mainstay here, with local bands such as the Remedies, Ratpak, and Hot Karma appearing on weekends.

THE TRADEWINDS
8210 Old Redwood Highway, Cotati
(707) 795-7878
www.tradewindsbar.com
Across the street from Spancky's (see listing above) is another established watering hole where live music reigns. Local bands like the Pulsators and Alameda All-Stars are usually worth the cover charge. The two clubs are good for each other's business: customers routinely trek back and forth across the narrow street that separates them to be entertained by two bands in one night.

A'ROMA ROASTERS AND COFFEEHOUSE
95 Fifth Street, Santa Rosa
(707) 576-7765
www.aromaroasters.com
Come down to Railroad Square on a Friday or Saturday night for live music and a hot cup of chai or joe. A'Roma does a lot of folk music, plus some world beat, jazz, and blues. Shows start at 8:30 p.m.

LAST DAY SALOON
120 Fifth Street, Santa Rosa
(707) 545-2343
www.lastdaysaloon.com
This is the northern outpost of the venerable San Francisco nightclub that's been rocking the Bay Area for more than 30 years. On a busy corner in Railroad Square, Last Day is 8,000 square feet of live music and food too. DJ music is provided a couple nights a week, with weekends dedicated to music of all kinds—you're likely to hear Motown, funk, blues, or new wave. Owner David Daher draws on his three decades in the music business to bring in some terrific acts that might have previously overlooked Santa Rosa on their tour itineraries. Recent legends appearing in the main music room have included Elvin Bishop, Nils Lofgren, the Tubes, Dr. John, and members of the Grateful Dead. The Sonoma County Blues Society has its weekly jam here on Wednesday nights. DJ nights usually carry a $5 cover; tickets for live shows can range from $10 to $20, depending on whether the artist is a household name. There's also a full menu of decent pub grub, and it's served until midnight—perfect for late-night diners.

SEVEN ULTRALOUNGE
528 Seventh Street, Santa Rosa
(707) 528-4700
www.sevensr.com
This dance club, which opened in early 2006 to much ballyhoo, recently made many changes. It began as a high-end, high-priced club aimed at twenty-somethings, complete with a velvet rope and a line around the block. The owners have tweaked the music lineup (mostly provided by DJs) to help reduce some of the frequent police presence that threatened to shut the place down. There's a colorful dance floor, and a strict dress code is enforced. The menu consists of appetizers and sandwiches.

FLAMINGO RESORT HOTEL
2777 Fourth Street, Santa Rosa
(707) 545-8530
www.flamingoresort.com
Sure, it's a hotel bar, but it's better than most. Count on rock, soul, or rhythm & blues bands on the weekends, and karaoke on Monday nights. Sundays are for salsa dancing; on Tuesdays it's West Coast swing (with lessons optional both nights). The spacious dance floor is one of the best around, and it's always packed with hoofers of all ages.

ELLINGTON HALL
3535 Industrial Avenue, Santa Rosa
(707) 545-6150
www.ellingtonhall.com
If you don't know how to dance but want to learn, or if you are a rising star looking to improve your style, waltz into Ellington Hall. You can take lessons almost every night, and you get to practice afterward during the nightly open dance parties. The choices include—but are not limited to—ballroom, hip-hop, belly dancing (women only), salsa, jitterbug, and Scottish dancing too. Call or check the Web site for prices and details. (As the address suggests, this dance hall is tucked into a light industrial and commercial area.)

JASPER O'FARRELL'S
6957 Sebastopol Avenue, Sebastopol
(707) 823-1389
www.jasperofarrellspub.com
This tiny pub keeps Sebastopol busy every night of the week—mostly blues, some rock, some reggae and world beat, some original songwriting, and even the occasional Celtic group. Tuesday is open-mic night. It's eclectic and very local. The stage and dance floor were recently expanded to make the live experience more enjoyable.

ACE IN THE HOLE CIDER PUB
3100 Gravenstein Highway N., Sebastopol
(707) 829-1223
www.acecider.com
I like this place. It's out in the country a bit, some distance north of Sebastopol (at the Graton turn-off). You can always count on live entertainment any night of the week, but earlier than at most clubs. Performers typically play from 6:00 to 9:00 p.m., though some nights the music begins at happy hour. It's a cider pub, the first of its kind in America, where delicious hard ciders are created, bottled, and available on tap. Beer and wine are also served if cider isn't your thing. The food is good, consisting largely of pizza, barbecue, and fish and chips. It's a small pub, so come early to get a seat and a parking spot.

MAIN STREET STATION
16280 Main Street, Guerneville
(707) 869-0501
www.mainststation.com
When Guerneville gets a little too hot, duck into the Station for some cool, breezy jazz or Celtic music. Out of the Blue Swing Band are regulars on Tuesday. Other hipsters blow in and out on Thursday, Friday, and Saturday.

RAINBOW CATTLE COMPANY
16220 Main Street, Guerneville
(707) 869-0206
www.queersteer.com/rainbow_cattle_company
This is where the Russian River's gay clientele have gathered for loud, uninhibited fun since 1979. The club has a DJ on Friday and Saturday nights and holidays.

MOVIE THEATERS
Napa County
NAPA CINEDOME 8
825 Pearl Street, Napa
(707) 257-7700
www.cinemark.com

CAMEO CINEMA
1340 Main Street, St. Helena
(707) 963-9779
www.cameocinema.com

Sonoma County
SEBASTIANI THEATRE
(historic building; occasional art movies)
476 First Street E., Sonoma
(707) 996-2020
www.sebastianitheatre.com

SONOMA CINEMAS 6
200 Siesta Way, Sonoma
(707) 935-1234
www.cinemawest.com

BOULEVARD CINEMA
Corner of Petaluma Boulevard S. and C Street, Petaluma
(707) 762-SHOW
www.cinemawest.com

ROHNERT PARK STADIUM 16
555 Rohnert Park Expressway W., Rohnert Park
(707) 586-0555
www.readingcinemasus.com

SONOMA FILM INSTITUTE
Sonoma State University, Darwin Theater, 1801 East Cotati Avenue, Rohnert Park
(707) 664-2606
www.sonoma.edu

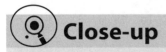 **Close-up**

Sip Wine by Day, Lift a Pint at Night: A Guide to Wine Country Brewpubs

You know you've wandered into serious microbrewery territory when you can sip—at the source—satisfying suds that bear such colorful names as Death and Taxes Black Beer, Twist of Fate Bitter, Hop 2 It, Damnation, Lunatic, Bony Fingers Malt, Rat Bastard Pale Ale, and Workingstiff Red.

The Wine Country ferments much more than just grape-based beverages. If you prefer ambers and blacks to reds and whites and put more stock in a drink's head than its legs, you'll feel right at home. Brewpubs are plentiful, and they have coexisted comfortably alongside the more established emporiums devoted to vino.

Following are descriptions of several microbreweries in Wine Country that craft unforgettable ales and lagers. Most serve better than average pub grub, and many offer live entertainment too, especially on weekends (see individual listings in this chapter for more information). After a day of sniffing, sipping, and chewing on Cabernets, these friendly establishments might be just the place to quaff a cold one.

Downtown Joe's
902 Main Street, Napa
(707) 258-2337
www.downtownjoes.com
Joe's has the standard pub fare (fish-and-chips, sandwiches), with fancier dinner items that range from chicken *pomodoro* to cioppino to sea bass. This establishment lays claim to the best hamburger in Napa, made from Niman Ranch beef. It's smothered with two slices of white cheddar and topped with onion rings. Wash it down with a pint of Ace High Pale Ale or Golden Ribbon (or the Golden Thistle Very Bitter Ale, if your palate prefers that) while enjoying the view of the Napa River outside.

Silverado Brewing Company
3020 St. Helena Highway N., Suite A,
St. Helena
(707) 967-9876
www.silveradobrewingcompany.com
This is a full bar with six beers made on-site—and 30 wines by the bottle, if you just can't get enough of the grape. It's located about a mile and a half north of St. Helena in the Freestone Abbey complex (watch for the sign—it can sneak up on you). I like the tap handle for the Blonde Ale—a babe in a red dress—and the warm ambience of the small bar. As they say in this neck of the woods, "It takes a lot of great beer to make good wine." The extensive menu has something for everyone, including meatloaf or gumbo pasta.

Calistoga Inn
1250 Lincoln Avenue, Calistoga
(707) 942-4101
www.calistogainn.com
This may be one brewery where the food gets more attention than the brews. Choose from a wheat ale, a pilsner, red ale, or a porter on most nights, with some seasonal recipes thrown in. To accompany your foamy brew, order the paella, a pork tenderloin, or pepper-crusted duck breast. Calistoga Inn can boast that it has "survived the Depression, periods of neglect, and five major wars." In other words, it's been around a few years.

Dempsey's Restaurant & Brewery
50 East Washington Street, Petaluma
(707) 765-9694
www.dempseys.com
This brewpub has been quietly serving Petalumans since 1994, combining its Red Rooster Ale and Petaluma Strong Ale with hearty

meals like a marinated pork chop. They also brew Ugly Dog Stout, no doubt a nod to the annual World's Ugliest Dog Contest, held each summer in this town (see Festivals and Annual Events). Much of the produce used in the cuisine is organically grown locally.

Third Street Aleworks Restaurant & Brewery
610 Third Street, Santa Rosa
(707) 523-3060
www.thirdstreetaleworks.com
There are lots of brews to choose from here, and the pub fare to go with it. Have a pint of Annadel Pale Ale or the Stonefly Oatmeal Stout, or sample one of the "occasional" ales, such as Drunken Weasel and Burgher's Kolsch. Use any of these fine brews to accompany English bangers and mash or a selection of pizzas. It's an ethnic menu here, with appetizers ranging from hummus to quesadillas. Burgers too, of course.

Russian River Brewing Company
725 Fourth Street, Santa Rosa
(707) 545-2337
www.russianriverbrewing.com
This brewery had its humble beginnings at Korbel Champagne Cellars near Guerneville, but now it's gone uptown, or more precisely, downtown in Santa Rosa. The hops are grown in Sonoma County, and the brews include an amber ale, a golden wheat ale (a gold medal winner at the 2001 Great American Beer Festival), a pale ale, and a porter. Check the chalkboard behind the bar for the current selection of suds. Live music, mostly acoustic or in the rockabilly genre, can be enjoyed here on weekends. Pizza rules the menu, with calzones and focaccia included too.

Bear Republic Brewing Company
345 Healdsburg Avenue, Healdsburg
(707) 433-2337
www.bearrepublic.com
There are usually 11 beers and ales on tap for sampling, most of them award winners (try the Red Rocket or Black Raven and see why). They added a new beer to the menu recently: Easy Ryeder, what the brewmasters believe is the world's first all-rye beer. If you like what you taste, you can usually get a one-gallon reusable box of your favorite to go. (For the kids, there's homemade root beer and cream soda.) In the shadow of Hotel Healdsburg, the patio is a relaxing spot to nosh on calamari fritti, a huge chicken sandwich called "the Press," or such specials as chicken Parmesan, lobster bisque, or chicken potpie. Tours of their new brewing facility in Cloverdale can be arranged. In 2006, Bear Republic won "Best Small Brewing Company" honors at the Great American Beer Festival.

Hopmonk Tavern
230 Petaluma Avenue, Sebastopol
(707) 320-2405
www.hopmonk.com
New in spring 2008 is this brewery founded by one of the duo that created the Gordon Biersch chain of brewpubs. Dean Biersch promises a lively atmosphere with lots of good food and a chance to chug from small batches of special brews he makes onsite. Lunch, dinner, and Sunday brunch are planned. This is also a music venue; Biersch remodeled the historic building to include a 2,000-square-foot room equipped specifically for live performances.

3RD STREET CINEMAS
620 Third Street, Santa Rosa
(707) 522-0330
www.northamericancinemas.com

AIRPORT STADIUM 12
409 Aviation Way, Santa Rosa
(707) 522-0330
www.northamericancinemas.com

RIALTO CINEMAS LAKESIDE
551 Summerfield Road, Santa Rosa
(707) 525-4840
www.rialtocinemas.com

ROXY STADIUM 14
85 Santa Rosa Avenue, Santa Rosa
(707) 522-0330
www.northamericancinemas.com

THE RAVEN FILM CENTER
415 Center Street, Healdsburg
(707) 433-5448
www.raventheater.com

CLOVER CINEMAS
121 East First Street, Cloverdale
(707) 894-7920
www.cinemawest.com

SEBASTOPOL CINEMAS 9
6868 McKinley Street, Sebastopol
(707) 829-3456
www.cinemawest.com

RIO THEATER
20396 Bohemian Highway (Highway 116),
Monte Rio
(707) 865-0913
www.sonomamovies.com

WINERIES

This is the chapter that was the excuse to create this book in the first place. In the Wine Country galaxy, the wineries are the sun around which all of our other attractions orbit. And just as the grape varietals that grow here are dramatically different from one another, so too are the wineries that produce them. If you take time to drop in at more than a few, you'll discover that each place has its own special story to tell. So when you visit Wine Country, set aside at least a day or two for a sampling of the region's wineries. On the outside they can range from rustic barns to grand estates resembling castles. Once inside you are warmly welcomed by genial guides and tasting-room hosts who gladly explain the mysteries of the craft. Whatever you do, please refrain from rushing through Wine Country. There's nothing to be gained from sprinting between tasting rooms. Take the time to learn about the winery, the winemaking process, and especially its people. Usually they are as mellow and unhurried as the wines themselves.

A TASTE OF EACH REGION

So . . . with hundreds of wineries within the region, how do you get started? First, I'll give you a taste of what separates this coverage area from the rest of the winemaking areas of California and the world—qualities that have given this region the undisputed title of California's Wine Country. Next, I'll provide a brief overview of the wine and wineries of each of the counties in our coverage area. Then comes the part where you get to pick and choose: detailed listings for more than 100 individual producers throughout Wine Country.

Despite the number of wineries here and the number of acres under viticulture, Wine Country's grape harvest represents only a relatively small contribution to California's total wine production. The annual grape harvest of Sonoma County adds up to a minuscule 4 percent of the state's total volume, about the same as neighboring Napa County. This deceptively small percentage stands in stark contrast with the lofty reputation Wine Country's vintages have deservedly attained.

There are scores of wineries here, but they are not the oil-refinery-scale tank farms of the jug wine, bulk business. With a few exceptions, nearly all our wineries are small- to medium-size operations, often family owned. This is as good a

reason as any to visit—you will nearly always find a tasty vintage to call your own personal discovery. Pour another glass of your favorite red, and read on about the climatology of fine wines.

What Are Appellations?

Understanding appellations is this simple: The quality of the grapes is the key to the quality of the wine. Where grapes are grown makes up almost 80 percent of the characteristics of a specific wine. The mellow in your Merlot? The zest in that Zinfandel? The panache of a particular Pinot Noir? It all can be traced back to the grapes, the climate that fostered their growth, and the soil from which they emerged.

Areas with hot days, warm nights, and deep, peat-rich soils might be good for growing corn and other vegetables (and even table grapes), but they produce wine grapes that are too high in sugar content and, therefore, not good for creating fine wines. A cooler, dryer climate and the volcanic soils so common in Napa and Sonoma Counties lead to the production of ultrapremium wines.

Within this two-county area, there are many microclimates. Each of these areas has specific characteristics that affect the wine grapes grown there. In the wine industry, these special growing regions are called American viticultural areas (AVAs). Around here we refer to them as "appellations," a French word you will run into frequently in this guide, but which is not used officially by the Alcohol and Tobacco Tax and Trade Bureau (formerly called the Bureau of Alcohol, Tobacco, and Firearms), the agency of the federal government that monitors these things.

How important is the term *appellation*? Some grapes grow better in one appellation than in another. Also, the same grape varietal grown in one appellation may produce a wine that is distinctly different from one made with the same grade of grapes grown in another appellation.

At first, it may sound to the novice as if the wine snobs are splitting hairs. But the differences in the wines from different appellations (and different winemakers within the same appellation), when tasted side by side, are distinct and remarkable.

Appellations also are important from a marketing standpoint. A wine labeled with a certain appellation name must be produced using a minimum of 75 to 85 percent of grapes from that region. For example, a Sonoma Valley Zinfandel must take at least 85 percent of its Zinfandel grapes from the Sonoma Valley AVA. Such distinctions add value to the wine and raise the shelf price. By comparison, a Zinfandel with the appellation "California" on the label means that the grapes could have come from anywhere in California. These wines often are produced with grapes from less-prestigious growing areas such as the San Joaquin Valley, where the long, hot summers allow production of massive quantities of grapes that are used primarily for jug wines and the so-called "fighting varietals" (wine industry jargon for lower-priced varietals).

The generally dryer and cooler microclimates of Napa and Sonoma Counties (and our neighbors to the north, Mendocino and Lake Counties) produce fewer grapes, but they are of a much higher quality for making fine wine. Grapes from these regions are more expensive (often as much as four to five times higher per ton), and they are in high demand.

Of course, grapes are not the only element that goes into making a fine wine. The object of the winemaker's craft—a blend of skill, experience, science, art, taste, and inspiration—is to take the special qualities of certain grapes and maximize their potential.

i **Another French word worth remembering is** *terroir* **(pronounced ter-WAR). Roughly translated, it refers to all the factors involved in growing the grape, such as soil, climate, water, topography, and sunlight. You will see and hear** *terroir* **used frequently as you visit tasting rooms.**

Napa County

When people hear the words "California Wine Country," they may first think of Napa, where the wines have been established as the yardstick by which other American vintages are measured. Compared to Europe, however, where vineyards have flourished for centuries, Napa Valley is still in its infancy. Yet it has grown quickly, and with approximately 250 wineries, it is believed to be the world's most densely concentrated winery region. Because of this, there is some concern that traffic and crowds will destroy the bucolic landscape, particularly in summer when the tourist count is high.

Motorists who know the region well are inclined at such busy times to abandon the main highway through the valley, Highway 29, and turn onto the Silverado Trail, which runs parallel to the east. From there they can cross over, using any of several connecting lanes that bind the two north–south roads. Silverado Trail is a delight in itself, winding between meadows and wooded slopes to the east and vineyards to the west. Its slight elevation produces some striking vineyard panoramas, eminently suited to photography. (For more on negotiating the byways of Wine Country, see the Getting Here, Getting Around chapter.)

Napa Valley boasts so many tasting rooms it is almost impossible to classify them as a group. They range in style from quaint to elegant, disarmingly casual to alarmingly commercial. This valley in particular has seen several over-the-top architectural palaces pop up in recent years, with more on the way. Among these are Quixote (tastings by appointment only) and Dalioush on the Silverado Trail, and Castello di Amorosa, south of Calistoga off Highway 29. More such grandiose statements by their owners are in the planning and building stages, including the controversial design by world-renowned architect Frank Gehry for Hall's new facility, which resembles two enormous wadded-up and discarded burlap sacks. But beyond atmosphere and physical trappings, the valley's tasting rooms provide the makings of a truly unique wine experience. In these pockets of hospitality, you will find an abundance of wines rivaling any in the world.

At its widest, Napa Valley is no more than 3 miles across. It is 27 miles from north end to south end, framed on both sides by hulking mountains. Most of the valley's three million annual visitors come to see its 42,000 acres of groomed vineyards—some newly replanted, some ancient, with gnarled vines that stand like regiments of old soldiers.

Food-and-wine pairings are staged in many wineries, and scores have picnic grounds that give new meaning to the great outdoors. Others have mini museums with historical and educational exhibits, and a few have elegant and eerie caves open for exploring.

Sonoma County

The Napa and Sonoma Valleys are separated by the Mayacmas Mountains, but much more distinguishes these two prime grape-growing regions. Napa, which enjoyed early prestige as a wine-growing region, is often considered the glitzier cousin of the more down-home Sonoma. Yet beneath Sonoma's rural charm is an elegance and sophistication that you can sample in both the wine and local culture. Saying that a wine comes from Sonoma doesn't say enough to those who know their wines. There are differences—sometimes subtle, sometimes dramatic—among the same types of wine produced

by different Sonoma County vintners in different appellations.

With the exception of the coastal bluffs overlooking the Pacific and the cool redwood forests, grapes grow in almost every corner of Sonoma County. Major grape-growing areas include the Russian River, where ocean fog makes the climate ideal for Pinot Noir and Chardonnay and for an exceptional Sauvignon Blanc; Los Carneros, where wind and fog from San Pablo Bay create conditions that produce intensely flavored Pinot Noir and Chardonnay; Sonoma Valley, whose many microclimates are suited to many grape varieties; Alexander Valley, known for its Cabernet Sauvignon and Sauvignon Blanc; and Dry Creek Valley, where the wines have earned much publicity and numerous gold medals.

Wineries here range from small, family-operated enterprises, where bottle labels still are applied by hand, to huge corporations where ageless winemaking skills are blended with computerized technology. If you are eager for some serious wine tasting, there are more than a half dozen small- and medium-size wineries within a short drive of Sonoma Plaza. These include Ravenswood, known for its excellent Zinfandels; Buena Vista; Gundlach Bundschu; and Bartholomew Park Winery (all are listed in this chapter). If you are headed south to San Francisco from the town of Sonoma, you will travel through the Carneros region with its many wineries. Stop in at Gloria Ferrer and Cline Cellars.

If you are able to visit and taste the wines of even half the places mentioned, you will have had a full and enjoyable day. The big-name producers in the county include Sebastiani, Clos du Bois, and Korbel, but don't neglect the smaller wineries: Benziger, Kenwood, Foppiano, Hop Kiln, Martinelli, and so on. Besides the wine itself, touring Sonoma County offers the sheer pleasure of driving along winding roads with views of vineyards and farms that alternate between the dramatic and the sweetly rural. From some mountaintops and parts of the Carneros district at the southern border, the skyline of San Francisco is visible on clear days (and nights).

PLANNING YOUR EXCURSION

Where to begin? To make your decision easier, I have listed only tasting rooms that are open to the public regularly, although many wineries now require appointments for tours. Tasting room hours at wineries generally range from 10:00 a.m. to 5:00 p.m. daily, but some have shorter hours, and some may be closed on certain weekdays and major holidays. If there's a particular winery you absolutely must visit, call ahead to find out how early or late you can arrive.

Most—but not all—Napa Valley wineries charge a fee for tasting, as well as some Sonoma County establishments. The fees can range from about $5 to $15—prices fluctuate depending on the wines being poured. (Reserve wines and library wines, if offered, run higher.) The tasting fee can usually be applied toward the purchase of a bottle, and you might get to keep the logo glass. More wineries are also enhancing the tasting experience by offering food pairings, cheese seminars, wine blending classes—the list goes on. There are extra charges for these events, and reservations are almost always required. Same with tours, which may also cost extra but sometimes include luscious bites to eat.

Many wineries also have picnic areas for enjoying munchies you bring along or buy on-site. If you want to wash down your cheese and bread with wine, however, please purchase a bottle of the winery's own product to go with your food. Not only is it just good manners, but the winery's license most likely prohibits alcoholic beverages other than its own to be consumed on the property.

If your time is limited, there is another way to sample the fruits of many wineries rather than visiting individual tasting rooms. Several independent tasting rooms, most of which feature tastes of limited-production wines, offer convenience for visitors seeking particular labels or those who prefer to do their tasting in one spot (see the close-up in this chapter for details). If you still want to sample the latest wines being produced by, say, Robert Mondavi Winery, you'll have to stop by his tasting room in Oakville.

Many wineries also operate their own clubs and publish newsletters so you can continue to enjoy the experience—and savor their wines—after you return home. If you find a favorite label during your Wine Country travels, sign up in the tasting room to receive shipments of new releases and invitations to members-only events. As done throughout the book, I arrange the winery listings in the geographical sequence explained in the How to Use This Book chapter. I begin with Napa County wineries, followed by those in Sonoma County.

NAPA COUNTY WINERIES

DOMAINE CARNEROS
1240 Duhig Road, Carneros
(707) 257-0101, (800) 716-2788
www.domainecarneros.com
This imposing winery was inspired by the Louis XV–style Château de la Marquetterie in Champagne, country estate of the Taittinger family, which founded Domaine Carneros in 1987. The atmosphere is très français, with a looming portrait of Madame de Pompadour in the main lobby. You can enjoy your beverage (with complimentary hors d'oeuvres) in the salon or on the patio, which is swept by breezes off San Pablo Bay. Domaine Carneros offers three types of sparkling wine (Brut Cuvée, Blanc de Blancs, and Brut Rosé) and its Famous Gate Pinot Noir. Tours are three times daily: 11:00 a.m., 1:00 p.m., and 3:00 p.m., at $25 per person.

ARTESA WINERY
1345 Henry Road, Carneros
(707) 224-1668
www.artesawinery.com
Dug into the top of a hill, with native grasses planted over its sloping walls, this winery looks like a half-unearthed Mayan ruin—until you get inside, where the breezy central atrium and reflecting pools are nothing but modern elegance. Artesa is owned by Codorniu, one of the world's biggest producers of champagne, or cava.

The Raventos family has been making wine since the 16th century (a Codorniu married a Raventos in 1659) and making *méthode champenoise* sparkling wine since 1872. In addition to some bubbly, the Napa outpost now bottles primarily still wines, including Chardonnay, Cabernet Sauvignon, Merlot, and Pinot Noir.

MONTICELLO VINEYARDS
4242 Big Ranch Road, Napa
(707) 253-2802
www.corleyfamilynapavalley.com
Proprietor Jay Corley is a big fan of Thomas Jefferson. So big, he named his winery Monticello and built a small-scale "Jefferson House," patterned after the founding father's Virginia mansion, to serve as the company's offices and culinary center. It's a pretty setting on Big Ranch Road, which heads north out of Napa city about halfway between Highway 29 and the Silverado Trail. There is a vivid rose garden and a shady picnic area called the Grove. Monticello makes Cabernet, Chardonnay, Merlot, Pinot Noir, and Syrah.

TREFETHEN VINEYARDS
1160 Oak Knoll Avenue, Napa
(707) 255-7700, (866) 895-7696
www.trefethenfamilyvineyards.com
When Capt. Hamden McIntyre built the Eshcol winery in 1886, the three-story, wooden, gravity-flow architectural design was standard. Grapes were crushed on the third floor, fermented on the second, and stored at ground level. Today the old Eshcol building is the centerpiece of Trefethen Vineyards, and it's one of the last gravity-flow winery buildings in Napa Valley. Trefethen is a throwback in another way too: Surrounding the winery are vineyards, plus gardens, walnut trees, and oaks. It was Eugene Trefethen, an executive for Kaiser (the massive construction firm responsible for Hoover Dam and the San Francisco–Oakland Bay Bridge), who bought the estate in 1968. His son, John, and John's wife, Janet, started the winery five years later.

THE HESS COLLECTION WINERY
4411 Redwood Road, Napa
(707) 255-1144, (877) 707-HESS
www.hesscollection.com
The "collection" is a stunning assemblage of modern art (see the Arts and Culture chapter). The Hess is Donald Hess, the Swiss millionaire whose holdings include Valser St. Petersquelle, one of Switzerland's most popular mineral waters. Hess keeps it simple as far as the wines go, with Chardonnay, Sauvignon Blanc, Syrah, and Cabernet Sauvignon.

i For a fabulous view of the Carneros region, it's worth the trip to Artesa Winery, an architectural wonder. Drink in the expansive vista while sipping cava on the tasting room patio.

BLACK STALLION WINERY
4089 Silverado Trail, Napa
(707) 253-1400, (888) 279-6272
www.blackstallionwinery.com
The newest winery and tasting room to open along Silverado Trail in the past couple of years is Black Stallion, an 11-acre site (once an equestrian center) surrounded by vineyards planted to Malbec, Petite Verdot, and Cabernet Franc. (These are the grapes that will compose a future meritage blend.) There's a huge outdoor tasting patio in addition to the large indoor visitor center, and a "petting" vineyard, too, where you can learn about grape-growing. The wines—Cabernet Sauvignon, Merlot, Syrah, Chardonnay, Pinot Grigio, and Muscat—are available only at the winery and online.

DARIOUSH
4240 Silverado Trail, Napa
(707) 257-2345
www.darioush.com
Rising from the vineyards alongside the Silverado Trail is a magnificent building that evokes Persepolis, the capital of ancient Persia. It's hard to miss

this architectural wonder, a 22,000-square-foot palace set off with 16 columns that act as stone trees, inviting visitors into the tasting room. The travertine stone that gives the building its warm glow was quarried in the region of Persepolis, then cut in Turkey and Italy before being shipped to Napa Valley. Named for its founder, Darioush Khaledi, who grew up in a wine-growing region of Iran, the winery produces exceptional reds, such as Cabernet Sauvignon and Shiraz, and whites such as Chardonnay and Viognier.

CLOS DU VAL
5330 Silverado Trail, Napa
(707) 259-2225, (800) 820-1972
www.closduval.com
Clos Du Val is French in more than name only. Founder John Goelet is descended from a distinguished Bordeaux wine merchant family, the Guestiers, and president/winemaker Bernard Portet is a sixth-generation vintner from the same French region. They crushed their first Napa Valley harvest together in 1972, and their ivy-covered, stone tasting room opened in 1983. Clos Du Val now produces several wines, including its signature Reserve Cabernet Sauvignon and Ariadne, a blend of Semillon and Sauvignon Blanc grapes. Tours are available in the demonstration vineyard; tasting room staff can hook you up.

CHIMNEY ROCK WINERY
5350 Silverado Trail, Napa
(707) 257-2641, (800) 257-2641
www.chimneyrock.com
At the foot of the hills east of the Silverado Trail— including the outcrop from which it draws its name—is Chimney Rock, a stately white structure of Cape Dutch style, cloaked (in the summer) or picketed (in the winter) by a row of poplars. Ask if you can see the wine cellar, where resides a faithful reproduction of the Ganymede frieze depicting the gods' cupbearer atop a fierce eagle. The winery makes Fumé Blanc, Cabernet Franc, and Cabernet Sauvignon, and its own Cabernet Sauvignon–Merlot–Petit Verdot blend called Elevage.

STAG'S LEAP WINE CELLARS
5766 Silverado Trail, Napa
(707) 944-2020, (866) 422-7523
www.cask23.com
Stag's Leap founder Warren Winiarski was a liberal arts lecturer at the University of Chicago, but his destiny should have been clear: In Polish, "winiarski" means "from wine" or "winemaker's son." Founded in 1972, Stag's Leap was a little-known family winery until 1976, when it outshone the best of French Bordeaux in the famous "Judgment of Paris" tasting in France. Since then it has been a Napa Valley landmark, though Winiarski recently sold the business to a joint venture of American and Italian wine companies. The winery produces several types of wine, red and white. Its reputation, however, is staked upon Cabernet Sauvignon, especially the versions made from the Stag's Leap and Fay vineyards, including the world-renowned Cask 23. (*NOTE:* Stag's Leap Wine Cellars is not to be confused with Stags' Leap Winery or the Stags Leap District, all of which get their name from the rock outcropping that overlooks the scene.)

i Every year the Home Winemakers Classic is held in Napa Valley for wine lovers to taste vino made by 60 amateur vintners. The 26th annual Classic was in 2008.

PINE RIDGE WINERY
5901 Silverado Trail, Napa
(707) 253-7500, (800) 486-0503
www.pineridgewinery.com
The pines aren't only high on the ridge. A grove of them surrounds the picnic area, making for a cool experience on a hot Napa Valley day. Winery and cave tours are by appointment only. Pine Ridge currently produces Chardonnay, Chenin Blanc-Viognier, Cabernet Sauvignon, Cabernet Franc, Malbec, Merlot, and Rosé. If you can't fit a tour into your schedule, investigate the Pine Ridge Demonstration Vineyard adjacent to the

winery. It displays various combinations of root-stock, clone, and trellising apparatus.

STELTZNER VINEYARDS
5998 Silverado Trail, Napa
(707) 252-7272, (800) 707-9463
www.steltzner.com
Dick and Christine Steltzner started making wines for bulk sale in 1977, and they opened their Silverado Trail winery in 1983. (The current structure was built in 1992.) Steltzner is noted for its reds, as are all labels within the Stags Leap appellation. Its wines include Cabernet Sauvignon, Claret, and a South African varietal called Pinotage.

SILVERADO VINEYARDS
6121 Silverado Trail, Napa
(707) 257-1770
www.silveradovineyards.com
This is no Mickey Mouse winery, despite ownership by Walt Disney's daughter, Diane Disney Miller, and Diane's husband, Ron Miller. The Millers are longtime Napa Valley denizens. Silverado offers great views above the trail and a winery crafted of native stone and redwood. It made its reputation with Chardonnay but probably is best known these days for its Sauvignon Blanc, Merlot, Sangiovese, and estate-grown Cabernet Sauvignon.

ROBERT SINSKEY VINEYARDS
6320 Silverado Trail, Napa
(707) 944-9090, (800) 869-2030
www.robertsinskey.com
This is another multigenerational operation, with founder Robert Sinskey, M.D., having passed the reins to his son, Rob. Sinskey Vineyards, which has been crushing grapes since 1986, is known for tackling Merlot and the tricky Pinot Noir, grown in the winery's Carneros vineyards. ("Heathens in the land of Cabernet," as they describe themselves.) Winemaker Jeff Virnig also creates small quantities of a half-dozen other varieties, including a late-harvest Zinfandel and a Pinot Blanc. The cathedral-like winery combines Napa Valley stone and California redwood.

DOMAINE CHANDON
1 California Drive, Yountville
(707) 944-2280, (800) 736-2892
www.chandon.com
Domaine Chandon, child of world-renowned Moët-Hennessy, is a trendsetter. It was California's first French-owned winery (established in 1973), and the first to use the champagne varietal Pinot Eunier in sparkling wine. It welcomes visitors to Le Salon, an open, terraced, cafe-style tasting room where you get samples of cuvées as well as complimentary hors d'oeuvres. On weekends Chandon's renowned tours run every hour (on the hour, except for opening and closing times), and they pretty much tell you everything you need to know about fermentation, aging, riddling, and disgorging. The scenic winery produces several types of sparkling wine plus brandy and pear liqueur. See the Restaurants chapter for information on Chandon's exclusive eatery, Étoile.

GOOSECROSS CELLARS
1119 State Lane, Yountville
(707) 944-1986, (800) 276-9210
www.goosecross.com
Goosecross Cellars likes to refer to itself as a microwinery, and the feeling is unquestionably intimate on this lonely lane off the Yountville Cross Road. The winery was established in 1985 by college buddies David Topper, the CEO, and Geoff Gorsuch, the winemaker. ("Goosecross" is an Old English derivation of Gorsuch.) They produce Chardonnay and Cabernet Sauvignon, in quantities that barely surpass 7,500 cases a year. If you have some free time Saturday (summer only) beginning at 10:30 a.m., sign up for the acclaimed Goosecross Wine Basics class, a hands-on crash course designed to remove the "snobbery and mysticism" from grape appreciation. The free class includes a full tour of the vineyard and winery. This winery asks that you phone ahead before stopping by for tasting (even if it's from your cell phone a mile away) anytime between 10:00 a.m. and 4:30 p.m. daily.

ℹ️ You've heard of Magnums and Double Magnums, yes? That's one bottle that holds the equivalent of 2 and 4 standard 750-milliliter wine bottles, respectively. But what about a Rehoboam, an Imperial, and a Nebuchadnezzar? These bottles hold 6, 8, and 20 standard bottles of wine, respectively. You will sometimes see a Nebuchadnezzar on display in tasting rooms.

COSENTINO WINERY
7415 St. Helena Highway S., Yountville
(707) 944-1220
www.cosentinowinery.com

Mitch Cosentino crafts a variety of wines and sells them in an affable, low-key setting next door to Mustards Grill (see the Restaurants chapter). Cosentino's Meritage reds ("The Poet") stand out, as do his Zinfandels. He also is no stranger to dessert wines. The winemaker prides himself on his "punched cap fermentation" process, a traditional, labor-intensive technique that involves continually dunking the floating grape skins (the cap) into the juice during fermentation.

SILVER OAK CELLARS
915 Oakville Crossroad, Oakville
(707) 944-8808, (800) 273-8809
www.silveroak.com

Wine & Spirits' 1996 poll of restaurants determined that Silver Oak produced the most popular Cabernet Sauvignon in America. The secret? Do one thing and do it well. Silver Oak is all Cabernet, all the time. It was founded in 1972 by Ray Duncan and Justin Meyer, who had recently abandoned his post as the Christian Brothers' Napa Valley winemaker. His company has two winery sites: one in Napa Valley at the site of the Oakville Dairy, and another in Alexander Valley in the old Lyeth Winery. The tasting room was being rebuilt in 2008, following a fire in 2006 at what had once been a dairy barn. Tours are by appointment only, and because the tasting room can get swamped

---

Wine Country Appellations

Wines labeled with a certain appellation name must be produced using a minimum of 75 to 85 percent of grapes (depending on the varietal) from that specific region. Below are the recognized appellations (American viticultural areas, or AVAs) of the two counties in Wine Country. Note that the North Coast AVA is a broad one, applying to wines from several different counties, including Napa, Sonoma, Mendocino, and Lake; Los Carneros is shared by Napa and Sonoma Counties.

Napa County

Atlas Peak, Chiles Valley, Diamond Mountain, Howell Mountain, Los Carneros, Mount Veeder, Napa Valley, North Coast, Oak Knoll District, Oakville, Rutherford, Spring Mountain District, St. Helena, Stags Leap District, Wild Horse Valley, Yountville

Sonoma County

Alexander Valley, Bennett Valley, Chalk Hill, Dry Creek Valley, Green Valley, Knights Valley, Los Carneros, North Coast, Northern Sonoma, Rockpile, Russian River Valley, Sonoma Coast, Sonoma Mountain, Sonoma Valley

---

on summer Saturdays, the winery suggests arriving early or calling ahead on those days. The tasting room is closed on Sunday.

FOLIE À DEUX WINERY
7481 St. Helena Highway S., Oakville
(707) 944-2565, (800) 535-6400
www.folieadeux.com

Give this one extra credit for a sense of humor. *Folie à deux* is a French term that means "shared madness." It's a psychiatric diagnosis that the original owners, two mental health professionals, found appropriate. They even requisitioned a logo that resembles a Rorschach inkblot. You don't have to be not-all-there to enjoy Folie à Deux's wines, however. The broad selection includes Merlot, Cabernet Sauvignon, and a special Amador Zinfandel from the oldest Zin vines in California, those of the 1870s Grandpere Vineyard. Whites include Chardonnay and Sauvignon Blanc. This winery produces a second label, called Ménage à Trois, that features a red, a white, and a rosé.

ROBERT MONDAVI WINERY
7801 St. Helena Highway S., Oakville
(707) 226-1395, (888) RMONDAVI
www.robertmondaviwinery.com

More than any other individual, Robert Mondavi is credited with educating the world about California wine. Now in its 42nd year, the winery in Oakville that bears his name has been a must-see stop along the Napa Valley wine road for decades. Wine-and-food programs have long been popular with visitors, as well as the many art exhibits and jazz and classical concerts. It's also known for its in-depth tasting tours that run three to four hours and include a picnic or sit-down dinner. You can also spend time at this iconic winery gazing at the sculptures and artwork. Mondavi bottles several varieties, not the least of which is a Fumé Blanc, so named by Robert himself several decades ago. The winery also produces Chardonnay, Pinot Noir, Merlot, Cabernet Sauvignon, and a Moscato d'Oro. In late 2004, the Robert Mondavi corporation was purchased by Constellation Brands, the world's largest owner of fine wine producers, in a deal that shook up the industry and ended a long family legacy.

OPUS ONE
7900 St. Helena Highway S., Oakville
(707) 944-9442
www.opusonewinery.com

When Robert Mondavi and Baron Philippe de Rothschild announced this joint venture in 1979, it created quite a stir in the wine world. But it also added credence to what the French had recently discovered: California wines are among the best in the world. Though the baron died in 1988, the business went forward, and groundbreaking on this architectural masterpiece took place in 1989. As you might expect from such a team of wine royalty, this is an elegant winery that produces one pricey product. Opus One is a big red wine—a blend that's predominantly Cabernet Sauvignon—that sells for $180 per bottle. You can try this hearty drink for $30 a taste in the winery's Partners' Room. A concierge greets you at the door and ushers you to the tasting room. Calling ahead is strongly recommended, as this showplace is frequently booked for private functions. There's also one daily tour, at $35 per person, beginning at 10:30 a.m.

TURNBULL WINE CELLARS
8210 St. Helena Highway S., Oakville
(707) 963-5839, (800) 887-6285
www.turnbullwines.com

The winery is located just north of the Oakville Crossroad, and its vineyards are primarily contained within the Oakville viticultural area. Turnbull's production is about 10,000 cases per year, with most of it in Cabernet Sauvignon, along with Merlot, Syrah, Sauvignon Blanc, and Viognier. Turnbull's Black Label wine is a blend of Cabernet Sauvignon, Petit Verdot, Cabernet Franc, Malbec, Merlot, and Syrah.

> **i** The wine and grape industries in the United States poured more than $162 billion into the American economy in 2005, according to a report by the Wine Institute and the Wine Grape Growers of America. That's a lot of juice.

ST. SUPÉRY VINEYARDS & WINERY
8440 St. Helena Highway S., Rutherford
(707) 963-4507, (800) 942-0809
www.stsupery.com
More than its intriguing historical setting and its rich lineup of wines, St. Supéry is known for its Wine Discovery Center. You can wander through the display vineyard and the exhibit gallery (the SmellaVision display is a must-do) or sign up for a $10 guided tour. St. Supéry (named for a onetime owner of the property) has a lengthy list of wines, with an emphasis on Sauvignon Blanc and Cabernet Sauvignon, plus surprises such as a dessert Moscato and a Merlot Rosé sold only at the winery.

PEJU PROVINCE WINERY
8466 St. Helena Highway S., Rutherford
(707) 963-3600, (800) 446-7358
www.peju.com
Herta Peju's prolific flower beds have been photographed for numerous garden magazines, while husband Tony sticks to winemaking. His Cabernet Sauvignon has won many awards, and he also makes Chardonnay, Cabernet Franc, Sauvignon Blanc, Merlot, and a Zinfandel Port. The Pejus opened their French provincial–style facility in 1991 and produce about 15,000 cases a year.

RUBICON ESTATE WINERY
1991 St. Helena Highway S., Rutherford
(707) 968–1100, (800) RUBICON
www.rubiconestate.com
A winemaker almost as long as he has been a filmmaker, Francis Ford Coppola and his wife, Eleanor, purchased the lavish Victorian and prime acreage in 1975, then discovered the story behind the locale. The house was built in 1881 by Gustave Niebaum, a Finnish sea captain who founded Inglenook, perhaps the most respected winery in California before corporate raiders used the name to sell jug wine. Enchanted by the history, Coppola invested the substantial profits from his film *Bram Stoker's Dracula* to reunify Niebaum's original estate in 1995. The purchase included the original château, which the director renovated (check out the staircase made from exotic Belizean hardwoods). It now houses the tasting room, with a $25 guest fee that includes tastings and a tour. Coppola releases several wines under different labels but is best known for Rubicon, the Cabernet Sauvignon–Merlot–Cabernet Franc meritage that is made to last 100 years.

ZD WINES
8383 Silverado Trail, Rutherford
(707) 963-5188, (800) 487-7757
www.zdwines.com
ZD might be last on the alphabetical list, but it has been first elsewhere, such as the Los Angeles County Fair, where the 1996 Chardonnay was named Best of Class. And the label is clearly bipartisan—it has been served at the White House during three presidential administrations. ZD got its start in Sonoma County in 1969, then moved to Napa County a decade later. Today it makes primarily Chardonnay, Pinot Noir, and Cabernet Sauvignon.

i Red wine grape varieties account for approximately 32,532 acres of fruit-bearing vineyards in Napa Valley, with 9,656 acres planted to white varieties. In Sonoma County, 37,950 acres are red, and 17,557 acres are white.

MUMM NAPA VALLEY
8445 Silverado Trail, Rutherford
(707) 967-7700, (800) 686-6272
www.mummnapa.com
The setting in Mumm's tasting salon is one of the most soothing in the valley, with a long wall of glass that faces uncluttered vineyard. Tours of the winery are offered on the hour; the last stop is the photo gallery, which is reason enough to make a pilgrimage (see the Arts and Culture chapter). Mumm Napa Valley was launched in 1979, a coventure between G. H. Mumm of France and Joseph E. Seagram and Sons of New York. The winery currently bottles three Bruts—Blanc de Blancs, Blanc de Noir, and Brut Prestige—and a vintage sparkler, DVX, its prestige cuvée.

BEAULIEU VINEYARD

1960 St. Helena Highway S., Rutherford
(707) 967-5230, (800) 264-6918
www.bvwines.com

The oldest continuously producing winery in Napa Valley isn't Charles Krug or Beringer. It's Beaulieu, which was founded by Georges de Latour in 1900 and survived Prohibition by turning out sacramental wines. By 1940 Beaulieu might have been the nation's most famous winery, a status no doubt aided by de Latour's recruitment of young, Russian-born enologist Andre Tchelistcheff, who was more or less the Luther Burbank of the wine industry. The winery's Napa Series is made up of Cabernet Sauvignon, Chardonnay, Pinot Noir, Sauvignon Blanc, Zinfandel, and Merlot; the BV Coastal Estates wines include Shiraz. (The Georges de Latour Private Reserve Cabernet, hunted by collectors, remains BV's benchmark product.)

GRGICH HILLS CELLAR

1829 St. Helena Highway S., Rutherford
(707) 963-2784, (800) 532-3057
www.grgich.com

The Grgich is Miljenko Grgich. The Hills, you might be surprised to learn, is a reference not to the rugged terrain around Rutherford, but rather to Austin Hills of the Hills Brothers coffee family. Hills added his business acumen to Grgich's winemaking skills back in 1977, and they have been making tasty wines ever since. Grgich Hills is known for its buttery, creamy Chardonnay, though it also produces Fumé Blanc, Zinfandel, Cabernet Sauvignon, and a late-harvest dessert wine. Visitors may purchase library wines, which are available only at the winery, which celebrated its 30th year of operation in 2007.

FRANCISCAN OAKVILLE ESTATE

1178 Galleron Road, Rutherford
(707) 967-3830, (800) 529-WINE
www.franciscan.com

Franciscan specializes in Cabernet Sauvignon and Merlot, with all the grapes for Magnificat (a meritage blend) coming from its 240-acre

estate in the heart of the Oakville appellation. It also sets itself apart through its experiments in "wild" yeast fermentation, using the native yeast of each vineyard to help ferment those particular grapes. The winery's Chardonnay is 100 percent wild yeast, barrel fermented. Outside the winery, which is right off Highway 29, you'll encounter the Rutherford Bench, a tongue-in-cheek reference to a local geologic feature.

RUTHERFORD HILL WINERY

200 Rutherford Hill Road, Rutherford
(707) 963-1871, (800) MERLOT-1
www.rutherfordhill.com

Rutherford Hill produces numerous varietals (including a Zinfandel Port), but the name has become nearly synonymous with Merlot. It's also known as one of the most pleasant places to visit, with picnic grounds amid shady oaks and olive trees, and stunning views of Napa Valley. Rutherford Hill's wine caves are said to be some of the most extensive in America, with nearly a mile of tunnels, galleries, and passageways.

Rutherford Hill hosts a regular "Blend Your Own Merlot" class for small groups to learn the basic principles of making wine. You get to create your very own blend to take home in a bottle. It's offered by reservations only, so call ahead to inquire about dates.

> **i** You will see the word *meritage* used frequently in this chapter. It's not a French word, but was cobbled together from "merit" and "heritage." A meritage wine is a blend of two or more red Bordeaux-style grape varietals, and two or more white wine grapes (Sauvignon Blanc, Sauvignon Vert, and Semillon) for a white wine.

RAYMOND VINEYARDS

849 Zinfandel Lane, St. Helena
(707) 963-3141, (800) 525-2659
www.raymondvineyards.com

Raymond has a strong reputation for Chardonnay and Cabernet Sauvignon, though it also bottles Sauvignon Blanc and Merlot. It produces under three distinct brands: Amberhill, R Collection, and Raymond Napa Valley Reserve. Raymond also bottles two late-harvest dessert wines: a Chardonnay and a Sauvignon Blanc. The winery's Napa Valley vineyards are supplemented by a large Chardonnay plot in Monterey County, on the Central Coast.

HALL WINERY
401 St. Helena Highway S., St. Helena
(707) 967-2626, (866) 667-4255
www.hallwines.com
Forget for a moment that the winery founded by Craig and Kathryn Hall produces fine wines. The big buzz here is its new Frank Gehry–designed winery that's going up, with completion scheduled for 2010. As briefly mentioned in the introduction of this chapter, the Halls are constructing a $100 million facility approximately 1 mile north of Zinfandel Lane. Initially controversial, when finished it's likely to be embraced as a symbol of a new era in design for Wine Country. It's certainly one of the oddest and most cutting-edge buildings you'll find in our region. Be that as it may, Hall has consistently produced mostly red wines—Merlot, Cabernet Sauvignon, Cabernet Franc—and Sauvignon Blanc, and the tastings take place in the existing facility while the Gehry project takes shape. The Halls were not born into the wine industry; he's also a real estate developer, and Kathryn was U.S. ambassador to Austria during the Clinton administration.

MILAT VINEYARDS
1091 St. Helena Highway S., St. Helena
(707) 963-0758, (800) 54-MILAT
www.milat.com
This is an intimate, family-run winery, 2 miles south of St. Helena. The Milats have been growing and selling grapes to Napa Valley wineries since 1949, and in 1986 they finally decided to affix their own label. Milat bottles Chardonnay, Chenin Blanc, Merlot, Zinfandel, Cabernet Sauvignon, a Port-style wine called Zivio, and a chocolate Port sauce, selling the bulk of their production from the tasting room.

V. SATTUI WINERY
1111 White Lane, St. Helena
(707) 963-7774, (800) 799-2337
www.vsattui.com
If you have made a few trips to Napa Valley, you probably know V. Sattui as the place with all the picnickers. It's a favorite for itinerant eaters, primarily because of an ample, shady picnic area and well-stocked deli featuring homemade items. The current wine list is immense, with two Chardonnays, two Johannisberg Rieslings, two Zinfandels, four Cabernet Sauvignons, and many others—all of them sold exclusively at the winery, online, and by mail order. In 2007, V. Sattui received the Golden Winery Award in the California State Fair Wine Competition, proclaiming it the top winery in California for number of medals won. Of the 28 wines it entered in the contest, 23 won awards.

WHITEHALL LANE WINERY
1563 St. Helena Highway S., St. Helena
(707) 963-9454, (800) 963-9454
www.whitehalllane.com
As wineries go, this one is a youngster in Napa Valley. The Leonardini family of San Francisco purchased Whitehall Lane Winery from foreign investors in 1993 and brought in new equipment, a new barrel program, and plans for expanding production and acquiring vineyards. It now produces award-winning Sauvignon Blanc, Chardonnay, Merlot, and Cabernet Sauvignon. There's even an orange muscat dessert wine, Belmuscato.

HEITZ WINE CELLARS
436 St. Helena Highway S., St. Helena
(707) 963-3542
www.heitzcellar.com
The winery you visit is not the current Heitz facility, but rather the original facility Joe and Alice Heitz opened in 1961. The winery built its reputation on Chardonnay, though now it is known more for its Cabernet Sauvignon. Three special Cabs are vineyard designated: Martha's Vineyard (near Oakville), Bella Oaks Vineyard, and

Trailside Vineyard (both near Rutherford). Heitz also makes Zinfandel and a Grignolino, a light red—and Port, too.

PRAGER WINERY & PORT WORKS
1281 Lewelling Lane, St. Helena
(707) 963-7678, (800) 969-7678
www.pragerport.com
Prager makes Chardonnay and Cabernet but is really known for its Port, which accounts for about 85 percent of production. One of the top sellers is the Royal Escort Port, produced from Petite Sirah grapes. Prager's facilities are inside an old carriage house, part of the John Thomann Winery and Distillery, constructed in 1865. The intimate tasting room is closed on Sunday.

SUTTER HOME WINERY
277 St. Helena Highway S., St. Helena
(707) 963-3104
www.sutterhome.com
What was once a small, family-run winery is now a gigantic family-run winery, thanks to unqualified marketing genius. The facilities date from 1874, the name from 1906, when the new Swiss-American co-owner named it after her father, John A. Sutter. Sutter Home has been owned by the Trincheros since 1947, and the family gets credit (or blame, depending on your outlook) for inventing White Zinfandel—which it originally called Oeil de Pedrix, "Eye of the Partridge"—in the 1970s. Sutter Home has numerous vineyards in Napa and Lake Counties but grows the bulk of its grapes in the Sacramento Valley, Sacramento Delta, and Sierra foothill regions. The company produces more than 10 varieties, including a regular Zinfandel, a White Merlot, and a White Cabernet Sauvignon.

LOUIS M. MARTINI WINERY
254 St. Helena Highway S., St. Helena
(707) 968-3361, (800) 321-WINE
www.louismartini.com
Louis M. was an Italian immigrant, born near Genoa, who founded the L. M. Martini Grape Products Co. in Kingsburg, California, in 1922. The "Grand Old Man" built his Napa Valley winery 11 years later. Three generations of Martinis have led the winery. The winery makes primarily Cabernet Sauvignon but also a Petite Sirah, a Chardonnay, and Gnarly Vine Zinfandel. It also produces Moscato Amabile, which it's been bottling for more than 70 years.

MERRYVALE VINEYARDS
1000 Main Street, St. Helena
(707) 963-7777, (888) 963-0576
www.merryvale.com
Merryvale is hard to miss, as it sits in Sunny St. Helena. That's not a reference to the town, but to the old winery that dates from the 1930s. The stolid stone structure took new life when it was founded as Merryvale by four partners (the same four who started San Francisco's Pacific Union Realty) in 1983. The facility produces several varietals, including Chardonnay, Cabernet Sauvignon, Merlot, and a dessert wine called Antigua under two labels: Merryvale (10,000 cases annually) and Starmont (more than 90,000 cases). There are no tours, but Merryvale does offer wine component tasting seminars every Saturday and Sunday at 10:30 a.m. The cost is $20, and reservations are recommended.

BERINGER VINEYARDS
2000 Main Street, St. Helena
(707) 963-7115
www.beringer.com
Just as you pass through the row of elms that forms a canopy over Highway 29 just north of St. Helena, what you'll see to the west is Beringer, arguably the most majestic of all Napa Valley wineries. Beringer produces a half-dozen wines that vary from high quality to high volume. Three types of tours are offered, with staggered starting times, and prices ranging from $15 to $35 per person—tastings included. They include an excursion into the wine caves tunneled into the hillside. The winery's Rhine House, the impressive structure that grabs your attention from the highway, is a preserved historical landmark built by Jacob and Frederick Beringer in 1876.

CHARLES KRUG WINERY
2800 Main Street, St. Helena
(707) 967-2229, (800) 682-KRUG
www.charleskrug.com

A lot of history is working at this 19th-century structure. It was Napa Valley's first winery, founded in 1861 by the eponymous Prussian immigrant, political theorist, and editor of *Staats Zeitung,* the Pacific Coast's first German-language newspaper. Charles Krug, the winery, also shares the history of the Mondavi family, that dynasty of California wine-making. Cesare Mondavi bought Krug in 1943; his wife, Rosa, took over upon Cesare's death in 1959, and their son, Peter, became general manager in 1966. Now Peter's sons, Marc and Peter Jr., oversee most of the winery's operations, including the wine-making, marketing, and sales. Charles Krug bottles at least 10 varieties of wine, including the full-bodied Vintage Selection Cabernet Sauvignon and Generations, a traditional Bordeaux blend.

i Who says great wine has to be expensive? Charles Shaw Chardonnay, more commonly known as "Two-Buck Chuck" because it retails for $1.99 per bottle, won a double gold medal for best Chardonnay in the 2007 California State Fair Wine Competition. Two-Buck Chuck is sold exclusively at Trader Joe's stores.

MARKHAM VINEYARDS
2812 St. Helena Highway N., St. Helena
(707) 963-5292
www.markhamvineyards.com

The fortress north of St. Helena, with its fountains and eucalyptus trees, has seen a lot of change in its 130-plus years. It was built of stone quarried from nearby Glass Mountain by Bordeaux immigrant and failed prospector Jean Laurent in 1874, but it was used for bulk wines until 1977. The tasting room is not in the old structure but rather in an addition on its north side. Markham's Merlot, Cabernet Sauvignon, Sauvignon Blanc, and Chardonnay make up the majority of production,

with Zinfandel, Petite Sirah, Syrah, and Pinot Noir in more limited quantities.

ST. CLEMENT VINEYARDS
2867 St. Helena Highway N., St. Helena
(707) 967-3033, (800) 331-8266
www.stclement.com

The St. Clement winery is eye-catching anytime, but especially at night, when the pristine Victorian is bathed by floodlights. The house dates from 1878, when it became Johannaburg winery, the eighth in Napa Valley. It was a private residence for most of the 20th century, until Dr. Bill Casey started St. Clement in 1975. The winery bottles seven varietals and is best known for its Carneros Chardonnay and Cabernet Sauvignon. It also produces Oroppas, a blend of Cabernet and Merlot.

FREEMARK ABBEY WINERY
3022 St. Helena Highway N., St. Helena
(707) 963-9694, (800) 963-9698
www.freemarkabbey.com

Freemark Abbey was never home to a group of monks. The name comes from a triumvirate that purchased the winery in 1939: Charles Freeman, Markquand Foster, and Albert (Abbey) Ahern. Long before that (starting in 1886, to be exact), the winery was known as Tychson Hill, named for California's first female vintner, Josephine Tychson. The winery concentrates on several varietals: Cabernet Sauvignon, Chardonnay, Merlot, Petite Sirah, Viognier, and a late-harvest Riesling. Among those are two esteemed single-vineyard wines—Cabernet Bosche and Sycamore Vineyards' Cabernet Sauvignon.

ROMBAUER VINEYARDS
3522 Silverado Trail, St. Helena
(707) 963-5170, (800) 622-2206
www.rombauervineyards.com

If the name rings a bell, think of food, not wine. Vintner Koerner Rombauer's great aunt, Irma Rombauer, has been in practically every kitchen in America: She's the author of *The Joy of Cooking.* Koerner makes six types of wine, including a Port

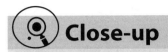 **Close-up**

A Glass of Ramazzotti Syrah, Please...

Before you give up trying to find a store that sells a particular cult wine you've heard about, step into one of the wine tasting collectives that have popped up in recent years in Wine Country. Boutique and artisan wines are the primary products sold in these comfortable establishments, which for a fee offer tastes of the fruits of small-production wineries that most likely do not have tasting rooms of their own. Fees can range from $2 to $20, depending on the number of pours you desire. With some exceptions, these tasting collectives differ from regular wine retail shops because they don't offer huge inventories of wine from around the world. Some also provide food pairings and light menus. (By the way, Ramazzotti Syrah can be sipped at Locals tasting room in Geyserville.)

Napa County

A Dozen Vintners
3000 St. Helena Highway N., St. Helena
(707) 967-0666
www.adozenvintners.com

Backroom Wines
1000 Main Street, Napa
(707) 226-1378, (877) 322-2576
www.backroomwines.com

Bounty Hunter
975 First Street, Napa
(707) 255-0622, (800) 943-9463
www.bountyhunterwine.com

Vintner's Collective
1245 Main Street, Napa
(707) 255-7150
www.vintnerscollective.com

Wineries of Napa Valley
1285 Napa Town Center, Napa
(707) 253-9450, (800) 328-7815
www.napavintages.com

Sonoma County

The Cellar Door
1395 Broadway, Sonoma
(707) 938-4466
www.sonomacellardoor.com

Family Wineries of Sonoma County
9200 Sonoma Highway, Kenwood
(707) 833-5504
www.familywineries.com

Locals
21023 Geyserville Avenue, Geyserville
(707) 857-4900
www.tastelocalwines.com

Sonoma-Enoteca
35 East Napa Street, Sonoma
(707) 935-1200
www.sonoma-enoteca.com

The Wine Room
9575 Sonoma Highway, Kenwood
(707) 833-6131
www.the-wine-room.com

Wine Spectrum
123 Fourth Street (Railroad Square), Santa Rosa
(707) 636-1064
www.winespectrum.com

Zinfandel and Joy, a late-harvest Chardonnay. Rombauer is at the end of a long, steep driveway, and its views of the Napa Valley floor are hard to match—bring lunch and take advantage of the picnic tables.

FRANK FAMILY VINEYARDS
1091 Larkmead Lane, Calistoga
(707) 942-0859, (800) 574-9463
www.frankfamilyvineyards.com
This one isn't as gargantuan as some of Napa's other champagneries, but it's a treat for visitors: a sublime spot on one of the valley's less-traveled crossroads; a charming picnic area behind the 1906 stone building, on the National Register of Historic Places; and sparkling and still wines sold almost exclusively on the premises (a few select wine shops and restaurants carry it). The winery was known as Larkmead Cellars back in the old days, when it produced still wines, then was operated as Hans Kornell Champagne Cellars. The champagne line includes Blanc de Noirs, Brut, and Rouge. Other wines produced are Pinot Noir, Zinfandel, Sangiovese, Cabernet Sauvignon, Chardonnay, and Sauvignon Blanc.

DUTCH HENRY
4310 Silverado Trail, Calistoga
(707) 942-5771, (888) 224-5879
www.dutchhenry.com
The family that owns Dutch Henry runs it like a mom-and-pop winery. They pour in the cellar, and a tour consists of looking in different directions while you get the lowdown. Named for nearby Dutch Henry Canyon, the winery produces only about 5,000 cases a year, and its line includes Chardonnay, Pinot Noir, Cabernet Sauvignon, and a meritage called Argos. Dutch Henry also makes its own olive oil, pressed from fruit on the property, and vinegar.

CASTELLO DI AMOROSA
4045 St. Helena Highway N., Calistoga
(707) 967-6272, (707) 942-8200
www.castellodiamorosa.com
The scale is immense, even for Napa Valley: 121,000 square feet of Tuscan medieval architecture with

107 rooms on eight levels, a drawbridge, a replica of a torture chamber, five towers, and gargoyles. Oh, and a tasting room, too, pouring Chardonnay, Sangiovese, Merlot, Cabernet Sauvignon, a "super Tuscan" blend, and Gewürztraminer. But it's the castle that's the big attraction here, with a tour-and-tasting package for $25 (you may also just taste for about half that). Construction of Castello di Amorosa was the passion of owner Daryl Sattui (of V. Sattui Winery fame), who spent 14 years and $30 million getting it off the ground. Opened to the public in 2007, the castle has hosted quite a few private events already, including a dinner for California Governor Arnold Schwarzenegger.

STERLING VINEYARDS
1111 Dunaweal Lane, Calistoga
(707) 942-3345, (800) 726-6136
www.sterlingvineyards.com
First-time visitors can be forgiven for unfailingly asking, "Is that a monastery up on the hill south of Calistoga?" Not exactly. It's Sterling Vineyards, with its white stucco, Ionic-style architecture, and knoll-top regality. Wine tasting here literally has been elevated to an event. A gondola takes you to the top of the hill, where you are free to sip samples and wander on a self-guided tour. Wide-angle views of the valley are worth the trip up the hill. It's $20 for adults for the aerial tram, self-guided tour, and a five-wine tasting. Most of Sterling's production falls among four wines— Cabernet Sauvignon, Chardonnay, Sauvignon Blanc, and Merlot, including several vineyard-designated versions. It also bottles small lots of lesser-known wines sold only at the winery, such as Malvasia Bianca and Charbono. Sterling was founded by English paper broker Peter Newton, who left behind a Brit legacy—the old bells of St. Dunstan's Church, which chime on the half hour.

CLOS PEGASE WINERY
1060 Dunaweal Lane, Calistoga
(707) 942-4981, (800) 366-8583
www.clospegase.com
Jan Shrem's winery is named for Pegasus, the winged horse whose hooves are said to have unleashed the Spring of the Muses, bringing both

wine and art to the masses. Shrem, who built his fortune publishing reference and technical books in Japan, is preoccupied with both wine and art. His collection of sculpture and painting is profiled in the Arts and Culture chapter, and his wines—Cabernet Sauvignon, Chardonnay, Merlot, and Sauvignon Blanc—are some of the best in the valley. The winery itself, designed by renowned Princeton architect Michael Graves (who was commissioned to build a "temple to wine"), is a stark, modern landmark of earth tones, angles, and curves.

CUVAISON WINERY
4550 Silverado Trail, Calistoga
(707) 942-2468, (800) 253-9463
www.cuvaison.com
When Silicon Valley engineers Thomas Cottrell and Thomas Parkhill started a small upvalley winery in 1969, they called it Cuvaison, a French term for the fermentation of wine on the grape skins. The winery is particularly known for Chardonnay, but it also produces reds: Cabernet Sauvignon, Merlot, Pinot Noir, and Syrah. Cuvaison gets most of its Chardonnay grapes from its 400-acre vineyard in Carneros. A second tasting room, by appointment only, is located there. The Silverado Trail location has a pleasant picnic area, shaded by centuries-old oak trees.

GRAESER WINERY
255 Petrified Forest Road, Calistoga
(707) 942-4437, (800) 898-4682
www.graeserwinery.com
Want to get a feeling for the Napa Valley wine industry circa 1890? Take a drive to Graeser, about 2 miles northwest of Calistoga. The tasting room is in an 1886 home. If no one answers, ring the doorbell, a rope attached to the bell tower over the house. It's a bucolic setting once known as La Perlita del Monte ("The Little Pearl of the Mountain"), and Richard Graeser can genuinely claim a unique mountainside microclimate for his grape varietals: Cabernet Sauvignon, Cabernet Franc, and Merlot. Winemaker Graeser also produces Chardonnay and Semillon. He will even autograph your bottle of wine if you ask nicely.

i With the success of the film *Sideways,* more movies about wine are being released. The latest is *Bottle Shock,* about Chateau Montelena's Jim Barrett (played by Bill Pullman), whose Chardonnay won the Paris tasting in 1976. Actor Alan Rickman portrays the wine merchant who arranged the tasting that shocked the industry. Most of the filming took place in Napa and Sonoma Counties.

CHATEAU MONTELENA
1429 Tubbs Lane, Calistoga
(707) 942-5105
www.montelena.com
Montelena was one of the two Napa Valley wineries—Stag's Leap being the other—that rocked the French establishment at a famous blind tasting in Paris in 1976. It was a Chardonnay that prevailed that day, and the winery still makes one of the valley's best, along with top-notch Cabernet Sauvignon and Riesling. Chateau Montelena's name and origins go back much further than 1976. The winery was started by Alfred L. Tubbs in the late 1800s, but no wine had been produced for 50 years when new owner Jim Barrett filled the barrels again in 1972. The building, nothing short of a hilltop castle with walls 3 to 10 feet thick, dates from Tubbs's day, and a subsequent owner added Jade Lake and its Chinese gardens, a must-see if you're seeking an oasis of tranquility (the picnic tables, however, are reserved for wine club members).

SONOMA COUNTY WINERIES

Southern Sonoma

BARTHOLOMEW PARK WINERY
1000 Vineyard Lane, Sonoma
(707) 935-9511
www.bartpark.com
Once called Hacienda Winery, the winery and adjacent park were renamed for Frank Bartholomew, former foreign correspondent with United Press International (later its president). The

winery's picnic sites, set among native oaks, are unequaled, with tables overlooking vistas of vineyards. A fascinating first-class museum next to the tasting room is dedicated to the property's colorful history. Look for a large display of Victorian-era photographs that document viticultural practices from that period. Wall murals, a display of soil samples, and a topographical map explain present-day vineyard practices. The winery is known for its vineyard-designated Cabernet Sauvignon, Merlot, Syrah, Zinfandel, and Sauvignon Blanc.

BUENA VISTA WINERY

18000 Old Winery Road, Sonoma
(707) 926-1266, (800) 926-1266
www.buenavistacarneros.com

Huge shade trees surround Buena Vista, the oldest premium winery in California, which celebrated 150 years of operation in 2007. It was established in 1857 by Count Agoston Haraszthy (see the close-up "The Father of California Viticulture," in the History chapter). Two of the winery's stone buildings are registered as state historic landmarks. Chinese laborers dug long tunnels into the hillside for wine aging, and Buena Vista's buildings are made from the salvaged rock. The Press House, built in 1862, houses a gift shop and displays a fine collection of art. Three levels of tasting are offered; fees range from $5 to $20. The winery's "Carneros quartet" of grapes are Pinot Noir, Chardonnay, Syrah, and Merlot. A Pinot Gris is also produced.

VIANSA WINERY & ITALIAN MARKETPLACE

25200 Highway 121 (Arnold Drive), Sonoma
(707) 935-4700, (800) 995-4740
www.viansa.com

When Sam Sebastiani visited the homeland of his grandfather in Italy, he was astounded to see that Farneta, Italy, looked exactly like the Sonoma Valley. The winery that Sam and his wife, Vicki (Viansa combines "Sam" and "Vicki"), established in 1989 is about as Italian in aura as you will find this side of the Atlantic. Olive trees were imported from Italy, the architecture is Italian, and the garden paths that wind between levels of the winery are in Tuscan style. The Sebastianis

no longer own the facility, but the new operators have kept much of the charm intact. The wine tasting room is also a tasting room for some stunning gourmet foods. Visitors can wander about, picking up samples of olive-anchovy pesto, hot sweet mustards, blood orange vinegar, and other aromatic foods. Plenty of tables are available at various patio levels overlooking Sonoma Valley and the award-winning wildlife preserve. The winery adheres to Italian-style wines; it produces Augusta Barbera, Aleatico, and Nebbiolo (the name of the grape and the wine), plus several other varieties. There are also specialty wine- and food-tasting programs.

CLINE CELLARS

24737 Highway 121 (Arnold Drive), Sonoma
(707) 940-4000, (800) 546-2070
www.clinecellars.com

After spending his childhood learning farming and winemaking from his grandfather Valeriano Jacuzzi (of spa fame), Fred Cline founded Cline Cellars in 1982 on the sandy soils of Contra Costa County. His brother Matt joined him in 1991 as winemaker, and they relocated to the Sonoma Valley. The tasting room is in an 1850s farmhouse with a large, old-fashioned porch. The gardens here are terrific, and the picnic grounds are surrounded by thousands of rosebushes. There are also sweeping views of the Sonoma Valley on a site that was once a Miwok village. Complimentary tastings feature Syrah and Mourvèdre—as well as several white wines. Cline also produces Red Truck, an inexpensive but delicious red table wine (the red truck depicted on the label is on display at the winery, if you care to look at it). Ask for a taste of Cashmere, a blend of Grenache, Syrah, and Mourvèdre. Allow extra time to wander through the California Missions Museum (see the Attractions chapter), on the winery grounds only a short stroll from the tasting room.

JACUZZI FAMILY WINERY

24724 Highway 121 (Arnold Drive), Sonoma
(707) 940-4061, (866) 522-8693
www.jacuzziwines.com

Combine the fortunes of the Jacuzzi family with

a history of growing wine grapes and you get Jacuzzi Family Winery, one of the newest facilities on the Sonoma Valley wine trail. (Cline Cellars across the street shares a similar pedigree; see previous listing.) Going back many decades, the Jacuzzi brothers manufactured airplane propellers used in World War I. During the Depression one of the brothers, Valeriano, turned to grapes and winemaking and planted his crops at Oakley, 40 miles east of San Francisco. He later went to work with his brothers in Berkeley, manufacturing water well pumps and, ultimately, the bath and spa products that still bear the Jacuzzi name. Some of these old products are on display and make for an interesting walk around the property. The building is modeled after the family's home in the Friuli region of Italy. In the tasting room, treat yourself to sips of Pinot Noir, Nebbiolo, Sangiovese, Barbera, Chardonnay, Pinot Grigio, and several other varietals.

GLORIA FERRER CHAMPAGNE CAVES

23555 Highway 121 (Arnold Drive), Sonoma
(707) 996-7256
www.gloriaferrer.com

The vineyards stretch across the hills, and from the hillock above, the Spanish-style winery overlooks the estate vineyards and the rolling Carneros appellation. Grab a glass of bubbly and soak up the vistas from the large veranda outside the tasting room. This is one of several wineries owned and operated by the Ferrer family of Barcelona, which has produced *méthode champenoise* sparkling wine for more than 100 years. You can tour the facility with its state-of-the-art caves and learn the secrets of the *méthode champenoise* process. In addition to sparkling wine, Gloria Ferrer produces still wines such as Chardonnay and Pinot Noir, including a limited amount of Pinot Noir Rosé.

GUNDLACH BUNDSCHU WINERY

2000 Denmark Street, Sonoma
(707) 938-5277
www.gunbun.com

Jacob Gundlach and his brother-in-law, Charles Bundschu, established this winery in 1858 on land east of Sonoma that they called Rhinefarm. In 2008, with six generations of family history behind it, the winery celebrated its sesquicentennial—150 years as one of the oldest family-owned wineries in California. Today Gundlach Bundschu produces 50,000 cases of premium, award-winning wines a year, specializing in Merlot, Pinot Noir, Chardonnay, Tempranillo, Syrah, Zinfandel, and Cabernet Franc. Picnic tables are in a grove of oak trees overlooking a lake. Two different tours are offered, and both require advance reservations. This winery is known throughout the community for its sense of humor and the wacky posters it creates to market its products. In one, a woman behind the wheel of an old car is exchanging words with a motorcycle cop, who says, "If you can't say Gundlach Bundschu Gewürztraminer, you shouldn't be driving."

ℹ Well-trained sniffer dogs are being used in Wine Country vineyards for their uncanny ability to locate vine mealybugs, a particularly insidious pest that can quickly ruin a valuable grape crop. Meanwhile, a Yountville winemaker is relying on her pet bloodhound to detect bad corks in wine bottles under storage.

RAVENSWOOD WINERY

18701 Gehricke Road, Sonoma
(707) 933-2332, (888) 669-4679
www.ravenswood-wine.com

It's hard not to like a winery that lives by the motto "No Wimpy Wines!" Ravenswood excels at antisnobbery behavior, with a friendly and funny tasting room staff and a down-to-earth winemaker, Joel Peterson, who believes "wine belongs on the table, not on a pedestal or in an ivory tower." The decidedly unwimpy wines produced by Ravenswood are primarily Zinfandel (not to be confused with White Zinfandel), and they refer to their winery as "Zinfomania Central." Tours may include samples of wines directly out of the barrel. You can also participate in the bottling of a special blend just for you (for a $25 fee). And if your nose is up to the challenge, there's a daily (2:00 p.m.) "smelling" seminar to help you learn more about the bouquet of wine and enjoy a lot of laughs in the process. On weekends from May through September, barbecues are held in the picnic facilities.

SCHUG CARNEROS ESTATE WINERY
602 Bonneau Road, Sonoma
(707) 939-9363, (800) 966-9365
www.schugwinery.com
This lifelong dream of owner-winemaster Walter Schug spans four decades and two continents. A native of Germany's Rhine River valley and a graduate of a prestigious German wine institute, Walter left for California determined to find success with his Pinot Noir, which has since been proclaimed no less than world class by critics in both the United States and Europe. The winery, built in 1990 of post-and-beam architecture, reflects the Schug family's German heritage. A daily cave tour is offered at 11:00 a.m., and picnic tables are available for visitors. The winery produces sparkling wine, Sauvignon Blanc, Chardonnay, Pinot Noir, Merlot, and Cabernet Sauvignon.

ROBLEDO FAMILY WINERY
21901 Bonness Road, Sonoma
(707) 939-6903
www.robledofamilywinery.com
Here's a true American success story. The founder of this winery, Reynaldo Robledo, came to the United States from Mexico at the age of 16. He spent years toiling in the vineyards, first pruning the vines and then slowly working his way up to vineyard manager and later becoming a respected viticultural consultant. He dreamed of one day owning his own winery and growing his own grapes, and with hard work and persistence, his dream became reality. Founded in 1997, the Robledo Family Winery opened its tasting room in 2004. In 2008, the president of Mexico, Felipe Calderon, stopped by the winery to check it out (Reynaldo and the president are from the same small town in Mexico). Reynaldo's wife and their seven sons and two daughters are all active in the business, which produces five wine varietals. Stop

by the tasting room to sample their delicious Seven Brothers Sauvignon Blanc, along with a Pinot Grigio and a Pinot Blanc.

SEBASTIANI VINEYARDS
389 Fourth Street E., Sonoma
(707) 933-3230, (800) 888-5532
www.sebastiani.com
One of the few original family wineries still remaining, Sebastiani is extremely proud of its wines and its Italian heritage. Founder Samuele Sebastiani learned winemaking from the monks in Farneta, Italy, before he came to America in 1894 at the age of 19 and went to work hauling cobblestones. In 1904 he bought the old Sonoma Mission vineyard, where the padres had been making altar wines for 80 years.

The winery is 3 blocks east of Sonoma Plaza, set amid the vineyards from which Sebastiani produces its special Cherryblock Cabernet wines. A great convenience for visitors is the winery's trolley (seasonal), which allows you to park at the winery and catch a shuttle to the plaza, or vice versa.

BENZIGER FAMILY WINERY
1883 London Ranch Road, Glen Ellen
(707) 935-3000, (888) 490-2739
www.benziger.com
You could easily spend hours at the Benziger Family Winery, which is perched on the side of Sonoma Mountain high above the Sonoma Valley floor and the town of Glen Ellen. It's a cluster of historic buildings accented with some rusty farm implements and lots of landscaping. The pace here is not frenetic. Guests can picnic in the redwood grove, visit an experimental vineyard, enjoy complimentary wine tasting, and take in a one-of-a-kind educational vineyard tour aboard a motorized tram. It's one of the few wineries you may encounter that is friendly to kids (see the Kidstuff chapter). The Benzigers emigrated from White Plains, New York, to their mountain ranch next to Jack London State Historic Park (see the Parks and Recreation chapter). In addition to their namesake label, the Benzigers have built

a reputation for grape-growing innovation that produces award-winning wines in the Imagery series (see listing in this chapter). Benziger is also renowned in the industry for its biodynamic wine-growing practices. Make sure you gaze up the hillside from the parking lot at the small Parthenon, then hightail it to the other Benziger winery, Imagery Estate (read on!).

B. R. COHN WINERY
15000 Highway 12 (Sonoma Highway), Glen Ellen
(707) 931-7924, (800) 330-4064
www.brcohn.com
When Bruce Cohn founded his winery in 1984, he brought with him the glamour of the music industry. Bruce has been the manager of the Doobie Brothers since 1969 but managed to establish a side career as a winery owner. This facility began as a modest tasting room, lined with gold records from the Doobies' long career. It was later expanded, with the tasting room and gift shop now separate. This is also where Bruce's annual Charity Fall Music Festival takes place, in an amphitheater behind the production facility. The Doobies usually headline the shows, with many other top acts on the bill, and it's a sellout every year. Now about the wine: B. R. Cohn produces SyrCab (a blend of Cabernet Sauvignon and Syrah), Pinot Noir, Zinfandel, Port, and its signature Olive Hill Estate Cabernet. Bruce was one of the first winery owners in these parts to market his own line of olive oils, available at the winery, made from the picholine olive trees found all over the property.

IMAGERY ESTATE WINERY & ART GALLERY
14335 Highway 12 (Sonoma Highway), Glen Ellen
(707) 935-4500
www.imagerywinery.com
The Benziger family operates two wineries in the Sonoma Valley—their namesake facility and this one, which is, for lack of a better word, hipper. The labels are the stars at Imagery, which combines a tasting room with an art gallery. The

winery's symbol is the Parthenon (see the Benziger Family Winery listing), and notable contemporary artists have been commissioned over the years to create interesting labels that include the image of the Parthenon within the design. Some are obvious, some not so, but all are intriguing. The original canvases from which the labels are taken are on display, and the gift shop sells many of the label images in small versions and on myriad wine accessories. Imagery produces Viognier, White Burgundy, Tempranillo, Sangiovese, Petite Verdot, Malbec, and a fabulous red dessert wine called Interlude.

WELLINGTON VINEYARDS
11600 Dunbar Road, Glen Ellen
(707) 939-0708, (800) 816-9463
www.wellingtonvineyards.com
Operating a small, family vineyard and winery producing approximately 9,000 cases a year, John and Peter Wellington nevertheless offer a wide range of wines, concentrating on reds like Zinfandel, Merlot, and Cabernet Sauvignon. They also produce a couple of unusual wines unique to the area, including Marsanne and Roussanne, and an Alicante Bouschet blend. Top off the tasting ladder with a sip of White Port. The winery and tasting room are surrounded by vines, some more than a century old.

KUNDE ESTATE WINERY & VINEYARDS
9825 Highway 12 (Sonoma Highway), Kenwood
(707) 833-5501
www.kunde.com
Louis Kunde arrived in California from Germany in 1884 and founded his ranch in 1904. Four generations of Kundes have worked the ranch, which stretches for 1.5 miles along Sonoma Highway and extends from the valley up into the mountains above. Today's tasting room is a replica of Louis Kunde's old barn, built on the site of the original. The Kunde family ages its wine in 32,000 square feet of caves dug into the hillside, providing an ideal environment for natural aging. Timbers from the old barn were used to

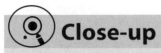

A Key Ingredient in the Making of Your Wine: Farmworkers

As you glide past Wine Country's thousands of tidy acres of vineyards, moving from tasting room to tasting room, take a moment to remember the people who are the backbone of the wine industry: the tireless farmworkers who pick the grapes, prune the vines, and maintain the fields year-round.

Farmworkers are the backbone of the wine industry.

JEAN SAYLOR DOPPENBERG

Farming by machinery is commonplace in California's hot interior valleys, where the wine grapes are less desirable and ultimately used in less flavorful wines. But the premium grapes grown in Wine Country are lovingly tended throughout their growing season by thousands of callused fingers and strong backs, making our wines truly a handcrafted commodity.

At harvest time, the most popular season for visitors, farmworkers dot the vineyards, quickly plucking the grape bunches off the vines with special cutting tools. They bring in the crop when the berries are at their peak of flavor and ready for crushing, working long hours to get the job done.

Every February, during the slow part of the growing season, grapevine pruning competitions are held in both counties to honor North Coast farmworkers and bestow upon two of them the "best pruner" championship title.

So when sipping your next glass of Napa Valley Cabernet or Sonoma County Pinot Noir, say a toast to the many farmworkers who had a hand in making these wines so great.

handcraft tables and benches. Free tours of the caves are available Friday through Sunday. Vineyards surround the tasting room, where samples are $10 to $20. Chardonnay, Zinfandel, Syrah, Viognier, Primitivo, and Barbera are among the many varietals made by Kunde.

KENWOOD VINEYARDS
9592 Highway 12 (Sonoma Highway), Kenwood
(707) 833-5891
www.kenwoodvineyards.com
When the Pagani brothers founded this winery in 1906, Jack London lived on the estate next door. Both estate owners are gone now, and the winery was bought by three college chums, all wine lovers, in 1970. The grapes they use are still grown on the London ranch, and the label on a special bottling shows a picture of Jack London's signature and a wolf, Jack's nickname. The tasting room is rustic, the sips are complimentary, and the atmosphere is charmingly informal. Kenwood is known for its Sauvignon Blanc, Zinfandels, and Cabernets.

CHATEAU ST. JEAN
8555 Highway 12 (Sonoma Highway), Kenwood
(707) 833-4134, (800) 543-7572
www.chateaustjean.com
Nestled against the tranquil slopes of Sugarloaf Ridge, Chateau St. Jean (named for former owner Ken Sheffield's sister and pronounced like my name and the popular dungarees) was founded in 1973. An elegant château on the grounds of this 250-acre estate was built in 1920 and is now a showplace surrounded by beautiful gardens. It's a lovely spot for picnicking. Chateau St. Jean's Cabernet Sauvignon has been served at the White House, and Queen Elizabeth has sipped its Chardonnay.

LANDMARK VINEYARDS
101 Adobe Canyon Road, Kenwood
(707) 833-0053, (707) 833-0218
www.landmarkwine.com
Perhaps the most spectacular aspect of this

Spanish mission–style winery is its expansive interior courtyard, facing onto dramatic, hulking Sugarloaf Mountain. The hospitality center at Landmark is a magnificent facility, featuring a granite tasting bar, a warm fireplace for chilly days, and a full-wall mural by noted Sonoma County artist Claudia Wagar. The pondside picnic area is a picturesque location for lunch or for just lounging and watching the clouds drift by. This winery began in Windsor, north of Santa Rosa. The owner, Damaris Deere Ford, the great-great-granddaughter of John Deere—whose name is on a million bright green farm implements worldwide—moved Landmark to this scenic spot. Production focuses on Chardonnay, and it's known for the Overlook and Damaris Reserve labels. It also produces Pinot Noir and Syrah.

KAZ VINEYARDS & WINERY
233 Adobe Canyon Road, Kenwood
(877) 833-2536
www.kazwinery.com
Ostentatious wineries have nothing on this place. When you're ready for a fun, down-home experience, seek out Kaz, which pours its wine in a barn just off Adobe Canyon Road. Bring your sense of humor, and check your attitude at the door. You'll be tasting reds and whites with whimsical labels and names such as "Dudes" and "Hooligans." Owner Richard "Kaz" Kasmier used to be a wine hobbyist, but now it's a full-time obsession, and his immediate family helps him out in the tasting room. Even so, production is still small—approximately 1,500 cases a year. The turnoff to Kaz is just beyond Landmark Vineyards (see previous listing); watch for the sign.

ST. FRANCIS WINERY & VINEYARDS
100 Pythian Road, Santa Rosa
(707) 833-4666, (800) 675-9463
www.stfranciswine.com
Joseph Martin, who left the corporate world in 1971 to become a vintner, named his winery after St. Francis of Assisi and San Francisco de Solano Mission in Sonoma. His first harvest came in 1979 with production of 4,000 cases. Today the benchmark varietals are Chardonnay and

a meritage called Anthem, but the portfolio also includes Cabernet Sauvignon and Cabernet Franc. The visitor center is a beauty, with terrific views and a huge gift shop and special reserve wine tasting bar.

LEDSON WINERY & VINEYARDS
7335 Highway 12 (Sonoma Highway),
Santa Rosa
(707) 537-3810
www.ledson.com
When this 16,000-square-foot French Normandy structure was first erected, it seemed ideally suited to be a fancy haunted castle, set far back from the highway and with rocky mountains as a mysterious backdrop. But that all changed when the castle opened and the warmth and beauty of the place became apparent. Owned by the Ledson family, longtime Sonoma Valley farmers, this hospitality center has several tasting bars, a clothing and gift boutique, and a terrific gourmet market. But what really sets it apart are the picnic grounds, where on any given weekend in summer there might be a jazz combo, art exhibit, or Corvette and Porsche auto shows to add to your wining and dining experience. Construction on the building, which was originally intended as a private home, began in 1989. The Ledsons soon realized the emerging castle was getting too much attention for their liking, so they decided it would work better as a winery open to the public. Ledson wines are sold only at the winery, are served at the Ledson Hotel's wine bar in Sonoma (see the Hotels, Motels, and Inns chapter), and are on the wine lists at many fine restaurants. The winery is known for its Merlot and Chardonnay, but it also produces Sauvignon Blanc, Johannisberg Riesling, and Madera Port.

MATANZAS CREEK WINERY
6097 Bennett Valley Road, Santa Rosa
(707) 528-6464, (800) 590-6464
www.matanzascreek.com
Ensconced at the base of Bennett Mountain, this environmentally friendly winemaking facility boasts one of the most sophisticated research laboratories in California. There, winemakers have conducted more than 100 experiments in progressive winemaking. In the early 1990s, Matanzas released a new wine, Journey, made in a radically progressive program. Although its $70 price raised some controversy, the first 1990 Chardonnay sold out on release and was hailed by some critics as the finest Chardonnay ever produced in America. Matanzas Creek also produces Merlot, Pinot Noir, and Cabernet Sauvignon. Picnic facilities are available as well as a self-guided garden tour that includes one of the largest plantings of lavender in Northern California. Look for handmade lavender products in the gift shop.

PARADISE RIDGE WINERY
4545 Thomas Lake Harris Drive,
Santa Rosa
(707) 528-9463
www.paradiseridgewinery.com
For Walter and Marijki Byck, Paradise came to be on the day in 1994 when they opened the doors to their new winery, a California-style structure with breathtaking views from the decks. In fact, the view is so exciting the winery stays open late some evenings just so visitors can catch the sunset. After purchasing a 156-acre ranch adjoining the old Fountain Grove Winery, the Bycks planted 18 acres of Sauvignon Blanc and Chardonnay grapes, determined to produce the finest wines possible. In addition to their award-winning wines, they also feature a historical exhibit and world-class sculpture garden. Paradise Ridge can be a little tricky to find, but it's worth the journey. It produces Syrah and Cabernet Sauvignon, among others, and even a sparkling wine.

Northern Sonoma
ARMIDA WINERY
2201 Westside Road, Healdsburg
(707) 433-2222
www.armida.com
Tastings here are charmingly casual, and the setting is spectacular. Built on the side of a hill, the winery looks out on the Dry Creek and Russian

River Valleys, with Alexander Valley, Geyser Peak, and Mount St. Helena to the east and south. High on the hillside, three geodesic domes house the winery, lab, and administrative offices. If you've been looking forward to a game of Italian bocce ball (or if you'd like to learn what it is), visit the bocce court near the picnic grounds. Armida is known for its "everyday" Zinfandel called Poizin (the reserve bottle comes resting in a coffin), as well as Chardonnay and Sauvignon Blanc.

FOPPIANO VINEYARDS
12707 Old Redwood Highway,
Healdsburg
(707) 433-7272
www.foppiano.com
This is one of the oldest family-owned wineries in Sonoma County, whose history reaches back to 1896. Founded by Giovanni Foppiano, a disenchanted gold miner who decided to get back to his farming roots, the winery is now being run by fourth- and fifth-generation Foppianos, producing 75,000 cases a year of Cabernet Sauvignon, Petite Sirah, Pinot Noir, Chardonnay, Sangiovese, and Sauvignon Blanc. Some of the producing vines are more than 100 years old.

KENDALL-JACKSON TASTING ROOM
337 Healdsburg Avenue, Healdsburg
(707) 433-7102
www.kj.com
The hugely successful Kendall-Jackson operation encompasses several wineries. The largest of these is Kendall-Jackson itself. It produces a Highland Estates label, for Chardonnay, Pinot Noir, Merlot, and Cabernet Sauvignon, as well as Grand Reserve and Vintner's Reserve lines in those same grape varieties and more. The Stature product is a meritage of five classic Bordeaux varietals. The friendly folks at the K-J store in Healdsburg will be happy to direct you to their other location: Kendall-Jackson Wine Center, 5007 Fulton Road, Fulton, (707) 571-7500. That facility features a viticulture exhibit, where students from Santa Rosa Junior College—and visitors—can become acquainted with 26 varietals and 19 trellising systems.

MARTINELLI WINERY
3360 River Road, northwest of
Santa Rosa
(707) 525-0570, (800) 346-1627
www.martinelliwinery.com
This family-run winery tends more than 350 acres of vines in the Russian River Valley, which it uses for its own wines and sells to other vintners. The winery specializes in Zinfandel—the Jackass Hill variety from the vineyard of the same name is considered by experts to be extraordinarily complex. They also produce a fine Sauvignon Blanc, Gewürztraminer, Chardonnay, Syrah, and Pinot Noir. The winery is housed in an old hop kiln, just a short hop from U.S. Highway 101 off the River Road exit.

MILL CREEK VINEYARDS
1401 Westside Road, Healdsburg
(707) 431-2121, (877) 349-2121
www.millcreekwinery.com
This beautifully landscaped winery is set on a rise above the vineyard, which has been operated since 1975 by the Kreck family. The tasting room, complete with working waterwheel and a mill pond, is in an air-conditioned, two-story redwood building. The bar top, trusses, and beams are all made from one redwood tree from the Kreck ranch on Mill Creek Road. A 3,000-square-foot picnic deck overlooks the Dry Creek Valley, Fitch Mountain, and Mount St. Helena. Buy a bottle of the winery's Sauvignon Blanc, Merlot, Cabernet Sauvignon, Chardonnay, Zinfandel, or Syrah and dig into your picnic basket.

EVERETT RIDGE VINEYARDS & WINERY
435 West Dry Creek Road, Healdsburg
(707) 433-1637
www.everettridge.com
Views, good wine, and Shona sculptures, too—that's Everett Ridge. The wines include Petite Sirah, Cabernet Sauvignon, Pinot Noir, Sangiovese, Zinfandel, a Harvest Fair gold medal–winning Syrah, and a meritage blend called Diablita. With a pastoral view of the Dry Creek Valley, the patio is a relaxing spot to unwind. African Shona sculptures dot the property, adding to the peaceful mood (they're for sale, too). Read more about

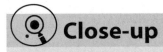 **Close-up**

Bored with Cabernet? Weary of Chardonnay?

Wine Country is busy experimenting with many wine-grape varietals beyond Chardonnay and Cabernet that are changing the climate in the wine world and soon will be more noticeable at your favorite wine shop. Leading the pack of white varietals taking the industry by storm is actually an old favorite: Sauvignon Blanc. "A lot of people had been predicting it, and now there's an interesting rebirth of Sauvignon Blanc and Fumé Blanc going on in Napa Valley," says Clay Gregory, former president of the board of directors of the Napa Valley Vintners Association and one-time general manager at Robert Mondavi Winery. "Frankly, consumers are getting a little tired of oaky Chardonnays." To illustrate his point, Clay says many acres of Chardonnay grapes grown north of the Carneros region are being pulled out in favor of other varieties that grow more successfully in the warmer valley air. He adds that the cooler Carneros appellation, shared by both Napa County and Sonoma County, is better suited to Sauvignon Blanc grapes than Chardonnay, although Chardonnay will continue to be grown there. "But a lot of wine people now prefer Sauvignon Blanc," he says. Nick Frey, president of the Sonoma County Winegrape Commission, agrees with Clay. "The movement now is toward Sauvignon Blanc rather than Chardonnay," says Nick. "Sauvignon Blanc is produced without oak, and it bursts with clean, crisp fruit. It's a food-friendly wine and a good value."

Among other white varietals, Viognier (vee-own-YAY) has been receiving its share of attention in the past few years, says Clay. "Viognier is very floral and aromatic—it smells like it's going to be sweet but it's actually dry." Yet instead of being "the next big white wine," as had once been predicted, Viognier will likely be used more for blending, especially with Sauvignon Blanc, Nick believes. Also flashing brightly on the wine industry radar are Pinot Gris, Marsanne, and Roussanne.

In red wines, Syrah (or *Shiraz*, as Australian vintners spell it) is generating the most excitement, says Clay. "Cabernet Sauvignon is still king in Napa Valley for the foreseeable future, but Syrah is coming up fast as the next big variety to plant. It grows well in many climates, the wines have a lot of character, and it's not as 'intellectual' as Cabernet." Nick agrees: "Syrah is going to be a very important wine very soon."

Bordeaux varieties getting more buzz these days include Petit Verdot, Cabernet Franc, and Malbec, while another old favorite, Zinfandel (not *White* Zinfandel) is making a welcome comeback. "There are still many old Zin vines around here that produce terrific wines, and most were planted by Italian immigrants," says Clay. Another small-production grape, the Spanish varietal Tempranillo, is likely to be a "next generation" wine, he adds.

Clay reminds wine lovers that, as in other types of perennial agriculture, ramping up to produce new varietals can take time. "But one of the hallmarks of Californians is our constant experimentation and desire to try new things." If you love wine, it can be fun to jump outside your comfort zone (Chardonnay and Cabernet) once in a while and try a new grape varietal.

Shona sculptures in the Shopping chapter under the Spirits in Stone listing.

RODNEY STRONG VINEYARDS
11455 Old Redwood Highway,
Healdsburg
(707) 431-1533, (800) 678-4763
www.rodneystrong.com

In 1959, long before Sonoma County was "discovered" as a premium grape-growing region, Rodney Strong began an exhaustive search for the very best vineyards. Ultimately he selected several vineyards in the Chalk Hill, Alexander Valley, and Russian River Valley appellations. The winery, a low-lying building with a roof spreading across it like the wings of a giant eagle, is situated among acres of prime vineyards. The winery's estate wines are named after the individual vineyards where the grapes grow—for example, the Charlotte's Home, a Sauvignon Blanc, and Alexander's Crown, a Cabernet. Picnic areas are available. For special occasions there's a garden area adjacent to the vineyards (contact the winery for details). This winery has gained fame in recent years for its annual summer concert series, with big-name acts such as Michael McDonald and Chris Isaak taking the stage.

DRY CREEK VINEYARDS
3770 Lambert Bridge Road, Healdsburg
(707) 433-1000, (800) 864-9463
www.drycreekvineyard.com
Opened in 1972, this was the first new winery in Sonoma County's Dry Creek Valley since the days of Prohibition, and it led to a dramatic wave of change in this long-neglected grape-growing region. The Stare family produces Fumé Blanc, Chenin Blanc, Cabernet Sauvignon, and other wines, including the estate-bottled meritage (a Bordeaux blend). Dry Creek Vineyards is known for its collection of sailboat labels, based on a personal long-standing love affair with the sport of sailing. The gray stone winery resembles a French country wine château, and the tasting room is casual and informal.

FERRARI-CARANO VINEYARD & WINERY
8761 Dry Creek Road, Healdsburg
(707) 433-6700, (800) 831-0381
www.ferrari-carano.com
The Wine Shop at Villa Fiore (the name of the château that houses the Ferrari-Carano operation) is one of California's friendliest and most enchanting Wine Country destinations. Visitors will discover magnificent gardens, critically acclaimed wines, and unique gifts. Allow extra time to walk through the Enclosed Garden with its parklike setting. If you time your visit just right, you'll see more than 10,000 tulips and daffodils in bloom (call ahead to find out precisely when the flowers unfurl). The spectacular underground

barrel cellar where the wines of Don and Rhonda Carano age is also a favorite. Among the wines poured at the wine shop are Fumé Blanc, Pinot Grigio, Siena (a Sangiovese-based blend), Chardonnay, Merlot, and a late harvest dessert wine called Eldorado Gold.

LAMBERT BRIDGE WINERY
4085 West Dry Creek Road, Healdsburg
(707) 431-9600, (800) 975-0555
www.lambertbridge.com
Established in 1975, the winery takes its name from a neighboring landmark bridge that spans Dry Creek. Many of the wines of this small, high-quality winery are available only in the charming tasting room, where the wine-stained tasting bar was made from oak casks. A crackling fireplace cheers on frosty days, and on sunny days the picnic grounds may be the most elegant in Dry Creek Valley. The tasting room pours Viognier, Merlot, Chardonnay, Cabernet Franc, Cabernet Sauvignon, and Zinfandel.

PRESTON VINEYARDS
9282 West Dry Creek Road, Healdsburg
(707) 433-3372, (800) 305-9707
www.prestonvineyards.com
According to the folks at family-owned Preston Winery, "Having fun is no scandal." They take pride in being known as the alternative winery: the place to go when you want something different and delicious. Not only can you taste some unusual wines, but you can also enjoy some freshly baked bread ("Lou's Bread," named for owner Lou Preston) and picnic among flowers, herbs, vegetable gardens, and olive trees. If that's not enough fun, you can play a game of bocce on the house courts.

Preston is slightly off the beaten path, but with so much going for it, the adventure is worth taking the drive. The 115 acres of grapes grow without insecticides and produce flavorful, eccentric wines such as Mourvèdre, Rousanne, Barbera, Cinsault, and Marsanne.

i Those large structures with propellers you see rising high out of vineyards are wind machines, which help protect delicate vines against frost. The wind machines keep the air circulating so the coldest air does not settle on the vines.

QUIVIRA VINEYARDS
4900 West Dry Creek Road, Healdsburg
(707) 431-8333, (800) 292-8339
www.quivirawine.com
For centuries, European explorers searched for the legendary New World land called Quivira. It was thought to be on the Pacific Coast in the region now known as Sonoma County. Three centuries ago European mapmakers placed it just about where the Quivira Winery is located now. Whatever else you find out here about the legends of Quivira, you will also encounter some excellent Sauvignon Blanc, Zinfandel, and Grenache. This is a great place for a picnic, complete with terrific views.

CLOS DU BOIS
19410 Geyserville Avenue, Geyserville
(707) 857-3100, (800) 222-3189
www.closdubois.com
Clos du Bois got its start in Sonoma County as a vineyard operation in the early 1970s, with 590 acres of vineyards in the Alexander Valley. Today, it is one of Sonoma County's most productive wineries, having begun a huge expansion in 2006 that will effectively double its capacity to 3.5 million cases of wine annually. It is located on a 40-acre site in the heart of the beautiful Alexander Valley and has approximately 1,000 prime acres of vineyard in Alexander and Dry Creek Valleys. The winery produces Sauvignon Blanc, Chardonnay (and a reserve), Gewürztraminer, Pinot Noir, Merlot, Zinfandel, and Cabernet Sauvignon (and a reserve). Clos du Bois also pours the J. Garcia line of wines in its tasting room, with labels featuring colorful artwork created by the late Jerry Garcia of Grateful Dead fame.

FRANCIS FORD COPPOLA PRESENTS ROSSO & BIANCO
Via Archemides at Independence Lane, Geyserville
(707) 857-1400, (888) 809-4637
www.rossobianco.com
The mighty Coppola name, long part of Napa Valley's wine trail, now has a large presence in Sonoma County. The filmmaker bought the former Chateau Souverain facility in 2006 and set out to convert it from a French-style winery to an Italian one. For the longest time after the acquisition, this winery had no official name. It now goes by Rosso & Bianco, and big plans are in the works for a redo of the property, pending all the usual county permit approvals. Poured in the tasting room are Coppola's Rosso & Bianco wines ("everyday wines," he says), the Diamond collection, Sofia (after his famous daughter), and limited reserve and Director's Cut labels. When you visit, it's likely that Coppola's movie memorabilia—once housed in his Napa Valley winery, Rubicon—will be on display here. The collection includes costumes, cars, and furniture taken from Coppola's many classic films, along with his five Academy Award Oscar statuettes. There's a decent cafe on-site, too. To get to the winery, take the Independence Lane exit off US 101 near Geyserville.

GEYSER PEAK WINERY
22281 Chianti Road, Geyserville
(707) 857-9400, (800) 255-9463
www.geyserpeakwinery.com
Though particularly known for its Chardonnay, Geyser Peak produces a number of fine varieties, including Merlot, Cabernet Sauvignon, Malbec, Sauvignon Blanc, Petite Verdot, and Petite Sirah. It sources its grapes from Alexander Valley, Dry Creek Valley, Russian River Valley, and the Sonoma Valley. A lovely picnic area overlooks the Alexander Valley, and the Panoramic Trail (winding up behind the winery) and the Margot Patterson Doss Trail (named for a well-known San Francisco walker and writer) will appeal to hikers.

HANNA WINERY
9280 Highway 128, Healdsburg
(707) 431-4310, (888) 854-3987
www.hannawinery.com

Dr. Elias S. Hanna, a Marin County surgeon who was born and raised on a farm in Syria, founded Hanna Winery in 1985. His estate winery now produces about 40,000 cases of Sauvignon Blanc, Chardonnay, Cabernet Sauvignon, Merlot, and Pinot Noir annually from its approximately 250 acres of vineyards. Jasmine, a rosé, is also available. You can taste Hanna wines at two hospitality centers, one at 5353 Occidental Road in Santa Rosa and the other at the address above. The patio of the visitor center in Healdsburg is a lovely place for a picnic, with panoramic views of the Alexander Valley and Hanna's magnificent hillside vineyard.

PEDRONCELLI WINERY
1220 Canyon Road, Geyserville
(707) 857-3531, (800) 836-3894
www.pedroncelli.com

In 1927 John Pedroncelli, a native of Lombardy, Italy, bought the vineyard property that was to bear his name. At that time the vines planted there had been yielding grapes for more than 20 years. During Prohibition, the winery sold grapes to home winemakers; after the repeal, it sold wine in bulk to other wineries. Today the winery uses grapes harvested from the Dry Creek Valley to produce primarily red wines, including excellent Cabernet Sauvignon, Zinfandel, Sangiovese, and Pinot Noir. Tucked 2 miles up Canyon Road from US 101, the charmingly rustic Pedroncelli Winery offers picnic tables for a pleasant lunch.

FRICK WINERY
23072 Walling Road, Geyserville
(707) 857-1980
www.frickwinery.com

On a narrow lane, up the road a piece from Pedroncelli Winery, is this gem of a property. It's a one-man operation with no frills but great hospitality. Bill Frick does just about everything here, from processing the grapes he makes into his wine (Viognier, Syrah, Cinsaut, Carignane,

Grenache, and others) to manning the tasting room (Saturday and Sunday afternoons only). Frick Winery has just a little over five acres of vineyards, with a production of 1,900 cases. As he pours, Bill will tell you the whole story of how he sold his beloved 1957 Chevy to buy the place. This is a delightful stop when you've had your fill of the glitzier wineries.

SIMI WINERY
16275 Healdsburg Avenue, Healdsburg
(707) 433-6981, (800) 746-4880
www.simiwinery.com

In 1881 two Italian immigrant brothers, Giuseppe and Pietro Simi, bought a winery near the grain depot in Healdsburg for $2,250 in gold coins. They built a magnificent, hand-hewn stone winery, and their business soon doubled. Then, in the midst of success, both brothers died, and Giuseppe's teenage daughter Isabelle took over. Prohibition was a blow for her, but when it ended, she had one of the winery's enormous redwood tanks rolled outside and created a retail tasting room. Isabelle could be found there until her late 80s, still selling Simi wines. In today's more modern tasting room you will find sips of Sauvignon Blanc, Chardonnay, Merlot, and Cabernet Sauvignon.

i The ideal serving temperature for Sauvignon Blanc is 45 degrees (7 degrees Celsius). By comparison, most red wines taste best served at a cool "room" temperature of 60 to 65 degrees.

TRENTADUE WINERY
19170 Geyserville Avenue, Geyserville
(707) 433-3104, (888) 332-3032
www.trentadue.com

Founded in 1969, the family-owned and -operated Trentadue has achieved an outstanding reputation not only for rare and unusual wines but also for highly regarded, better-known varieties. Visitors are offered complimentary tastings of classic reds (including Petite Sirah, Cabernet Sauvignon, and Sangiovese), and for a small charge you may try Ports. The Chocolate Amore Port in particular is darn good.

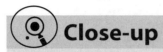 **Close-up**

A Wine Tasting Primer

"Quaffable, but far from transcendent." That's how the character of Miles in the Academy Award–nominated and Golden Globe–winning film *Sideways* described a particular Chardonnay he was sampling in a winery tasting room. The hit movie about two buddies—one obsessed with Pinot Noir and the other clueless about wine but always thirsty—made for entertaining fiction about the tasting room experience. Lofty statements such as those Miles uttered in the movie may be the reason some people shy away from wine. They believe, wrongly, that it's a drink only for snobs and that tasting rooms are for characters with raised pinkies and attitude. I'm not sure where this misconception comes from, but I can assure you that most tasting rooms are friendly places—fun, educational, and decidedly nonsnobby. You needn't feel silly or self-conscious about sipping wine among strangers—tasting room personnel are patient and friendly, and they enjoy chatting with visitors and answering questions. You may also meet interesting wine tasters from around the world and strike up conversations with like-minded folks you would not have had the chance to meet otherwise. For instance, the person pouring your Syrah could be the vintner who created it (a good example is Frick Winery's Bill Frick). Another way to enrich the tasting experience is to take your glass out to the winery's patio or deck and share a table with others.

But let's get down to the nitty-gritty of tasting. During your enological experience, remember that the pleasure of wine comes from several senses—sight, smell, taste, and touch. Here are a couple of suggestions to keep you from feeling completely lost during your first winery adventures. (Rest assured that you will learn much more as you travel from one tasting room to another.) And remember, if you're a designated driver, don't swallow the wine. You can taste the sample as described below, then pour it into the handy "spit" bucket provided.

Sight: Hold the glass to the light and enjoy the wine's color.

Smell: Swirl the wine gently in the glass to release its fragrances. Sniff sharply to carry the aroma to the nerve endings high in the nose.

Taste: Take a drink and roll it in your mouth to reach all the taste bud areas. Connoisseurs learn to draw in air over the wine still in their mouth. It looks silly (remember Miles's exaggerated behavior?), but it carries fumes to the nasal cavity, where most of the subtle olfactory differences emerge. Try to pick out tastes that are familiar to you, such as berry or pepper. Ask the tasting room staff if they have an "aroma wheel" handy to help you identify even more elusive flavors (soy sauce, bacon, artichoke?).

West County/Russian River

HOP KILN WINERY
6050 Westside Road, Healdsburg
(707) 433-6491
www.hopkilnwinery.com

Housed in an old stone building that was once a hop-drying kiln, the tasting room at Hop Kiln displays a fine collection of winemaking tools and a gallery of old photos showing the history of the hop industry, which bustled in Sonoma County during the early 1900s. The Hop Kiln was declared a state historic landmark in 1977 and has been used in several motion pictures. The tasting room is cool and rustic, serving samplings of Zinfandel, Chardonnay, and two popular blends, Big Red and Thousand Flowers. Hop Kiln's grounds are a great place to have a picnic. A picturesque pond inhabited by local wildfowl sparkles next to the tasting room, and trees provide plenty of shade around the outdoor tables.

Touch: Chew the wine, just as if you were munching on some mashed potatoes. Note the amount of astringency present and get its "feel."

Aftertaste: Swallow the wine and note the taste sensations remaining, also known as "the length." The aftertaste should always be pleasant, though it's often quite different from your first impression upon sipping.

(You may now pop that wad of Dentyne back in your mouth.)

Scott Chafen (center), winemaker at Dutch Henry, conducts an informal tasting for visitors in the winery's barrel room. JEAN SAYLOR DOPPENBERG

KORBEL CHAMPAGNE CELLARS

13250 River Road, Guerneville
(707) 824-7000, (800) 656-7235
www.korbel.com

When the three Czech Korbel brothers emigrated from Bohemia, they settled in a redwood forest along the Russian River, tried several different enterprises—including cigar-box manufacture—and finally resolved to become winemakers. They built their handsome brick winery in 1886, including a quaint turreted tower at the south end. The story behind this tower is interesting. Before leaving Prague, the youngest Korbel inadvertently fired his pistola in the midst of the townfolk, who had gathered to hear the news called out by the town crier. He was jailed briefly, and upon his release the three brothers fled the country. The tower of the winery is a sentimental duplicate of the jail where young Joseph spent his last days in his home country. Korbel has an excellent tour of both the champagne cellars and the antique rose garden that surrounds the old summer house.

The sparkling wine is produced in the *méthode champenoise,* the traditional French method in which the second fermentation takes place in the same bottle. If you're hungry, there's a good deli on-site. Be aware that this is a popular spot and it can be jam-packed with visitors on weekends.

WINE SHOPS

As you would expect, they don't just make 'em, pour 'em, and sell 'em in Wine Country—a variety of stores are also dedicated to the display, presentation, storage, and properly outfitted enjoyment of wines. In addition, some shops offer amazing selections of wines from our region and beyond, along with all the decadent accoutrements. Many of the retail stores are also licensed to pour, so you can sample before buying. Here are only a few of the places you will find merchandise to make the wine collecting experience enjoyable and educational.

Napa County

JV WINE
301 First Street, Napa
(707) 253-2624, (877) 4-MY-WINE
www.jvwine.com
A store with a long pedigree, JV Wine began in 1983 as the distribution center for Napa's decades-old Vallerga's Market. When it first opened it was warehouse-style with no frills, but it offered great wine deals to the locals. It continues to offer great deals, now in a new location not far from the old site. Two sommeliers are on staff, and the wine is sold mostly at discount prices. There's a tasting bar, too, open every day from 1:00 to 6:00 p.m., serving 40 boutique wines.

V WINE CELLAR
6525 Washington Street, Yountville
(707) 531-7053, (800) WINE-4-US
www.vwinecellar.com
Inside the V Marketplace is this large store devoted to wines from around the world, not only Napa Valley—as many as 3,000 are available.

On the shelves you might find everything from $5 bottles to an imperial of Mondavi 1978 Reserve Cabernet Sauvignon that goes for $1,000. At the tasting bar, daily "flights" are offered from 11:00 a.m. to 7:00 p.m. Cigars are sold here as well.

ST. HELENA WINE MERCHANTS
699 St. Helena Highway S., St. Helena
(707) 963-7888, (800) 729-9463
www.sthelenawinemerchants.com
Across the road from V. Sattui Winery is this unpretentious purveyor of wines. Merchants aims to carry the sort of small-availability labels that out-of-state visitors read about but can't find at home—Harlan, Dominus, and Maya come to mind as examples. Don't be surprised if you bump into a local winemaker or two during your visit.

DEAN & DELUCA
607 St. Helena Highway S., St. Helena
(707) 967-9980
www.deandeluca.com
When these classy New Yorkers set up shop in Wine Country (see the Shopping chapter), it changed the face of retail wine sales in Napa Valley. D&D has the most extensive collection of California wines you could ever hope to see: 1,200 labels, and that's just 750-milliliter bottles. The wines are arranged alphabetically within varietal categories. Forget about trying to note every wine; by the time you make it to the last Zinfandel, they probably will have added a few more bottles.

THE WINE GARAGE
1020 Foothill Boulevard (Highway 29), Calistoga
(707) 942-5332, (888) 690-WINE
www.winegarage.net
What was once a pet store is now a well-stocked wine shop with an inventory of 3,000 bottles. Owner Todd Miller handpicks everything he sells, and just about every bottle in the store is under $25. Much of the wine comes from small California producers, but Todd also stocks labels from around the world.

CALISTOGA WINE STOP

1458 Lincoln Avenue, No. 2, Calistoga
(707) 942-5556, (800) 648-4521
www.calistogawinestop.net

Before you even get to the wine, there's a lot of history worth noting here. The Wine Stop is in the Depot, that big wood building that was what it claims to be. Built in 1868, it's the second-oldest train station left in California (though no trains have stopped here since 1963). The wine shop itself is jammed mostly inside a 19th-century boxcar, which limits the elbow room but doesn't impair the Napa-Sonoma-concentrated selection. (Owner Tom Pelter estimates that 75 percent of his stock is made in those two counties.) Pelter is something of a Port aficionado, which explains the high density of Portugal's fortified wine in his store.

ENOTECA WINE SHOP

1348 Lincoln Avenue, Calistoga
(707) 942-1117
www.enotecawineshop.com

Enoteca is an Italian word meaning "wine cellar" or "wine library." This store tends toward artisanal vintners who produce hundreds of cases rather than tens of thousands, and they draw from all over the world. The inventory is continually changing, and the store motto is "life is too short to drink even above-average wines."

Sonoma County

THE WINE EXCHANGE OF SONOMA

452 First Street E., Sonoma
(707) 938-1794, (800) 938-1794
www.wineexsonoma.com

Interested in a place that carries hard-to-find wines and will even ship them anywhere allowed by law? The Wine Exchange is the place for you, with some 800 premium wines and 280 beers in stock. It's opposite the Sonoma Plaza, with a tasting bar that features 18 wines and 6 draft beers.

SONOMA WINE HARDWARE

536 Broadway, Sonoma
(707) 939-1694, (866) 231-9463

NAPA VALLEY WINE HARDWARE

659 Main Street, St. Helena
(707) 967-5503, (866) 611-9463
www.winehardware.com

You just scored your first case of great Cabernet Sauvignon—now how can you store it properly back home? Your next stop should be at one of these shops. The stores do not sell wine (they leave the buying up to you); their main focus is wine storage systems. Under the same ownership, both stores have similar inventories, but the Sonoma store features a slightly larger showroom and a larger library of wine books. On display in both are a multitude of cabinets, racks, and other hardware for storing and enjoying wine, and lots of accessories too.

TAYLOR & NORTON WINE MERCHANTS

19210 Highway 12 (Sonoma Highway), Sonoma
(707) 939-6611
www.taylorandnorton.com

You'll have no trouble finding every local and regional wine you've been looking for in this wine shop. More than that, Taylor & Norton carries wines from other U.S. areas as well as wines from Europe and other foreign wine-producing regions. While shopping for wine, you might want to browse through a handsome selection of antique wine decanters and glasses, some from the Victorian era.

THE WINE SHOP

331 Healdsburg Avenue, Healdsburg
(707) 433-0433

It's all wine here, and it's also a wine bar, meaning it's licensed by the state to serve and charge for full glasses of wine, not tastings. But the selection is enormous: The shop specializes in hard-to-find small production wines worldwide, with more than 600 wineries represented. They will ship your selections too.

> **i** Not every state will allow interstate wine shipments into its territory, so ask your wine merchant in advance.

ATTRACTIONS

So you've had a go at wine tasting, feasted on some fabulous food, and now you're ready for something completely different. You've come to the right chapter. Sure, the wineries, mud baths, and world-class restaurants are attractions in their own ways, and all those selling points are detailed elsewhere. In this chapter, however, you'll find everything worth visiting that defies categorical lumping. That might be a culturally rich historical site (such as Fort Ross), a museum (such as the Sharpsteen Museum in Calistoga), or even a chance to hit the jackpot at River Rock Casino. Please note that some of the attractions are seasonal, so always call ahead before planning your itinerary.

Price Code

The price code below reflects the admission price or fees for two adults in high season, not including gratuities, where appropriate.

$	Less than $15
$$	$15 to $50
$$$	$51 to $150
$$$$	More than $151

MAIN EVENTS

Napa County

SEGUIN MOREAU NAPA COOPERAGE   FREE
151 Camino Dorado, Napa
(707) 252-3408
www.seguin-moreau.fr
You've seen how the wine is blended, now take a good look at how the barrels get toasted. The only U.S. outpost of the famed French wine-barrel makers, Tonnellerie Seguin Moreau Cooperage, is located in Napa. Watch the crew of skilled coopers bend, shave, and roast the oak staves over open flames in the floor, then hammer them together using steel hoops. It's a craft that has changed little in hundreds of years of winemaking. Self-guided tours are offered Monday through Friday between 9:30 a.m. and 12:30 p.m. If your group numbers 10 or more, there's a small fee.

NAPA FIREFIGHTERS MUSEUM   FREE
1201 Main Street, Napa
(707) 259-0609
www.napafirefightersmuseum.org
This museum will give you a deeper appreciation of the folks who fight the flames. Inside you'll see a hand pumper and a steamer, hose carts, engines, ladder trucks, old fire equipment and uniforms, and photos from many eras of puttin' out fires. The museum is open 11:00 a.m. to 4:00 p.m. Wednesday through Saturday.

NAPA VALLEY MUSEUM $
55 Presidents Circle, Yountville
(707) 944-0500
www.napavalleymuseum.org
A major capital project that was years in the planning, the nonprofit museum celebrates the valley's artistic, historical, and cultural heritage with a permanent exhibit called "The Land and People of the Napa Valley." Its central, permanent exhibition is "California Wine: The Science of an Art." Using music, the spoken word, and the power of technology, it effectively presents the winemaking process in near entirety. The Napa Valley Museum is open Wednesday through Monday 10:00 a.m. to 5:00 p.m. Admission is $4.50 for adults, $3.50 for students and seniors age 60 or older, and $2.50 for youths ages 7 to 17. Kids under 7 get in free.

SILVERADO MUSEUM   FREE
1490 Library Lane, St. Helena
(707) 963-3757
www.silveradomuseum.org

A California museum devoted to a Scottish novelist might seem a bit strange, but, hey, Robert Louis Stevenson did help immortalize the area with his *The Silverado Squatters*. He also penned classics such as *Treasure Island, Dr. Jekyll and Mr. Hyde*, and others you'll read all about at the museum. It has first editions, artifacts from the Stevenson home, personal letters and photographs, and a few original manuscripts (though most of those reside at Yale University). The museum is closed Monday but open the rest of the week from noon to 4:00 p.m.

CULINARY INSTITUTE OF AMERICA AT GREYSTONE $
2555 Main Street, St. Helena
(707) 967-1100, (888) 424-2433 (store)
www.ciastore.com

You can learn more about the educational possibilities of the CIA in the Relocation chapter, but this listing is to encourage you to make a stop at the huge stone building on the north edge of St. Helena and soak up its grandeur. There are a few options: The Spice Islands Marketplace is the CIA's culinary store, where you will find anything and everything needed to become—or improve your skills as—a gourmet chef. A huge selection of cookbooks takes up one corner of the store, and even chef's "whites" and toques are for sale if you want to dress the part at home. Cooking demonstrations are ongoing, for an extra charge. If you made a prior reservation, enjoy fine dining at the Wine Spectator Restaurant (see the Restaurants chapter). A smaller cafe sells pastries and baked goods prepared by the student chefs on-site. If you have a thing about corkscrews, you'll be enchanted by the huge collection of historic wine-bottle openers on display. It's free to walk in and look around the CIA; cooking demos cost about $15 per person.

i More than 1,000 corkscrews from around the world, some dating to the 18th century, are on display at the Culinary Institute of America at Greystone in St. Helena. The collection was amassed by Brother Timothy, cellar master and educator with Christian Brothers, the original occupants of the huge stone building.

BALE GRIST MILL STATE HISTORIC PARK $
3369 Highway 29, St. Helena
(707) 942-4575
www.parks.ca.gov/?page_id=482

The friendly miller will tell you how this park is a working reminder of the days when "milling" involved more than driving to Safeway for a bag of all-purpose flour. Dr. Edward Bale built the wood-frame mill in 1846, and it has been painstakingly refurbished. The park is open 10:00 a.m. to 5:00 p.m. daily, but the best times to visit are weekend days at 11:30 a.m. and 1:00, 2:30, and 3:30 p.m. That's when the park cranks up the wooden, 36-foot waterwheel and gets those original quartz stones to grinding wheat or corn. Admission is $2 for adults; children under 16 free. From here you can hike to adjacent Bothe-Napa Valley State Park (see the Parks and Recreation chapter).

THE SHARPSTEEN MUSEUM $
1311 Washington Street, Calistoga
(707) 942-5911
www.sharpsteen-museum.org

If every small town in America had a museum as lively and authentic as the Sharpsteen, maybe we wouldn't be so ignorant of history. The museum was founded in the 1970s by Ben Sharpsteen, who produced such films as *Fantasia* and *Snow White* for Walt Disney. (Sharpsteen's Academy Award Oscar statuette from his days with Disney gleams inside a special display case.) The crowning piece of his legacy is a 32-foot scale-model diorama that lays out the grounds of Sam Brannan's Calistoga spa, circa 1860 (see the History chapter for more on Brannan). One of the original cottages from that spa serves as a museum annex. The museum is open daily from 11 a.m. to 4 p.m. Admission donations accepted.

OLD FAITHFUL GEYSER OF CALIFORNIA $
1299 Tubbs Lane, Calistoga
(707) 942-6463
www.oldfaithfulgeyser.com

About every 30 minutes on the yearly average (depending on how much water is in the aquifer), the earth gurgles, puffs, and blows a stream of boiling water (350 degrees hot!) from 60 to 100 feet into the air off Tubbs Lane. Welcome to Calistoga's geyser, one of only three in world that can call themselves Old Faithful without shame. There is a working seismograph in the entryway (the geyser is said to predict earthquakes), and outside near the erupting pond, for some reason, is a pen of Tennessee Fainting goats, a rare breed suffering from myotonia, which causes them to lock up and topple when startled. The Old Faithful complex is open 9:00 a.m. to 6:00 p.m. daily in the warm months, closing an hour earlier in winter. Admission is $8 for adults, $7 for seniors, and $3 for kids ages 6 through 12.

VILLA CA'TOGA $$
Off Tubbs Lane, Calistoga
(707) 942-3900
www.catoga.com

Italian artist Carlo Marchiori is one of the eminent trompe l'oeil artists in the world, and Villa Ca'Toga—a mansion and work in progress on the outskirts of Calistoga—is his vision come to life. Faux pillars, staircases, and hanging plants are painted in three-dimensional realism on two-dimensional walls. Alcoves end abruptly at painted backdrops, and surprises lie around every corner. The house is open Saturday from May to October for a one-hour tour that begins at 11:00 a.m. Reservations are necessary, and you pick up your tickets and a map to the property at the Ca'Toga Galleria D'Arte at 1206 Cedar Street in downtown Calistoga (see the Arts and Culture chapter). Tickets are $25 per person, and children over 12 are welcome. No pets, please.

PETRIFIED FOREST $
4100 Petrified Forest Road, Calistoga
(707) 942-6667
www.petrifiedforest.org

It's not as spooky as it sounds, unless you think too hard about the advancing wall of muddy volcanic ash that leveled these trees about three million years ago, following massive eruptions to the northeast. The trees lay unmolested until 1870, when a gent later known as "Petrified Charlie" Evans happened upon a rock-hard stump while tending his cows. The rest is tourist-industry history. A short loop takes you past all the highlights, including the Monarch, a petrified, 105-foot redwood with a diameter of 6 feet. The museum and store are open daily 9:00 a.m. to 7:00 p.m. (closing at 5:00 p.m. in winter). Admission is $6 for adults, $5 for youngsters ages 12 through 17 and seniors 60 and over, and $3 for kids under 12.

Sonoma County
Southern Sonoma

CALIFORNIA MISSIONS MUSEUM
AT CLINE CELLARS FREE
24737 Highway 121 (Arnold Drive), Sonoma
(707) 939-8051
www.californiamissionsmuseum.com

If you can't find the time to visit California's historic missions found up and down the state, you can see them all at this museum. A bit of background: The missions were built during a 50-year period beginning in 1769, when they were designed as settlements to convert American Indians to Catholicism and the Spanish way of life. The models you see in this museum, of all 21 missions, were first unveiled at the World's Fair in 1939. In storage since 1971, the collection went on the auction block in 1998, and Nancy Cline of Cline Cellars bought the whole shebang. The building in which they are housed, behind the winery's tasting room and grounds, opened to the public in 2006. These are fascinating reproductions of some of California's most enduring structures. The museum is open daily from 9:30 a.m. to 4:00 p.m. (11:00 a.m. to 4:00 p.m. in summer).

VINTAGE AIRCRAFT CO. $$$$
23982 Highway 121 (Arnold Drive), Sonoma
(707) 938-2444
www.vintageaircraft.com
You step back into the 1940s when you step onto the tarmac and check out Christopher Prevost's fleet of authentic 1940 Boeing-built Stearman biplanes. One of the planes is a North American–built World War II Navy SNJ-4, designed to train pilot candidates for the air force and navy. Meticulously restored and maintained, the planes tempt thrill seekers to take one of several rides offered by Prevost. For the truly brave, Prevost offers a variety of aerobatic flights—the most intense is appropriately named Kamikaze. Weekday flights are by appointment. You can take off for about $175 for a single passenger for 20 minutes, up to $295 for 40 minutes.

INFINEON RACEWAY $$$
Highways 37 and 121, Sonoma
(707) 938-8448, (800) 870-7223
www.infineonraceway.com
Each year you'll see some of the top names in the racing world compete at Infineon (formerly known as Sears Point Raceway) on the grueling road course, the rugged motocross dirt track, and the drag strip. Legends such as Mario Andretti, Al Unser (Sr. and Jr.), and Jeff Gordon have all toured the track, as well as Hollywood celebrities such as Paul Newman, Clint Eastwood, and James Garner. Annual events include NASCAR road races and sports car racing by the Sports Car Club of America with TRANS-AM, Formula Atlantic, and Pro Formula Ford entrants. Bike events include AMA motorcycle road races and several motocross races. Prices for events vary. (See the Spectator Sports chapter for more details.)

DEPOT PARK MUSEUM FREE
270 First Street W., Sonoma
(707) 938-1762
www.vom.com/depot
This is more than a museum; it's an authentic piece of Sonoma city's history. Originally the depot was on the downtown plaza, much to the chagrin of Sonomans, who felt the plaza had been turned into a railroad yard, turntable and all. After some pressure, the depot was moved in 1890 to its present site. The museum now houses a terrific collection of historic memorabilia focusing on the 19th century. Several rooms are furnished in Victorian style, and a good deal of emphasis is placed on the life of Gen. Mariano Vallejo (see the History chapter). Pioneer artifacts and exhibits of Native American culture are nicely displayed. Temporary exhibits shed light on specific historical periods, crafts, and events. The museum is open 1:00 to 4:30 p.m. Wednesday through Sunday. Admission donations are welcome.

TRAIN TOWN $
20264 Broadway, Sonoma
(707) 938-3912
www.traintown.com
Train Town is the most well-developed scale railroad in America—a joy for anyone of any age. You climb into a miniature train, one-fourth the normal size, and chug your way through 10 acres of planned landscaped park filled with thousands of native trees, animals, bridges over lakes, tunnels, waterfalls, and replicas of historic buildings. Two miniature engines and handcrafted railroad cars take passengers on the 20-minute ride to Lakeville, a pint-sized, western-flavored hamlet populated with geese and ducks. Along the way there's a stop to pet some llamas and goats. Trains operate daily in summer from 10:00 a.m. to 5:00 p.m. In winter it's a shorter, weekend schedule. The fare is $3.75 for all ages.

HISTORIC TOWN OF SONOMA $
Various sites
A national landmark and the largest square of its kind in California, the Sonoma Plaza evokes the feel of Old Europe. It is an ideal picnic spot, with numerous tables under nearly 200 trees, a playground, and a duck pond. Surrounding the plaza are some of the buildings that marked the start of the village, then owned by Mexico and ruled by Gen. Mariano Vallejo. It makes a lovely walking tour, and one $2 ticket, available at any

of the following sites, will give you access to the mission, the barracks, Vallejo's home, and the Petaluma Adobe.

Mission San Francisco Solano, founded in 1823 as the last of California's Franciscan missions, is diagonally opposite the plaza's northeast corner. Today's mission is a faithful re-creation of the original. Only the priests' quarters date from the founding. It's open 10:00 a.m. to 5:00 p.m. daily.

Sonoma Barracks, across from the mission, housed Vallejo's Mexican troops, sheltered the Bear Flag soldiers, and served as a U.S. military headquarters in the 1840s and 1850s. Today the barracks are restored to their Mexican-era appearance, with exhibits inside and an attractive gift shop with California items. Grizzly bears once battled bulls in the enclosed courtyard behind the barracks, while spectators gambled on the outcome. It's open 10:00 a.m. to 5:00 p.m. daily.

On the north side of the Plaza, the Swiss Hotel has a bar and restaurant that have long been favorites of residents and visitors alike. Originally built as a home for General Vallejo's brother, Salvador, in the late 1830s, it has been known as the Swiss Hotel since the 1880s. The locally famous drink, "Bear's Hair" sherry, is served in the saloon.

Referred to as the Salvador Vallejo Adobe when it was built in the early 1840s, what is now the El Dorado Hotel on the west side of the Plaza is a Monterey colonial adobe. Once a home for Salvador and his family, the structure went on to have a checkered history as a government office, college, winery, and hotel. Subsequently it was occupied by Bear Flag party members and U.S. Gen. John C. Frémont during the opening days of the Mexican-American War. Presbyterian settlers operated Cumberland College at the adobe from 1858 until 1864.

El Paseo de Sonoma (Pinelli Building) is one of several plaza structures built of native stone. The building survived a 1911 fire when Augustino Pinelli let firefighters douse flames with his barrels of wine. Today several shops and restaurants can be found on the passageway behind First Street East and Spain Street. Blue Wing Inn, on East Spain Street across from the mission, was once a rowdy gold rush–era saloon visited by future President Ulysses S. Grant, Lt. William Tecumseh Sherman, Kit Carson, and notorious bandit Joaquin Murietta.

Gen. Vallejo's Home (Lachryma Montis) is not on the plaza but 3 blocks down West Spain Street. Vallejo built this Gothic revival home at a cost of $50,000 in 1851 and named it Lachryma Montis ("tears of the mountain") because of a spring on the property. Abandoning Spanish-style architecture, he built a grand Victorian and furnished it with European imports. He had redwood lumber hauled in from the port at Vallejo, while bricks and marble mantels were shipped from Hawaii. Landscaping, a glass pavilion (now gone), and every convenience of the time were included. The Vallejos' 15th and 16th children were born at Lachryma Montis.

Vallejo's once-great holdings eventually were reduced to only the acreage around this home. Many of the original furnishings are still in place. The kitchen located in a separate building kept the heat of cooking away from the rest of the house. A charming little guesthouse remains on the property, and a short walk up the hill leads to the room of one of the Vallejo children. Picnic tables are set around a stream that runs through the property. Now a state historic park, Lachryma Montis is open 10:00 a.m. to 5:00 p.m. daily.

JACK LONDON STATE HISTORIC PARK $
2400 London Ranch Road off Arnold Drive, Glen Ellen
(707) 938-5216
www.jacklondonpark.com
www.parks.ca.gov/?page_id=478
This is my favorite park in all of Sonoma County, the kind of place where you can spend an entire day. Jack London called it his Beauty Ranch, but he wanted to achieve more than aesthetic satisfaction here. His goal was to create a scientifically operated ranch where new techniques could be developed. Many buildings remain from his experiment in ranching: stone stables where he kept his prize horses, the last vestiges of his famous scientific piggery, and the farmhouse where he lived for five years, wrote most of

his stories, and died. In the center of the 1,400 acres is the rubble of Wolf House, the lava-stone mansion he had hoped to live in, which burned to the ground in 1913. The half-mile trail to the Wolf House ruins passes through a forest of oak, madrone, and buckeye trees. Nearby is London's grave, marked only by a stone from the ruins of the house.

At the top of the hill, as you enter the state park, is the House of Happy Walls, built by London's wife, Charmian, after his death. It contains memorabilia of his life as a war correspondent, his abortive trip around the world with Charmian in a ship he designed himself, and a load of information about his writing life. Displayed are some of the 600 rejection slips he received, the first from the *Saturday Evening Post*. Seven miles of hiking, mountain biking, and equestrian trails are available. The museum is open daily except for major holidays from 10:00 a.m. to 5:00 p.m., and admission is $6 per car.

PETALUMA HISTORICAL MUSEUM   FREE
20 Fourth Street, Petaluma
(707) 778-4398
www.petalumamuseum.com
A large, freestanding, stained-glass dome accents the beauty of this 1906 Carnegie Free Library—one of the hundreds that philanthropist Andrew Carnegie built and donated in the early 20th century. You'll find a 19th-century horse-drawn fire wagon here, along with Native American artifacts, pioneer relics, and displays describing Petaluma's dairy and poultry beginnings. An exhibit about the Petaluma River illustrates how the town became an important manufacturing and trading hub when Petaluma was one of California's largest cities.

The museum offers brochures for self-guided walking tours of the city, featuring the famous Iron Front buildings and beautiful Victorian homes. In addition, docents costumed in Victorian attire lead guided tours of historic downtown on weekends. It's free, but donations are accepted. Hours are 10:00 a.m. to 4:00 p.m. Thursday through Saturday, noon to 3:00 p.m. Sunday.

PETALUMA ADOBE STATE HISTORIC PARK $
3325 Adobe Road at Casa Grande Road, Petaluma
(707) 762-4871
www.petalumaadobe.com
www.visitpetaluma.com
Once the headquarters of Gen. Mariano Vallejo's 100-square-mile Rancho Petaluma, this enormous two-story adobe overlooking Petaluma stands as a monument to California's early history. A self-guided tour of the structure offers views of the period-furnished kitchen, the living quarters where the Vallejo family stayed when they spent their summer holiday at the rancho, and the guest rooms. The rustic chairs and candle sconces are of Spanish motif. Outside you will find replicas of the beehive ovens where cooks baked bread for rancho residents. Occasionally the ranger in charge may put in a loaf or two, using the same recipe the Vallejo servants used. The ranch is open daily (except Thanksgiving, Christmas, and New Year's Day) from 10:00 a.m. to 5:00 p.m. The $3 admission fee entitles you to visit any of the sites on historic Sonoma Plaza (see previous listing).

LUTHER BURBANK HOME AND GARDENS $
Santa Rosa and Sonoma Avenues, Santa Rosa
(707) 524-5445
www.lutherburbank.org
During his 53 years in Santa Rosa, horticulturist Luther Burbank changed the plant world, improving and hybridizing more than 800 varieties (see the close-up "Genius in the Garden" in this chapter). This National Historic Landmark features Burbank's home, a carriage house, and the greenhouse where he performed his experiments. Outside you'll find a lovely garden filled with the plants Burbank introduced to the world. Docent-led house tours are offered on the half hour Tuesday through Sunday from April through October. House tours, which are $4 for adults and free for children 12 and younger, run 10:00 a.m. to 3:30 p.m. The gardens are open daily at no charge or $3 for an audio self-tour.

JESSE PETER NATIVE AMERICAN
ART MUSEUM   FREE
Santa Rosa Junior College, 1501
Mendocino Avenue, Santa Rosa
(707) 527-4479
www.santarosa.edu/museum

Dedicated to arts and crafts created by Native Americans from the 19th century up to the present day, this museum contains an extensive assortment of baskets, including the extraordinarily beautiful baskets of the Pomo tribe. Most items displayed represent the work of California tribes, although beadwork of the Plains and Plateau tribes is on hand as well as some Eskimo art. There are replicas of a southwestern pueblo, a Pomo roundhouse, and a Klamath River *xonta* (a family shelter). This museum was undergoing renovation in 2008; please call the number above for an update.

SONOMA COUNTY MUSEUM $
425 Seventh Street, Santa Rosa
(707) 579-1500
www.sonomacountymuseum.org

Housed in the old post office built after the 1906 earthquake, the museum was moved and restored as a part of local grassroots activities. The lower floor is devoted to an extensive collection of art exhibits, history and heritage of the county, and photographs of the local landscapes and people. The second floor is given over to exciting temporary exhibits. Past ones have included displays of cartoon art and a woodworking exhibit of bowls, boxes, and furniture. The Museum Shop has a particularly intriguing assortment of books and items with Sonoma County themes. The museum and gift shop are open 11:00 a.m. to 5:00 p.m. Wednesday through Sunday year-round. Admission is $5 for adults, $2 for seniors and students.

REDWOOD EMPIRE ICE ARENA $$
1667 West Steele Lane, Santa Rosa
(707) 546-7147
www.snoopyshomeice.com
www.snoopygift.com

Outside of Charlie Brown, who will always be universally loved, the Redwood Empire Ice Arena may be the most appreciated gift cartoonist Charles Schulz (1922–2000) gave Sonoma County. Even if you don't have time to lace up skates and take a spin around the arena, it's fun to drive by for a quick look at the building and a visit to Snoopy's Gift Shop nearby, which sells hundreds of items honoring the Peanuts gang. Schulz's career started in Minnesota and ballooned to fame, with his work appearing in more than 1,800 newspapers in 65 countries worldwide. The arena offers a full range of skating, and many world champions have glided across the ice here. Open daily, but hours vary, with mornings reserved for special programs and classes. The cost is $9 for adults and teens and $7 for children younger than 12 (weekends); prices are slightly lower weekdays.

CHARLES M. SCHULZ MUSEUM
AND RESEARCH CENTER $$
2301 Hardies Lane, Santa Rosa
(707) 579-4452
www.schulzmuseum.org

Peanuts creator Charles Schulz didn't live long enough to see this museum dedicated to his legacy come to life (he died in early 2000), but he would be humbled by the result. Adjacent to Schulz's Redwood Empire Ice Arena (see previous listing), the $8 million museum opened in 2002. Within its 27,000 square feet are permanent and temporary displays of the cartoonist's 50-year body of work; a research library and archives for students, cartoonists, and scholars; and classrooms. Worth seeing is the 17-by-22-foot mural crafted from more than 3,500 individual Peanuts comic strips printed on ceramic tiles. Also on display is the wooden drawing board where Schulz drew his one-dimensional characters, in a re-creation of his art studio. Admission is $8 for adults, $5 for seniors and children under 18, and free for toddlers. Closed Tuesday.

i Inside the Charles M. Schulz Museum is a wall from a Colorado house where the cartoonist briefly lived, on which he painted some of his early cartoon characters in 1951. The artwork was later discovered under layers of paint, and the wall was carefully removed and shipped to Santa Rosa for display in the museum.

SAFARI WEST $$$

3115 Porter Creek Road, Santa Rosa
(707) 579-2551, (800) 616-2695
www.safariwest.com

This is a little different from those drive-through safari parks where tourists outnumber perplexed animals by about 100 to 1. Safari West is a private preserve and working ranch dedicated to conservation and propagation of endangered species—the 400 acres of Safari West are home to 400 exotic mammals and birds. You can gaze at herds of zebra or watch a giraffe crane its mammoth neck to eat out of your hand.

Guests spend an unparalleled two-and-a-half hours on a unique educational trek through the rolling hills of the preserve. Accompanied by a naturalist, groups get the rarest of opportunities to photograph herds of antelope, eland, gazelle, zebra, and many more types of animals. Because the critters live in vast acreage, they are comfortable with vehicles and can be seen up close. (One group was even treated to the birth of an antelope.) Wear comfortable clothing and bring sunscreen and a hat. Oh, and the proprietors can customize tours if you have a particular interest in, say, springboks. Cost of a basic tour is $65 for adults, $30 for children three to nine, and $10 for toddlers. Safari West also includes overnight accommodations. The South African–made "tents" feature hardwood floors, bathrooms, and king-size beds. Visits are by appointment only. Leave your pets at home.

PACIFIC COAST AIR MUSEUM $

2330 Airport Boulevard, Santa Rosa
(707) 575-7900
www.pacificcoastairmuseum.org

Located next to Sonoma County's Charles M. Schulz Airport, the Pacific Coast Air Museum was formed by local aviators interested in restoring and preserving retired military aircraft. The collection ranges from a Korean War–era RF-86 Sabre and Huey helicopter—which saw combat in Vietnam—to an F-16 Viper flown by the commander of the navy's Top Gun flight school, and an F-14A Tomcat that saw duty on several U.S. carriers. The museum is open every Tuesday, Thursday, Saturday, and Sunday from 10:00 a.m. to 4:00 p.m. On the third weekend of each month, museum staff unlatch the canopy of a featured aircraft and let visitors climb aboard to get a feel of what it's like behind the wheel of a war bird. The museum also sponsors a weekend air show—Wings over Wine Country—each August (see the Festivals and Annual Events chapter).

Northern Sonoma

HEALDSBURG MUSEUM   FREE

221 Matheson Street, Healdsburg
(707) 431-3325
www.healdsburgmuseum.org

This museum is in a refurbished Carnegie library building and features both permanent and changing exhibits. The county's history is depicted from prehistoric times to the present, and displays include antique firearms, 19th-century clothing, tools, and an outstanding collection of Pomo basketry and crafts. The archives contain more than 5,000 historical photographs and newspapers dating to 1865. Healdsburg Museum is open Thursday through Sunday 11:00 a.m. to 4:00 p.m.

THE HAND FAN MUSEUM   FREE

327-A Healdsburg Avenue, Healdsburg
(707) 431-2500
www.handfanmuseum.com

Small but mighty, this tiny museum tucked into the north side of Hotel Healdsburg is a personal favorite. Claiming to be the only museum in the United States dedicated to the hand fan, it is overflowing with rare and historic fans, and most are considered pieces of art. Every type imaginable is on display. It might sound like an

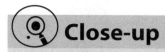

Close-up

Genius in the Garden

Luther Burbank (1849–1926) knew plants not just for what they were but for what they could become. The nation's most renowned and prolific horticulturist, he dedicated his life to the propagation of new plant varieties, many of which are still valued today for their extraordinary beauty and utility.

Born in Lancaster, Massachusetts, Luther began his career at the age of 21, when he accidentally discovered a potato that had sprouted a seed ball on his farm. From the 23 seeds he found in the seed ball, Luther developed a hardy, high-yielding variety of potato, the "Burbank potato," which eventually became the predominant type grown in the United States—today's russet potato is a descendant of the Burbank variety. But this was only the beginning for a man whose name would become associated with nearly a thousand other new plants. Perhaps sensing his destiny, Luther quickly sold the rights to his new potato for $150 to a local seed dealer and used the proceeds to finance a trip to Santa Rosa, where his brother had been living.

Inspired by his brother's letters describing a gardener's paradise, Luther had dreamed of California for years. When he finally set foot in Santa Rosa in 1875, he found it beyond even his expectations. It wasn't long before Luther acquired some land near "downtown" Santa Rosa—then a jumble of 726 houses, 6 hotels, 7 churches, and 22 saloons—and began his work. Though he had achieved some notoriety through early efforts, it wasn't until 1893, when he published his catalog *New Creations in Fruits and Flowers*, that he achieved widespread fame. At the time the propagation of new plant varieties was a slow, tedious process, and such a large offering—more than a hundred varieties—by a single individual was a surprise, if not downright shocking. Among individuals and groups who believed that God alone could "create" a new plant, Luther was considered an infidel. But the results quickly trumped the skeptics. Gardeners from coast to coast and abroad bought Luther's plants, which were exceptionally hardy and high yielding. The catalog turned Luther into a popular hero, and his stature ranked with such greats as Thomas Edison and Henry Ford—Edison and Ford both personally admired Luther and visited him at his home in Santa Rosa.

Luther's plant varieties are legion, and it is difficult to do justice to the breadth and inventiveness of his creations. Varieties such as elephant garlic, plumcot (a cross between a plum and apricot), and the ubiquitous Shasta daisy are still popular today. At the time of his death in 1926, Luther had more than 3,000 experiments under way and was growing more than 5,000 species. He is buried near the house in an unmarked grave.

Throughout his long career Luther sought to produce high-quality plant varieties that would help increase the world's food supply. But more important, his work was inspired by a deep love of beauty. "The urge to beauty," he wrote, "and the need for beautiful and gracious and lovely things in life is as vital as the need for bread."

attraction only ladies will enjoy, but gentlemen find it fascinating too.

RIVER ROCK CASINO　　　　　　　　　**FREE**
3250 Highway 128, Geyserville
(707) 857-2777
www.riverrockcasino.com
I wouldn't normally encourage you to play fast

and loose with your hard-earned cash, but River Rock is such a different sort of attraction—or distraction, if you will—that it's worth mentioning. When you've had enough worshipping of the grape, head up the hillside outside Geyserville for some Las Vegas–style gambling (watch the signs for Dry Creek Rancheria). The casino was first erected in 2002 as an extravagant tent, and

The Luther Burbank Home and Gardens in Santa Rosa stand as a testament to the nation's greatest horticulturist. JOHN NAGIECKI

I firmly believe, from what I have
seen, that this is the chosen spot
of all this earth as far as Nature is
concerned.

—Luther Burbank

a huge parking structure soon followed. In spring 2008, the Indian tribe that owns the casino broke ground on a $300 million luxury resort hotel at the site. Disputes between the casino's rural neighbors and battles with the county board of supervisors have been going on for years, but River Rock looks like it's here to stay. It's free to walk in the door, but after that the cost is up to you.

West County/Russian River

LUTHER BURBANK GOLD RIDGE EXPERIMENT FARM   FREE
7781 Bodega Avenue, Sebastopol
(707) 829-6711
www.wschs-grf.pon.net
On this 18-acre experimental farm, horticulturist

Luther Burbank built a cottage and worked to perfect Gravenstein apples, plums, cherries, grapes, and lilies. Although he lived and worked in Santa Rosa, this is where he conducted his horticultural research between 1895 and 1926. Free guided tours, available by appointment from April through mid-October, explore Burbank's gardens and visit his restored cottage. The gardens are open for free self-guided tours year-round.

WEST COUNTY MUSEUM FREE
261 South Main Street, Sebastopol
(707) 829-6711
www.wschs-grf.pon.net
A restored railroad depot houses the collections of the Western Sonoma County Historical Society. The Triggs Reference Room contains books, photographs, magazines, newspapers, audiotapes, and videotapes on local history. West County Museum is open 1:00 to 4:00 p.m. Thursday through Sunday. There is no admission fee, but donations are welcomed.

CHILDREN'S BELL TOWER FREE
2255 Highway 1, Bodega Bay
(707) 875-3866
www.sonomacoastguide.com/childrensbell
tower/childrensbelltower.htm
In 1994 Nicholas Green, a seven-year-old boy from Bodega Bay, was tragically shot and killed by robbers during a vacation with his family in Italy. Nicholas's parents bravely chose to donate his organs to seven sick Italians, who were given a new chance to live a full life. The heartbreaking yet life-affirming tale received worldwide media attention and was turned into a movie. It also gave birth to this moving monument dedicated to the memory of Nicholas and the positive aftermath of his death. Families, schools, and churches around Italy donated all of the 140 bells that ring the 18-foot-high tower. The large bell in the center, blessed by Pope John Paul II, is inscribed with the names of the seven recipients of Nicholas's organs. The memorial is behind the Bodega Bay Community Center, at the north edge of town on the ocean side of the highway. Park in the small lot behind the center and stroll down to the tower. (Nicholas is buried in Bodega, a short distance inland. His grave is also an inspirational sight.)

FORT ROSS STATE HISTORIC PARK $
19005 Highway 1, north of Jenner
(707) 847-3286
www.fortrossstatepark.org
www.parks.ca.gov/?page_id=449
On a grassy, windswept bluff north of Jenner stands a ruddy, wooden stockade, its main gate facing the Pacific Ocean. The 14-foot walls are made of weather-beaten redwood. Inside is a small chapel dedicated to St. Nicholas and topped with an orthodox cross. In another building, seal and otter pelts hang on walls above casks marked in Cyrillic characters. Now part of a state historic park, Fort Ross provides a fascinating glimpse into the history of the settlement founded with the aim of supplying food for the fledgling Russian colony in Alaska, where Russia's eastward push ended in the early 1800s (see the History chapter). The museum in the visitor center exhibits Russian and Native American artifacts, and the gift shop offers crafts made by the local Pomo tribe as well as goods imported from Russia.

Join more than 100 costumed participants for the annual Cultural Heritage Day—held on the third or last Saturday of July—to get a taste of what life was like for the Russians 200 years ago (see the Festivals and Annual Events chapter). The park is open daily 10:00 a.m. to 4:30 p.m. There is no entrance fee for cyclists or hikers. Vehicles pay $6 for parking.

BERRY'S SAW MILL FREE
Highway 116 and Cazadero Highway,
Cazadero
(707) 865-2365
www.berrysmill.com
This authentic sawmill offers visitors an opportunity to see trees sawed, split, and planed into usable lumber. Visitors can explore the mill on an informal basis—guided tours are not offered. It's

open at no charge Monday through Friday 7:45 a.m. to 4:30 p.m. Call ahead first to make certain the sawmill is running on the particular day you wish to visit.

HOT-AIR BALLOONS

It's hard to find a Wine Country brochure that doesn't include a photo of a multicolored hot-air balloon drifting over vine-scored hills. Somewhere along the way, ballooning became part of the everyday scenery. The flying machines are quite safe, and most pilots are FAA certified; feel free to ask about their qualifications when you phone. It is true that balloon pilots have limited control over the direction of their rigs, except on a vertical scale. This means there is always a chance you'll make an unscheduled stop in an open field, but it will likely be a gentle one, and the company's chase team will be right on your heels.

As for capacity, the balloon gondolas accommodate anywhere from 4 to 16 passengers. Those of average size hold 6 to 8 people. Dress in layers when riding in a balloon—the shifts in altitude, the breezes, and the heat from the fire make it hard to predict what level of clothing will be comfortable. And if you are a tall person, be sure to bring a cap—radiant heat from the burner can be unpleasant after an hour or so. Count on rates starting at approximately $200 per person (kids a bit less), which might include a preflight continental breakfast or postflight champagne brunch, and a souvenir photo. There are many balloon companies in the two-county Wine Country region, but here are a few that can lift you up:

Napa County
BALLOONS ABOVE THE VALLEY
(707) 253-2222, (800) 464-6824
www.balloonrides.com

NAPA VALLEY ALOFT
(707) 944-8638, (900) 627-2759
www.nvaloft.com

NAPA VALLEY BALLOONS
(707) 944-0228, (800) 253-2224
www.napavalleyballoons.com

Sonoma County
A BALLOON OVER SONOMA
(707) 546-3360
www.aballoonoversonoma.com

ABOVE THE WINE COUNTRY
(707) 538-7359, (888) 238-6359
www.balloontours.com

UP & AWAY
(707) 836-0171, (800) 711-2998
www.up-away.com

OTHER WAYS TO SEE THE SIGHTS

Napa County
WINE COUNTRY HELICOPTERS $$$$
2030 Airport Road, Napa County Airport, Napa
(707) 226-8470
www.winecountryhelicopters.com

Here's a chance to get above the traffic and see Napa Valley and Sonoma County the way birds do. This service offers a wide range of tours and will also arrange custom tours. Certified pilots steer a four-passenger Bell Jet Ranger or a six-passenger Bell Long Ranger to just about any place in Wine Country. Most flights begin and end at Napa County Airport; other arrangements can be made to your specifications. A basic 45-minute tour over Napa Valley is $1,200; a more extensive flight over Napa Valley and Sonoma Valley, lasting approximately 65 minutes, is $1,600. Other options include a trek to the Russian River for a picnic, flying to and from the Rockpile appellation in Sonoma County for wine tasting, or a six-hour chopper tour to a working cattle ranch with horseback riding thrown in. They will even whiz you to Lake Tahoe or the Hearst Castle (San Simeon) in Southern California, if you so desire. The sky's the limit, weather permitting.

NAPA RIVER ADVENTURES $$$
2399 Streblow Drive, Napa
(707) 224-9080
www.napariveradventures.com
Ready to watch some wildlife along the Napa River? Adventures await during regularly scheduled two-hour cruises for up to 11 people aboard an electric boat. Bring along a bottle of wine, if you'd like, and explore nature in comfort, spotting herons, river otters, and egrets as you float gently on tidal waters (no rapids on this river). This is a great adventure for the kids too, who ride for half price if they are 12 or younger. Several package deals are available, including a golf-and-cruise combo and a wine-tasting/cruise package. Reservations for all cruises are a must.

NAPA VALLEY & SONOMA BIKE TOURS $$$
6488 Washington Street, Yountville
(800) 707-2453
www.napavalleybiketours.com
You feel the breeze, you burn the calories, but someone else wrestles with the logistics. Sound all right? These winery tours begin at 9:30 a.m., end about 3:00 p.m., and cost $139 per person. Along with a bicycle and helmet, you'll get a fully catered picnic, a friendly guide, and a support van to lug bottles of wine (and bodies of worn-out riders). Bring along some cash for the tasting fees. Napa Valley Bike Tours also rents cycles for two hours ($20) and by the day ($30)—tandems run $40 and $65.

CALISTOGA COOL WINE TOUR $$$
Calistoga Bike Shop, 1318 Lincoln Avenue, Calistoga
(707) 942-9687, (866) 942-2453
www.calistogabikeshop.com
With this tour you get complimentary wine tasting at up to eight wineries that are slightly more off the beaten track (and therefore safer for two-wheelers). The bike shop will pick up your wine purchases from the wineries so you don't have to figure out an imaginative way to bring them back on the bike. Even if you tire out, the shop

will come and get you. It's an affordable tour, too: $79 per person.

Sonoma County

SONOMA SEGWAY $$$
524 Broadway, Sonoma
(707) 938-2080
www.sonomasegway.com
You've probably seen them, those goofy two-wheeled people movers called Segways. Well, somebody thought the machines would make great touring vehicles, and they were right. With this guided tour, costing $99 per person, you get more than two hours of rolling time. After a quick lesson in the idiosyncrasies of the Segway, you visit a winery and a cheese factory, and end your tour with a free bottle of wine. There's just one tour a day, beginning at 10:00 a.m. Children age 12 and up are welcome.

SCENIC AERIAL TOURS $$$
5010 Flightline Drive, Santa Rosa
(707) 542-8687
www.northcoastair.com
Pick your pleasure—coast, vineyards, or San Francisco? Sweeping over our beautiful scenery from the air in a small plane is a wonderful way to drink in the sights, especially if your time is limited. This service flies seven days a week, as long as the weather cooperates. Flat rates (not per person) begin at $235 for a 45-minute tour over the coastal waters or above numerous wine-growing valleys. A more extensive vineyard-gazing tour lasts about 100 minutes and costs $283.

GETAWAY ADVENTURES $$$
2228 Northpoint Parkway, Santa Rosa
(707) 568-3040, (800) 499-2453
www.getawayadventures.com
The folks at Getaway do winery tours on bikes (one in upper Napa Valley and another in Dry Creek Valley near Healdsburg), and even a couple of kayak tours on portions of the Russian River. Basic prices start at $125 for the hybrid bike rides; kayak tours start at $145.

HEALDSBURG WALKING TOURS $$
P.O. Box 2097, Healdsburg, CA 95448
(707) 484-6249
www.healdsburgwalkingtours.com
Here's a novel idea: Save gas and walk. That's exactly what Darla Meeker, your intrepid tour guide, would like you to do. She has a variety of walking tours around Healdsburg to choose from: food and wine, chocolate, homes and gardens, even a ghost walk (starting at twilight). The walks range from $20 to $30 per person, and reservations are recommended.

FLYING HORSE CARRIAGE TOURS $$$$
Alexander Valley Vineyards, 8644 Highway 128, Healdsburg
(707) 849-8989
www.flyinghorse.org
The horse-drawn carriage, with seating for six, departs from the winery at 12:30 p.m. and takes a slow route through vineyards. A gourmet picnic lunch is included, and the carriage stops at three additional wineries throughout the four-hour tour. The per-person cost is $125.

BIG RED ENGINE WINE TASTING ADVENTURES $$$
Hoffman House Cafe, 21712 Geyserville Avenue, Geyserville
(707) 857-3099
www.bigredengine.com
If you've ever wanted to ride in a vintage fire engine, here's your chance. For $75 per person, this company will whisk you away on a five-hour tour that begins in Geyserville at 11:00 a.m. The engines—a 1947 American LaFrance and a 1933 Seagrave—accommodate eight adults and stop at five to seven tasting rooms along the way through the Alexander, Dry Creek, and Russian River Valleys. The tours are available between April and September.

FESTIVALS AND ANNUAL EVENTS

In Wine Country every season brings its share of special events. From January to December there's always some kind of music, food, or farm celebration going on. In late winter we have wine barrel tastings and olive-themed events, and in autumn it's the "crush" and a slew of harvest fairs. When spring blossoms begin to appear—whether apple, pear, or the venerated mustard blossom—they are saluted in grand style. Summer is for wine auctions, county fairs, an ugly dog contest, and a rodeo, too. Animals also make a good excuse for a party. If it swims, flies, or crawls, chances are there's a festival in this region to honor it. Once upon a time, we even had an annual Slug Festival, complete with chefs cooking up the large and slimy creatures—called "banana" slugs around these parts—into tasty recipes. But animal rights activists were not amused, and the good time eventually came to an end. Wineries play a major role in this celebratory milieu, sponsoring concerts and other major cultural events. Their lovely courtyards, grand estate lawns, and unique wine caves cry out for special events, and they are some of the best places to listen to music, whether it's a symphony, chamber music, or jazz. Some weekends there are so many festivals going on, it's difficult to choose which to attend. But I've selected some popular favorites to get you started. For more information, check with the local chambers of commerce listed in the Area Overview chapter.

JANUARY

Sonoma County

SONOMA VALLEY OLIVE FESTIVAL
Various locations, Sonoma
(707) 996-1090, (866) 996-1090
www.sonomavalley.com/olivefestival
In case you didn't know, we grow lots of olives in Wine Country. So holding a shindig to salute the mighty olive seemed like a natural thing to do. The first annual Sonoma Valley Olive Festival took place during winter 2001-02, with oil tastings, special dinners, demonstrations of olives being turned into oil, a visual arts contest with olives as the theme, and more. The Feast of the Olive Dinner is the most expensive event, at $175 per person; the wrap-up event is VinOlivo, a gala with food, wine, and olives, of course. Other festivities vary in price. The whole affair begins in early December and ends in late February.

WINTER WINELAND
Various locations, Russian River and Healdsburg area
(707) 433-4335, (800) 723-6336
www.wineroad.com
During the sometimes gloomy days of winter, the Russian River wine-growing region comes alive for Winter Wineland. On a weekend in mid-January, rain or shine, wine lovers can stop in at more than 100 wineries for special tastings of wine and food. The latter might include tri-tip steak, beef stew, or andouille sausage. The 2008 event was the 16th annual. It's $50 per person for the weekend, $40 for Sunday only, and $20 for designated drivers (who at least get to sample the food). With a wristband and a logo glass, you move at your own pace from one location to another. This is strictly a 21-and-over event; no infants and no children, please, and leave the dogs at home, too.

OLD-TIME FIDDLE CONTEST

Cloverdale Fairgrounds, 1 Citrus Fair Drive, Cloverdale

(707) 894-2067

www.cloverdalehistoricalsociety.org/fiddle

Dozens of contestants, novice to pro, gather at the fairgrounds on Citrus Fair Drive for an old-fashioned fiddling contest that's been taking place for more than 30 years. But some of the best action is not on the stage; it's in a side room where curious visitors can look in on some wild, free-form jamming. This event is sponsored by the Cloverdale Historical Society on the last weekend of January. General admission is $12.50 for one day, $20.00 for both days. For $8.00 more you can kick up your heels at the Saturday-night dance.

FEBRUARY

Napa County

MUSTARD MAGIC

The Culinary Institute of America at Greystone, 2555 Main Street, St. Helena

(707) 938-1133

www.mustardfestival.org

When the mustard begins carpeting the vineyards with its eye-popping yellow blossoms, it's time to party! This grand fete officially launches the annual Napa Valley Mustard Festival on a Saturday in late January or early February. The focus is on the arts, including an exhibition and silent auction of entries in the Mustard Festival Fine Art Contest. Other pleasantries include hors d'oeuvres and desserts created by prominent local chefs, ultrapremium wine tastings, and music (live opera, for instance). Admission to Mustard Magic is $150 in advance, $175 at the door.

CHOCOLATE CABERNET FANTASY

Sterling Vineyards, 1111 Dunaweal Lane, Calistoga

(707) 942-3345, (800) 726-6136

www.sterlingvineyards.com

Looking for a little decadence? Nero might have been attracted to this three-hour get-together off Dunaweal Lane, about 2 miles south of Calistoga. Feed your face with luscious desserts (mostly chocolate) and Sterling's renowned Cabs, and surrender to the mix of flavors. There is dance music too. The fantasy is held on a Friday or Saturday night around Valentine's Day. Tickets are $20, with all proceeds going to charity.

Sonoma County

WILD STEELHEAD FESTIVAL

Healdsburg area

(707) 484-6438

www.healdsburgsteelheadfest.org

The annual return of wild steelhead, a threatened species, is celebrated on a weekend in early February in Healdsburg. It begins with a gala dinner at Hotel Healdsburg on Friday night ($100 per person), moving into Saturday with all manner of fun: fish cooking demonstrations, wine tasting, demonstrations of fly-fishing, education booths, and a free trout pond for the kids to enjoy. Most of the action takes place in Healdsburg Plaza. The 2008 event was the first year for this festival, but based on its success, I believe it's a keeper.

CITRUS FAIR

Cloverdale Fairgrounds, 1 Citrus Fair Drive, Cloverdale

(707) 894-3992

www.cloverdalecitrusfair.org

Here's how to brighten up winter. On the weekend nearest Presidents' Day, the citizens of Cloverdale come together in a jolly event organized by the Citrus Fair Association. It starts off with a downtown parade, then moves out to the fairgrounds, with square dancing, country-western dancing, line dancing, and regular dancing. There is a carnival for young people and beer tasting and wine tasting for grownups. Live entertainment can range from clowns to local blues or rock bands. Admission is $6 for adults, $5 for seniors and kids ages 6 to 13, and $3 for kids 5 and under. Carnival wristbands are $25.

ROMANTICA AND LE GRAND DÎNER
Meadowood, St. Helena and Domaine
Chandon, Yountville
(707) 938-1133
www.mustardfestival.org

These two events, a couple weekends apart in February, continue the mustard worship during the Mustard Festival. Romantica is a five-course meal and party at Meadowood loosely tied to Valentine's Day, with tickets fetching $200 per person. Le Grand Dîner goes even further, with a seven-course meal prepared at Étoile, the restaurant at Domaine Chandon, and wine galore. Seating is limited; tickets are $350 per person.

i Grapevine pruning competitions are held every February in Sonoma and Napa Counties to honor North Coast farmworkers and bestow upon two of them the "best pruner" championship title.

MARCH

Napa County

THE AWARDS
Black Stallion Winery
4089 Silverado Trail, Napa
(707) 938-1133
www.mustardfestival.org

Should your springtime excursions begin to convince you that mustard is merely a treat for the eyes, here is an evening that pits Napa Valley's best chefs in a spread-off, and it's also the worldwide mustard competition awards ceremony. Champion mustard makers descend on Napa Valley from all over the world to vie for awards. Guests get to taste the entries, along with food and wine. There is live music as well. The event costs $100 ($150 at the door) and is held the night before the Marketplace (see next listing).

THE MARKETPLACE
Robert Mondavi Winery
Highway 29, Oakville
(707) 938-1133
www.mustardfestival.org

This is the Mustard Festival's signature event, and the most popular (and affordable). Enjoy cooking demonstrations by celebrity chefs, wine and mustard tastings, gourmet food products, microbrews, fine art, local crafts, horse-drawn carriage rides, eclectic musical offerings on three stages, historical displays, and barrel-making demonstrations. It's a two-day event (11:00 a.m. to 5:00 p.m. both days) on a weekend in mid-March. Admission is $35 for adults, $10 for students, and $5 for children under five. Net proceeds benefit a wide range of nonprofit groups.

A TASTE OF YOUNTVILLE
Washington Street, Yountville
(707) 944-0904
www.mustardfestival.org

Yountville likes to boast that it has more gourmet restaurants and premium wineries than any other town of comparable size. So on the third weekend in March, the hamlet sets up a solid-mile gauntlet of food, olive oil, vinegar, mustard, wine, and beer to prove it. Local merchants get into the act with fashion shows, tours, furniture restoration displays, and even tips on table setting. Most demonstrations for this Mustard Festival event are free, and tasting tickets are reasonable. Even if you are beyond temptation, it might be worth your time to stroll the 6 blocks through downtown just to hear the live music and watch the entertainment.

THE PHOTO FINISH
Mumm Napa Valley, 8445 Silverado Trail,
Rutherford
(707) 938-1133
www.mustardfestival.org

With this grand finale, the Mustard Festival usually leaves 'em longing for more as it heads into hibernation for a year. Mumm's hallways and visitor center are filled with lovers of photography, food, wine, and music (doesn't leave many of us out, does it?) on the last Saturday in March or the first in April. The food is by Napa Valley chefs, the wine is primarily from Silverado Trail labels, and the camera work is by the contestants in the annual Napa Valley Mustard Festival Photography Contest. Awards are presented in the tasting room at about 9:00 p.m. Tickets to the Photo Finish cost $90 per person in advance, $125 at the door.

Sonoma County

RUSSIAN RIVER BARREL TASTING
Alexander, Dry Creek, and Russian
River Valleys
(707) 433-4335, (800) 723-6336
www.wineroad.com
This annual event sponsored by the Russian River Wine Road Association has become a victim of its own success. It's so popular that in 2007 it was expanded to two weekends in early March instead of just one. The backroads of Sonoma County's famous wine regions become clogged with wine lovers seeking a day or two of tasting, entertainment, and viticulture education. The tasting focuses on unreleased wines from wineries located in the Alexander, Dry Creek, and Russian River Valleys, offering participants the opportunity to taste the juice straight from the barrel and to purchase "futures." There may be some light munchies here and there, but food is not the point. You can also expect live entertainment at a few places. You pay $20 for a special logo glass at the first participating winery you visit, then take the glass with you for free tastes at many more wineries.

ARTISAN CHEESE FESTIVAL
Sheraton Sonoma County Hotel, 745 Baywood Drive, Petaluma
(707) 283-2890
www.artisancheesefestival.com
Wine and cheese were meant for each other. So what better place to hold a cheese festival than in Wine Country? Besides wine, olives, and mustards, this region is brimming with fabulous award-winning cheeses crafted by small producers. This festival also includes cheesemakers from throughout California. The weekend begins on Friday night with a reception and tasting,

followed on Saturday by educational tastings and seminars that cover such topics as easy beginning cheesemaking and basic wine-and-cheese pairings. Prices vary, but plan on $40 for the all-day events on Saturday.

APRIL

Napa County

APRIL IN CARNEROS
Various locations
(800) 909-4352
www.carneroswineries.org
The Carneros area, in the bay-cooled hills between Sonoma and Napa, is one of Wine Country's most interesting appellations. You can judge for yourself over one weekend in mid-April, when 20 or more wineries open their doors and stage special events. About a quarter of the participating producers are normally open by appointment only, and others don't even have proper wineries there—guests are welcomed instead to production facilities. New vintages are released, accompanied by barrel tastings, food pairings, arts and crafts, and music. Tickets are $40 per person, valid for both days. Pay at your first stop, then take the logo glass along for admission into the next.

i The men-only Bohemian Grove encampment of some of the world's most powerful leaders and household names, held annually in west Sonoma County near Monte Rio, was lampooned in a 2002 film called *Teddy Bear's Picnic*—the creation of actor/comedy writer Harry Shearer.

KITCHENS IN THE VINEYARDS TOUR
Various locations
(707) 258-5559
www.napavalleymusic.com
The emphasis is on food during this all-day affair in late April or early May that gives you a peek into one-of-a-kind kitchens, dining rooms, and gardens from Napa to St. Helena. Five homes are typically featured, and shuttle buses might

take you to a couple of them. The event, now in its 11th year, benefits Music in the Vineyards' Chamber Music Festival, held in August. A limited number of tickets at $65 are made available.

Sonoma County

SHEEPSHEARING AT THE ADOBE

Petaluma Adobe State Historic Park,
3325 Adobe Road, Petaluma
(707) 762-4871
www.petalumaadobe.com
www.visitpetaluma.com

On a Saturday in mid-April, 4-H'ers and docents gather at the adobe building that was once the ranch home of Gen. Mariano Vallejo (see the History chapter) to demonstrate the arts of wool cleaning, weaving, and sheepshearing (from 11:00 a.m. to 1:00 p.m.). It's all done to pay homage to an age-old craft. Looms are available for those who want to try their hand at it. Bring along a picnic and make a day of it. Admission is $2 for adults.

BUTTER AND EGG DAYS

Various locations, Petaluma
(707) 763-0344
www.petalumadowntown.com
www.visitpetaluma.com

Petaluma celebrates its storied past through this popular event. Once known as the world's egg basket, Petaluma is now largely dairy country, thus the hometown Butter and Egg Days parade. This includes an egg toss in downtown and a parade of marching bands, floats, and (best of all) residents dressed as chickens and pats of butter. Contests for the Cutest Little Chick in Town and cow-chip tossing add to the fun. It all happens the last complete weekend in April, and there are food booths, other entertainment, and an antiques fair.

APPLE BLOSSOM FESTIVAL

Various locations, Sebastopol
(877) 828-4748
www.sebastopol.org

It's a weekend in late April, and it's a salute to the apple and its snow-white blooms. Festivities include the crowning of the Apple Blossom Queen, a mile-long parade down Main Street, and two days of good-time partying with plenty of blues, country, and gospel music. There's an art show, crafts made by local artisans, and plenty of products made from apples. The festival is sponsored by the local chamber of commerce, and events are held in Ives Park (282 High Street) and at the Veterans Memorial Building next door. Admission is $7 for adults, $5 for seniors and students, and free for kids 10 and under.

BODEGA BAY FISHERMEN'S FESTIVAL

Westside Park, Bodega Bay
(707) 875-3866
www.bodegabay.com
www.bbfishfest.com

This annual event takes place at Westside Park during a weekend in April. It features foot races, the Blessing of the Fleet, a boat parade, and a bathtub race that includes tubs crafted out of anything that floats—from Styrofoam to milk cartons. A wreath is dropped into the bay to honor fishermen who have lost their lives. Directions to the park are well posted. It's been going on a long time—the 2008 festival was the 35th. Admission is $8 for adults, $5 for seniors, and kids under 12 get in free.

MAY

Napa County

ITALIAN STREET PAINTING FESTIVAL (LA STRADA DELL'ARTE)

(707) 224-8735
www.napastreetpainting.org

Talented madonnari (street artists) are welcome at this family-friendly, two-day event that offers pros and amateurs alike a chance to show their creative skills with chalk on the sidewalk. There is no cost to participate and the chalk is provided. You can draw as an individual or bring along a team of madonnari. The festival includes a kids' area, where free boxes of chalk are handed out for little ones to do their thing. Expect lots of food, wine, and entertainment, too. On Saturday night an auction is held, with tickets costing $40 per person in advance. The 2008 festival, a fundraiser for New Technology High School in Napa, was the 4th annual.

Sonoma County

PASSPORT TO SONOMA VALLEY
Various locations between Sonoma and Santa Rosa
(707) 935-0803
www.sonomavalleywine.com
Need another excuse to visit more wineries? This is a good one, as it's the wine valley nearest and dearest to my heart (and my home). Held on a weekend in mid-May, Passport gives you access to some wineries not typically open to the public, along with some of the popular locations, too. There are usually more than 40 participating wineries pouring about 200 wines, along with food pairings. The passport costs $50 for the weekend, or $45 for one day; designated drivers pay only $10. The ticket includes your passport and a commemorative wineglass for unlimited tastings.

LUTHER BURBANK ROSE PARADE & FESTIVAL
Downtown Santa Rosa
(707) 542-7673
www.roseparadefestival.com
Find a spot along Santa Rosa's streets on a mid-May weekend to watch a parade that dates from 1894 and now draws more than 20,000 people. Floats created with thousands of roses are the highlight of the parade, which begins in front of Burbank's home on Santa Rosa Avenue and winds its way through town to the Veterans Memorial Building. The event honors the world-famous horticulturist who improved 800 plant varieties, including the Santa Rosa rose, while living in Santa Rosa (see the Attractions chapter). Other festival events take place at various sites in the downtown area and include street fair exhibits, food booths, performances by singing groups, carnival rides, folk dancing, an antiques fair, a firefighter competition, and displays of firefighting equipment.

HEALDSBURG COUNTRY FAIR AND TWILIGHT PARADE
Various locations, Healdsburg
(707) 433-6935
www.healdsburg.com
Scheduled for the last weekend in May, this is the longest-running event in Healdsburg and the only fair in California that's nonprofit. The Future Farmers of America sponsor this event, in which everything's free except the food. There's a parade on Thursday, a livestock show and auction on Friday, and kids' activities on Saturday. Food and game booths are run by local youth organizations.

JUNE

Napa County

AUCTION NAPA VALLEY MEADOWOOD
900 Meadowood Lane, St. Helena
(707) 963-3388
www.napavintners.com
Since it began nearly 30 years ago, the auction has raised more than $77 million for local agencies and nonprofits in health care, youth services, and housing. The auction weekend (the first Thursday-through-Sunday block in June) draws high rollers from around the world, who have the means to bid on limited-production cult wines and wine/dinner/travel packages. There are usually big names from show business at the podium to encourage high bidding, such as Jay Leno and Teri Hatcher in 2005, Geena Davis and Ryan Seacrest in 2006, and Dana Carvey in 2007. (Leno was lured back for another shot at it: He emceed the 2008 auction.) Other celebrities might be milling about too. A limited number of tickets are made available and are usually gone within days. The full four-day package of fun is $5,000 for two; the "daytime" package including the live auction is $2,000 per couple; and the "Friends of Napa Valley" package, for Friday-only events, is $250 per person. (See the close-up in this chapter for more about wine auctions.)

V MARKETPLACE FATHER'S DAY INVITATIONAL AUTO SHOW

V Marketplace, 6525 Washington Street, Yountville
(707) 944-2451
www.vmarketplace.com

Throw out the loud ties and cheap cologne. Take Dad to a car show for Father's Day. The parking lot of V Marketplace will be double-parked with 85 to 90 cars—from Vipers to DeSoto Coupes and from a 1939 Packard limousine to a boss old Woody. While you examine the cars, you can eat, drink (everything from Calistoga water to margaritas), and listen to music. The show runs from 11:00 a.m. to 4:00 p.m. and is free to the public, excluding food.

Sonoma County

OX ROAST

Sonoma Plaza, Sonoma
(707) 938-4626
www.sonomavalley.com

For 40 years, the first Sunday in June has been marked by aromatic smoke rising from the town's central plaza. The annual Ox Roast is one giant picnic with barbecued beef, corn on the cob, and plenty of beer and wine. You'll pay $4 to $10 for the meal (beer and wine are extra), and it all goes to benefit the local community center.

SONOMA LAVENDER FESTIVAL

Near Chateau St. Jean Winery, Kenwood
(707) 523-4411
www.sonomalavender.com/festival.html

Aaaaaah . . . the aroma! For one weekend a year, Sonoma Lavender, a commercial lavender-growing company, swings open its gate for the public to immerse themselves in all things lavender, from soap to food (you haven't lived till you've tried lavender sausages followed by lavender ice cream). The five acres of the fragrant herb are bursting with blooms, ready for picking. There's a gift shop, along with crafts, cooking demonstrations, and more. Parking is $5 per car; pay as you go for the other activities and food. To reach the farm, turn at the entrance to Chateau St. Jean Winery and follow the signs.

WORLD'S UGLIEST DOG CONTEST

Sonoma-Marin Fairgrounds, Petaluma
(707) 283-3247
www.sonoma-marinfair.org

The hairless Chinese Crested is not an attractive pooch. That's why this annual contest, held in late June, with 2008 being its 20th year, attracts so many of these small, homely creatures and their proud owners. The Cresteds may have regular dog names like Archie and Rascal and Lulu, but their tongues hang involuntarily from their typically toothless mouths. Generally the only hair on their bodies are tufted crests on their heads, and most are cursed with unsightly warts to boot. I've watched the competition from the sidelines, and I've seen this ugliness firsthand. Breeds other than the Chinese Crested are encouraged to enter, but it's tough to beat those truly wretched-looking Archies and Lulus. This contest is so popular it's been covered by international media and broadcast on the Animal Planet network. Competitors come from throughout the nation to vie for the coveted title. The Ugliest Dog contest is free with paid admission into the Sonoma-Marin Fair ($14 for adults, $9 for kids, $8 for seniors).

HARMONY FESTIVAL

Sonoma County Fairgrounds, Santa Rosa
(707) 861-2035
www.harmonyfestival.com

For more than two decades, loyal throngs of locals have been buying hemp clothing, eyeing belly dancers, and pounding the drums of world-beat music at this Sonoma County institution. For some, the annual affair in mid-June is like returning to the hippie days of 1967—but the hippies all sport gray ponytails these days. There's always plenty of free music on several stages (Jefferson Starship, Rickie Lee Jones, and Brian Wilson, for example) and a huge number of vendors selling everything from holistic health products to Indian cottons. Admission is about $32 in advance, $37 at the gate.

CLOVERDALE HERITAGE DAY
124 South Cloverdale Boulevard, Cloverdale
(707) 894-4470
www.cloverdale.net
The citizens of Cloverdale close off the main boulevard of town one day each year to celebrate the memory of days past. Events include a pancake breakfast, wine tasting, cow-chip tossing (the local Boys and Girls Club collects the chips), a gold-rush foot race, and a barbecue. There's also country music and dancing outdoors on the plaza. It's all free except the food.

STUMPTOWN DAZE
Main Street and Rodeo Grounds, Guerneville
(707) 869-9000, (707) 865-9854
www.russianrivertravel.com
A parade, with school bands and preschool kids on bikes, starts at 11:00 a.m. Saturday and follows a route that's subject to local politics, so you might want to call in advance to find out where to park your folding chair. After the parade everyone heads over to the town of Duncans Mills, about 6 miles west of Guerneville on Highway 116. At 2:00 p.m. the rodeo starts, with all those events you expect—calf roping, bull riding, and barrel racing. On Sunday there's more free rodeo and some horseback games. Where'd the name originate? Guerneville gained the moniker "Stumptown" in its early days when redwood trees were mercilessly chopped down, leaving only a forest of stumps.

JULY

Napa County

NAPA COUNTY FAIR
Napa County Fairgrounds, 1435 North Oak Street, Calistoga
(707) 942-5111
www.napacountyfairgrounds.com
This celebration (during Fourth of July weekend) features plenty of wine to taste, but there's also the usual assortment of carnival rides, livestock exhibits, arts and crafts, and cavity-creating snacks. The fair includes one or two nights of sprint-car racing and two nights of concerts, with recent headliners such as country music heavyweights LeAnn Rimes, Toby Keith, and Faith Hill. Admission is $7 for adults; $3 for kids ages 6 to 12; 6 and under get in free.

FOURTH OF JULY CELEBRATIONS
Napa (707) 226-7455
Calistoga (707) 942-6333
www.napachamber.org
www.calistogachamber.com
Veterans Park is the gathering place for a slew of activity in Napa, including food, carnival games, and wine tasting. Since 1995 the patriotism has expanded to include eight hours of music at the park by a lineup of five or six bands. Serving as interlude to the Napa County Fair is a sublime slice of Americana in Calistoga. People come from miles around for the town's annual Silverado Parade, placing lawn chairs along the route hours in advance. Past parades have featured the sparkling rigs of the volunteer fire department, horsemen, bikers, clowns, a kazoo corps, and floats ranging from sweet to absurd. The procession starts at 11:00 a.m.

Sonoma County

OLD-FASHIONED FOURTH OF JULY PARADE AND PLAZA CELEBRATION
Sonoma Plaza
(707) 938-4626
www.sonomavalley.com
You'd think someone rolled back the clock a few decades to see how Sonoma celebrated Independence Day. In fact, some locals say the Fourth of July is their favorite holiday. Arrive early for a good place to watch the 10:00 a.m. parade that circles Sonoma Plaza. After the parade, townsfolk assemble in the plaza for more band music, the singing of the national anthem, a patriotic speech, and the presentation of awards for parade entrants. There's plenty of fun for kids, including vintage carnival games.

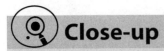 **Close-up**

Wine Auctions for Charity: From Ultrachic to Down-home

Napa Valley and Sonoma Valley are only a few miles apart, yet the two regions are worlds apart when comparing their annual wine auctions for charity. Auction Napa Valley is the big kahuna of charity wine auctions, one of the largest of its kind in the world. On the quieter side of the Mayacmas range, the smaller Sonoma Valley Harvest Wine Auction shares the same noble goal as its neighbor: to raise gobs of money for local charities.

The number of lots (or packages) up for bid at each auction varies significantly; some are wine only, from one bottle to many, perhaps in custom-designed boxes. Other lots can be a combination of wine, travel, luxury cars, and even a shot at greatness: a lot at the 2007 Napa Valley auction included a walk-on role in the TV series *Ugly Betty*. Bids such as the $650,000 paid for eight double magnums—that's 24 liters—of Screaming Eagle Cabernet Sauvignon really add up: In 2005 the Napa Valley auction raised more than $10 million for charity in one weekend. In 2007 the total was down a bit, but no less impressive: $7.48 million. That included a record-breaking single bid of $1.1 million for a trip to Italy for four and three 3-liter bottles of Stagliano Sangiovese from the Staglin Family Vineyard lot. It was purchased by the chairman of Symantec Corp.

While the Napa Valley auction weekend has always had "chic" written all over it, the Sonoma Valley affair by comparison is more "down home." The Sonoma Valley is no less refined when it comes to wine affairs and winemaking talent, but the Sonoma vintners decided long ago that their auction wouldn't be as big or as highfalutin as Napa's. Each year they set out to raise a serious pile of cash, just like Napa, but they have a lot of laughs doing it. You can count on the vintners to provide the goofy entertainment and the stand-up comedy, complete with elaborate costumes and props. (A Las Vegas–themed auction recently showcased more amateur Elvis impersonators than you might find in Vegas itself.) As in Napa, auction attendees can dress in "Wine Country casual" attire, but in Sonoma that means just about anything goes, from Hawaiian shirts and shorts for the men to sundresses for the ladies.

SALUTE TO THE ARTS

Sonoma Plaza

(707) 938-1133

www.salutetothearts.com

On the third or fourth weekend in July, the entire Sonoma Plaza in the heart of town is transformed into an elegant, lively outdoor setting, featuring five stages filled with theater troupe performances and a variety of music and dance. Fine art by Sonoma Valley artists, children's activities, and the best in local cuisine, wine, and handcrafted beers are available. A tasting package for food and wine may be purchased for $30 in advance, or $35 at the event, or you can choose pricier

packages that include a reception for the artists, a live auction, and more.

FORT ROSS CULTURAL HERITAGE DAY

Fort Ross State Park, north of Jenner

(707) 847-3286

www.fortrossstatepark.org

On the last Saturday in July, some 100 volunteers and staff participants don period attire and reenact a typical day at Fort Ross in the mid-1800s, during the days of Russian settlement when the commandant and his wife lived elegantly in the wilderness surroundings (see the History chapter). Bring a picnic! Coastal weather is unpredictable,

Yes, the big bucks really do go to local charities. The beneficiaries in Napa Valley include 49 health care, youth, and housing nonprofit agencies. In Sonoma Valley the good causes range from community health centers to vineyard workers' services to the regional Boys and Girls Club. If you decide to attend one of these events, you may walk away not only with some fabulous wine but also with the knowledge that you contributed significantly to improving the quality of life for the less fortunate, and you had a great time doing it.

You can learn more about these auctions—and request an invitation—by visiting their respective Web sites: www.napavintners.com and www.sonomavalleywine.com.

Silliness is expected at the Sonoma Valley Harvest Wine Auction. JEAN SAYLOR DOPPENBERG

so pack a sun hat and warm clothes. Admission is $6 per vehicle.

SONOMA COUNTY FAIR
Sonoma County Fairgrounds,
1350 Bennett Valley Road, Santa Rosa
(707) 545-4200
www.sonomacountyfair.com
This 10-day event begins the last week in July and features carnival rides, a flower show, horse racing, livestock competitions, lots of live music, and a wide array of food and other vendors. This fair is a long-standing Sonoma County institution, and it is not to be missed. General admission is $7 for

adults, and free for children 12 and under; parking fees range from $5 to $8, depending on the lot.

AUGUST

Napa County

NAPA TOWN AND COUNTRY FAIR
Napa Valley Exposition, 575 Third Street, Napa
(707) 253-4900
www.napavalleyexpo.com
You can join the 65,000-odd people who come to the Exposition over five days in early to mid-

August—just don't call it a county fair. Napa's one and only official county fair is in Calistoga in July (see previous listing), but this is a more-than-reasonable facsimile. There are homemade jams and oversize zucchini, 4-H livestock, crowd-pleasers such as a lumberjack competition, a high-diving exhibition, wine tasting, and a kiddie carnival. Headliners at this event have spanned genres from Chubby Checker to Chinese acrobats to the Village People. Admission is $8 for adults and teens and $5 for seniors and children ages 6 to 12; free for children 5 and under. There is an additional charge for events in the grandstand, specifically drag racing and a demolition derby.

DAY FOR THE QUEEN AT SILVERADO
Silverado Country Club & Resort,
1600 Atlas Peak Road, Napa
(707) 257-4044, (707) 251-1882
www.qvhf.org
For one day in August, Silverado Country Club becomes a large, lush hat passed for Queen of the Valley Medical Center. The full bill includes a fashion show, tennis tournament and golf tournament, lunch, an evening barbecue, dancing, and a silent auction. The cost depends on how many events you mix and match. The fashion show and lunch are $75; evening events and the barbecue are $85; golf, lunch, evening events, and the barbecue are $265; and so on.

i Want to find out for yourself what it's like to bring in the grape harvest? Sign up for Grape Camp, a three-day, hands-on adventure for approximately 30 people put on each autumn by the Sonoma County Winegrape Commission and other local organizations. You'll pick grapes during "crush" and blend your own wine, and enjoy behind-the-scenes access to food and wine purveyors. Visit www.sonomagrape camp.com to learn more.

Sonoma County

WINGS OVER WINE COUNTRY AIR SHOW
Charles M. Schulz–Sonoma County
Airport, 2330 Airport Boulevard,
Santa Rosa
(707) 575-7900
www.pacificcoastairmuseum.org
This two-day air show sponsored by the Pacific Coast Air Museum (see the Attractions chapter) showcases a variety of daredevil performances that will have you craning and squinting in disbelief. In addition to the aerial demonstrations by a variety of WW II aircraft and other vintage fighters, the event features an outstanding demonstration of an F-16 fighter jet in action, courtesy of the air force demo team. Bring your earplugs. Admission is $12 per day—children 12 and under are free, and seniors are $5.

SONOMA COUNTY BLUEGRASS AND FOLK FESTIVAL
Sebastopol Community Center, Sebastopol
(707) 829-8012
www.socofoso.com
Renowned throughout the United States since 1986, this is a wonderful indoor music festival— a one-day event held in August, with a varied lineup of musicians. You'll hear everything from traditional and original acoustic music to blues, Caribbean grooves, country, and '40s music. Instrumental workshops offer a chance to learn to play folk instruments from dulcimer to banjo, and there is a kids-for-kids concert. Tickets are $27 in advance; $32 at the door.

BODEGA SEAFOOD, ART & WINE FESTIVAL
Watts Ranch, 16855 Bodega Highway
(Highway 12), Bodega
(707) 824-8717
www.winecountryfestivals.com
Not to be confused with the Bodega Bay Fishermen's Festival held along the water, this celebration takes place a few miles inland, in the tiny town of Bodega. There's a large wine-tasting tent, plenty of microbrews, a clam chowder cook-off, booths selling seafood concoctions, and crafts

galore. Three stages feature entertainment that might include Pete Escovedo, Pride & Joy, and flame-throwing acrobats. This is a benefit for the Stewards of the Coast and Redwoods and the Bodega Volunteer Fire Department. Tickets are $12 for adults, $10 for seniors, $8 for ages 12 to 16, and free for the kids.

COTATI ACCORDION FESTIVAL
La Plaza Park, West Silva Avenue and
Redwood Highway, Cotati
(707) 664-0444
www.cotatifest.com
On the weekend before Labor Day, accordion players from around the world descend on La Plaza Park. For them, this is a world classic—a two-day extravaganza with professionals playing tangos, Irish clogging music, and all else in between. Expect such luminaries as Big Lou's Polka Casserole, the Great Morgani, and the Mad Maggies. The event's appeal is largely to a mature crowd, but on the morning of the second day, kid players show what they can do. Admission is $17 for one day, $25 for both. Kids 15 and under are admitted free with an adult.

GRAVENSTEIN APPLE FAIR
Ragle Ranch Park, 1 mile north of Bodega
Highway, Sebastopol
(800) 207-9464
www.farmtrails.org/gravensteinapplefair/
default.html
Traditionally scheduled for a mid-August weekend at Ragle Ranch Park in Sebastopol, the Apple Fair features local cuisine and food demonstrations, an animal petting zoo, arts and crafts, and of course lots of Gravenstein apples and plenty of pie. Music and kids' activities fill the day. Admission is $10 for adults, $8 for seniors, $5 for kids 6 to 12, and free for kids younger than 6. Pets not allowed.

i One of the oldest wine harvest celebrations in the nation, the Valley of the Moon Vintage Festival, is held every September around the plaza in Sonoma.

SEPTEMBER

Napa County

NAPA VALLEY OPEN STUDIOS TOUR
Various locations
(707) 257-2117
www.nvopenstudios.com
Come see real live artists in their natural habitats! On successive weekends in mid- to late September, Napa Valley creative types throw open the doors to their studios and welcome the self-guided with refreshments. The format tends to be upvalley one weekend and downvalley the next. The Arts Council of Napa Valley distributes maps prior to the free event; all you do is drive and gawk. At least 90 artists usually participate.

MUSIC FESTIVAL FOR MENTAL HEALTH
Staglin Family Vineyard, 1570 Bella Oaks
Lane, Rutherford
(707) 944-0477
www.staglinfamily.com,
www.music-festival.org
It's not a very sexy title, but the event itself is rather divine. On a Saturday or Sunday in mid-September, a reception and dinner are staged in a big, open-sided tent overlooking the winery and Napa Valley. Past entertainment has included the Ramsey Lewis Trio and classical music performed under the baton of a celebrity guest conductor. Proceeds from this event go to much-needed research into brain disorders and mental illness. Some 60 to 70 ultrapremium Napa Valley wineries pour their goods throughout. The base price is $300 per person for the reception and concert, $3,500 if you stay for dinner, and the best tables (for 10) are reserved for $50,000. Nobel Prize winner John Nash, subject of the book and movie *A Beautiful Mind*, attended the 2002 event, which raised $2.4 million. The 2007 benefit raised more than $4 million.

Sonoma County

SONOMA VALLEY HARVEST WINE AUCTION
Cline Cellars, Sonoma
(707) 935-0803
www.sonomavalleywine.com
www.sonomawinecountryweekend.com
Events during the Labor Day weekend occur at various wineries and vineyards and include a wine auction, celebrity-chef dinners, entertainment, and wine tasting panels. It's four days of irreverent fun and frivolity to raise money for various charities. Sunday's auction culminates with an extravagant dinner buffet and live dance band. (See the close-up in this chapter.) Prices and package deals vary widely year to year, as do the charities that benefit. Get information on tickets from Sonoma Valley Vintners & Growers Alliance at the listed number and Web sites (see next item).

TASTE OF SONOMA COUNTY
MacMurray Ranch, 9015 Westside Road, Healdsburg
(800) 939-7666
www.sonomawinecountryweekend.com
When combined in 2008 with the event listed directly above, a new name was coined for the Labor Day weekend: Sonoma Wine Country Weekend. Two vintner organizations—the Sonoma Valley Vintners & Growers Alliance and the Sonoma County Vintners (yes, that's two separate groups)—decided to merge in the same weekend their different extravaganzas that had previously occurred a few weeks apart. Taste of Sonoma County—dubbed "a flavor event"—features more than 110 wineries pouring and 60 chefs cooking. Taste of Sonoma County features wine seminars, cooking demonstrations, and a top-chef competition. Held on Saturday afternoon of the holiday weekend at the ranch once owned by actor Fred MacMurray, the event costs $150 per person.

HEIRLOOM TOMATO FESTIVAL
Kendall-Jackson Wine Center,
5007 Fulton Road, Santa Rosa
(800) 769-3649
www.kj.com
The lowly tomato is elevated to superstar status at this annual festival dedicated to the enjoyment of the juicy fruit that comes in many shapes and colors. In early September, at the height of the tomato harvest in local backyards, as many as 170 varieties can be sampled in some fashion. For five hours, nearly 40 restaurants and purveyors of gourmet food offer tomato-inspired goodies in bite-size portions, along with cooking demonstrations, wine tasting, food and wine seminars, and even an art show. Amateur gardeners can enter their own tomato crop in a "beauty" contest with categories such as Ugliest Tomato. The 2008 festival was the 12th. Tickets are sold in advance only for $40 per person.

RUSSIAN RIVER JAZZ FESTIVAL
Johnson's Beach, Guerneville
(707) 869-1595
www.russianriverfestivals.com
At least eight internationally recognized jazz artists get together the first week in September for two all-day concerts on the Russian River. Food and drinks are available. Prices for jazz under the redwoods range from $50 to $100 for two days.

VALLEY OF THE MOON VINTAGE FESTIVAL
Sonoma Plaza
(707) 996-2109
www.sonomavinfest.org
At 110 years and counting, Valley of the Moon Vintage Festival, held annually on the last weekend in September on the plaza in Sonoma, is among the oldest wine harvest celebrations in the nation and the second-oldest festival in California, right behind the Rose Parade. It features a traditional Friday-evening wine tasting party and a full weekend of historical pageants, the blessing of the grapes, stomping of said grapes, parades, concerts, and wine and food tastings. If you want to attend the Friday-night wine tasting

event ($65 per person), however, you'll need to order tickets at least a month in advance—it's a sellout every year.

OCTOBER

Napa County

OLD MILL DAYS
Bale Grist Mill State Historic Park,
3369 St. Helena Highway N., St. Helena
(707) 942-4575
www.parks.ca.gov/?page_id=482
The folks at the Bale Grist Mill celebrate the end of harvest by partying like it's 1869. Coopers, weavers, storytellers, and old-time fiddlers don period costumes to lend a touch of authenticity to the 19th-century goings-on. The kids can make cornhusk dolls or dye wheat. And the park rangers offer nonstop tours of the mill, which will be busy grinding whole wheat flour and cornmeal. It's a two-day event in mid-October. The cost is $4 for adults and $2 for children.

HOMETOWN HARVEST FESTIVAL
Adams Street, St. Helena
(707) 963-4456, (800) 799-6456
www.ci.st-helena.ca.us/
This festival, a one-day event on a Saturday in October, includes arts and crafts, a fun run, a carnival, wine tasting, and a canine Frisbee-catching contest. The highlight is the pet parade, an advancing column of dogs, cats, horses, llamas, roosters, and lizards. Most of the action swirls around St. Helena Elementary School, on Adams Street between Oak and Stockton Streets. There is no admission fee, and most of the proceeds from vendor sales go toward building St. Helena a new community center and supporting the school.

Sonoma County

SONOMA COUNTY HARVEST FAIR
Sonoma County Fairgrounds,
1350 Bennett Valley Road, Santa Rosa
(707) 545-4203
www.harvestfair.org

This harvest festival on the first full weekend in October features a world-championship grape stomp, wine tasting, produce exhibits, food, arts, crafts, amateur beer and wine booths, music, and kids' exhibits. This bustling fair brings in droves of wine lovers from the Bay Area and beyond to taste many limited-production wines that just won gold medals in the Harvest Fair awards. Wine- and food-tasting tickets are extra, but you get a souvenir glass, and you will sip the top award winners in their specific categories—perhaps the only chance you'll get, because the wines might be difficult to find after the event. General admission is $6, but it's $2 for seniors on Friday and $2 for kids ages 7 to 12.

NOVEMBER

Napa County

TASTE FOR KNOWLEDGE ANNUAL WINE FESTIVAL
Napa Valley Exposition, 575 Third Street, Napa
(707) 253-3563
www.napavalleyexpo.com
Encouraging kids to drink is not good, but encouraging kids through a drinking festival is another matter altogether. This gig on the first Saturday in November raises about $50,000 a year for the Napa Valley Unified School District. The fun includes live and silent auctions, with about 30 valley wineries pouring and 1,000 guests sipping; student-provided music as a backdrop; and hors d'oeuvres for sustenance. Tickets are $45 in advance, $50 at the door.

WINE COUNTRY KENNEL CLUB
Napa Valley Exposition, 575 Third Street, Napa
(707) 253-4900
www.napavalleyexpo.com
If you can't make it to that big Westminster Kennel Club show in New York City, this is a good substitute, with some 2,000 well-groomed pooches strutting around the halls and grounds

of the Expo. There are separate shows on Saturday and Sunday, each from 8:00 a.m. until about 6:00 p.m., with eight age-and-experience classes (including two puppy classes) and seven dog groups: sporting, hound/working, terrier, toy, nonsporting, herding, and miscellaneous breeds. The animals vie for points, ribbons, trophies, and the ever-popular pat on the head. There is no charge to spectators. The Lions Club provides food, including a pancake breakfast.

FESTIVAL OF LIGHTS
Downtown Yountville
(707) 944-0904
www.yountville.com
This isn't so much the lighting of a tree as the lighting of a town. At about 6:00 p.m. the day after Thanksgiving, all of Yountville flicks its switches and is bathed in fairy lights. Christmas is beckoned with singers, street performers, horse-drawn carriage rides, and roasted chestnuts from 2:00 to 9:00 p.m. Santa makes an appearance, too. There is no admission fee, and much of the food and wine tasting is complimentary. The extravaganza sets off a month of special dinners, musical performances, and the like around Yountville.

Sonoma County
SANTA'S ARRIVAL
Petaluma Riverfront, Petaluma
(707) 769-0429
www.visitpetaluma.com
On the last Saturday in November, at noon sharp, Santa and Mrs. Claus make their way into Petaluma by boat. While awaiting the jolly one's arrival, the children stay busy with a variety of entertainment options. As might be expected, Santa's first move is to start handing out candy canes. Then he steps into an antique wagon chosen from the collection at the county museum (considered the largest collection in North America) and leads a parade of beautiful wagons in a circular route around town. It ends in historic Petaluma, where merchants hold a Share the Spirit event with an array of treats for all.

WINE & FOOD AFFAIR
Various locations in the Alexander,
Dry Creek, and Russian River Valleys
(707) 433-4335
www.wineroad.com
What a great excuse to cop a free cookbook. *Tasting Along the Wine Road* is complimentary when you buy your ticket to this weekend of food and wine pairing at about 100 wineries, celebrating its 10th year in 2008. The cookbook features recipes submitted by most of the wineries, so it's a terrific souvenir of the weekend, along with a logo glass. Tickets are $60 for the two-day event, $40 for Sunday only, and $20 for designated drivers. Get an early start to taste the best goodies.

DECEMBER

Napa County
CAROLS IN THE CAVES
Various Napa and Sonoma wineries
(707) 224-4222
www.cavemusic.net
The "Improvisator" is a multi-instrumentalist likely to play two dozen musical devices including dulcimers, pan pipes, and psalteries. As you might guess, he specializes in unusual folk instruments, and he brings out the best of each in the flawless acoustic environment of wine caves. The Carols in the Caves series consists of simple, informal concerts in various locations. Cost for each show is about $40 per person.

HOLIDAY CANDLELIGHT TOUR
Various locations, Napa
(707) 255-1836
www.napacountylandmarks.org
On the second Saturday in December, Napa County Landmarks (a local preservation society) organizes a 2:00 to 7:00 p.m. walking tour in a selected historic neighborhood. The stroll and open houses are usually in Napa but can turn up anywhere in the county. Many of the hosts put out cookies or cider. Expect eight or nine stops, with strolling carolers and glowing luminaries

along the way. The cost is $30 for Napa County Landmarks members, $40 for everyone else signing up in advance. It's $45 if you pay at the door.

PIONEER CHRISTMAS
Bale Grist Mill State Historic Park,
3369 St. Helena Highway N., St. Helena
(707) 942-4575
www.parks.ca.gov/?page_id=482
Ever wonder how Americans celebrated Christmas in the 1850s? What you can expect are Christmas carols sung to the accompaniment of mandolin and fiddle. You can string popcorn and cranberries, drink apple cider, and, for a nominal charge, decorate gingerbread cookies. The miller will probably be there giving tours, and he may be grinding out fresh flour and cornmeal too. Adults pay $4; it's $2 for the kids.

Sonoma County
SONOMA VALLEY OLIVE FESTIVAL
Various locations, Sonoma
(707) 996-1090, (866) 996-1090
www.sonomavalley.com/olivefestival
December is the official kickoff month for this several-weeks-long annual event (see more details under the January listing).

SHOPPING

A trip to Wine Country isn't complete without at least a day or two of serious shopping. But please skip the malls and browse instead in our one-of-a-kind shops and stores around small town squares or housed in fascinating old structures. The picturesque plazas of Healdsburg and Sonoma, together with the charming main drags in St. Helena and Calistoga, are some of the best places to find just the right gift for someone back home or a special remembrance of Wine Country to keep for yourself. This chapter also includes some of the many antiques stores and bookstores around the region. Don't forget to peruse the possibilities in countless winery gift shops. Many stock their own private-label olive oils and vinegars, as well as logo apparel, kitchen accessories, wine-oriented cookbooks, and a plethora of other items. The stores listed here keep reasonably regular hours daily, but some may be open shorter hours (or closed) on Sunday. It's best to call ahead if you're in doubt.

UNIQUE SHOPS

Napa County

SHACKFORD'S KITCHEN STORE
1350 Main Street, Napa
(707) 226-2132

World-class restaurants necessitate a lot of chefs, and most Napa Valley kitchen whizzes do their shopping at Shackford's. So do the common cooks, and one step into the store will show you why. This is the nirvana of pots and pans. You'll find whole aisles of knives (Wusthof-Trident, Sabatier, Forschner, and many more), pans (Calphalon, All-Clad, LOOK, etc., etc.), and cutting boards (wood, acrylic, poly, yada yada yada). The KitchenAid mixers are lined up like a panzer division, and the pot racks hang like chandeliers. It's all priced competitively.

THE BEADED NOMAD
1238 First Street, Napa
(707) 258-8004

There aren't many stores where prices start at three cents. The Nomad stocks more types of beads than you thought existed on the seven continents of the planet—beads of metal, thread, plastic, glass, wood, fimo (a polymer clay), ceramic, and even hemp. You can assemble your beads right there in the store (mixing is encouraged), and staff will provide design assistance and repair. The shop even offers classes in basic and advanced stringing. It also carries masks and jewelry from exotic locales, as well as Indian cottons and premade jewelry.

PATINA NAPA VALLEY
1030 Clinton Street, Napa
(707) 257-1151
www.napavalleysoapcompany.com

The aromas here will intoxicate you. There's everything for making yourself squeaky clean and deliciously scented in style. It's both a retail store and a soap production facility, so the products are as fresh as they come. Select gifts for all ages, all circumstances (even a Honeymoon Gift Bag), and for four-legged friends. (The owner created a line of pet products for getting dogs *really* clean and sweet smelling.) Ask about the Vintage Harvest bath gel, made with Cabernet grape seeds (that one's for you).

BETTY'S GIRL BOUTIQUE
1239 First Street, Napa
(707) 254-7560

Return to a time in fashion when petticoats and bust darts were all the rage. Vintage clothing, accessories, and jewelry fill every corner of the small shop, named in memory of owner Kim Northrop's mother, Betty. It really is for girly-girls, and ladies who want to feel like girls again (gents may wait patiently on the sidewalk outside). You can't help but smile when you walk in, as you will no doubt recognize something your mother once wore, or a purse she once carried. Betty's is retro with a capital R.

INTI
1139 First Street, Napa
(707) 258-8034
That this store was named for the Incan sun god tells you all you need to know about the business. It's a hodgepodge of imported multiethnic crafts popular with children of the '60s and their children—and anyone else looking for interesting decorations that won't devastate their checkbooks. Inti has jewelry, wood carvings, furniture, musical instruments, purses, candles, incense, batiks from Bali, and rugs from Peru. Oversize tapestries hang on the walls, and clothing from India and Indonesia hangs on racks.

THE MUSTARD SEED CLOTHING COMPANY
1301 Napa Town Center, Napa
(707) 255-4222
www.mustardseedclothing.com
Well-dressed women have been flocking to this store since 1996. It carries casual and dressy clothing, from denim to sequins, and has reasonably priced merchandise. Though it stocks labels such as Eileen Fisher and Scala, the store prides itself on not being a "cookie cutter" clothing boutique. A thoughtful small-town touch: The owner photographs customers who buy outfits for special events so they won't be likely to sell the same outfit to another customer attending the same event.

OVERLAND SHEEPSKIN COMPANY
6505 Washington Street, Yountville
(707) 944-0778
www.overland.com
If it once bleated, you'll find it here. Overland's

Jim Leahy began making sheepskin coats by hand in Taos, New Mexico, in 1973. Now the family-owned company sells its woolly wear at 13 locations around the nation, including this locale in Yountville. Try on the sheepskin slippers, or sit on a stack of amazingly plush rugs. Almost everything is 100 percent sheepskin, from the car seat covers to the coats (even the lining). Overland sells leather goods made by other manufacturers, including Australian outback dusters, hats, footwear, and water buffalo bags from India.

V MARKETPLACE
6525 Washington Street, Yountville
(707) 944-2451
www.vmarketplace.com
Careful on those cobblestone walkways in your spike heels. This is technically a shopping center, but it's small, quaint, and historical. Constructed in 1870, the building was once part of the Groezinger Winery complex and is listed on the National Register of Historic Places. Enough about the past. Today it's a collection of galleries, fashion boutiques, home decor options, a children's store (Hansel & Gretel), bridal and evening couture (Vianett), and the latest addition, NapaStyle (see next entry). When you've cased out all the shops, stop in for ice cream at Cups & Cones and peruse the silly toys and trinkets. Be sure to browse for wine at V Wine Cellar, then grab a bite to eat at Pacific Blues restaurant, just outside.

NAPASTYLE
V Marketplace
6525 Washington Street, Yountville
(866) 776-1600
www.napastyle.com
Here are two words gourmet chefs know all about: gray salt. It's the best type of salt for cooking, says Michael Chiarello, and he should know. He founded Tra Vigne restaurant in St. Helena, among other achievements in the food world. He's since gone retail, with several NapaStyle stores on the West Coast, including this new one in Yountville's V Marketplace (see previous listing). Chiarello is devoted to entertaining with style—Napa style—and the stores feature glassware, table linens,

 **Close-up**

Don't Miss Downtown Napa's Sweet and Savory New Public Market

It's somewhat inspired by the Ferry Plaza Marketplace in San Francisco, considered one of the best farmers' markets in the United States, and some have even compared it to Seattle's Pike Place. The Oxbow Public Market in downtown Napa might best be described as a big food court or food mall, but that really doesn't do it justice. It's big, yes—about 40,000 square feet of shopping space. The market opened slowly during the winter of 2007–08, with a couple of merchants stocking shelves and perfecting their product lines, then another and then another. Before long, it was filled with more food purveyors and culinary accessories than you could shake a spatula at.

There are many reasons to wander through the market at any time of day. It's designed for locals and visitors, and you can't pass by all these vendors without seeing *something* to covet. There's just too much great stuff to pick from. For produce, the emphasis is on freshness, with 10 farm stands outside. The dining options inside range from an ice cream vendor (Three Twins Organic Ice Cream) to rotisserie chicken dinners (Rotisario). Wine and cheese are well represented, of course (Wine Merchant and Wine Bar, and Cheese Merchant, which share a common room). A ring-binder notebook of the wine selections sits on every table for easy browsing before deciding on a particular label. My favorite stores are Tillerman Tea and Whole Spice, the latter featuring a wall of spices available by the ounce or the pound. The tea shop is equally charming, with bright red canisters of special blends direct from China. If you visit on a day when owner David Campbell is manning the shop, you're in luck. He will explain the mystique and appeal of tea, and offer complimentary tastings, too (try some of his roasted pumpkin seeds that have been coated in green tea).

Red-meat eaters will appreciate the steaks and chops on display from Five Dot Ranch, growers of all-natural beef products raised without antibiotics or hormones. Home decor and gift items with cooking and entertaining themes are available at Fete, the Kitchen Library, and Heritage Culinary Artifacts. Heritage has an assortment of large copper cookware that would look right at home in your chateau in France. Folio Enoteca & Winery is reportedly the world's smallest bonded winery, at only 80 square feet. Owner Michael Mondavi, son of Robert, serves wines from the Isabel Mondavi (I'M), Hangtime, and Oberon labels. The food menu includes soups, salads, hot and cold sandwiches, and pasta—with most of the provisions for the meals coming right from the vendors within the market.

Outside the main building are two outposts of famous St. Helena eateries: Taylor's Automatic Refresher and the Model Bakery (see the Restaurants chapter). If my recent explorations of Oxbow Public Market are any indication—when the place was humming with locals and visitors each time—it promises to be a winner. Oxbow Public Market is located at 610 First Street, near McKinstry Street, in Napa. For more information, visit www.oxbowpublicmarket.com.

and small appliances, along with staples such as gray salt (harvested from France's Normandy coast), olive oils and vinegars, pasta, marinated Parmesan dips, and a slew of sauces and spreads. There are kitchen accessories of all kinds, seasonal decor, conversation club chairs, dining furniture, and much more. This location also has a specialty wine shop and tasting room, a salumeria offering house-made salami and other cured meats, and a salt bar. Yes, a salt bar, for selling specialty salts by the pound. At press time, Chiarello had plans to open a restaurant near this store in V Marketplace, but details were still sketchy.

NAPA VALLEY GRAPEVINE WREATH COMPANY

8901 Conn Creek Road
(Rutherford Cross Road), Rutherford
(707) 963-8893, (877) 776-NAPA
www.grapevinewreath.com

While most grape growers are pruning, stacking, and burning vines in the winter, this company is building its inventory. The Wood family (a partner in the original Freemark Abbey investment group) trims its 80 acres of Cabernet Sauvignon plants, strips the leaves, and fashions the vines into decorative wreaths—and a whole lot more. They make dozens of styles of baskets, plus cornucopias, hearts, crosses, stars, wine carriers, even reindeer and magic wands. All of it is handmade, distinct, and highly durable.

ST. HELENA OLIVE OIL CO.

8576 Highway 29, Rutherford
(707) 967-1003, (800) 939-9880

1351 Main Street, St. Helena
(707) 968-9260
www.sholiveoil.com

Olive oil is as ancient a pursuit as wine, and it gets the same reverent treatment at St. Helena Olive Oil Co. This is one place where you can sample some of the best. Most of the fruit comes from the Central Valley, but the company contracted with a Napa Valley olive grower to produce the high-end Cask 85 line. St. Helena Olive Oil also imports balsamic vinegar from Italy and makes a few types of its own, including five flavored balsamics (with fresh berries) and a Cabernet vinegar. Everything is natural—no sugars or preservatives—and available in 60-, 250-, or 375-milliliter vessels. There are soaps and wooden wine-barrel products, too.

DEAN & DELUCA

607 St. Helena Highway S., St. Helena
(707) 967-9980
www.deandeluca.com

Twenty years after the first Dean & DeLuca opened in SoHo in 1977, the ultrapremium food purveyors brought their act to Napa Valley. And while the massive wine section is what sets this one apart from the other branches, there is plenty more to woo your senses—such as jam and marmalade jars by the dozen and an ocean of olive oil compartmentalized into 16-ounce bottles. You can find dried beans and rice, dried fruit, tins of dried herbs, teas and coffees, cigars, chocolates, and sweetly packaged edibles you never knew existed. And you can complete the experience with a high-quality cooking utensil, cookbook, or basket. Dean & DeLuca has an espresso bar and bakery, fresh produce, and a central deli with no end of meats, cheeses, and olives. But most of all it has its reputation for service, a commodity delivered by a squadron of friendly attendants in white chef's coats. This is a great place for assembling a delicious feast to enjoy at your favorite winery's picnic area.

JAN DE LUZ

1219 Main Street, St. Helena
(707) 963-1525
www.jandeluz.com

Ooh la la! Named for its owner, this store features inventory that is all imported from France. Linens are the specialty, in a couple basic styles that can be mixed and matched and personalized with embroidery right in the store. Linens, kitchen accessories, and bath products dominate one side of the store, home decor and furniture the other. The antiques, the lavender, the spices, the colorful tableware—it's all from the old country. Look for the copper bathtub in the window. Jan de Luz has a second location in Carmel.

FOOTCANDY

1239 Main Street, St. Helena
(877) 517-4606

452 First Street E., Sonoma
(707) 963-3876
www.footcandyshoes.com

A woman cannot own too many shoes and purses, right? If you must have more, and money is no object (I mean, really, no object), step into Footcandy. Most of us might walk on by in our arch-friendly Birkenstocks, but there's a thriving market for stores like Footcandy, and it's proven successful with two other shops in the Bay Area in addition to the Sonoma outpost. You know the names: Kate Spade, Jimmy Choo, Marc Jacobs, Lilly Pulitzer, and Emilio Pucci are only a few of the many designers represented. Like the heels, the prices are steep. Maryjanes by Manolo Blahnik, for instance, will set you back $615; to complete the ensemble, add a Jimmy Choo Congo clutch at the sale price of $1,197.

FRECKLES CHILDREN'S BOUTIQUE
1309 Main Street, St. Helena
(707) 963-1201
www.frecklesboutique.com
In a town targeted to more mature shoppers, there's this sweet little store for kids. Freckles has the usual adorable outfits for boys and girls, along with books and toys. They also carry Rody ponies, those inflatable riding toys from Italy, available in several colors. Freckles is located at the corner of the entryway to Hotel St. Helena (you can't miss the vertical HOTEL signs).

GOODMAN'S
1331 Main Street, St. Helena
(707) 963-1750
There is no shortage of women's clothing stores along St. Helena's Main Street, but I like this store for its big selection of apparel for women *and* men. The sale racks are always worth a look, too. If your passion is aloha shirts, they usually have a large collection. The store is housed in the historic Richie Block building, built in 1892 and hands-down the best looking facade on Main Street.

WOODHOUSE CHOCOLATE
1367 Main Street, St. Helena
(800) 966-3468
www.woodhousechocolate.com
Stepping into Woodhouse is like walking into Tiffany & Company, but you won't spend as much, and the experience will be sweeter. Inside, beautiful display cases fit for fine jewelry are filled with stunning chocolates lined up like rows of soldiers. The confections are all made on-site in

a production kitchen behind the "salon," as the owners refer to it. The Andersons are longtime Wine Country residents who jumped from the wine industry into chocolates several years ago. I'm glad they did. The storefront display window is always entertaining.

OLIVIER NAPA VALLEY
1375 Main Street, St. Helena
(707) 967-8777
www.oliviernapavalley.com
The olive is celebrated here in many ways, from cookbooks to soaps, candles, and ceramics. Check out the handcrafted tableware from Provence and other beautiful serving pieces. Though some of the products are imported, Olivier has its own label of gourmet oils and savories, tapenades, and so forth.

FIDEAUX
1312 Main Street, St. Helena
(707) 967-9935

43 North Street, Healdsburg
(707) 433-9935
Greeting customers on a recent visit to this shop was a shirt that read, I KISS MY DOG ON THE LIPS. If that sentiment warms your heart rather than turns your stomach, come on in. Dogs and cats are shaggy royalty here. Fideaux (pronounced "Fido"—get it?) offers numerous squeeze-and-squeak toys, a wide selection of pet collars, collapsible dog dishes for hiking, pet futon beds (made for the Fideaux label), and even wine-barrel doghouses. Take home a bag of scoopable snacks for your mutt, too. Fideaux also stocks the basics: shampoo, food, kitty litter, etc.

PENNALUNA
1220 Adams Street, St. Helena
(707) 963-3115
www.pennalunanapavalley.com
Just around the corner from the main shopping street in St. Helena is this sun-filled gift shop named for the owner's grandmother. It's the type of place that's hard to categorize. There's some kitsch (pillows, dish towels, and glasses printed with touristy Napa Valley maps), stuff for kids,

greeting cards, desk accessories, great jewelry, and the store's own fragrance, called Pennaluna. Lots of Jaag plush animals, too.

CALISTOGA POTTERY
1001 Foothill Boulevard, Calistoga
(707) 942-0216
www.calistogapottery.com
Sally and Jeff Manfredi run this pottery studio from the back of their home, and although popularity has surged, in some ways it's all very similar to how it was in 1980. Everything is fired on-site. The company aims for utilitarian stoneware—platters, plates, pitchers, bowls, mugs, kettles, etc.—that complements food. (Sally used to be a painter, Jeff a chef.) Much of the work is made to order, but you can always find some pots for sale on the shelves.

HURD BEESWAX CANDLES
1255 Lincoln Avenue, Calistoga
(707) 942-7410, (800) 977-7211
www.hurdbeeswaxcandles.com
Get your candles and wine here: This store combines the art of beeswax candle crafting with a tasting bar that pours On the Edge wines produced by the same family that owns the candle business. There are all-beeswax candles by the score, in an endless combination of sizes and styles. A demonstration beehive is mesmerizing, with the bees busy at work generating some of the raw material from which the two-legged artisans create their masterpieces. For an up-close look at the making of these fine candles, tours of the factory in St. Helena are offered; inquire at the numbers above.

THE CANDY CELLAR
1367 Lincoln Avenue, Calistoga
(707) 942-6990
If you have not just one sweet tooth but a whole mouthful of them, abandon all hope when you enter this place. You'll see barrels filled with saltwater taffy, jawbreakers, swirls, crunches, bubble gum, lollipops, and all the Jelly Bellies of the rainbow. Most of it is sold by weight, so you can mix and match. But you'll probably head straight for the award-winning fudge—up to 30 flavors to choose from, depending on the day, mixed right on the spot, including the likes of chewy praline, maple nut, rocky road, and caffe latte.

MUDD HENS
1348 Lincoln Avenue, Calistoga
(707) 942-0210, (800) 793-9220
www.muddhens.com
Want some mud to take back home? Mudd Hens has jars of all sizes filled with volcanic ash and pine needle extract for adding to your personal soaking tub. Combine that with their seaweed mask and a bar of mud scrub and you'll feel like new again. It's a way to recapture the mud-bath experience you enjoyed while a visitor in Calistoga. Mudd Hens also has a collection of Tired Old Ass products, incense and candles, and the Cowgirl line of kooky western-inspired gifts.

A MAN'S STORE
1343 Lincoln Avenue, Calistoga
(707) 942-2280
The name says it all. In a valley where women's clothing stores dominate, here's one for the guys. The owners opened this store to fill a niche they felt was missing in the upper valley: a place for local men to find affordable rugged work clothes and other accessories. But there's plenty for the short-term visitor too, starting with a greeting from the store's mascot, a German shorthaired pointer. If there's any doubt this is A Man's Store, just ask to scan their cigar collection, which includes Cheap Bastard, Arturo Fuente, and Montecristo.

AMERICAN INDIAN TRADING COMPANY
1407 Lincoln Avenue, Calistoga
(707) 942-9330
www.aitcoc.com
This long, narrow store along Calistoga's main shopping street is overflowing with jewelry made of turquoise, charoite, spiny oyster, amber, and lots of other gems. Native American culture is represented in many ways, with kachinas, clothing, artifacts, pottery, white sage, and handcrafted flutes and drums.

Sonoma County
Southern Sonoma

THE OLIVE PRESS
24724 Highway 121 (Arnold Drive), Sonoma
(in the Jacuzzi Family Vineyards facility)
(707) 939-8900, (800) 965-4839

610 First Street, Napa
(in the Oxbow Public Market)
(707) 226-2579
www.theolivepress.com

It's a twofer when you visit the Highway 121 location. You get to taste olive oil at Olive Press, then skip across the entryway to try Jacuzzi Family wines (see the Wineries chapter). Watch olives being crushed into oil when you visit between October and January. Any time of the year you can sample at least six oils at the tasting bar and select from all sorts of olive-themed gifts, including long-lasting soap "rocks." (The Oxbow location is merchandise only.)

ARTEFACT DESIGN & SALVAGE
23562 Highway 121 (Arnold Drive), Sonoma
(at Cornerstone Place)
(707) 933-0660
www.artefactdesignsalvage.com

Any store with the word *salvage* in its name might make you think twice about stopping. If you have no other reason to pull into Cornerstone Place (see the Arts and Culture chapter), this is one store at the collective that's definitely worth some browsing time. Take a stroll through the antique architectural pieces, odd bits culled from the owner's world travels and other resources, many of them huge (such as an ornate copper cornice torn from a condemned Manhattan high-rise, and a 10-foot-diameter, 19th-century cast-iron clock face). Much of the inventory is on a grand scale, but there are also smaller gift items and scads of books on architecture. Don't forget to walk through the treasures outside. Artefact is guaranteed to give you design inspiration for your own home and garden.

SPIRITS IN STONE
452 First Street E., Sonoma
(707) 938-2200, (800) 474-6624

401 Healdsburg Avenue, Healdsburg
(707) 723-1723, (877) 774-6627

3111 St. Helena Highway N., St. Helena
(707) 963-7000, (800) 974-6629

6526 Washington Street, Yountville
(707) 944-9924, (888) 574-6625
www.spiritsinstone.com

Laura and Tony Ponter are on a mission: to import the best in elegant, simple sculpture from the Shona ("people of the mist") tribe in Zimbabwe and to demonstrate that "the spirit in stone" has much to teach us all about dignity, compassion, and peace. There is something almost magnetic about these profound sculptures—a feeling that you must reach out and touch them, and you are encouraged to do so. Large pieces are pricey, but the smaller sculptures are affordable and tempting for any lover of fine things. (See the gallery listings in the Arts and Culture chapter for more information.)

TIDDLE E. WINKS VINTAGE 5 & DIME
115 East Napa Street, Sonoma
(707) 93-WOWEE
www.tiddleewinks.com

Spanning approximately 50 decades of American pop nostalgia, Tiddle will have you pointing and laughing, then snatching up a few keepsakes— your favorite old candy, for instance, that you probably can't find anywhere else. More good memories can be found in vintage metal lunch boxes, advertising signs and displays, board games, and other novelties. Don't forget to buy a Moon Pie on your way out.

CHURCH MOUSE THRIFT SHOPS
15 East Napa Street, Sonoma
(707) 938-9797

10 Boyes Boulevard, Sonoma
(707) 938-9839

As thrift stores go, these are exceptional. St. Francis Solano Parish operates four Church Mouse locations in the town of Sonoma, but the two listed are the handiest for visitors to seek out. One is on the south side of the plaza, while the Boyes Boulevard shop is just across from Big 3 Diner at Fairmont Sonoma Mission Inn. There are basic thrift shop items, to be sure, but much of the merchandise is of an upscale nature at bargain prices. After brunch at the Big 3, I like to pick up an item or two from the huge kitchen accessories/glassware/housewares department and see what's new in jewelry. The plaza location is just as intriguing.

VELLA CHEESE COMPANY
315 Second Street E., Sonoma
(707) 938-3232, (800) 848-0505
www.vellacheese.com
Some of the best cheese in the world is made on East Second Street, around the corner from the main drag, by Thomas Vella and his son, Ignazio. The family has operated out of the same 1905 rough-cut stone building since 1931; it's an architectural wonder in shaky, earthquakey California. The Vella Dry Jack has won international prizes, and the cheddar is so sharp it makes your mouth pucker.

MILAGROS GALLERY
414 First Street E., Sonoma
(707) 935-8566, (877) 939-0834
www.milagrosgallery.com
Following the covered passageway called El Paseo, which winds between East Spain and East First Streets, you'll suddenly believe you've wandered into another country and another time. Milagros is a fabulous store of affordable fine Mexican folk art, featuring whimsical Oaxacan wood carvings, Spanish colonial sconces, handcrafted jewelry from all over Latin America, Talavera bowls, and wonderful masks. This shop also displays a rare collection of religious Mexican folk art. Milagros, which means "miracles" in Spanish, is named after the figures sold in front of churches in Mexico.

SONOMA ROCK & MINERAL GALLERY
414 First Street E., Sonoma
(707) 996-7200
El Paseo courtyard has another shop worthy of a visit, particularly if you're interested in things lapidary. It's hard to believe the earth holds such wondrous rocks and stones. The display is professionally arranged in a spacious setting, with beautiful polished stones to buy. There are also beads galore for jewelry making.

BAKSHEESH HANDCRAFTED GIFTS FROM THE DEVELOPING WORLD
423 First Street W., Sonoma
(707) 939-2847

106-B Matheson Street, Healdsburg
(707) 473-0880

1327 Main Street, St. Helena
(707) 968-9182
www.vom.com/baksheesh
Fair trade for artists in approximately 35 developing nations is the business of these stores. There's a little bit of everything, and at reasonable prices—home decor, jewelry, toys and games, garden accessories and planters, musical instruments, and year-round holiday ornaments. The owners work with trade organizations that guarantee living wages to the artists for their crafts, which are magnificent. I drop in frequently for the affordable jewelry and garden pots.

SIGN OF THE BEAR KITCHENWARE
435 First Street W., Sonoma
(707) 996-3722
Beautiful Italian ceramics mingle with kitchen doodads of all kinds in this popular store. It's packed to the rafters with merchandise *and* shoppers, all searching for gourmet gadgets. I can lose myself here for an afternoon, gazing at the shelves of cookware and must-haves and wondering where in my own kitchen I might find room for it all.

Other Southern Sonoma Shops

WINE COUNTRY CHOCOLATES
14301 Arnold Drive, Glen Ellen
(707) 996-1010

414 First Street E., Sonoma
(707) 933-4475
www.winecountrychocolates.com
Mother and daughter chocolatiers Betty and Caroline Kelly serve up the best truffles around, thanks to a special ingredient: wine. Take your pick of formed and pressed truffles made with sparkling wine, Zinfandel, Port, or Cabernet Sauvignon. There's also cappuccino-tiramisu, raspberry, apricot, fresh orange, and more. A selection of four truffles in a discreet takeaway box will have you swooning.

RAYMOND & CO. CHEESEMONGERS
14301 Arnold Drive, Glen Ellen
(707) 938-9911
www.raymondcheesemongers.com
Just steps from the chocolate shop described above is the aromatic domain of John Raymond, a delightful character who can converse about cheese like some men talk about baseball or football. If you're a cheese neophyte, John's your man. It's his passion, and cheesemongering is his profession. He doesn't *make* the cheese; he selects artisan cheeses from around the world—many produced in Sonoma County—and presents the best in this small shop. As John puts it, "I believe that just as great fruit begets great wine, great cheese can only come from great milk."

SNOOPY'S GALLERY AND GIFT SHOP
1665 West Steele Lane, Santa Rosa
(707) 546-3385, (800) 959-3385
www.snoopygift.com
Snoopy's Gallery features a museum containing awards, drawings, and personal memorabilia from Peanuts creator Charles M. Schulz. The gift shop has the largest selection of Snoopy products in the world. The Redwood Empire Ice Arena is next door, and the Charles M. Schulz Museum and Research Center is steps away (see the Attractions chapter).

GADO GADO INTERNATIONAL
129 Fourth Street (Railroad Square),
Santa Rosa
(707) 525-8244
www.gadogadointl.com
When you pass through the doors of Gado Gado, you are enveloped in another world. Browse among exotic Asian furniture, much of it crafted from recycled teak taken from ancient dismantled dwellings. Hand-carved puppets are everywhere in every size, as are tribal artworks and sculptures, architectural elements, beaded boxes, hats, baskets, and countless other decorative accessories.

SONOMA OUTFITTERS
145 Third Street, Santa Rosa
(707) 528-1920, (800) 290-1920
www.sonomaoutfitters.com
The inventory in this 22,000-square-foot store is sure to cover everything you need for just about any sport. There's an enormous amount of boating and camping equipment—tents and sleeping bags, hiking boots and climbing shoes, canoes, rubber and plastic kayaks, ski clothing, in-line skates, you name it. It's sports equipment from wall to wall. Find it in the Railroad Square district of downtown Santa Rosa.

Northern Sonoma

The pretty plaza that makes Healdsburg so charming was built in 1852 by Harmon Heald, who sold lots for $15. Today, $15 will barely cover lunch, and the stores that sold harnesses and hardware in Heald's day are occupied by charming shops filled with jewelry, books, fine art, clothing, and home furnishings. Here are a few to seek out:

OAKVILLE GROCERY CO.
124 Matheson Street, Healdsburg
(707) 433-3200

7856 St. Helena Highway, Oakville
(707) 944-8802, (800) 736-6602
www.oakvillegrocery.com

The Healdsburg location is a branch of the same wonderful gourmet grocery store whose jam-packed shelves in the Napa Valley have attracted passersby for decades. The Healdsburg location has metamorphosed into a gentrified, glossy emporium of most everything gourmet and delicious. Here you can stock your kitchen pantry with exotic mustards, duck pâté, caviar, Greek olives, and more. You can eat lunch here too, selecting salads, sandwiches, and yummy desserts to be eaten under umbrellas on the sun-drenched patio.

SAINT DIZIER HOME FURNISHINGS
259 Center Street, Healdsburg
(707) 473-0980
www.saintdhome.com
Please, honey, can I buy that gorgeous wood chandelier? I bet the staff behind the counter at this store hears pleas of that nature all the time. Besides a large assortment of Ralph Lauren fabrics and that designer's home collection, this beautiful showroom has furniture and decorative accessories made locally, as well as antiques from faraway places. The tableware is lovely, too.

FABRICATIONS & WINE COUNTRY FABRICS
116 Matheson Street, Healdsburg
(707) 433-6243
www.stitchbitch.net
I used to sew, once upon a time, so I still get a little thrill when I first walk into a fabric store, even a tiny one such as Fabrications, in this same spot since 1981. It may be small but the bolts of fabric are stacked into every crevice and high up on the walls. It's a great place for quilters looking for unusual small pieces of fabric at reasonable prices.

VIGNETTES
110 Matheson Street, Healdsburg
(707) 433-8552
www.vignetteshealdsburg.com
Vignettes is a combination gallery/gift shop with plenty of collectible pieces, such as local artist Gail Packer's multiplate etchings and the watercolors

of Douglas Chun. Owner Dyanne Celi has also stocked her store with whimsical wire sculptures, and regionally produced arts and crafts of all kinds: jewelry, photographs, illustrations, pottery, ceramics, and tilework.

SEASONS OF THE VINEYARD
113 Plaza Street, Healdsburg
(707) 431-2222
www.seasonsofthevineyard.com
Here's a store that embodies all the gifts and decorative objects that can turn a house into a home. Owned by Rhonda Carano, of Ferrari-Carano Vineyards, it's a cornucopia of fabulous table settings, wreaths, furniture, linens, and other home accents. And don't forget to look up—the ornate tin ceiling dates from 1883.

ART AND ALL THAT JAZZ
119 Plaza Street, Healdsburg
(707) 433-7900
www.artandallthatjazz.com
Jessica Felix, whose works have been shown at the Smithsonian Institution as well as prominent galleries across the country, has been designing spirited jewelry since 1970. Her shop serves as a gallery that includes the work of others in art glass, ceramics, photography, and collage, and it offers an eclectic selection of jazz and Brazilian music.

POWELL'S SWEET SHOPPE
322 Center Street, Healdsburg
(707) 431-2784

720 McClelland Drive, Windsor
(707) 836-0808

151 Petaluma Boulevard S., Petaluma
(707) 765-9866
www.powellssweetshoppe.com
The comparisons to *Willy Wonka's Chocolate Factory* are unavoidable, because the movie and its music are in fact playing while you shop. But this store is really about rekindling fond memories of childhood and favorite sweets. The first store opened in Windsor in 2003, followed soon by many others in the region as its popularity

reached far and wide. I guarantee you will find candy you once coveted but haven't seen in years. Maybe that's not such a good thing for your dental work, but your heart will leap with joy.

JIMTOWN STORE
6706 Highway 128, Healdsburg
(707) 433-1212
www.jimtown.com
Not only can you find American antiques, folk art, and primitives here, you can also have some "real food" (as they advertise) and a truly good cup of coffee. Owner/artist Carrie Brown started this store in 1989 with her late husband, John, and it's only gotten more popular with time. Built more than 100 years ago, the building was once a general store and post office. Carrie makes her own line of condiments, and the lunch selections are terrific, and reasonable, too. Look for the yellow building with one or two vintage automobiles parked outside.

West County/Russian River

INCREDIBLE RECORDS & CDS
112 North Main Street, Sebastopol
(707) 824-8099
Forget the Rock and Roll Hall of Fame in Cleveland. Sonoma County has its own "museum" masquerading as a record/CD store in Sebastopol. Owner Jonathon Lipsin had a similar store in Toronto for many years, with much of the same priceless rock memorabilia on display. It's not exhibited in fancy style; it's mostly a jumble of taped and pushpinned treasures, creating a mosaic of the weird and the wonderful, with no wall space left unused. There are vintage rock posters aplenty; a rare collection of early Beatles photos (including the proof sheets) taken by photographer Dezo Hoffmann, who accompanied the moptops around the world; the Who's contract to perform at Woodstock in 1969 (they earned $12,500, by the way); a fringed vest worn by Steve Miller in the '60s; a guitar used by Randy Bachman in the '70s; and an assortment of odd pencil drawings made by Jim Morrison at the tender age of 14, which foretold his future legacy as

the Lizard King. And that's just for starters. Don't be surprised to find Carlos Santana or Tom Waits standing next to you at the racks—they pop in from time to time to do their music shopping.

CALIFORNIA CARNIVORES
2833 Old Gravenstein Highway, Sebastopol
(707) 824-0433
www.californiacarnivores.com
It's been called "Little Shop of Horrors," and it's billed as the largest carnivorous plant shop in the United States. About 550 carnivorous plants grow here, with about 120 varieties for sale. These are the meat eaters of the plant world and are endless fun to watch. An unsuspecting fly circles above the Venus flytrap and makes what will be its final landing. Other plants, like the pitcher plant or the bladderwort, are even more unkind to insects. The plants are easy to care for and inexpensive—you could get a dandy one for between $10 and $20 and perhaps be fly-free forever. If you'd like to send one to a friend, a mail-order service is provided.

HAND GOODS
3627 Main Street, Occidental
(707) 874-2161
Proclaiming a "distinctive mall-free experience," Hand Goods is located in the tiny hillside hamlet of Occidental. Since 1971 the shop has offered a wide variety of fine, locally made handcrafts, featuring the work of more than 100 artists. The ceramics encompass everything from functional tableware to ornamental sculpture, from painted oil lamps to ikebana vases. You'll also find Shaker boxes and fine furniture, embroidered Thai jackets, and batik baby clothing. If it's jewelry you're looking for, Hand Goods offers local and imported earrings, necklaces, pins, and bracelets in every price range.

STUDIO NOUVEAU
25195 B Street, Duncans Mills
(707) 865-2461
www.studionouveau.com
Tucked behind the Cape Fear Cafe in a hobbit-

size cottage sits Studio Nouveau, which owner Andrea Record describes as carrying "objects of beauty." She has so much it spills out of the tiny store and onto a deck. Much of it she created herself, especially the pottery. There are also classic wooden wall hangings, candles, scarves, and unique garden planters. She also has a large array of liquid-metal jewelry and cool purses.

ANTIQUES

Napa County

ANTIQUES ON SECOND
1370 Second Street, Napa
(707) 252-6353

Described as having everything under the sun, "even rust and peeling paint," this shop also displays some attractive home furnishings, along with a baby grand piano and an 1840s pump organ. There's pottery and glassware, Shabby Chic, and textiles. Inside the store is a new section called Accessoire, featuring vintage clothing and jewelry.

THE ANTIQUE SHOPPE
1408 Second Street, Napa
(707) 256-0811

If you're looking for an old *Life* magazine, step right this way. Inside the shop are more than 23,000 back issues of the popular periodical, dating from 1936. The store also has an assortment of cranberry and Depression glass, tools, primitives, and lots of furniture.

> **i** Vintage wine-related accessories can sometimes be found among the treasures in Wine Country antiques stores.

ANTIQUE FAIR
6512 Washington Street, Yountville
(707) 944-8440
www.antiquefair.com

This shop has been around for a long time (since 1971), but not as long as its merchandise. Antique Fair specializes in high-quality French antiquities from *la crème* of Lyon, Toulouse, and Paris estates.

The proprietors have jewelry, statuettes, silverware, armoires, and bookcases. Ask to see their collection of walking sticks.

Sonoma County
Southern Sonoma

SONOMA COUNTRY ANTIQUES
23999 Arnold Drive, Sonoma
(707) 938-8315
www.sonomacountryantiques.com

Looking for English and Victorian or Georgian pine designs and furnishings from the period 1820 to 1900? This dealer either has it or can obtain it for you. It's a one-of-a-kind showplace of unique pine antiques that would fit perfectly in the modern home.

CHELSEA ANTIQUES
148 Petaluma Boulevard N., Petaluma
(707) 763-7686

This collective of more than 30 dealers features a wonderful selection of decorative antiques, collectibles, and architectural and garden items in three buildings. Chelsea represents just about every field of antiques collecting.

VINTAGE BANK ANTIQUES
101 Petaluma Boulevard N., Petaluma
(707) 769-3097

It's one of those wonderful old banks that has ceilings two stories high and a small window on the second level overlooking the bank floor— so the manager could monitor his tellers and cashiers. Today it's a collective for approximately 40 dealers, giving you two full floors (at 5,000 square feet each) and the mezzanine level to explore. What you'll find is estate jewelry, furniture, vintage clothing, porcelain, gentlemen's collectibles, dinnerware, and lots more.

WHISTLE STOP ANTIQUES
130 Fourth Street, Santa Rosa
(707) 542-9474
www.railroadsquare.net

This is where it all began—Sonoma County's original collective, now nearly three decades old.

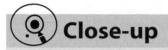
Our Other Nectar

Color, bouquet, and *taste*—the words traditionally associated with wine tasting. But there's another nectar grown and bottled in Wine Country that is judged in much the same way: olive oil.

Color refers to the tinged green from the chlorophyll found in green olives or the yellow of mature olives. As the oil becomes oxidized, a red tint may appear.

Bouquet is determined by the volatile compounds in the oil, such as alcohols, ketones, and esters.

Taste involves the bouquet in combination with the four gustatory senses: salty, acidic, bitter, and sweet.

Today's emphasis on improved health and better eating has brought a new appreciation for olive oil—not only the one- and three-liter bulk offerings found in most supermarkets but the hand-harvested, finely milled, flavorful, creatively bottled, and limited-availability artisan varieties found in places such as Wine Country. Indeed, countless wineries now bottle their own brands and feature them prominently in their gift shops. The oils may be infused with many flavors, ranging from lemon to hot chili. Other creative combinations may blend orange and thyme, basil and chili, and mixed herbs and sun-dried tomato.

Olive trees are grown for oil production in all Wine Country counties, and the olives are generally harvested following the autumn wine-grape crush. Newly pressed olive oils, which have the strongest flavors, are sometimes known as one- or two-cough oils. When the oil hits the back of your throat, the bitterness may produce an involuntary cough . . . or two—much like gulping down a shot of whiskey. But with olive oil, bitter is often considered a desirable trait. Once limited to only a handful of locations, olive oil tasting can now be found in a multitude of shops, wineries, and other attractions in Napa and Sonoma Counties.

There is no shortage of oil in Wine Country; distinctive homegrown olive oils dominate the shelves in most upscale groceries. LOREN DOPPENBERG

With 10,000 square feet of space and more than 35 dealers, Whistle Stop is a collector's paradise with thousands of items from dishes to doorknobs. You'll find clock repair, refinishing supplies, antique books, and a wonderful assortment of glassware, jewelry, furniture, and collectibles.

RAILROAD SQUARE BASEMENT ANTIQUES & COLLECTIBLES
100 Fourth Street, Santa Rosa
(707) 569-9646
You enter this shop on Wilson Street. It features a fine collection of vintage furniture, glassware, pottery, kitchenware, china, and cookbooks. Closed Tuesday.

Northern Sonoma

MILL STREET ANTIQUES
44 Mill Street, Healdsburg
(707) 433-8409
Inside a big orange building, approximately 38 dealers showcase their wares in 10,000 square feet of space. You'll find furniture—classic to country—glass, china, silver, fine oil paintings by listed artists, plus some eccentric goodies that need a home, such as gas station collectibles, metal signs, and 1950s memorabilia.

HEALDSBURG CLASSICS
226 Healdsburg Avenue, Healdsburg
(707) 433-4315
www.hbg.sonoma.net
This is an enormous warehouse with a roster of some 20 dealers. It would be difficult to name something that isn't here, rather than what is. However, anyone looking for indoor-outdoor furniture or yard pieces will not be disappointed.

ANTIQUE HARVEST
225 Healdsburg Avenue, Healdsburg
(707) 433-0223
Items range from country pine to Victorian, with lamps, brass, art deco furnishings, and Maxfield Parrish prints to boot. Meander through and check out the wares of more than 25 dealers.

i The Jimtown Store near Healdsburg is an old-fashioned, side-of-the-highway, rural store with a twist: gourmet food and coffee, unusual gifts, and antiques.

Sonoma Coast

WOODEN DUCK ANTIQUE SHOP
132 Bodega Lane, Bodega
(707) 876-3176
You'll spot the big yellow house (once a Druids hall) from the highway as you head toward the ocean. The store is open only Saturday and Sunday, but you'll find some fine 18th- and 19th-century furniture, plus a lot of Americana— pewter, glass, silver, whale oil lamps, and some English Staffordshire china. There's also a fine collection of antique guns. It's across the narrow lane from the old Potter School, made famous in the movie *The Birds*.

West County/Russian River

LLANO HOUSE ANTIQUES
4353 Gravenstein Highway S. (Highway 116), Sebastopol
(707) 829-9322
Housed in the oldest wooden building in Sonoma County, Llano House Antiques deals mainly in American oak furniture, Depression glass, and kitchen collectibles.

ANTIQUE SOCIETY
2661 Gravenstein Highway S. (Highway 116), Sebastopol
(707) 829-1733
www.antiquesociety.com
Antique Society is right when it claims "there's no place quite like" its collective. With approximately 125 dealers, it is simply immense. You'll find just about anything you're looking for here, and the dealers claim to have "country prices."

BOOKSTORES

Napa County

COPPERFIELD'S BOOKS

Bel Aire Plaza Shopping Center, Trancas
Street and Highway 29, Napa
(707) 252-8002

1330 Lincoln Avenue, Calistoga
(707) 942-1616
www.copperfields.net

Wine Country literati have been relying on Copperfield's for years. The Napa Valley stores (there are also four locations in Sonoma County; see next section) are well stocked and well staffed. Expect new, used, and rare books as well as excellent children's sections.

MAIN STREET BOOKS

1315 Main Street, St. Helena
(707) 963-1338

This business has been around since 1983. It's an extremely small shop that emphasizes used items, and it's the only upvalley used-book store. The cramped quarters and carefully selected titles are bound to remind you of a classic London bookstall.

RIVER HOUSE BOOKS

1234 Adams Street, St. Helena
(707) 963-1163
www.riverhousebooksnapavalley.com

Duck into this bright and airy store a few steps off the main drag and sample the cookbooks, tomes on the science of winemaking, and beautiful Napa Valley souvenir volumes. Looking for an old-fashioned potboiler for reading in your spa tub? You'll find those here, too, along with a good selection of magazines and a corner for kids.

Sonoma County

Southern Sonoma

SONOMA BOOKENDS BOOKSTORE

201 West Napa Street, No. 15, Sonoma
(707) 938-5926
www.sonomabookends.com

It's a general interest bookstore with an eye toward tourists in the wide selection of Wine Country books. The store's travel section focuses on California, and there's also a fine selection of U.S. Geological Survey maps.

READERS' BOOKS

130 East Napa Street, Sonoma
(707) 939-1779
www.readersbooks.com

Described by *Travel & Leisure* as a "honey pot" ("You can't help but get stuck there"), Readers' is a bookstore with many rooms, one of which is strictly for children's books and serves as a gathering room for youngsters. The store has gained some fame for its authors' readings.

JACK LONDON BOOKSTORE

14300 Arnold Drive, Glen Ellen
(707) 996-2888

Used and new books are sold here, with a special concentration of books dealing with the life of author Jack London.

COPPERFIELD'S BOOKS

140 Kentucky Street, Petaluma
(707) 762-0563

2316 Montgomery Drive, Santa Rosa
(707) 578-8938

138 North Main Street, Sebastopol
(707) 823-2618

104 Matheson Street, Healdsburg
(707) 433-9270
www.copperfields.net

Copperfield's has built its business on customer service and is highly respected in Sonoma County. The shelves are filled with general-interest publications, and there's a great children's section with occasional special events for children. The Petaluma store deals in new and used books. The Santa Rosa store also has an intriguing assortment of greeting cards and gift items of a bookish nature, as well as a cafe serving yummy lunches. The Healdsburg store expanded recently, taking over the space formerly occupied by Plaza Farms and anchored by Bovolo restaurant, owned and operated by chefs John Stewart and Duskie Estes (see the listing and the close-up in the Restaurants chapter). At press time, Bovolo planned to remain where it is, in the back of the store with both indoor and outdoor seating.

Northern Sonoma

LEVIN & COMPANY
306 Center Street, Healdsburg
(707) 433-1118
It would be hard to find a more appealing bookstore—a large, airy room displays books on three large islands in the center of the store. Beyond that there's a cozy room with a comfortable couch in the mystery novel section, and a children's room. Levin & Company offers primarily new books—quality fiction, interior design, and garden titles. Upstairs in the loft you'll find an art gallery displaying the works of local artists.

Sonoma Coast

FORT ROSS BOOK & GIFT SHOP
19005 Highway 1, north of Jenner
(707) 847-3437
www.fortrossstatepark.org
Located 11 miles north of the town of Jenner, the state-park shop has a unique selection of books highlighting the Russian settlers and Native Americans, plus the natural history of the Fort Ross area (see the History chapter).

ARTS AND CULTURE

Beauty and creativity seem to naturally go together. The scenery and tranquility of Napa and Sonoma Counties have stirred the soul and inspired the imagination of numerous writers, artists, musicians, and thespians. A hundred years ago it was wordsmiths such as Jack London and Robert Louis Stevenson (read more about them in the History chapter). Today, all sorts of creative types call this home. On any given day you may see watercolor artists perched on coastal bluffs, capturing as best they can the unmatchable majestic blues and greens of the sky and ocean. Talented local actors stalk the stages of our community theaters, putting heart and soul into their performances.

More famous creative people have also put down roots here. Don't be surprised to bump into blues guitarist and singer Boz Scaggs in Glen Ellen or see actor/director Robert Redford biking along Highway 29. You might encounter the gravelly voiced entertainer Tom Waits while shopping in Sebastopol, see comedy legend Tom Smothers while dining in Sonoma Valley, or come face-to-face with former Grateful Dead percussionist Mickey Hart as you stroll through Occidental—all are local residents. Filmmaker Francis Ford Coppola has a high profile in Wine Country, as the owner of two wineries and an interest in a few other business concerns. (He even tried to buy Madrona Manor awhile back—see the Bed-and-Breakfast Inns chapter—but the deal fell through.)

Speaking of filmmakers, we also have our share of film festivals. These events attract movie directors and actors, and the fans who love the silver screen. Wine Country has been the backdrop for many films over many decades, so it's a natural fit to showcase new movies here (see the close-up in this chapter). Winery tasting rooms frequently double as art galleries, and the winery courtyards and surrounding grounds often serve as theaters and concert halls. Several examples are spotlighted in this chapter. Here is a rundown of some of the Wine Country's best arts and culture, presented in four categories: theater, music and dance, visual arts, and film festivals.

THEATER COMPANIES AND VENUES

Napa County

DREAMWEAVERS THEATRE
1637 Imola Avenue, Napa
(707) 255-5483
www.dreamweaverstheatre.org
This is Napa's only nonprofit live theater, supported by memberships, donations, and ticket sales—and completely staffed by volunteers. The troupe incorporated in 1987, and in 2000 it renovated a former nightclub in the River Park Shopping Center. There is a main theater for big

productions and a "black box" area for smaller shows. Dreamweavers has traditionally staged five shows a year for four weekends each, with smaller projects filling the gaps. Recent shows have included *Agnes of God*, *Rhinoceros*, and *The Gin Game*. Tickets typically run $18 to $20. Dreamweavers also sponsors a young actors' theater, with performances by the kids.

NAPA VALLEY OPERA HOUSE
1030 Main Street, Napa
(707) 226-7372
www.napavalleyoperahouse.org
Thanks to the deep pockets of Robert Mondavi

and his wife, Margrit Biever, this landmark building was completely renovated and reopened in 2002. Built in 1879 in the Italianate style, the opera house had been dark for *88 years*, the victim of earthquake damage and the decline of vaudeville. There are two venues here—a 183-seat theater and a 500-seat theater. Musicals, jazz, cabaret, family shows, world music and dance, and comedy are just some of the entertainment offered. Recent shows have included stagings of the *Barrage*, Mozart's *Cosi fan tutte*, and *Winnie the Pooh*, and the music of Arlo Guthrie, Asleep at the Wheel, and the Cowboy Junkies. Tickets are reasonable—from $15 to $45, generally—and other shows can run higher. Allow yourself extra time for parking; two city garages are close by.

NAPA VALLEY COLLEGE THEATER
2277 Napa-Vallejo Highway, Napa
(707) 259-8077
www.napavalley.edu
The drama students of Napa Valley College stage several events at their campus theater during the academic year, August through May. Some examples of recent undertakings are *Our Town* and *La Cage Aux Folles*. Prices range from $15 to $18; ask about student and senior discounts. See the Music and Dance section for more NVC productions.

LINCOLN THEATER
100 California Drive, Yountville
(707) 944-1300
www.lincolntheater.com
Restored to the tune of $20 million, Lincoln Theater reopened in 2005 as a world-class venue with all-new lighting and sound systems, and an extra 30,000 square feet with balcony seating. Home to the Napa Symphony, the 1,200-seat theater has attracted major musical performers and theatrical troupes since the renovation. The repertoire is all over the place, so there's something for everyone: One night it might be Garrison Keillor pontificating about fictional Lake Wobegon, two nights later it could be a staging of Mozart's *Don Giovanni*, or even a burnin'-down-the-house performance by the Temptations. Tickets can range from $20 to

$100, depending on the artist. The theater is on the grounds of the California Veterans Home, a bit of an attraction in its own right.

WHITE BARN
2727 Sulphur Springs Avenue, St. Helena
(707) 251-8715, (707) 963-3408
Originally a carriage house built in 1872, it's now a 75-seat theater for stage and musical performances, located in a rural setting. A Celtic musical group, Kith and Kin, is one musical act that appeared in 2008. Seats are not reserved, and tickets run about $25.

TUCKER FARM CENTER
1201 Tucker Road, Calistoga
(707) 942-0977
Nobody is trying to be facetious here. It really is a theater, but for most of its existence it has served as a working support center for local farmers. The stage company, mostly Calistogans, performs original works in the summer, fun musicals and comedies in the spring and fall. The theater building, which doubles as a meeting hall or whatever else the growers need it for, holds about 120 patrons for most performances. Admission is $10 to $20. The center is off Highway 29, just north of Bothe–Napa Valley State Park.

Sonoma County

ANDREWS HALL AT SONOMA COMMUNITY CENTER
276 East Napa Street, Sonoma
(707) 938-4626
www.sonomacommunitycenter.org
A classic brick structure, Andrews Hall is a leftover from 1916, when it was the Sonoma Grammar School. More recently it achieved modest national exposure when it was selected as one of the settings for the hit movie *Scream*. It's a small theater that's now part of the Sonoma Community Center and will seat up to 299—it takes on no airs for being grand. The stage is small, so plays generally run to those requiring few actors and uncomplicated sets such as *Mame, A Child's Christmas in Wales*, and murder mysteries.

December usually brings a Christmas-themed production. Occasional musical evenings bring the internationally recognized Brass Works of San Francisco or a performance by the Baguette Quartet. The intimate, 50-seat Black Box Theater behind Andrews Hall stages one-act plays, sometimes written by local authors. Admission is set at $10 to $12 per event at Andrews Hall, or a season of five performances is $60.

AVALON PLAYERS SHAKESPEARE COMPANY
Gundlach Bundschu Winery, Sonoma
(707) 996-3264
www.sonomashakespeare.com
Performing Shakespeare's plays since 1980, this group has become something of a tradition among theater lovers. A lighthearted spirit of fun prevails, and whole families attend, kids and grandparents included. This is "Shakespeare with a twist"—the audience can expect an occasional actor to leave the stage and carry on the performance amidst the viewers. In 2008 the group performed *A Midsummer Night's Dream.*

Seating at the winery is at picnic tables on a first-come, first-served basis. It has become the custom among those who attend often to bring fanciful picnic fare and elaborate table settings. Tickets are approximately $12 to $20, depending on the show.

SONOMA STATE UNIVERSITY
1801 East Cotati Avenue, Rohnert Park
(707) 644-2353
www.sonoma.edu/PerformingArts/
Performing arts get top billing at Sonoma State, with works from the pens of local playwrights and international favorites performed year-round, along with dance recitals and musical concerts. The school's Everett B. Person Theatre seats 475 and has featured such Broadway plays as *You're a Good Man, Charlie Brown* and *Scapino.* A smaller theater seating 175 presents plays in the round, mostly student productions suitable for the more intimate stage. *Romeo and Juliet* and *West Side Story* are good examples. There is also Warren

Auditorium, which is devoted to music events throughout the year, from jazz to chamber music. Prices of tickets vary but generally run in the range of $25 to $35.

SPRECKELS PERFORMING ARTS CENTER
5409 Snyder Lane, Rohnert Park
(707) 588-3400
www.spreckelsonline.com
This is one Sonoma County building designed specifically for the arts. When the city of Rohnert Park was developed in the late 1970s, an $8 million performing arts complex of 35,000 square feet was included in the master plan. The center houses two theaters designed and built exclusively for dance, music, and theatrical performances. The Nellie W. Codding Theatre seats 511 patrons and offers performances from nationally known arts groups. The innovative Bette Condiotti Experimental Theatre seats 175 and presents more unusual and creative programming. Main Stage ticket prices usually run $15 to $26.

6TH STREET PLAYHOUSE
52 West Sixth Street (Railroad Square), Santa Rosa
(707) 523-4185
www.6thstreetplayhouse.com
Take two theater companies, add a million dollars and an old building, and you get the newest theatrical venue in Sonoma County—the 6th Street Playhouse. After moving from venue to venue for more than 20 years, two longtime acting troupes now have a permanent home to showcase their talents. The Santa Rosa Players and Actors Theatre teamed up in 2004 to renovate a former cannery building more than 100 years old in Santa Rosa's historic Railroad Square, where they collaborate and present semiprofessional and community theater productions. One month it might be the Actors Theatre mounting a staging of *Stones in His Pockets* or other experimental shows; the next month it could be a rousing production of such classic musicals as *Little Shop of Horrors* or *The Grapes of Wrath.* Ticket prices range from $14 for children to $26 for adults at weekend performances.

 **Close-up**

Now Starring in a Theater Near You: Wine Country

Ever since Alfred Hitchcock put sleepy Santa Rosa on the map in 1942, when he came to town to make his classic thriller *Shadow of a Doubt,* Hollywood moviemakers have returned again and again to Wine Country to capture its rural charms and natural beauty on film.

The list of movies partially or entirely filmed here over the past 50 years is lengthy and impressive. From simple love stories to megaprojects that lean to computer-generated imagery, nearly every genre of motion picture has featured Northern California locations in a starring role.

Here's a brief list of some better-known theatrical movies of the last four-plus decades—and more recent blockbusters—in which Napa Valley, Sonoma County, and our neighbor to the north, Mendocino County, served as a backdrop in one way or another:

American Graffiti	*The Goonies*
The Animal	*Grand Avenue* (HBO)
Apocalypse Now	*The Horse Whisperer*
Bandits	*I Know What You Did Last Summer*
Basic Instinct	*Inventing the Abbotts*
The Beverly Hillbillies	*It's a Mad, Mad, Mad, Mad World*
The Birds	*Lolita*
Black Rain	*The Majestic*
Bottle Shock	*Mumford*
Braveheart	*Peggy Sue Got Married*
Bronco Billy	*Phenomenon*
The Candidate	*Pollyanna*
Cheaper by the Dozen (2003 version)	*Racing with the Moon*
Cujo	*The Russians Are Coming, the Russians Are Coming*
Die Hard 2	
Dying Young	*Scream*
East of Eden	*Shoot the Moon*
Flatliners	*True Crime*
Forever Young	*Tucker: The Man and His Dream*
	A Walk in the Clouds

In addition to full-length feature films, many TV commercials are shot here. Particularly popular is the Sonoma County coastline—its ultragreen hills, rocky cliffs, and switchbacked highway make a snazzy setting for car commercials.

i The Uptown Theater in downtown Napa was expected to open in 2009 after a slow restoration over the years that came to a standstill several times. With 900 seats, the old movie house should be a great venue for live concerts and feature films.

WELLS FARGO CENTER FOR THE ARTS
50 Mark West Springs Road, Santa Rosa
(707) 546-3600
www.wellsfargocenterarts.com
This elegant center became a reality in 1981 when a religious organization was forced to sell the

property as part of its bankruptcy proceedings. The Luther Burbank Foundation moved in and reopened it as a regional arts hub. Wells Fargo added its moniker in 2006, bringing with it an infusion of cash to make much-needed structural upgrades to the building. It's still going strong, with concerts and cultural events of all kinds. Multilayered chandeliers light up the expansive 6,000-square-foot lobby, which is matched by the huge 1,500-seat main theater. Expect the finest in ballets, choral performances, symphonies, films, operas, and concerts of all kinds in this inviting setting. Comics Dana Carvey and the late George Carlin have taped HBO specials at this venue. Tickets run from $15 to $100, depending on the event.

SANTA ROSA JUNIOR COLLEGE SUMMER REPERTORY THEATRE
1501 Mendocino Avenue, Santa Rosa
(707) 527-4419
www.santarosa.edu/srt
With more than 35 seasons under its belt, the SRT is a longtime local favorite. Running from mid-June into early August, plays rotate throughout the season and include musicals, dramas, and comedies. The lineup for the 2008 season included *The Producers, The Crucible, The Women,* and *Kiss Me Kate*. Performances are held variously at the college, Wells Fargo Center for the Arts (see previous listing), or local high schools. This is a professional training program geared to actors in graduate school, all of whom come on scholarships for summer work. Paid directors are well known and usually work on a rotating basis—six work each season. Ticket prices range from $10 to $25.

SONOMA COUNTY REPERTORY THEATRE
104 North Main Street, Sebastopol
(707) 823-0177
www.the-rep.com
Once voted Sonoma County's best theater troupe, Main Street Theatre was formed in 1991, then in 1996 teamed up with a sister company to form Sonoma County Repertory Theatre. The group offers an intriguing selection of fare—the 2008 season featured *Moonlight and Magnolias, Shirley*

Valentine, and *Rabbit Hole*. In addition, the theater offers year-round multidisciplinary training for both children and adults, plus children's theater and a summer Shakespeare festival. Admission prices are generally $18 to $23.

MUSIC AND DANCE ORGANIZATIONS AND VENUES

Napa County

JARVIS CONSERVATORY
1711 Main Street, Napa
(707) 255-5445
www.jarvisconservatory.com
The Jarvis Conservatory was founded in 1973 as a nonprofit generator of scholarships for students of the performing arts. The corporation took a great leap in 1994 when it acquired its own educational facilities. And what facilities they are, centered around the Lisbon Winery, a registered historic landmark built in 1882. Performances are in a 221-seat theater in the acoustically superb, expensively equipped, stone winery building. The conservatory's offerings feature a mix of students and visiting professionals. The first Saturday of each month is opera night, and the specialty of the house is zarzuela, a splendidly costumed, melodramatic form of Spanish opera. Admission for shows can range from $10 and $30.

NAPA VALLEY SYMPHONY
1100 Lincoln Avenue, Napa
(707) 226-8742
www.napavalleysymphony.org
Conducted by Asher Raboy, the symphony plays with an assurance and aptitude you might not expect to find in a city of 75,900. Its primary venue is the refurbished Lincoln Theater at the Veterans Home of California. The Napa Valley Symphony has tackled Beethoven, Tchaikovsky, and Mahler; baroque chamber music; and jazzy compositions by Artie Shaw. It has welcomed guests such as trumpeter Chris Botti, Pink Martini, pianist Ursula Oppens, clarinetist Todd Palmer, and violinist Amy Oshiro. Tickets are generally from $25 to $110.

NAPA VALLEY COLLEGE THEATER
2277 Napa-Vallejo Highway, Napa
(707) 259-8077
www.napavalley.edu

The college's esteemed music program puts on a variety of performances, such as orchestra and vocal recitals, even cabaret nights, during the August-through-May academic year. The theater also has lured independent groups, such as the North Bay Philharmonic Orchestra and the North Bay Wind Ensemble. Occasionally events are staged off campus, usually at wineries. Prices average about $15. Ask about senior and student discounts.

CHAMBER MUSIC IN NAPA VALLEY
Napa Valley Opera House
1030 Main Street, Napa
(707) 963-1391
www.chambermusicnapa.org

This group brings the soothing sounds of chamber music to Wine Country. Artists performing in 2008 included the Takacs String Quartet, Helsingborg Symphony Orchestra, pianist Garrick Ohlsson, and soprano Camilla Tilling. Tickets are sold by subscription only (five concerts cost $100), but some tickets are available for $10 on a first-come, first-served basis the night of the performance.

> **i** Filmmaker Woody Allen left New York City long enough to make an appearance with his New Orleans Jazz Band at the Napa Valley Opera House in 2007.

Sonoma County

SONOMA VALLEY CHORALE
Veterans Memorial Building
126 First Street W., Sonoma
(707) 935-1576
www.sonomavalleychorale.org

This professional-level, 110-member chorus has been singing together since the early 1970s. Its annual concert series brings audiences to their feet with music that might be classical, sacred, or Broadway. The chorale has sung with the Napa Valley and Santa Rosa Symphonies (see listings in this section) and even for the opening ceremony at a Giants baseball game. They've made two European tours, singing their way through France, Italy, and Great Britain. Their regular venue is the Veterans Memorial Building auditorium, which has tiered theater seating for 400. Tickets are $18 for adults and $14 for seniors and children.

CINNABAR THEATER
3333 Petaluma Boulevard N., Petaluma
(707) 763-8920
www.cinnabartheater.org

In the summer of 1970, Marvin Klebe abandoned his career singing baritone with the San Francisco Opera Company, bought a 60-year-old, two-room schoolhouse surrounded by dairy cows and chickens on the outskirts of Petaluma, and began transforming the structure into a theater. Disenchanted with the usual regimentation of grand opera, Marvin's goal was to provide a stage for experimental works that would involve the local community. Today Cinnabar Theater features an outstanding array of entertainers, performing everything from Bach to rock. Theater is also on the schedule, with performances of *Cosi fan tutte*, *The Bluebird*, and *Private Lives* in 2008. Performance tickets are $20 to $35.

SANTA ROSA SYMPHONY
50 Santa Rosa Avenue, Suite 410, Santa Rosa
(707) 546-8742
www.santarosasymphony.com

The Santa Rosa Symphony was founded by George Trombley in 1927. Thirty-two eager (and some talented) amateur musicians played for the first time at the local Elks Club. It is said that Mr. T (as his players called him) was fond of spirited selections. Under his direction the orchestra played Dvořák's Slavonic Dance at most concerts. These performances were enlivened by the gusto of Mr. T, who stomped his foot on the podium until the dust flew. Trombley's tenure lasted 30 years, when Maestro Corrick Brown took over the baton and held it for another 37 years. Today,

Bruno Ferrandis is the orchestra's conductor. The orchestra has long since left the Elks Club and now makes its home at the Wells Fargo Center for the Arts (see listing under Theater Companies and Venues in this chapter). The concert season consists of seven three-day events plus a pops concert and picnic in June (table seating and lawn seating are available), a Redwoods Music Festival in August, and other special events in August and September. There is also a Youth Symphony Orchestra, providing two free concerts for children (particularly popular with kindergarten through third-grade students). Adult ticket prices range between $25 to $50.

VISUAL ARTS ORGANIZATIONS, VENUES, AND GALLERIES

Wine Country is dotted with art galleries, from elegant storefront varieties to the larger "museum" type, to special exhibits at many wineries and even at a couple of roadside attractions. It's impossible to include them all here, but within the listings for each county below are organizations that can supply you with an exhaustive list of places to view, contemplate, and purchase art. Also look for gallery guides and maps at visitor centers.

Napa County

DI ROSA PRESERVE
5200 Highway 121/12, Napa
(707) 226-5991
www.dirosapreserve.org
The subtitle of this collection is Art & Nature, and indeed many of the pieces are blended into the scenery of Carneros, that cool-climate grape-growing region on the north side of San Pablo Bay (see the Wineries chapter). Rene and Veronica di Rosa gathered artwork for more than 40 years, and their current display tends to the whimsical, even outrageous. The indoor space includes a circa-1886 winery the di Rosas converted into their home plus some contemporary galleries full of works of various media. Ticket prices range from $10 to $15; free for children under 12 (except on Wednesdays, when everyone gets

in free). The preserve offers two tours—the Discovery tour, which offers extended time in the main gallery, the di Rosa residence, Courtyard, and North Lawn; and the Arts and Meadows tour, for extended time in the main gallery and the sculpture meadow.

JESSEL MILLER GALLERY
1019 Atlas Peak Road, Napa
(707) 257-2350, (888) 702-6323
www.jesselgallery.com
On the road to Silverado Country Club, in a stately, vine-covered, white-brick building, is the studio of esteemed watercolorist Jessel Miller. The gallery shows the work of both emerging and established artists, in media from oil to collage to jewelry. It also offers public tours, lectures, and demonstrations. The gallery is open 10:00 a.m. to 5:00 p.m. daily.

NAPA VALLEY ART ASSOCIATION
1520 Behrens Street, Napa
(707) 255-9616
www.nvart.org
The Napa Valley Art Association was formed as a nonprofit corporation in 1953 to provide local artists with satisfactory facilities. At the association's once-a-month meetings, guest artists demonstrate their skills and ideas. Those demonstrations are often videotaped for future observation. You can pay a $35 annual fee for membership or surrender a nominal charge to attend a single meeting. The association hosts occasional shows of its members' work—everything from still lifes to portraits and landscapes to abstracts, in all sorts of media. Member galleries are located in downtown Napa at 710 First Street and at the Town Center shopping center at First Street and Randolph Street. Call the association for more information.

ARTS COUNCIL OF NAPA VALLEY
1041 Jefferson Street, Napa
(707) 257-2117
www.artscouncilnapavalley.org
This nonprofit organization strives to provide information to art lovers, as well as support

artists themselves—visual, literary, music, dance, and so forth. Artists are encouraged to register with the council and participate in the annual Open Studios Tour (see the Festivals and Annual Events chapter).

THE HESS COLLECTION WINERY
4411 Redwood Road, Napa
(707) 265-3489
www.hesscollection.com

Donald Hess, the Swiss businessman who made his millions bottling water before he turned to wine, is a passionate art collector, and some of the best of his collection is here in Napa Valley. The three-story, 13,000-square-foot gallery is part of the winery and just as much of a draw to visitors. Hess collects only works by contemporary artists, and the list is impressive: Francis Bacon, Frank Stella, Robert Motherwell, Henri Machaux, and Theodoros Stamos, to name a few. Some of the outstanding conceptual pieces include a group of oversize headless figures fashioned by Polish artist Magdalena Abakanowicz, and a vintage Underwood typewriter going up in flames, a work by Argentinian Leopoldo Maler. There is no charge to enter the museum, which is open 10:00 a.m. to 4:45 p.m. daily.

IMAGES FINE ART
North: 6540 Washington Street, Yountville
(707) 944-0404

South: 6505 Washington Street, Yountville
(707) 944-0606
www.imagesnapavalley.com

North and south have never been closer than at these twin galleries in downtown Yountville, two of the three galleries that compose the Images Collection (see gallery listing for Art on Main in St. Helena). The north gallery opened first, in 1990, and the south gallery soon followed to meet the demand of discriminating art collectors. Neither has a specialty, showcasing works by more than 200 artists. Sculpture and fine art furniture are part of the mix.

MUMM NAPA VALLEY
8445 Silverado Trail, Rutherford
(707) 967-7700, (800) 686-6272
www.mummnapa.com

This winery is probably Napa Valley's premier venue for photography. Luminaries such as Imogen Cunningham, Galen Rowell, Sebastio Salgado, Baron Wolman, and William Neill have been represented on the walls. But the rotating exhibitions have a hard time diverting attention from the winery's Ansel Adams collection. There is no admission charge to the galleries, which are open from 10:00 a.m. to 5:00 p.m. daily.

I. WOLK GALLERY
1354 Main Street, St. Helena
(707) 963-8800
www.iwolkgallery.com

This gallery is known for tasteful art presented in lovely, immaculate spaces. Expect everything from paintings and works on paper to photography and sculpture. The gallery is open 10:00 a.m. to 5:30 p.m. Wednesday through Monday. I. Wolk also operates galleries at the Auberge du Soleil and MacArthur Place spa resorts, and at Cliff Lede Vineyards (1473 Yountville Crossroad in Yountville.)

ART ON MAIN
1359 Main Street, St. Helena
(707) 963-3350
www.imagesnapavalley.com

As one of St. Helena's most prominent and centrally located spaces, Art on Main focuses on, but is not limited to, images of vineyards and wine. It's primarily a venue for Northern California artists working in traditional watercolors and oils. Gail Packer's extensive series of multiplate etchings are featured, with frames designed by artist Hildy Henry. Other contributors include Garberville's Josh Adam and Hopland's Ray Voisard. Open daily 10:00 a.m. to 5:00 p.m.

RASMUSSEN ART GALLERY
Pacific Union College, Angwin
(707) 965-6311, (800) 862-7080
www.puc.edu
Pacific Union College's stylish art gallery is largely a showplace for its own students, faculty, and alumni. It isn't limited to these groups, however. Other recent exhibitions have included the woodcut collages of Harry Clewans. Admission is free, and the gallery is open 1:00 to 5:00 p.m. on Tuesday, Thursday, Saturday, and Sunday.

CLOS PEGASE WINERY
1060 Dunaweal Lane, Calistoga
(707) 942-4981, (800) 366-8583
www.clospegase.com
Art is everywhere at Clos Pegase, from the winery itself—something of a huge modern sculpture—to French and Italian carvings of Bacchus tucked into the wine caves. The variety is impressive too, from granite sculptures to watercolors and collages. Clos Pegase offers a self-guided walking tour of the premises, as well as guided tours of the facility and wine caves at 10:30 a.m. and 2:00 p.m. (no reservation required). Among the pieces are a giant bronze thumb by Cesar Baldachini (designer of the "Cesar," the French equivalent of the Oscar); Michael Scranton's *Wrecking Ball*, an enervating installation in the Reserve Room; and a Henry Moore sculpture (*Mother Earth*) in the portico.

CA'TOGA GALLERIA D'ARTE
1206 Cedar Street, Calistoga
(707) 942-3900
www.catoga.com/galleria
Escape into a world of Renaissance, baroque, and neoclassic styles of painting in Carlo Marchiori's fabulous gallery off Lincoln Avenue. You may recognize his work—he has been commissioned to produce murals found in the world's finest hotels and attractions, including San Francisco's Westin St. Francis and Tokyo's DisneySea. Beautiful ceramics and art furniture are the draw, along with more affordable gifts such as greeting cards.

(Their intricate pop-up cards that unfold to make a stand-up gallery are always a hit when I give them to friends and family.) Marchiori also lives in Calistoga, and his Villa Ca'Toga outside of town is open for weekly tours in summer (see the Attractions chapter). The gallery is open 11:00 a.m. to 6:00 p.m. Thursday through Monday.

LEE YOUNGMAN GALLERIES
1316 Lincoln Avenue, Calistoga
(707) 942-0585, (800) 551-0585
www.leeyoungmangalleries.com
Owner Lee Love Youngman has long been surrounded by creative men. Her father, Ralph Love, was a painter from the early California school who has work hung in major museums. And her husband, Paul Youngman, is noted for his contemporary landscapes, architectural renderings, and marines. The gallery represents more than 60 full-time artists working primarily in traditional oils, watercolors, pastels, and casting sculptures. The gallery is open 10:00 a.m. to 5:00 p.m. Monday through Saturday and 11:00 a.m. to 4:00 p.m. Sunday.

Sonoma County
Southern Sonoma

CORNERSTONE PLACE
23570 Highway 121 (Arnold Drive), Sonoma
(707) 933-3010
www.cornerstoneplace.com
Art goes outdoors at this unique marriage of sculpture and landscaped gardens. The nearly 10-acre site mixes contemporary artwork with nature, such as the *Blue Tree* by Claude Cormier—a real tree completely covered in blue plastic balls. There's also a maze of screen doors surrounded by hay bales, and the Daisy Border, a field of more than 300 common garden pinwheel daisies creating a blur of color on windy days. You've got to see it all to believe it. This property is hard to pigeonhole, and it seems to be evolving as well. Art certainly takes center stage, but

there are also interesting stores and wine tasting, too. The outdoor gallery is located across the highway from Gloria Ferrer Champagne Caves. Admission is $9.00 for adults, $7.50 for seniors, $6.50 for students, and $4.00 for children. Open daily 9:00 a.m. to 5:00 p.m.

SONOMA VALLEY MUSEUM OF ART
551 Broadway, Sonoma
(707) 939-7862
www.svma.org

Located in a former furniture store, this art museum has already staged scores of exhibits in its short life. The first major show was an exhibition of 90 Latin American drawings and paintings by 30 renowned artists. There have also been displays of pottery, textiles, photography, wood, and toys on loan from the Mexican Museum of Art in San Francisco. In summer 2008 the museum featured a large collection of ceramics fired and painted by Pablo Picasso. The museum is open 11:00 a.m. to 5:00 p.m. Wednesday through Sunday. Admission is $5 per person or $8 for families; come on Sunday and it's free for everyone.

SPIRITS IN STONE
452 First Street E., Sonoma
(707) 938-2200, (800) 474-6624

401 Healdsburg Avenue, Healdsburg
(707) 723-1723, (877) 774-6627

3111 St. Helena Highway N., St. Helena
(707) 963-7000, (800) 974-6629

6526 Washington Street, Yountville
(707) 944-9924, (888) 574-6625
www.spiritsinstone.com

"Must touch to appreciate" is the byword when visiting this collection of Zimbabwe Shona sculpture. The form's sleek surface is beyond description. *Newsweek* once called Shona sculpture "the most important new art form to emerge from Africa this century." The *London Evening Standard* says, "These giant stone sculptures are the most hauntingly evocative images . . . the greatest contemporary collection of African art ever seen

in this country." In addition to sculptures, there are African photographs, paintings, and music at these museum-quality galleries, which are open daily 10:00 a.m. to 6:00 p.m.

ARTS GUILD OF SONOMA
140 East Napa Street, Sonoma
(707) 996-3115
www.artsguildsonoma.com

The guild's exhibits change monthly to showcase many artists in many media. Wacky metal sculpture by Martin Munson or the delightful creations made by Thena Trygstad from gourds are only two examples. This location is the gallery for the nonprofit group, Sonoma's oldest continuously operating artists' guild. The gallery is open six days a week (closed Tuesday), from 11:00 a.m. to 5:00 p.m. (until 9:00 p.m. Friday and Saturday).

SONOMA STATE UNIVERSITY ART GALLERY
1801 East Cotati Avenue, Rohnert Park
(707) 664-2295
www.sonoma.edu/artgallery

Changing exhibits of contemporary art are combined with works by artists known regionally, nationally, and internationally. The gallery is open Tuesday through Friday 11:00 a.m. to 4:00 p.m. and noon to 4:00 p.m. on weekends. Admission is free.

ARTS COUNCIL OF SONOMA COUNTY
404 Mendocino Avenue, Santa Rosa
(707) 579-2787
www.sonomaarts.com

Curating new exhibits every eight weeks, the council serves as a resource center for artists and provides a gallery for their work. A typical art competition commissioned by the Sonoma Land Trust challenged artists to portray imagery inspired by Sonoma County's agricultural environment. It's not just two-dimensional art. The council supports not only visual arts but the performing arts, too, with an emphasis on music and poetry. The gallery is open Wednesday through Friday from noon to 5:00 p.m. and Saturday from noon to 4:00 p.m. Admission is free.

Northern Sonoma

PLAZA ARTS CENTER
130 Plaza Street, Healdsburg
(707) 431-1970
www.plazaartscenter.org
I never miss a chance to stop by this gallery when I'm in Healdsburg. It's an all-volunteer nonprofit organization that maintains two galleries under one roof: one for resident artists, who contribute space fees for exhibiting their work, and another for juried shows. Proceeds from sales are shared with local schools, and a couple of student shows are featured each year. The center also conducts art classes for kids and adults throughout the year.

CLOVERDALE ARTS ALLIANCE
P.O. Box 446, Cloverdale, CA 95425
(707) 894-4410
www.cloverdaleartsalliance.org
More artists have discovered the charms of Cloverdale, and this nonprofit group was founded in 2001 to promote painting, sculpture, music, poetry, photography—the whole gamut. The alliance puts on several events, including Friday Night Live, the Twilight Poets Society, and arts and lecture series.

Sonoma Coast

THE REN BROWN COLLECTION
1781 Highway 1, Bodega Bay
(707) 875-2922, (800) 585-2921
www.renbrown.com
Housed in a building with shoji screens and a small Japanese garden, this gallery is dedicated to showing contemporary art from both sides of the Pacific. The major focus is on modern Japanese prints by artists such as Shigeki Kuroda, Toko Shinoda, and Ryohei Tanaka, whose works often appear in prominent museums. The items shown at Ren Brown represent the largest selections of contemporary Japanese prints in California. Also featured are the works of several regional California artists. You'll see watercolor; sculpture in stone and bronze; acrylic paintings; as well as woodcut, silk screen, mezzotint, and lithograph

art. All in all, some 75 artists are represented on two floors of the gallery, which is open 10:00 a.m. to 5:00 p.m. Wednesday through Sunday.

CHRISTOPHER QUEEN GALLERIES
John Orr's Garden, No. 4, Duncans Mills
(707) 865-1318
www.christopherqueengalleries.com
On Highway 116 in historic Duncans Mills, this gallery features both contemporary and early California art, from names such as Don Ealy, Paul Kratter, Joanna Matthews, and Wanda Westberg. The galleries are open every day but Tuesday from 11:00 a.m. to 5:00 p.m., and by appointment.

SEA RANCH LODGE
60 Sea Walk Drive, Sea Ranch
(707) 785-2371, (800) 732-7262
www.searanchlodge.com
Various artists and photographers display their work in the Sea Ranch Lodge's Fireside Gallery and the Front Gallery, a joint venture with Gualala Arts Center, just a few miles north in Mendocino County. New exhibits are posted each month, introduced with a reception of wine and hors d'oeuvres. Call for a list of upcoming exhibits.

FILM FESTIVALS

Mix together innovative independent films with wine, and the result is film festivals in "Hollywood North." Tickets can usually be purchased individually for these events, and passes for multiple screenings are available.

NAPA-SONOMA WINE COUNTRY FILM FESTIVAL
Various locations in the two-county area
(707) 935-3456
www.winecountryfilmfest.com
Entering its 22nd year in 2008, this festival, held during a couple weeks in late July and early August, features documentaries, shorts, and animation in several categories, including Eco Cinema. Screenings might take place outside at Frazier Winery in Napa (picnics welcome).

SONOMA VALLEY FILM FESTIVAL
Venues near Sonoma Plaza
(707) 933-2600
www.sonomafilmfest.org
Big names in moviedom have passed through this festival during its 12 years in existence. In mid-April approximately 65 films are screened over five days, most in venues around the plaza or within walking distance. Robin Williams and Bonnie Hunt made appearances at the 2007 event; Michael Keaton was guest of honor at the 2008 festival.

WEST COUNTY FILM FESTIVAL
Sebastopol Cinemas, 6868 McKinley Street, Sebastopol
(707) 483-1290
www.westcountyfilmsociety.org
Approximately 35 films are shown on four screens during a two-day weekend in October.

SEBASTOPOL DOCUMENTARY FILM FESTIVAL
Sebastopol Cinemas
6868 McKinley Street, Sebastopol

Sebastopol Center for the Arts
6780 Depot Street, Sebastopol
(707) 829-4797
www.sebastopolfilmfestival.org
Focused on documentaries, 40 films are screened in early November at the venues listed.

PARKS AND RECREATION

Some people's idea of recreation in Wine Country is to repeatedly lift a glass of Cabernet while soaking in a Jacuzzi spa. But as you no doubt are aware, Wine Country also offers a phenomenal outdoor environment. From picturesque inland mountains to the crashing waves of an unspoiled and awe-inspiring coastline, you won't find a better place to breathe in fresh air while getting a little exercise. If you're itching to hike, bike, or otherwise become one with nature, this chapter will point you in the right direction. I begin first with the water attractions, specifically the majestic Pacific Ocean and the region's rivers and lakes. Those are followed by the primary parks and recreation areas, then information on golf, bicycling, bowling, horseback riding, swimming, and tennis. There is no individual section on hiking, as almost all of the parks offer trails. Although campgrounds and primitive camping sites are mentioned in these listings, more specific information may be found in the Camping chapter.

THE PACIFIC OCEAN AND SONOMA COAST

If you're thinking of palm-studded sandy beaches, think again. This section of California's coastline bears little resemblance to its southern counterpart—that relatively mild stretch of oceanfront lined with sunbathers from Santa Barbara to San Diego. North of San Francisco the continent drops precipitously to the sea, with narrow crescents of beach occasionally flanking the rocky bluffs—you will not see a single high-rise hotel along this coast. And the ocean is rarely even-tempered here, alternating between violent fits of rage and quiet moods of calm. The summer months, when the sun burns through the morning fog and the wind is low, can be the most pleasant.

The Sonoma coast is hilly, almost mountainous at times, with coastal ranches stretching for miles along the bluffs. Bodega Bay, the county's largest coastal town, is home to a couple hundred commercial fishing boats. Its protected harbor is also an attractive spot for sporting activities. The shoreline on the west side of the harbor is great for windsurfing or launching a kayak. There's

hardly a day when you don't see the fluorescent sails of a sailboard darting about or the rhythmic movements of a kayaker plying the waters.

Surfers looking for the perfect wave will not be disappointed. Two of the most popular spots are Salmon Creek, just north of Bodega Bay, and Goat Rock State Beach, farther up the coast near Jenner. But it's always a good idea to contact a local surf shop for advice—it's a long coastline, and you can spend a lot of time looking.

Sportfishing is big at Bodega Bay. Charter boats sail most days and, depending on the season, will return to port with a mix of rock cod, lingcod, halibut, albacore tuna, and crab.

North from Bodega Bay is a series of state beaches accessible from clearly marked parking areas. These are a part of the Sonoma Coast State Beach, and they are ideal spots for fishing, beachcombing, picnicking, and parties. Unfortunately, the chilly waters are unsafe for swimming, and there are no lifeguards (see the close-up in this chapter about beach safety). You can get maps and information at a ranger station just north of Bodega Bay at Salmon Creek.

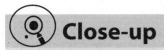 **Close-up**

Don't Get Swept Away by the Lure of the Ocean

The Pacific Ocean along the Sonoma coast is for looking, not touching. Trust me, I know from firsthand experience. The ocean is unsafe for swimming, and even wading is dangerous. The water is cold, about 50 degrees, and the forceful currents will whisk you off toward Japan before you can say *sayonara*.

The strong attraction for landlubbers to splash in the water, to laugh and giggle as they try to outrun a breaking wave along the sand, can be irresistible. But this behavior frequently has tragic outcomes.

Large and powerful waves—called "sleeper," "sneaker," or "rogue" waves—can occur without warning, occasionally sweeping beachcombers off coastal rocks and sand shores. These waves knock you down, disorient you, pull you under. Hypothermia sets in almost immediately, and survival time in the chilly water can be as short as 15 minutes.

A few years back, the ocean nearly took me away in this fashion. I had gone out too far onto a stack of boulders in search of tide pools to amaze friends visiting from out of town. While looking down into a calm pool of water, mesmerized by the sight of a brilliantly colored starfish, I was struck unmercifully by a rogue wave, nearly sucked right off the rock, and drenched to the bone. I hadn't been paying attention, didn't hear or see the wave coming. Even if I had, it might have been too late. I was very, *very* lucky, and I've never made that idiotic mistake again.

These deadly waves are unpredictable, and they are *always* likely to happen, even on calm-weather days.

Sure, there are posted signs along our coast with warnings about rogue waves and the cold water, but many visitors who come from long distances to see the ocean up close sometimes get, to put it bluntly, arrogant and careless. "That doesn't apply to *me*," they tell themselves. More times than not, it is precisely these visitors who lose their lives under largely preventable circumstances: innocently walking a dog near the surf (the dog is swept away, too), chasing a youngster who gets too close to the water (the child survives, the parent perishes), strolling hand-in-hand with your sweetie (one is yanked into the surf, and the other loses his or her life trying to save the first victim). The ocean is lovely to look at, but unforgiving.

Even if they heed the signs and stay away from the water, some visitors decide to climb the rocks—for instance, Goat Rock. This, too, can lead to disaster. The Sonoma County Sheriff's rescue helicopter is all-too-frequently called upon to pluck stranded climbers off the rocks, or retrieve the bodies of hikers or climbers. One misstep on slippery or unstable earth can mean the loss of a loved one.

If you're heading down to the beach, repeat this to yourself over and over before you go: *I'll never turn my back on the water.* And stay off the rocks, too. This is the best advice I can give you.

THE RIVERS

Napa County

Napa River

Though most of the Napa River's length snakes from Mount St. Helena to the town of Napa, the big-time angling is confined mostly to extreme points south, especially as the river broadens between the Butler Bridge (the airborne stretch of Highway 12/29) and Carquinez Strait. Summer fishing isn't great in these tidal waters, but autumn brings hungry striped bass and sturgeon. Try live bait, such as mudsuckers or bullheads for the stripers, live bass shrimp or mud shrimp for the sturgeon. The many sloughs that feed into Napa River in this marshy area are also good bets for striped bass.

Sonoma County
Russian River

Called *Slavyanka* (Slavic girl) by Russian settlers in the 19th century, the Russian River begins in Mendocino County just above Ukiah. Below Hopland, the Russian falls precipitously through a narrow canyon—alongside U.S. Highway 101—and then slows to a more languid pace for the rest of the trip through Sonoma County. It rolls past small wineries, campgrounds, and several towns before reaching the sea at Jenner. During the summer months canoeists, kayakers, rafters, and innertubists converge on the river. The more ambitious paddle the entire 70-mile stretch of relatively flat water below Cloverdale to Jenner, while most visitors opt for a one-day trip of about 10 miles—often between Forestville and Guerneville.

April through September is the best time to canoe the Russian. It's a beautiful run through quiet waters among redwoods, past summer resorts, quaint old homes, and the occasional nude beach. (See the Provisioners listings in this chapter for information on area river outfitters.)

i Be advised that when water levels in streams and tributaries are running low, particularly in the fall, many are off-limits to fishing. To find out if angling is permitted in certain streams, call the Department of Fish and Game at (707) 944-5533 or (707) 442-4502 for a recorded update.

THE LAKES

Napa County

Lake Hennessey

About 5 miles east of St. Helena is an 850-acre reservoir owned by the city of Napa and surrounded by rolling hills covered with grass and dappled with oak trees. Lake Hennessey was formed by the construction of Conn Dam. The Department of Fish and Game stocks Lake Hennessey with trout in the fall, winter, and spring, and you'll find a few bass, bluegill, and catfish as well. Motorized boats are allowed on the water if they don't exceed 18 feet and 10 horsepower; sailboats are permitted if they are 16 feet or shorter. Swimming and kayaking are prohibited, as are waterskiing and windsurfing. There is a $4 access fee for visiting the lake, and an additional $1 special fishing permit is also required. There is no particular place to pay for the fishing permit, so just be ready to fork over the buck if you see the Lake Hennessey caretaker.

Lake Berryessa

It was nearly 50 years ago that Putah Creek was dammed, creating Lake Berryessa between two legs of California's Coast Range (and drowning the town of Monticello). The ragged perimeter gives Berryessa 165 miles of shoreline, more than surrounds massive Lake Tahoe. The north end of the lake is shallow, with gentle, grassy hills sloping down to the water. Contrast that with the south end and its steep, rocky terrain dotted with manzanita and oak. The eastern shore of the lake, meanwhile, is off-limits to the public.

The Federal Bureau of Reclamation owns the shoreline of Lake Berryessa, and major redevelopment plans are in the works. Within the next few years, the bureau intends to redesign and refurbish the lake's recreational areas and restore the natural environment.

The trout and salmon fishing are great here in the spring; in the fall the trout feed on shad near the surface early in the day. Cast between the dam and the Narrows, or trawl in Markley Cove or Skiers Cove. Look for largemouth bass in the coves, smallmouth and spotted bass on the big island in the middle of the lake or at steep, jagged points in up to 40 feet of water. Bluegill usually hang out in the backs of shallow coves all around the lake, and catfish are plentiful at Capell Cove, Pope Creek, and Putah Creek.

There are several marinas and a couple of provisioners where you can rent boats, Jet Skis, wakeboards, inflatables, and other devices for frolicking in the water. Keep in mind that this lake is heavily trafficked, especially in the summer, when the water temperature can be 75 degrees and perfect for swimming. Berryessa welcomes more than 1.5 million visitors each year.

Sonoma County
Lake Sonoma

Designed to control Russian River flooding, the Warm Springs Dam has created some 3,600 surface acres of scenic recreational waters. Located 11 miles north of Healdsburg on Dry Creek Road, this is primarily a boating lake, although water-skiers and Jet Skiers are allowed in designated areas. Skiing is not always considered desirable because of the many large trees that have been partially submerged. Kayakers, however, have no trouble paddling their way through the treetops.

Fishing is the main recreational sport. Generally speaking, boat fishing is more successful than shore fishing, and the upper reaches of the lake usually produce the best results. Fish include smallmouth bass, red ear sunfish, green sunfish, and rainbow trout. A public boat ramp is available, as well as the full-service Lake Sonoma Marina. The fish hatchery is always great fun (see the Kidstuff chapter), and there's an interesting visitor center. Swimming is a possibility, but much of the shoreline is rocky.

Camping is another option at Lake Sonoma. Liberty Glen Campground has 97 campsites for RVs and tent campers, but no electrical or water hookups are available. Primitive campers have 109 sites accessible by boat and/or trail only. You must pack in your own fresh water. These campsites must be reserved through the National Recreation Reservation Service at (877) 444-6777, or at www.recreation.gov.

i February and March are typically the best months to spot large numbers of whales off the coastlines of Sonoma and Mendocino Counties. Watch long enough and you may see a whale "breach," or leap out of the water.

PROVISIONERS: CHARTERS, WATERCRAFT, LESSONS

Here's a sampling of businesses that cater to the aqua-nut. You'll find information on renting everything from a surfboard to kayaks, and lots of these folks will either guide you along or teach you what you need to know to have a safe and enjoyable experience.

Sonoma County
RIVER'S EDGE KAYAK & CANOE TRIPS
13840 Old Redwood Highway, Healdsburg
(707) 433-7247
www.riversedgekayakandcanoe.com
The company offers a wide range of canoe and kayak outings on the Russian River. Owner Lollie Mercer is a third-generation river local, so she knows the territory. You can choose from afternoon, half-day paddles for two to three hours; full days from four to six hours; or even a two-day canoe excursion. Extras such as box lunches are optional; package deals (river trips plus goodies like hats, wineglasses, etc.) are also available. Lollie has a retail store where you can pick up items you may have forgotten to make the trip more pleasant.

BURKE'S RUSSIAN RIVER CANOE TRIPS
8600 River Road, Forestville
(707) 887-1222
www.burkescanoetrips.com
Burke's provides the canoe, paddles, and life jackets starting at just $58 per canoe. Your trip begins at the Burke's base near Forestville and ends 10 miles downstream at Guerneville. Burke's then shuttles you back to your car at Forestville. It's a leisurely four- to five-hour downstream paddle, with the opportunity for many stops on warm, sunny beaches. Bring your own sunscreen, water, hats, towels, cooler, and food. But don't bring your dog—please.

BODEGA BAY SPORTFISHING CENTER
1410-B Bay Flat Road, Bodega Bay
(707) 875-3344
www.usafishing.com/bodegasportfishing
.html

These folks operate charter boats out of Bodega Bay for either full-day or half-day fishing trips for bay or ocean fishing. You'll be going after rock cod, lingcod, halibut, and Dungeness crab. Fishing tackle is available. Whale-watching trips run from November to February. The cost of excursions begins at $85 if you're going for the fish listed above, and you can fish for them in combinations. Going out 60 to 80 miles for halibut would require a negotiated cost. These trips on the sometimes rough and windy ocean waters are not for the queasy; motion-sickness medication is highly recommended.

BODEGA BAY SURF SHACK
1400 Highway 1, Pelican Plaza,
Bodega Bay
(707) 875-3944
www.bodegabaysurf.com

BODEGA BAY KAYAK
1580 East Shore Drive, Blue Whale Shopping Center, Bodega Bay
(707) 875-8899
www.bodegabaykayak.com

These two shops are a must-stop for any visitor eager to glean the optimum amount of local surfing or kayaking knowledge. Bob Miller, the Surf Shack's friendly and welcoming owner, has been surfing nearby Salmon Creek Beach and other primo wave spots since 1984. His shop offers surfboards, wetsuit rentals, and surfing lessons. Bike rentals also are available, along with a great selection of men's and women's beachwear and casual clothing. The nearby kayak shop offers single and tandem kayaks for half-day and all-day rental on sheltered Bodega Bay. More adventurous paddlers may want to consider signing up for the shop's guided tour of the coast.

NORTHERN LIGHT SURF SHOP
17191 Bodega Highway, Bodega
(707) 876-3032, (707) 876-3110 (surf report)
www.northernlightsurf.com

Of the few businesses in the tiny town of Bodega, this one has the most personality. Owner Nick

Marlow built a surf shop that began as 200 square feet into a store chockablock with surfboards, wetsuits, and everything you could want for surfing the Sonoma coastline. The staff always knows the wave conditions and can steer you to the right spots at the right time. Rentals begin at $15 for a surfboard, bodyboard, skimboard, or wetsuit.

i You may wonder about our coastal waters and the likelihood of encountering "Jaws" during your visit. Yes, sharks happen. Though attacks are rare, great white sharks along the Sonoma coast have been known to attack anything that resembles prey, including kayaks and surfboards. If you go into the water, stay alert.

KING'S SPORT AND TACKLE SHOP
16258 Main Street, Guerneville
(707) 869-2156
www.guernevillesport.com

For more than 50 years, this shop has been supplying just about anything you need for the outdoor life. Whether you're a camping, fishing, or archery enthusiast, or you don't know a striped bass from a catfish, King's friendly and knowledgeable staff can provide you with sportswear, footwear, camping gear and accessories, fresh- and saltwater bait and tackle, and guns and ammo. Or select custom, hand-tied flies, dry bags for river activities, and equipment for abalone diving. King's also provides guide service for fishing on the Russian River during steelhead, salmon, and bass season. A local hunting guide is available to help you stalk wild boar, deer, and turkey. King's rents kayaks ($30 a day for one-person kayaks, $50 for two) and gives guided river tours at any time of year, weather permitting.

i Planning to fish? To make certain you don't reel in more than the legal limit, check the latest regulations on the California Fish and Game Web site at www .fgc.ca.gov.

PARKS

Like the statewide system as a whole, the California state parks within Wine Country offer an almost inconceivable diversity of ecosystems. See the grasslands of Austin Creek one day and the redwood canopy of the Colonel Armstrong Tree the next, and try to convince yourself you're on the same planet. And that doesn't even address the historic parks, which are listed in the Attractions chapter.

Included in this section, along with the state lands, are major regional parks and recreation areas that offer more than a lawn and a playground. You're never far from one of them. (You're probably even closer to a municipal park—consult a local map or ask around.) Deciding where to go might depend on when you'll be there. All the parks have a chance of being wet and dreary between November and February, while spring and autumn are always safe bets. Summer takes more thought. The coastal parks and state beaches are wonderful retreats from the heat, but some of the valley parks will put you right into the oven.

With millions of jittery city folks visiting California's parks each year, the campgrounds are often filled to the brim, especially between Memorial Day and Labor Day. You can make reservations up to seven months in advance by phoning ReserveAmerica (see the number listed in the box in this chapter). All major credit cards are accepted.

In Sonoma County, several regional parks with camping facilities take reservations. Because the nearly 200 campsites at the county's four coastal campgrounds are occupied by more than 100,000 people each year, reservations are a must. You can call (707) 565-CAMP (2267) to reserve a camping spot at these Sonoma County regional parks: Gualala Point, Stillwater Cove, Doran, and Spring Lake. (All are profiled in this chapter and in the Camping chapter.)

NOTE: Early in 2008, California Governor Arnold Schwarzenegger raised a ruckus by proposing the closure of 48 state parks to cut the state budget. Three state parks in Wine Country—Armstrong Redwoods State Reserve, Austin Creek State Recreation Area, and Petaluma Adobe State Park—were on the "Terminator's" hit list, along with such popular attractions as San Simeon (the Hearst castle on the state's central coast). But Arnold underestimated the public outcry and several months later reversed his decision. The parks were still open at press time.

Napa County
BOTHE–NAPA VALLEY STATE PARK
Highway 29, 4 miles south of Calistoga
(707) 942-4575
www.parks.ca.gov/default.asp?page_id=477
A trail of cars crawls along Highway 29, but you can leave it behind by exploring this 1,900-acre retreat. Follow shady Ritchey Creek with its redwoods and maples, then venture deeper into terrain covered by oak, hazel, laurel, and madrone. From Coyote Peak you can gaze east into a rugged canyon. And in summer you can enjoy the cool, spring-fed swimming pool in the picnic area. There is a campground (see the Camping chapter) and a horse concession with guided rides. Bothe is just off Highway 29, between Calistoga and St. Helena. Parallel to the highway runs a 1.02-mile trail that connects Bothe with the Bale Grist Mill State Historic Park.

ROBERT LOUIS STEVENSON STATE PARK
Highway 29 between Calistoga and Middletown
(707) 942-4575
www.parks.ca.gov/default.asp?page_id=472
Between Calistoga and Middletown, at the crest of Highway 29, is Stevenson State Park. Less than a mile from the trailhead rests a memorial to the noted author, who in 1880 spent his honeymoon squatting here and weathering a long illness. (His experience wound up as the basis for The Silverado Squatters; see the History chapter.) A steep 100 yards from the memorial, you will encounter a fire road/trail that winds 5 miles to the top of Mount St. Helena, offering brilliant views throughout. If you spin in a circle at the 4,343-foot summit, you'll probably be able to see

the snowcapped Sierra Nevada to the east, the shining Pacific Ocean to the west, Mount Diablo to the south, and, on good days, Mount Shasta 192 miles to the north. The trail is highly exposed, so bring plenty of water and sunblock. The picnic area near the highway is lovely, although a bit noisy. Be advised there are no restrooms and parking is limited, but the vistas at the top are usually worth the trouble.

Sonoma County
Southern Sonoma

SONOMA VALLEY REGIONAL PARK
13630 Highway 12, Glen Ellen
(707) 565-2041
www.sonoma-county.org
A 162-acre spread just outside Glen Ellen, Sonoma Valley has a paved, 2-mile bicycle trail and about 5 miles of hiking trails through meadows and oak-dense terrain, plus a picnic area and dog park. Dogs must be leashed. Open daily from sunup to sundown. Parking is $5.

SUGARLOAF RIDGE STATE PARK
2605 Adobe Canyon Road,
11 miles north of Sonoma on Highway 12
(707) 833-5712
www.parks.sonoma.net/sugarlf.html
www.parks.ca.gov/?page_id=481
Standing at the summit of Bald Mountain, you don't have to choose between Sonoma and Napa Valleys—you can see them both at the same time. The startling view is aided by identifying signs. If you know where to look, you may even see the Golden Gate Bridge, some 50 miles distant. And speaking of distant vistas, Sugarloaf has an observatory with the most powerful publicly accessible telescope in the state. The park as a whole is rugged and steep, an adventurous contrast to the gentle valleys below. The chaparral can get hot in the summer, but you'll be shaded (sometimes by redwoods) if you stay next to Sonoma Creek. Because day parking is limited, the road entering Sugarloaf Ridge tends to congest with spillover traffic, so try to arrive early on weekends. The 7-mile Bald Mountain

loop is the highlight of the park's numerous and well-marked trails. The park is on Adobe Canyon Road, 9 miles east of Santa Rosa or 11 miles north of Sonoma on Highway 12.

HELEN PUTNAM REGIONAL PARK
411 Chileno Valley Road,
1 mile southwest of Petaluma
(707) 565-2041
www.sonoma-county.org
Just outside downtown Petaluma, 216-acre Helen Putnam Park has hiking, biking, and horse trails that lead to exceptional views of town and farmland. There is a playground and a picnic area with a gazebo. The park is open sunrise to sunset. From Petaluma Boulevard, go west on Western Avenue and turn left on Chileno Valley Road. Parking is $5. Dogs must be leashed.

CRANE CREEK REGIONAL PARK
5000 Pressley Road, east of Rohnert Park
(707) 823-7262
www.sonoma-county.org
No, Rohnert Park isn't made up entirely of Home Depots and Wal-Marts. This pleasant, 128-acre park is just east of Sonoma State University, in the foothills of Sonoma Mountain. It has a picnic area and 3 miles of trails open to people on foot, bicycles, and horses. Follow the creek past buckeye, oak, and maple. Crane Creek is on Pressley Road; take Roberts Road east from Petaluma Hill Road. The park is open sunrise to sunset. Parking is $5. Dogs must be leashed, and drinking water is not available in the park.

ANNADEL STATE PARK
Channel Drive, southeast of Santa Rosa
(707) 539-3911
www.parks.ca.gov/?page_id=480
One minute you're in Santa Rosa—the largest city in Wine Country—and the next you're hiking in the solitude of a 5,000-acre parcel of undulating meadow and oak woodland. Within Annadel, you'll find one large natural marsh and one man-made lake, Ilsanjo, stocked with black bass and bluegill. One of the best hikes is the Warren

Richardson–Ledson Marsh Loop, a 7.5-mile outing that takes you to Ledson with its bulrushes, cattails, and bird life. Primary trail junctions are marked, but you should think about carrying a park map to help you sort out the details. There are several picnic sites in the park, which is open 9:00 a.m. to sunset daily. Get there by taking Montgomery Drive to Channel Drive on the east side of Santa Rosa.

SPRING LAKE REGIONAL PARK
Summerfield Road, Santa Rosa
(707) 539-8092
www.sonoma-county.org
Most of this 320-acre park is consumed by the central lake, popular with boaters and swimmers in the summer and with a reputation for harboring huge, *huge* bass. Around the lake are a 2-mile bike path and a parcourse plus about 15 miles of hiking and equestrian trails. Spring Lake also has a developed campground, scads of picnic tables, and a visitor center that's open on weekends. The park is attached to the north end of Annadel State Park. The west entrance is on Newanga Avenue, off Summerfield Road in Santa Rosa; the east entrance is on Violetti Drive, off Montgomery Road. Parking is $6 for day use. Leash your dog, please.

Northern Sonoma

LAKE SONOMA
Stewarts Point–Skaggs Springs Road,
off Dry Creek Road, west of Geyserville
(707) 433-9483
www.parks.sonoma.net/laktrls.html
The 18,000-acre park that surrounds the lake is filled with possibilities, including more than 40 miles of trails with views of the lake. The visitor center has Pomo Indian artifacts, and the California Department of Fish and Game operates a nearby fish hatchery (see the Kidstuff chapter). A self-guided nature trail begins at the center. Lake Sonoma also has a large developed campground and several primitive campgrounds around the lake. From Geyserville, go west on Canyon Road, turn right on Dry Creek Road, and after about

3 miles bend left onto Stewarts Point–Skaggs Springs Road.

Sonoma Coast

DORAN REGIONAL PARK AND WESTSIDE REGIONAL PARK
Highway 1, south and west of Bodega Bay
(707) 875-3540
www.sonoma-county.org
These two recreation areas are on the south and northwest sides, respectively, of ultraprotected Bodega Bay. The parks feature wavy sand dunes and, at Doran, a 2-mile stretch of beach. Each park has a campground, with 47 sites at Westside and 133 at Doran (see the Camping chapter). Each is reached from Highway 1. For Doran Park, turn west at Doran Park Road; for Westside Park, turn west at Bay Flat Road. Parking is $6 in summer, $5 the rest of the year. Dogs must be leashed.

SONOMA COAST STATE BEACH
Off Highway 1
(707) 875-3483
www.parks.sonoma.net/coast.html
www.parks.ca.gov/?page_id=451
The 100-foot bluffs, the ruinous offshore rocks and arches, the coastal scrub plateaus, the black-sand coves—it all adds up to a dramatic oceanside landscape. The park stretches 17 miles along the jagged coastline and offers three trails. The main attraction is Goat Rock, a large, wave-battered massif near the main parking lot. In spring the bluffs are decorated with lupine, sea pinks, and Indian paintbrush. Bodega Head offers whale watching, and a seal colony is at the mouth of the Russian River. Numerous marked and unmarked roads provide access to the beaches, some of them ending in parking lots, some not. All are found off Highway 1 between Bodega Bay and the high bluffs 4.8 miles north of Jenner. There are two campgrounds, at Bodega Dunes and Wrights Beach. There also are two environmental camps. A final word: To get in this water, you'd have to be a lunatic, a harbor seal, or a surfer in a wetsuit (see the close-up in this chapter about beach safety).

When It's Time to Park It

Here are some helpful numbers and Web sites to keep in mind when considering a visit to one of the state parks.

California State Park Information
(916) 653-6995, (800) 777-0369
www.parks.ca.gov

ReserveAmerica Camping
Reservations
(800) 444-7275
www.reserveamerica.com

ReserveAmerica Customer Service/
Cancellations
(800) 695-2269

Special Services for the Handicapped
(916) 653-8148

Caltrans Road/Weather Information
(800) 427-7623

STILLWATER COVE REGIONAL PARK
22455 Highway 1,
approx. 15 miles north of Jenner
(707) 847-3245
www.sonoma-county.org
Even if you're not an abalone diver or a surf fisher, Stillwater Cove is a worthwhile stop. It has a picnic area and 5 miles of hiking trails amid the redwoods. It also has one developed campground with showers and flush toilets. In the park is a preserved one-room schoolhouse from the 19th century. Day-use parking is $5. Dogs must be leashed.

SALT POINT STATE PARK
25050 Highway 1,
approx. 20 miles north of Jenner
(707) 847-3221
www.parks.sonoma.net/coast.html
www.parks.ca.gov/default.asp?page_id=453

Salt Point and neighboring Kruse Rhododendron State Reserve (see the following listing) have a little bit of something for everyone. Salt Point has about 10 miles of rocky coastline featuring sea stacks, arches, and tafoni—those eerily sculpted knobs, ribs, and honeycombs that look like they were crafted for horror movies. The inland portion of the 6,000-acre park has hiking trails through coastal brush, Bishop pine, and Douglas fir, not to mention a ridgetop pygmy forest with half-pint cypress, pine, and redwood. Salt Point also boasts one of California's first underwater parks, Gerstle Cove Marine Reserve, a favorite for scuba divers (and for fish, which are fully protected there). The park has two campgrounds plus walk-in campsites; see the Camping chapter. It straddles Highway 1, about 20 miles north of Jenner or 18 miles south of Gualala.

KRUSE RHODODENDRON STATE RESERVE
Off Highway 1 on Kruse Ranch Road
(707) 847-3221
www.parks.sonoma.net/coast.html
www.parks.ca.gov/?page_id=448
This 317-acre reserve near Salt Point State Park was donated in 1933 by Edward P. E. Kruse, whose family raised sheep, logged, and harvested tanbark there. From April through June the pink and violet rhododendron blossoms brighten the shady forest of fir and second-growth redwood. Five miles of hiking trails offer great opportunities to view the blooms. The reserve is off Highway 1, toward the north end of Salt Point, and is open sunup to sunset.

GUALALA POINT REGIONAL PARK
42401 Highway 1, 1 mile south of Gualala
(707) 785-2377
www.sonoma-county.org
Located just south of the town of Gualala, the park offers both seaside and riverside environments. Anglers show up for saltwater and freshwater fishing. Hikers enjoy 6 miles of trails. Picnickers have several site options, some with barbecue pits. And campers are greeted by a developed area in the redwoods. The visitor center is open 10:30 a.m. to 3:00 p.m. Friday through Monday.

Day-use parking is $5. Dogs must be leashed and have proof of rabies vaccination.

West County/Russian River

RAGLE RANCH REGIONAL PARK
500 Ragle Road, 1 mile north of Bodega
Highway, Sebastopol
(707) 565-2041, (707) 823-7262
www.sonoma-county.org
This 157-acre park offers the usual family-oriented facilities—baseball diamonds, playgrounds, a soccer field, a volleyball court, and picnic sites—but also claims hiking and equestrian trails through rugged oak woodlands and marshes. There is a parcourse too. Each August the park hosts the annual Gravenstein Apple Fair (see the Festivals and Annual Events chapter). The park is off Ragle Road, 1 mile north of Bodega Highway on the western perimeter of Sebastopol, and is open sunup to sunset. Parking is $5. Your dog must be leashed outside of the dog park.

ARMSTRONG REDWOODS STATE RESERVE
17000 Armstrong Woods Road,
near Guerneville
(707) 869-2015
www.parks.sonoma.net/Armstrng.html
www.parks.ca.gov/?page_id=450
In the 1870s lumberman Col. James Armstrong saw the errors of his clear-cutting ways and preserved a large chunk of old-growth redwood forest for posterity. Today it forms the core of 805-acre Armstrong Redwoods Reserve. Don't forget to say hello to two of the most impressive specimens in the park: the 1,400-year-old Colonel Armstrong Tree and the tallest tree in the area, the 310-foot Parson Jones Tree (named for the colonel's son-in-law). Next to the Jones Tree is a gigantic log cross section, whose growth rings chart the course of history back to the first millennium—unfortunately, the tree was cut by vandals in the 1970s. To get to Armstrong from Guerneville, turn north off River Road onto Armstrong Woods Road and proceed 2.2 miles. The reserve is open daily 8:00 a.m. to one hour after sunset.

AUSTIN CREEK STATE RECREATION AREA
17000 Armstrong Woods Road,
near Guerneville
(707) 869-2015
www.parks.sonoma.net/austin.html
www.parks.ca.gov/?page_id=452
Directly adjacent to Armstrong Redwoods Reserve is 5,683-acre Austin Creek State Recreation Area. Austin Creek has 22 miles of trails that hikers must share with horses, which often come in large groups. (Mountain bikes are allowed only on paved roads and on a 5-mile dirt road called the East Austin Creek Trail.) Keep an eye open for deer, wild turkeys, raccoons, and possibly even world-famous ceramic artists. One of the latter, Marguerite Wildenhain, lived here, and her home and workshop—Pond Farm—are within the park, though off-limits since Wildenhain's death. There is a drive-in campground and four backcountry campsites within the recreation area. To get to Austin Creek, follow the directions for Armstrong Woods and, after reaching the entrance, continue another 3.6 miles to Bullfrog Pond Campground.

GOLF

Wine Country isn't a hacker's mecca in the way of a Scottsdale or a Myrtle Beach. On the other hand, the mild climate and the stunning terrain do lend themselves to the links, especially for those who consider walking from fairway to green a form of exercise. The facilities in our coverage area range from nine-hole pitch-and-putts to manicured, PGA-caliber courses. Most have some sort of refreshment option—either a snack bar or a full-service restaurant. And practically all of them have pro shops where you can buy anything you forgot to pack. Following are some basic descriptions of the public courses.

Napa County

EAGLE VINES GOLF CLUB
580 S. Kelly Road, Napa
(707) 257-4470
www.eaglevinesgolfclub.com
Designed by golf legend Johnny Miller, this course opened in 2004 following an extensive makeover

of the property. It's an 18-hole, par 72 course running 7283 yards and dotted with oak trees, creeks, vineyards, and wildlife, making it one of the most scenic courses you will find in this region. Because of its attraction to wild creatures, a canine team patrols the grounds to shoo the Canada geese off the greens. The dogs even have their own cart, marked "Geese Patrol." Green fees are $55 weekdays, $70 on Friday, and $85 on Saturday, cart included. Sundays and holidays are $70. Twilight fees and senior rates are $30 to $60.

NAPA GOLF COURSE AT KENNEDY PARK
2295 Streblow Drive, Napa
(707) 255-4333
www.playnapa.com

With John F. Kennedy Memorial Regional Park and the Napa River to the west and the open spaces of Napa Valley College to the north, this is a nicely placed 18-hole, par 72 course that runs about 6730 yards. Fees range from $33 to $43. A cart is an additional $13 per person. Ask about the reduced senior rates. Napa Golf Course is easy to walk but quite difficult to shoot.

VINTNERS GOLF CLUB
7901 Solano Avenue, Yountville
(707) 944-1992
www.vintnersgolfclub.com

This is a nine-hole course with true, fast greens and a backdrop of the historic Veterans Home of California buildings. Total yardage is 2700; par is 34. Vintners is full of amenities, including a clubhouse that serves breakfast, lunch, and appetizers (including alcohol), and a full pro shop. A lighted, covered, 36-stall driving range has been joined by a smaller grass range. Here are your green fees: $25 for 9 holes and $35 for 18 holes during the week; $35 for 9 holes and $45 for 18 holes on Saturday and Sunday. Rent an electric cart for 9 holes ($20) or 18 ($26).

MOUNT ST. HELENA GOLF COURSE
Napa County Fairgrounds,
1435 North Oak Street, Calistoga
(707) 942-9966
www.napacountyfairgrounds.com

The course itself is modest—nothing special, one might go so far as to say—but Calistoga's scenic situation, within a horseshoe toss of rugged hills, makes this a fine place to spend a few hours. Play all day for $18 during the week, $24 on weekends (seniors play for a few dollars less). Carts are $15. The nine-hole course is 2759 yards and par 36. Enter the course off Grant Street.

Sonoma County

LOS ARROYOS GOLF COURSE
5000 Stage Gulch Road, Sonoma
(707) 938-8835
www.thegolfcourses.net/golfcourses/
CA/11501.htm

This nine-hole course is just southwest of Sonoma, adjacent to Highway 116. It's a par 29, 1539-yard course with weekend green fees of $17 for 9 holes and $20 for 18. Play during the week for slightly less. Pull carts are $2. Los Arroyos has a snack bar and a driving range.

ADOBE CREEK GOLF & COUNTRY CLUB
1901 Frates Road, Petaluma
(707) 765-3000
www.adobecreek.com

Adobe Creek, designed by Robert Trent Jones Jr., is an 18-hole, par 72, 6886-yard course on the southeast edge of Petaluma (just south of Petaluma Adobe State Historic Park). It has a grass driving range, and green fees range from $36 to $56 depending on time of the week and day. Carts are $10 to $14. Collared shirts and soft spikes are mandatory.

ROOSTER RUN GOLF CLUB
2301 East Washington Street, Petaluma
(707) 778-1211
www.roosterrun.com

Rooster Run opened in 1998 and has since become Wine Country's supreme public-golf bargain. Situated across the street from Petaluma Airport, the course is subject to the same afternoon winds that bedevil its neighbor, Adobe Creek Golf Course. The front nine includes an island green on the par 3 number 6. You'll need an oasis after number 5—rated the course's most difficult. Rooster Run management likes to boast that the course includes "the toughest four finishing holes in Northern California golf." Believe it. Regular rates are $37 Monday through Thursday, $41 Friday, and $57 on weekends. Seniors play for $25 Monday through Thursday, and $27 on Friday. Juniors pay $10 after 2:30 p.m. Monday through Thursday. Carts are $14 per rider.

FOXTAIL GOLF CLUB
100 Golf Course Drive, Rohnert Park
(707) 584-7766
www.playfoxtail.com
Extensive renovations on the two courses at this establishment now make for a more satisfying game. The South Course is a par 71, 6492-yard layout with new tees, contoured fairways, and 14 new bunkers. The North Course has new drainage and 45 new bunkers. The lush redwood trees are still there among newly recontoured greens. Weekday fees range from $23 to $35; weekend fees are from $33 to $52. The cart fee is $14 per person.

BENNETT VALLEY GOLF COURSE
3330 Yulupa Avenue, Santa Rosa
(707) 528-3673
www.bvgolf.org
Bennett Valley is the perfect place for a golf course, with the peaks of Annadel State Park forming a backdrop to the east. This course underwent updating recently, gaining a new clubhouse, pro shop, and restaurant. It's an 18-hole, par 72 course that runs 6600 yards. You'll pay $39 on weekends, $25 during the week if you're an out of towner; residents pay slightly less. A cart costs an additional $13 per rider.

OAKMONT GOLF CLUB
7025 Oakmont Drive, Santa Rosa
(707) 539-0415 (West Course),
(707) 538-2454 (East Course)
www.oakmontgc.com
With two 18-hole courses—the championship, par 72 West Course and the executive, par 63 East Course—this is one of the Santa Rosa area's

premier facilities. Oakmont is just southeast of town, off Highway 12 where it starts to wind down toward the Sonoma Valley. Prices range from $50 to $65 on weekends for the west course's 18 holes; twilight fees (any day) are $15 to $30. Fees on the east course are less. Carts are $26 each. You can choose between a snack bar and a sit-down restaurant.

FAIRGROUNDS GOLF COURSE AND LEARNING CENTER
1350 Bennett Valley Road, Santa Rosa
(707) 284-3520
www.fairgroundsgolfcourse.com
Remodeled in 2006, this 9-hole course at the Sonoma County Fairgrounds was reworked at a cost of $3 million with two sets of tees so golfers can enjoy a full 18-hole round. The white tee is a par 29, running 1500 yards. Green fees are the best deal around: 18 holes for $18 on weekdays and $20 on weekends and holidays. Seniors play for $12 and $18. Pull carts are $5 per player for 18 holes, $3 for 9 holes. The on-site Learning Center offers a variety of golf instruction for individuals and groups.

WIKIUP GOLF COURSE
5001 Carriage Lane, Santa Rosa
(707) 546-8787
www.thegolfcourses.net/golfcourses/
CA/11489.htm
Wikiup is a cul-de-sac neighborhood just north of Santa Rosa, and the community pretty much revolves around the nine-hole, par 29 executive golf course. Green fees range from $27 to $30. Walking is preferred here, with no metal spikes.

WINDSOR GOLF CLUB
1340 Nineteenth Hole Drive, Windsor
(707) 838-7888
www.windsorgolf.com
This is a challenging and well-maintained facility— a par 72, 6650-yard championship course—that has hosted the Nike Tour on several occasions. Nontournament green fees are $36 to $56. Twilight (after 2:00 p.m.) rates are several bucks less.

A full cart will cost you $28, $10 twilight. Windsor has a restaurant and a snack bar, and golf lessons are available.

HEALDSBURG GOLF CLUB AT TAYMAN PARK
927 South Fitch Mountain Road, Healdsburg
(707) 433-4275
www.taymanparkgolfcourse.com
Sonoma County's oldest golf course (dating to 1923) has been significantly renovated over the past few years. Recent additions were a three-tiered driving range and a clubhouse with some of the best views in the county. At the eastern edge of central Healdsburg, about a quarter mile from one stretch of the Russian River and a half mile from another, the course is a par 70 nine-holer. It's also one of the best golf bargains you'll find in the area: weekdays it's $15 for 9 holes, $18 for 18; weekends it's $21 and $25. Carts are $6 per person for 9 holes.

THE LINKS AT BODEGA HARBOUR
21301 Heron Drive, Bodega Bay
(707) 875-3538, (800) 503-8158
www.bodegaharbourgolf.com
This seaside course offers wonderful salty breezes and ocean sparkle. Designed by Robert Trent Jones Jr., Bodega Harbour has rolling fairways, cavernous pot bunkers, native coastal rough, and marshlands. (Players are prohibited from entering the marsh on holes 16, 17, and 18.) The 18th has been voted the best finishing hole in Northern California. The par is 70, and the yardage measures 6275 from the black tees. Green fees are $60 Monday through Thursday, $70 on Friday, and $90 on Saturday and Sunday (all rates include cart rental). The clubhouse restaurant, Bluewater Bistro, serves lunch daily, dinner on Friday and Saturday nights, and breakfast on weekend mornings. Bodega Harbour has golf-and-lodging packages in conjunction with several hotels in Bodega Bay and with vacation rental agencies that offer private homes bordering the course.

SEBASTOPOL GOLF COURSE
2881 Scott's Right-of-Way, Sebastopol
(707) 823-9852
www.thegolfcourses.net/golfcourses/CA/11493.htm
This is your one and only option in Sebastopol. It's a 9-hole, par 66 for 18 holes course. Weekdays you'll pay $19 for 9 holes, $22 for 18 holes. Carts are $10 for 9 holes; $15 for 18. There's also a driving range.

NORTHWOOD GOLF COURSE
19400 Highway 116, Monte Rio
(707) 865-1116
www.northwoodgolf.com
Set in an elbow of the Russian River and surrounded by redwood trees, this is one of the more beautiful Wine Country courses. The wind is almost always gentle and the temperatures are moderated by the tall trees. Northwood is a par 36, nine-hole course designed by Alister Mackenzie. Weekday walking fees are $19 for 9 holes to $28 for 18 holes; riding fees are $26 and $40. Weekend walking/riding fees are $38 and $50 for 18 holes. Northwood Lodge is next door (see the Hotels, Motels and Inns chapter).

BICYCLE RENTALS

You may not be Levi Leipheimer, an internationally renowned bicycle racer favored to win the Tour de France someday, but you may still want to traverse the scenic roads of Wine Country on two wheels, as Levi does on a regular basis. From the seat of a rented bike, you'll see for yourself why pro cyclists such as Levi love living and training here. In general, our roads are conducive to biking, with ample shoulders along some of the more scenic and popular roads, and light car traffic on others. Rentals are easy to find, and many establishments offer maps and sound advice. The listings below will get you started planning your two-wheeled adventure. Also check with your hotel or inn—many in Wine Country offer bicycles for their guests to borrow.

Napa County

NAPA RIVER VELO
796 Soscol Avenue, Napa
(707) 258-8729
www.naparivervelo.com

NAPA VALLEY BIKE TOURS
6488 Washington Street, Yountville
(800) 707-BIKE
www.napavalleybiketours.com

ST. HELENA CYCLERY
1156 Main Street, St. Helena
(707) 963-7736
www.sthelenacyclery.com

CALISTOGA BIKE SHOP
1318 Lincoln Avenue, Calistoga
(866) 942-BIKE
www.calistogabikeshop.com

Sonoma County

GOODTIME TOURING COMPANY
Sonoma
(707) 938-0453, (888) 525-0453
www.goodtimetouring.com

RINCON CYCLERY
4927 Highway 12 (Sonoma Highway), Suite
H, Santa Rosa
(707) 538-0868
www.rinconcyclery.com

GETAWAY ADVENTURES
2228 Northpoint Parkway, Santa Rosa
(707) 568-3040, (800) 499-2453
www.getawayadventures.com

SPOKE FOLK CYCLERY
201 Center Street, Healdsburg
(707) 433-7171
www.spokefolk.com

WINE COUNTRY BIKES
61 Front Street, Healdsburg
(707) 473-0610, (866) 922-4537
www.winecountrybikes.com

BOWLING

The lanes below rent all the gear you need for knocking down pins and tallying up strikes.

Napa County

NAPA BOWL
494 Soscol Avenue, Napa
(707) 224-8331

Sonoma County

AMF BOULEVARD LANES
1100 Petaluma Boulevard S., Petaluma
(707) 762-4581
www.amf.com

DOUBLE DECKER LANES
300 Golf Course Drive, Rohnert Park
(707) 585-0226
www.doubledeckerlanes.com

WINDSOR BOWL
8801 Conde Lane, Windsor
(707) 837-9889

HORSEBACK RIDING

Many of the trails in the state parks, state forests, and recreation areas of Wine Country are open to horses, and there are a few outfits that will rent you a steed. Prices begin at approximately $40 per person for a one-hour ride. You provide the cowboy hat and the harmonica.

TRIPLE CREEK HORSE OUTFIT
Sonoma/Napa locations
(707) 887-8700
www.triplecreekhorseoutfit.com
A new owner took over this longtime business in 2003 but kept the horses and the popular routes through three state parks (the name of the

business refers to three creeks in the three parks): Bothe–Napa Valley, Jack London, and Sugarloaf Ridge (see previous listings and the Attractions chapter). All the rides are offered April through October. The Jack London rides skirt vineyards owned by the author's descendants. The Bothe ride offers the shade of Ritchey Creek and the peace of the Mayacmas Mountains. The views from the saddle during the Sugarloaf Ridge ride are fabulous. The rides are $67 for one hour in a group; $110 if you want a private ride. A half-day ride with lunch in Sugarloaf is $350. Reservations are a must. Riders must be at least eight years old. Open-toed shoes are not permitted, and the weight limit is 240 pounds.

CHANSLOR GUEST RANCH AND STABLES
2660 Highway 1, Bodega Bay
(707) 875-2721, (707) 875-3333
www.chanslor.com
You can lead a horse to the water, but you can't make him surf. Chanslor offers four daily beach rides from its inland property—over the dunes to Bodega Bay and back. There are other options too: the one-and-a-half-hour Salmon Creek Trail, which winds into a canyon and around much of the company's 378 acres; the one-hour Eagle View ride, where you are likely to spot a couple of resident bald eagles; and a half-hour trek through the Wetlands Preservation Habitat. Prices are about $60, $60, and $40, respectively. Private rides are more expensive than rides in groups of six. Chanslor also rents vacation homes on the ranch, ranging from $150 to $900 per night.

SWIMMING

If you are not fortunate enough to be staying (or living) next to any Wine Country lakes during those summer hot spells, you might feel the need to jump into a different body of water—specifically, the rectangular, chlorinated kind. Below is a partial list of public swimming facilities. Call for more information on lessons, admission fees, and no-kids or kids-only periods.

Also, some spas permit walk-in (dive-in?) swimmers who pay for day use of their mineral pools. Search out the Spas and Resorts chapter for relevant information.

Napa County

ST. HELENA COMMUNITY POOL
1401 Grayson Avenue, St. Helena
(707) 963-7946
www.ci.st-helena.ca.us

Sonoma County

PETALUMA SWIM CENTER
900 East Washington Street, Petaluma
(707) 778-4410
www.cityofpetaluma.net

ALICIA POOL
300 Arlen Drive, Rohnert Park
(707) 795-7265
www.rpcity.org

BENICIA POOL
7469 Bernice Avenue, Rohnert Park
(707) 795-7582
www.rpcity.org

LADYBUG POOL
8517 Liman Way, Rohnert Park
(707) 664-1070
www.rpcity.org

HONEYBEE POOL
1170 Golf Course Drive, Rohnert Park
(707) 586-1413
www.rpcity.org

i When visiting coastal parks, be prepared for sudden changes in the weather. It's best to dress in "California layers," as it may be sunny and warm, then foggy, then chilly and windy—sometimes all within a few minutes.

MAGNOLIA POOL
1501 Middlebrook Drive, Rohnert Park
(707) 795-8619
www.rpcity.org

FINLEY AQUATIC COMPLEX
2060 West College Avenue, Santa Rosa
(707) 543-3760
www.ci.santa-rosa.ca.us

RIDGEWAY SWIM CENTER
455 Ridgeway Avenue, Santa Rosa
(707) 543-3421
www.ci.santa-rosa.ca.us

HEALDSBURG MUNICIPAL SWIMMING POOL
360 Monte Vista Avenue, Healdsburg
(707) 433-1109
www.ci.healdsburg.ca.us

CLOVERDALE MEMORIAL POOL
105 West First Street, Cloverdale
(707) 894-3236, (707) 545-9622

IVES POOL
7400 Willow Street, Sebastopol
(707) 823-8693
www.ivespool.org

TENNIS

Because of the geographic enormity of Wine Country, a complete list of available public tennis courts would be harder to handle than an Anna Kournikova first serve. So here's a list of city recreation departments throughout the region. The folks on the other end of the line will tell you where the courts are—many of them are after-hours high school facilities—whether you need reservations, what it costs to play there, and whether the courts are lighted.

Napa County
CITY OF AMERICAN CANYON RECREATION
(707) 647-4566

CITY OF NAPA PARKS AND RECREATION
(707) 257-9529

TOWN OF YOUNTVILLE RECREATION
(707) 944-8712

CITY OF ST. HELENA RECREATION DEPARTMENT
(707) 963-5706

CITY OF CALISTOGA PARKS AND RECREATION
(707) 942-2838

Sonoma County
SONOMA CITY HALL
(707) 938-3681

CITY OF PETALUMA PARKS & RECREATION
(707) 778-4380

CITY OF COTATI
(707) 792-4600

CITY OF ROHNERT PARK RECREATION DEPARTMENT
(707) 588-3456

CITY OF SANTA ROSA RECREATION & PARKS OFFICES
(707) 543-3282

TOWN OF WINDSOR PARKS AND RECREATION
(707) 838-1260

CITY OF HEALDSBURG
(707) 431-3300

CITY OF CLOVERDALE
(707) 894-2521

CITY OF SEBASTOPOL RECREATION INFORMATION
(707) 823-1511

SPECTATOR SPORTS

The Wine Country approach to spectator sports varies from the occasional world-class bicycling event to the more populist sprint-car racing. And professional-level happenings are always available in the Bay Area and Sacramento. Several pro sports franchises take the field (or diamond, or court, or rink) within two or three hours of Wine Country—each is covered in this chapter. Though the list goes on and on, I had to draw the line somewhere. Some sports outings seemed more appropriately included in the Festivals and Annual Events chapter, and if the activity is more participatory than vicarious in nature, look for it in the Parks and Recreation chapter. The radio stations listed below every franchise name are the teams' English-language flagship stations. The team's Web sites usually have podcasts for downloading, too. The phone numbers are ticket sources, and for major events you also can try Ticketmaster at (415) 421-8497 or visit www.ticketmaster.com.

BASEBALL

SAN FRANCISCO GIANTS
AT&T Park, 24 Willie Mays Plaza,
San Francisco
(415) 972-2000
www.sfgiants.com
KNBR 680 AM

One of two franchises—the Los Angeles Dodgers being the other—to open major-league baseball to westward expansion in 1958, the Giants have been a team of individual standouts but little collective success. The team has won several National League West championships and two pennants in its 40-plus years in San Francisco, losing the World Series to the Yankees in 1962, to the Oakland A's in 1989, and to the Anaheim Angels in 2002. The team celebrated its 50th anniversary playing in San Francisco in spring 2008.

The 1960s squads had big clout from legendary center fielder Willie Mays, first basemen Willie McCovey and Orlando Cepeda, and brilliant pitcher Juan Marichal. In this century, Barry Bonds became a one-man draw. He went down in the history books in 2001 for hitting 73 home runs during regular season play. Bonds hit his 600th career home run in 2002, joining an exclusive club of only three other players in the history of the game: Babe Ruth, Willie Mays, and Hank Aaron. Finally, in 2007, Bonds broke Aaron's 33-year-old home-run record (755) by hitting his 756th homer in the fifth inning of a home game. But even as he was making his victorious run around the bases, his image was tarnished by allegations that he used performance-enhancing steroids. He left the Giants shortly afterward, and early in 2008 was awaiting trial for perjuring himself before a grand jury.

The Giants do their thing at AT&T Park. Designed by the renowned architectural group of HOK Sports Facilities, the ballpark hugs San Francisco Bay—so close, in fact, that prodigious drives to right field end up in salt water, retrieved by a canine employee. The stadium includes a brewpub, a bayside promenade that allows fans to peek through the fence for no charge, and, unlike the 49ers' Candlestick Park, ample public transportation options. Current Giants ticket prices range from $10 in the view reserve outfield, to $75 to $95 in the best behind-the-plate seats (if you can find one).

OAKLAND ATHLETICS

McAfee Coliseum, off Interstate 880, about 5
miles south of Interstate 980, Oakland
(510) 638-4900
www.oaklandathletics.com
www.coliseum.com
KFRC 610 AM

The Athletics' history in Oakland has been the
steepest of roller-coaster rides. The A's had been
unqualifiedly dreadful in Kansas City, but they
immediately posted their first winning record in
16 years after moving to the Bay Area in 1968.
Reggie Jackson hit the home runs and made
the headlines, but the strength of the team was
pitching, led by starters Jim "Catfish" Hunter and
Vida Blue, and handlebar-mustachioed reliever
Rollie Fingers. But the Athletics soon sank into
ineptitude. They played games in the late 1970s
that drew fewer than 1,000 fans. The A's became
Major League Baseball's best team from 1988
to 1990. Dave Stewart won 20 or more games
four straight years, Dennis Eckersley was reborn
as baseball's eminent closer, Rickey Henderson
returned to his hometown to steal bases and
runs, and hitting giants such as Jose Canseco and
Mark McGwire drove opposing pitchers into deep
depression. Oakland was upset by the Dodgers in
'88 and the Reds in '90 but flattened the Giants in
1989's "Bay Bridge Series," which was interrupted
by the 7.1-magnitude Loma Prieta earthquake.
McAfee Coliseum lies south of downtown Oakland, right off I-880. The cheapest A's ticket is $9;
the most expensive is $55.

i If you're going to either the Coliseum
or the Arena in Oakland to catch a
game, consider taking BART, the Bay Area
Rapid Transit system. You can park in
Richmond, at the northwest tip of what is
commonly called the East Bay, and take a
train to the coliseum's doorstep. Call (510)
236-2278 or visit www.bart.gov for schedules and directions.

FOOTBALL

SAN FRANCISCO 49ERS

Candlestick Park, off U.S. Highway 101,
about 1.5 miles south of Interstate 280, San
Francisco
(415) 656-4900, (800) 746-0764
www.sf49ers.com
KNBR 680 AM, KSAN 107.7 FM

The caps, the T-shirts, the bumper stickers, and
the bar decorations are there to make sure you
don't forget, not even for a minute, that Wine
Country is Niners country. It wasn't always this
way, of course. The team had its core following
for decades, but it wasn't until the harmonic
convergence of Bill Walsh and Joe Montana that
the serious adulation began. The 49ers were in
the Super Bowl by January 1982, and they'd be
back four times in the next 13 seasons. Along the
way, Montana was replaced by scrambling Steve
Young, now retired from the game. Wide receiver
Dwight Clark was replaced by Jerry Rice, maybe
the best player ever to wear an NFL uniform. Even
Walsh was replaced with protégé George Seifert,
who was in turn supplanted by Steve Mariucci
in 1997. Through it all, the team hardly missed a
beat—until 1999, when it sank to the bottom of
the NFL. The team took another hit in 2001, when
Jerry Rice defected to the Oakland Raiders. Single
tickets to a game are approximately $113 along
the sidelines, $86 above the end zones, and $56
in the nosebleed seats. Allow at least 90 minutes
to Candlestick Park from either Napa or Santa
Rosa, progressively longer from points farther
north. And for heaven's sake, take along a jacket
and a thermos of something hot.

OAKLAND RAIDERS

McAfee Coliseum, off I-880,
about 5 miles south of I-980
(510) 864-5000, (510) 625-8497
www.raiders.com, www.coliseum.com
KSFO 560 AM

That wasn't a tremor you felt in June 1995, it
was the earth shifting back onto its proper axis
upon the Raiders' return to Oakland—the first
time a pro sports franchise had come back to a

city it once fled. The team's pinnacle was 1972 to 1976, when the blustery John Madden coached at least seven Pro Football Hall of Fame players: center Jim Otto, guard Gene Upshaw, tackle Art Shell, wide receiver Fred Biletnikoff, kicker George Blanda, linebacker Ted Hendricks, and cornerback Willie Brown (not to be confused with San Francisco's iconoclastic former mayor of the same name). Stars of the 1980s included soft-spoken quarterback Jim Plunkett, relentless defensive end Howie Long, and incomparable running back Marcus Allen. The Raiders' rich on-field history notwithstanding, the best reason to come to Oakland on an autumn Sunday always has been the spontaneous circus that erupts in the parking lot and the cheap seats. It's a freak show of the highest order. Expect to see Darth Vaders, Grim Reapers, dangling bronco effigies, and more Harley-Davidsons and pirate tattoos than you can shake a cutlass at. Tickets range from $26 to $96. Finally, take note that the Raiders moved their summer training camp to Napa in 1996. The team has an annual fan day in July—and perhaps a couple of open workouts—at Memorial Stadium, which is near the intersection of Jefferson Street and Pueblo Avenue.

BASKETBALL

GOLDEN STATE WARRIORS
Oracle Arena, off I-880,
about 5 miles south of I-980, Oakland
(510) 986-2200
www.warriors.com
KNBR 680 AM/1050 AM

Born in Philadelphia in the 1940s, the Warriors moved west, becoming the San Francisco Warriors from 1962 to 1971, before floating across the bay to Oakland to become Golden State. The team that brought Wilt Chamberlain from Philadelphia in 1962 has won only one NBA title on the West Coast. That came in 1975, when superstar Rick Barry and a gang of overachievers shocked the Washington Bullets in a four-game sweep. Big-time performers such as Nate Thurmond and Cazzie Russell came before 1974–75, Bernard King and World B. Free after, but no other Warriors team has gone all the way. Things seemed to be looking up under coach Don Nelson in the early 1990s, but the situation blew up when Nelson feuded with star forward Chris Webber in 1994–95. Warriors tickets range from $15 to $100.

SACRAMENTO KINGS
ARCO Arena, near the northeast corner of
Interstate 5 and Interstate 80, Sacramento
(916) 928-6900
www.nba.com/kings
KHTK 1140 AM

Game after game, ARCO Arena is filled to the rafters with screaming, maniacal Kings fans. Finally, they've got something to shout about. In their first 13 seasons in Sacramento the Kings never had a winning season. But the love of hoops was unconditional here. Sellouts are practically a Sacramento city ordinance. Existing franchises in various sports, including the Raiders and the A's, certainly have taken notice, making overtures to Sacramento in the recent past regarding possible moves. (Sacramento has been the Kings' home since 1985, but they've moved before—from Rochester, Cincinnati, and Kansas City.) ARCO Arena is just north of Sacramento. From Wine Country, take I-80 to Sacramento and turn off on I-5 north. Take the Del Paso Road exit and follow the signs. Tickets range from $10 to $165 per game, though all but the cheapest seats are usually snapped up by season-ticket holders.

HOCKEY

SAN JOSE SHARKS
H-P Pavilion, off I-880, San Jose
(408) 287-7070, (800) 366-4423
http://sharks.nhl.com
KFOX 98.5 FM, KVON 1440 AM, KNBR
680/1050 AM

The Sharks made a reputation as giant-killers as they knocked off high-ranked opponents—Detroit and then Calgary—in the opening rounds of the 1994 and 1995 NHL playoffs. But the problem for San Jose has been getting to the playoffs. The Sharks have been known as the bottom feeders of the Western Conference, though coach Darryl Sutter's 1999–2000 squad was eminently respectable. In 2008 the team came within minutes—in quadruple overtime—of making the playoffs, losing to the Dallas Stars. H-P Pavilion is a tidy venue smack-dab in the middle of a tidy city, and professional hockey has been an incongruous hit in Silicon Valley. To get to the arena, exit I-880 at Coleman Avenue, turn left on Coleman, right on Julian, and follow the parking signs. Be advised that San Jose is about 40 miles south of San Francisco or Oakland, so getting there and back from Wine Country takes an investment of a full day or a very long evening. Sharks tickets range from $19 for the most distant upper-reserved seats to $102 for sideline club seats. Many others are in the $39 to $81 range.

SOCCER

SAN JOSE EARTHQUAKES
Two locations, depending on game:
Buck Shaw Stadium in Santa Clara, or
McAfee Coliseum in Oakland
(408) 556-7700
http://web.mlsnet.com
KLIV 1590 AM

When Major League Soccer officially set up shop in spring 1996, the fledgling league chose San Jose as the site of its inaugural game. The city had everything MLS was looking for: an established soccer tradition, a first-rate stadium, and a well-run organization headed by transplanted Englishman Peter Bridgwater. More than 31,000 fans showed up for the first game on April 6, 1996, and the Clash (as they were then known) did not disappoint, leaving with a 1–0 victory over D.C. United. Midfielder Eddie Lewis was named to the U.S. National Team for 1999 while gifted forward Ronald Cerritos played for El Salvador. In 2000 they meshed under the tutelage of Bay Area favorite Lother Osiander. The Earthquakes won the MLS Cup in 2001 over the L.A. Galaxy, on Cerritos's winning goal. In 2003, with the phenomenal Landon Donovan, they earned the cup in a victory over the Chicago Fire. Adult tickets range from $20 for goal-view seats to $60 for the "premier" category. The Major League Soccer schedule runs from March through October.

LACROSSE

SAN JOSE STEALTH
H-P Pavilion, off I-880, San Jose
(925) 460-8290
www.sjstealth.com
KLIV 1590 AM

One of 13 lacrosse teams in the National Lacrosse League in the United States and Canada, the Stealth plays a 16-game regular schedule, followed by a championship playoff. The season runs from December through April. Lacrosse is played inside the confines of an ice hockey rink, but with special turf placed on top of the ice. The game is rather hockey-like, combined with the fast pace of basketball. Tickets range from $23.50 to $33.50, with discounts for students and seniors.

GOLF

CHARLES SCHWAB CUP CHAMPIONSHIP
Sonoma Golf Club, Sonoma
(707) 939-4131, (800) 868-7563
www.charlesschwabcupchampionship.com
This is the final event on the Champions Tour (what used to be called the PGA Seniors Tour), a four-day party in late October at the Sonoma Golf Club, a private par 72, 7,093-yard course built in 1928. Tour players 50 and older have included Hale Irwin, Tom Watson (2005 winner), Jim Thorpe (2003, 2006, and 2007 winner), and Gil Morgan. In 2004 a relative youngster to the tour, Mark McNulty, shot a final-round 66 to win the $2.5 million championship by a stroke over Tom Kite. Ticket prices vary depending on what you want to see; a grounds pass is $30 for the tournament weekend. Add access to the wine festival and it goes up to $45 per day. Taking part in the whole enchilada costs between $100 and $150. This event has raised more than $1 million for local charities.

MOTOR SPORTS

Don't be surprised if the still air of your summer evening is suddenly torn apart by the growl of a 750-horsepower engine, the scent of ripening grapes replaced by a whiff of high-octane fuel. Love 'em or hate 'em, racing machines are here to stay in Wine Country.

CALISTOGA SPEEDWAY
Napa County Fairgrounds, 1435 North Oak Street, Calistoga
(707) 942-5111
www.napacountyfairgrounds.com
Calistoga is a gathering point for devotees of sprint cars, those miniature, winged beasts that evolved from old Indy 500 roadsters. Pound for pound, sprint cars pack as much power as modern-day Indy cars, and they seem to be as loud. They produce downward force, which helps the car grip the track; the larger one also happens to provide handy space for advertising.

Calistoga Speedway's half-mile dirt track hosts at least three sprint-car nights a year: one in mid-June and two in August. A typical program might include four 10-lap heat races, a feature-inversion dash, a 12-lap semi-main event, and a 25-lap feature event. Tickets run about $20 for a single race.

INFINEON RACEWAY
Highways 37 and 121, south of Sonoma
(800) 870-RACE
www.infineonraceway.com
If it's nitro-burning, rubber-ripping, and asphalt-grabbing, chances are you'll find it here. This might be the world's busiest raceway, with an average of 340 days a year of activity including 50 of 52 weekends. Much of that is devoted to the resident Jim Russell Racing Drivers School, but there is plenty of competition among a variety of internally combusting machines. Annual events at this raceway that draw huge crowds include the NASCAR Nextel Cup and the FRAM Autolite NHRA Nationals. Besides the twisting, 12-turn, 2.52-mile road course and the quarter-mile drag strip, Infineon offers 700,000 square feet of coexisting shop space and posh, tower VIP seats. The facility is in a beautiful corner of lush rolling hills at the southern tip of Sonoma County. If you just want a look, it's open to the public free of charge on weekdays. If you want to get truly revved, race tickets range from $25 to $180 for major events like NASCAR, with other events in the $10 to $85 range.

PETALUMA SPEEDWAY
Petaluma Fairgrounds,
100 Fairgrounds Drive, Petaluma
(707) 733-7223
www.petaluma-speedway.com
Check the notes about sprint cars listed in the Calistoga Speedway section and apply them here. The three-eighths-mile, semi-banked track is located at the fairgrounds, just west of US 101 on East Washington Street. Weekly shows (Saturday nights) are $13 for adults, $9 for kids 6 to 11, $7 for seniors, and free for kids 5 and under. Special event tickets run a couple bucks higher.

MARATHONS AND RUNNING EVENTS

VINEMAN IRONMAN TRIATHLON
Northern Sonoma County
(707) 528-1630
www.vineman.com
This popular event—celebrating its 20th year in 2009—attracts more than 2,000 participants from throughout the world. It is set mostly on the backroads of northern Sonoma County, with the swimming portion held in the Russian River at Guerneville. The full course includes a 112-mile cycle, 26.2-mile run, and 2.4-mile swim. A Half Vineman is also featured.

KAISER PERMANENTE NAPA VALLEY MARATHON
Calistoga to Napa
(707) 255-2609
www.napavalleymarathon.org
If you're gonna torture yourself, you might as well do it in Eden. This is an unbeatable course: 26.2 miles due south along the Silverado Trail, hills

hugging the left side of the road, and a yellow sea of blooming mustard to the right. Only the last half mile, the approach to the finish line at Vintage High School, is within any city limits. And after three moderate hills in the first 6 miles, the course offers a gently rolling descent. *Runner's World* magazine named this one of the top 20 marathons in America in 2002. The Napa Valley Marathon usually takes place the first Sunday in March. The 2008 run was the 30th annual. You can park at Vintage High and take a shuttle bus to the start line (just south of Calistoga on the Silverado Trail) but be punctual—the last bus leaves at 5:30 a.m. Weather can vary, of course, but bet on lifting fog and temperatures in the mid-40s at start time (7:00 a.m.), progressing to warm sunshine later in the morning. Early entry costs $85, and it jumps to $100 two months before the race.

THE RELAY
Calistoga to Santa Cruz
(650) 508-9700
www.TheRelay.com
The marathon doesn't present enough of a challenge for you? Try the Relay, a 199-mile trek that winds through seven counties and 36 cities from Calistoga to Santa Cruz, past cow pastures and redwoods and across the Golden Gate Bridge. Everything about this race is unique, except for sore feet and sweaty bodies. Start times are staggered, and teams of 12 competitors split up 36 3- to 7-mile legs, with vans leapfrogging runners to their next start position. The race heads south from Calistoga on the Silverado Trail, with competitors running through the night and the first finishers reaching the Pacific Ocean early the next morning. Several Silicon Valley companies have been involved, presenting more peculiarities: This was the first race in which runners wore bar codes and got scanned at checkpoints. The Relay is run under a full moon in the spring—the 2008 event was April 19–20. The entry fee is $50 per runner, due by April 1. Individuals looking for a team have two options: Find one yourself at the Web site, or mark the appropriate box on your application and organizers will place you.

BICYCLE ROAD RACES

CHERRY PIE CRITERIUM
Napa Valley Corporate Park, Napa
(707) 815-4828
www.eaglecyclingclub.org
The carbo-loading comes after the race at this event. Besides the $6,000 or so in prize money and goodies, the top three finishers in each class are awarded fresh cherry pies. The 1-mile course, which includes one modest hill, is bounded by Napa Valley Corporate Drive, Napa Valley Corporate Way, and Trefethen Way. The simplest way to find the start/finish line is to look for the famous Grapecrusher statue south of Napa. Approximately 650 racers split up into 16 divisions for men, women, and children. The criterium is run the second or third Sunday in February, and the 2008 Cherry Pie was the 33rd annual. Entry fees are reasonable, from $15 to $25 in advance depending on age; add $10 if you wait to register on race day. Spectators watch for free.

AMGEN TOUR OF CALIFORNIA
Sonoma County into Napa County, and beyond
(707) 577-8674
www.amgentourofcalifornia.com
Big-time bicycle racing entered Santa Rosa with a bang in 2006 with this major annual event, dubbed the "Tour de France of North America." The race attracts the best professional riders in the sport, including Santa Rosa's own Levi Leipheimer, an international cycling star some believe is destined to soon win that big race across the pond. The eight-day Tour of California route changes from year to year but is usually 600 to 700 miles up and down the state, with Santa Rosa hosting the end of stage 1 and the kickoff of stage 2. It costs nothing to watch the crowded field of approximately 180 pros zip up, down, and around rural Sonoma County roads to finish in a blur in downtown Santa Rosa. The cyclists also glide quickly through Napa County on their way to inland areas of the state. The first three years of the event were held in mid-February; the 2009 race may take place in the spring.

HORSE RACING

SONOMA COUNTY FAIRGROUNDS

Highway 12, east of US 101,
Santa Rosa
(707) 545-4200
www.sonomacountyfair.com

If the hoofbeat of the thoroughbreds should happen to draw your attention in midsummer, heed the call to the colors. What you'll find at the Sonoma County Fair in late July and early August is one of the country's most entertaining horse-racing meets. Wagering on the competition is optional. First post is 12:45 p.m.

THE JOCKEY CLUB

1350 Bennett Valley Road, Santa Rosa
(707) 524-6340, (800) 454-7223
www.sonomacountyfair.net/jockeyclub.php

This is where Wine Country's wise guys and other hip handicappers amuse themselves when the shed rows across the street aren't booked with blood stock. It's a year-round off-track concession offering races live via satellite TV from major courses in California (e.g., Golden Gate Fields, Bay Meadows, Santa Anita, Hollywood Park, Del Mar), New York, and Florida. A small cover charge gets you through the door and into a well-kept room stocked with eight projection big-screen TVs, 70 monitors, a full bar, and complete food and beverage services. Friendly clerks will take your wagers, or you may purchase a voucher and have at the auto-tote self-serve screens yourself. Either way, remember: There's a winner in each race.

COLLEGE SPORTS

Wine Country isn't exactly a hotbed of collegiate sports. But if you really feel like waving a pom-pom and belting out fight songs, here are some of your options.

SONOMA STATE UNIVERSITY

1801 East Cotati Avenue, Rohnert Park
(707) 664-2521
www.sonomaseawolves.com

With a couple players going on to the NFL, including Pro Bowl guard Larry Allen of the Dallas Cowboys, the NCAA Division II Seawolves reached a respected place among small football programs. That came to an end in 1997, when the university dropped football in the face of formidable travel expenses. Sonoma State still has plenty of athletics. Soccer is king and queen there: The women, who made it to the Division II championship game in 1998, enjoyed great success in the '90s, winning six straight Northern California Athletic Conference titles from 1990 to 1995 and a national championship in 1990. The men won five of seven NCAC titles between 1990 and 1996, and went on in 2002 to win the NCAA Division II national championship—the first ever for any SSU men's team.

PACIFIC UNION COLLEGE

1 Angwin Avenue, Angwin
(800) 862-7080
www.puc.edu

Tiny PUC has to scramble to come up with funding for sports, but the NAIA Division II school does what it can. It fields men's and/or women's teams in soccer, volleyball, cross-country, and basketball. The Pioneers have produced recent California Pacific Conference champions in women's basketball and men's golf.

UNIVERSITY OF CALIFORNIA

2223 Fulton Street, Berkeley
(800) 462-3277
www.calbears.com

Known primarily for its academics and tradition of radical politics, Cal also has a rich sports heritage, with Rose Bowl victories dating to 1921 (28–0 over Ohio State). The Golden Bear's football program produced such stars as Craig Morton, Steve Bartkowski, Wesley Walker, and Chuck Muncie. Bears basketball produced Jason Kidd (now an NBA star) in the early '90s. Cal claims 74 national team titles in 13 sports and can boast 159 individual, relay, and doubles titles.

KIDSTUFF

Wine Country is not Orlando, but if you have kids in tow, this region has some suitable diversions for little ones. Many of the entries in this chapter are reliable kid pleasers, guaranteed to put a smile on small faces while also keeping the big kids entertained. In addition, check out the Attractions chapter, which features information on other family-oriented places, such as Safari West, the Pacific Coast Air Museum, and Train Town. And read about great outdoor destinations for all ages in the Parks and Recreation chapter.

Price Code

Many of these attractions are free to enter (such as toy stores and some parks). Other places may charge various prices, depending on the activity you choose. Take this breakdown of per-person costs as merely a guide.

$	Less than $5
$$	$6 to $10
$$$	More than $11

NAPA COUNTY

NAPA SKATE PARK   FREE
Vajome and Clinton Streets, Napa
(707) 257-9529
www.cityofnapa.org

If they're bouncing off the walls, just put a skateboard or a scooter under their feet and give 'em a gentle nudge. The skate park is just about what you'd expect: a cemented city block with an assortment of hills, dips, ramps, and pathways. This is a free, do-it-yourself attraction. Bring your own gear, supervise your own children, bandage your own boo-boos. Roller skates and Rollerblades are welcome too.

JOHN F. KENNEDY MEMORIAL
REGIONAL PARK   FREE
Streblow Drive off Highway 121, Napa
(707) 257-9529
www.cityofnapa.org

The largest of Napa's municipal parks at 340 acres, Kennedy has four group picnic areas, hiking and jogging trails, volleyball courts, a lighted baseball diamond, and a multiuse ball field. It also has a duck pond and playground for the really young ones, plus a boat ramp for family outings. It's a tranquil, breezy setting adjacent to the Napa River.

PLAYGROUND FANTÁSTICO   FREE
Old Sonoma Road at Freeway Drive, Napa
(707) 261-7048
www.playgroundfantastico.com

When a city the size of Napa can pull together more than 1,500 volunteers for an intensive six-day community project, you know the result will be something special. In this case the result is a world-class, 15,000-square-foot playground with an estimated worth of $2 million, built in 2002 entirely with donated materials and labor. There are two themed sandboxes, two castles, one area for tots and another for older children, a tree house, a train station, and much more. No shortcuts were taken in the quality of the materials and creativity—nearly everything is tastefully constructed from wood. It's fun, and it's free.

CAROLYN PARR NATURE MUSEUM   FREE
3107 Browns Valley Road, Napa
(707) 255-6465

This modest facility a mile west of Highway 29 is sponsored by the Napa Valley Naturalists. People come here to see the museum's dioramas, which show five habitats: grassland, chaparral, marshland, riparian, and woodland/forest. Inside each diorama are examples of native plants and animal specimens, from raccoons and wood ducks to king snakes and badgers. There is an extensive raptor display and a special kids' section with such hands-on items as pelts and skulls. Adults enjoy the Carolyn Parr museum too, but the small scale seems ideally suited to children. Admission is free. The museum is open 1:00 to 4:00 p.m. Saturday and Sunday and for group tours by appointment. It is at the entrance to Westwood Hills Park, a 111-acre green space with picnic facilities and a self-guided nature trail.

LEARNING FAIRE   FREE
1343 Main Street, Napa
(707) 253-1024
www.learningfaire.com

Under the same ownership for more than 20 years, this Napa store prides itself on selectivity. All products are prescreened for safety, and they sell nothing that promotes violence. Learning Faire stocks Brio, Thomas wooden trains, Legos, plenty of other toys, and lots of games, puzzles, crafts, books, cassettes, and CDs. There are hands-on stations and the occasional market-research play day—when manufacturer reps bring new toys for kids to sample.

ROCKZILLA $$
849 Jackson Street, Napa
(707) 255-1500
www.climbrockzilla.com

It's not the Sierra Nevada but it's the next best thing if you're in Wine Country. With more than 8,000 square feet of climbing surface and 120 routes, Rockzilla offers indoor rock climbing for all ages and skill levels. Helmets are available, and optional. Rockzilla is open from 10:00 a.m. to 10:00 p.m. seven days a week (except on Sunday, when it closes at 6:00 p.m.). A kids' day pass is $8 (13 and under); students 14 and older climb for $10; and adults (18 and above) make the ascent for $13.

CRANE PARK   FREE
Highway 29 and Grayson Avenue,
St. Helena
(707) 963-5706
www.ci.st-helena.ca.us

St. Helena families and kids of every stripe gather at this well-kept sanctuary. The 10-acre park has two baseball diamonds, horseshoe pits, lighted bocce courts and tennis courts, substantial picnic setups, a playground, and restrooms. On Friday mornings in summer the farmers' market is here.

SMITH'S MOUNT ST. HELENA TROUT
FARM AND HATCHERY $$
18401 Ida Clayton Road, Calistoga
(707) 987-3651

Smith's has been raising trout for private ponds for six decades. On weekends the staff opens up the three-quarter-acre lake to the public, and locals have learned that it's one of the best diversions in the area for children. The proprietors provide poles and bait, and they even clean and bag the trout for you afterward. All you do is bait, cast, and reel. You pay only for the fish you take—$1 to $6, depending on size. From Highway 128 in Knights Valley, just north of Calistoga, go 7 miles north at the big sign for Smith's. On Saturday and Sunday from March through September, the fun lasts 10:00 a.m. to 5:00 p.m.

PETRIFIED FOREST $$
4100 Petrified Forest Road, Calistoga
(707) 942-6667
www.petrifiedforest.org

The trees died a few million years ago, but they remain alive forever as stone sculptures of what they used to be. Paths wind in and out through the fossilized forest (see the Attractions chapter). Visitors can take a quarter-mile loop that requires about 20 minutes to stroll. Almost as interesting as the forest is the museum and gift shop, where you can buy all kinds of good stuff—stones you've never seen before and pieces of wood turned to stone. There's also a good selection of books. Guided walks are offered on Sunday at

2:00 p.m. The museum and store are open daily 9:00 a.m. to 6:00 p.m. Admission is $6 for adults; $5 for youngsters ages 12 through 17 and seniors 60 and over; and $3 for kids under 12.

SONOMA COUNTY

Southern Sonoma

MAXWELL FUN CENTER $$
19171 Highway 12 (Sonoma Highway), Sonoma
(707) 996-3616

When's the last time you paid less than 10 bucks for 18 holes of golf? The course is laid out to look like historic Sonoma, with ponds, fountains, and a lifelike city hall. Not just for kids, it's a great place for teens. The Clubhouse features the latest video games as well as sports video games for air hockey, basketball, and football. To put an extra spin on a great family day, have a hot dog at the pondside picnic area. The course and game room are open noon to 8:00 p.m. Monday through Friday, and 11:00 a.m. to 8:00 p.m. Saturday and Sunday. Special packages are available for family groups and birthday parties. The Fun Center is located next door to Lucky's in the Maxwell Village Shopping Center.

TRAIN TOWN $
20264 Broadway, Sonoma
(707) 938-3912
www.traintown.com

It's difficult to say who gets the most fun out of this train ride, kids or adults. The whole layout is so cleverly crafted that it's a marvel of dedication to the art of the train buff. The miniature train travels through scenic landscapes of trees, lakes, bridges, a 140-foot-long tunnel, and a small-scale replica of a turn-of-the-20th-century Sonoma Valley town called Lakeville. Midway along, the best part for many kids is the petting zoo. For five minutes the train stops and everyone hauls out to pet llamas, horses, and miniature goats and to feed the ducks and geese. Back at the station there's a carousel and Ferris wheel and some interesting

mechanical exhibits. Trains operate 10:00 a.m. to 5:00 p.m. every day in summer. Winter hours are 10:00 a.m. to 5:00 p.m. Friday through Sunday. Trains leave every 30 minutes. The fare is $3.75 for all ages.

BENZIGER FAMILY WINERY $$
1883 London Ranch Road, Glen Ellen
(888) 490-2739
www.benziger.com

A winery for kids? Well, no—most are not set up to welcome little ones (nor would that be legal). But this one is somewhat kid-friendly, complete with a children's play area. Benziger is an inviting, sprawling ranch oozing with history as opposed to some of the more recently erected architectural showplaces where wine tastings take place. This is a real working farm, a pretty compound with the original farmhouses and outbuildings. It's delightful to wander through on your own, or take a 45-minute vineyard tram tour that escorts you through vines, gardens, and wildlife sanctuaries. The $15 tram fee includes a look inside the winery's underground cave and wine tasting. (Read more about this winery and the Benziger family in the Wineries chapter.) Benziger Family Winery is just down the road from Jack London State Park, another great place to take the kids (see the History and Parks and Recreation chapters).

MORTON'S WARM SPRINGS RESORT $$
1651 Warm Springs Road, Glen Ellen
(707) 833-5511
www.mortonswarmsprings.com

One of the last of the natural mineral-water swimming holes, Morton's has three beautiful pools—for toddlers, for kids, and for the family. More fun can be had at the volleyball and basketball courts, horseshoe pits, baseball field, bocce ball court, and game room with video games. There are 11 naturally landscaped picnic areas (one by a stream) with barbecue pits and shaded tables. Morton's is well known locally as a family gathering place and for hosting family and corporate picnics. Parking is available at no extra charge. The snack bar is conveniently close to the pools with ice-cold drinks and a wide selection of hot dogs, hamburgers, chips, and all those picnic eats that make a family day so much fun. Morton's is open from the first weekend in May through most of September. Admission is $8 for adults; $7 for seniors and kids under 12; and free for kids under 3.

EARLY WORK TOY STATION   FREE
90 Sycamore Lane, Petaluma
(707) 765-1993, (800) 711-1933
www.earlywork.com

Early Work was formerly a shop for teachers looking for educational materials, but it is now open to the public. It's a great favorite with children because of its selection of creative toys and learning materials. There's something for everyone here, from age 1 to 100. Toys and books cover art, science, math, and language. An event schedule changes from month to month—call the store for times or check its Web site.

JUNGLE VIBES   FREE
136 Petaluma Boulevard N., Petaluma
(707) 762-6583, (800) 804-0007
www.junglevibes.com

They call it a nature and science store, but it's really an adventure where nature and science meet world culture. At this unique Petaluma emporium, walking in the door is like entering another country. A taste of adventure and multicultural exploration goes a long way in our busy lives, and Jungle Vibes is set to help the community explore the world, using nature and science toys and books to complement an authentic collection of ethnic arts and sounds.

MRS. GROSSMAN'S STICKER
FACTORY   FREE
3810 Cypress Drive, Petaluma
(707) 763-1700, (800) 429-4549
www.mrsgrossmans.com

Millions of colorful and popular stickers have been produced in this hometown facility, the oldest and largest of its kind in the nation. There really is a Mrs. Grossman, a graphic artist with a stellar résumé who went out on her own in 1975 to design stationery. When one of her projects for a client was mistakenly printed on sticker rolls instead of flat sheets, the idea for this enterprise was born. The factory produces 15,000 miles of sticker rolls each year in the 24-hour printing plant. The one-hour tour is by appointment only, so call ahead for hours and directions to the tour entrance gate. Great for all ages, 5 and up.

VICTORIA'S FASHION STABLES
430 Sprauer Road, Petaluma
(707) 665-0600, (707) 481-3579
www.fashionstables.com

No, it's not related to that tantalizing fashion catalog. This place is pure, clean barnyard fun, featuring good stuff for good kids—small, medium, or large. It's primarily an equestrian operation, with pony rides suitable for even very small children—the staff will walk beside the horse to hold Junior steady if necessary. There is also a petting zoo. The stables are open every day except Tuesday. Appointments are preferred, though drop-ins can usually be accommodated.

i You can't beat Sonoma's Train Town for family fun. In addition to miniature trains, there's a petting zoo, Ferris wheel, and merry-go-round.

CAL SKATE $$
6100 Commerce Boulevard, Rohnert Park
(707) 585-0494
www.calskate.com

Kids of all ages love to roller-skate here. The arena is open from 9:30 a.m. to 8:00 p.m., and it offers special sessions—such as the tiny tots session for kids 10 and under. There is also plenty of open skating. Adult prices are $5 to $7.

SCANDIA FAMILY FUN CENTER $$$
5301 Redwood Drive, Rohnert Park
(707) 584-1398
www.scandiafunland.com

There's fun for everyone here: miniature golf, batting cages, go-karts, a video arcade, an Indy raceway, Tidal Wave bumper boats, and a snack bar. It opens every day at 10:00 a.m. and stays open until 9:00 p.m. on weekdays and 11:00 p.m. on weekends. Prices vary by attraction.

ℹ️ Courts for bocce ball, which can be fun for kids of all ages, have become commonplace at some public parks and at such wineries as Imagery Estates, Landmark, and Pedroncelli.

ENVIRONMENTAL DISCOVERY CENTER $
Spring Lake Regional Park, Violetti Road, Santa Rosa
(707) 539-2865
www.sonoma-county.org/parks/edc.htm
Here's a treat for the kids and the parents too. The former visitor center on the eastern edge of this park was creatively converted into a terrific facility for children to learn about the environment around them. Exhibits are always changing, but one of the most popular is a tide pool populated with interesting sea creatures that can be picked up and examined. Expect interactive games, an aquarium, puzzles, and many other activities geared to youngsters. The center is open noon to 5:00 p.m. Wednesday through Sunday. Admission is free; parking at Spring Lake is $4.

HOWARTH PARK $
630 Summerfield Road, Santa Rosa
(707) 543-3425
www.ci.santa-rosa.ca.us
One of 27 parks in Santa Rosa, Howarth is the big one, a 152-acre retreat into the world of nature. There's a 25-acre lake where families can rent canoes, rowboats, paddleboats, and sailboats and even take sailing lessons. Kids and parents can also fish for trout, bluegill, and bass throughout the year. In another part of the park, a simulated steam train follows a quarter-mile track over a bridge and through a tunnel. The latest addition to the park is the Land of Imagination, with an elaborate climbing structure, a frontier town, a Mexican rancho facade, and life-size animal sculptures. Bring a picnic and have a great day! The park is open 6:00 a.m. to 9:00 p.m. in

summer and 6:00 a.m. to 6:00 p.m. in winter. Boat rentals (fishing is optional and subject to state regulations) and amusement rides are in operation 11:00 a.m. to 5:00 p.m. Tuesday through Sunday during summer and on weekends in spring and fall.

REDWOOD EMPIRE ICE ARENA $$
1667 West Steele Lane, Santa Rosa
(707) 546-7147
www.snoopyshomeice.com
Charles Schulz, famous for his Peanuts cartoons, grew up in Minnesota and never lost his love for ice-skating. The rink he built in Santa Rosa is a beautiful venue compared to the outdoor rinks he knew in his youth. A full range of skating is offered, with mornings reserved for programs and classes (many world champions have trained here). The arena is open daily, but hours vary. The cost is $9 for adults and teens and $7 for children younger than 12 (weekends). Aside from the ice arena, there's a wonderful Snoopy's Gallery gift shop that's appealing to all ages (see the Shopping chapter). You can also buy skates here, both ice and roller. (For more information on the arena and the Charles M. Schulz Museum next door, see the Attractions chapter.)

RILEY STREET ART SUPPLIES   FREE
103 Maxwell Court, Santa Rosa
(707) 526-2416
www.rileystreet.com
This is a great place to pick up children's craft supplies, including face-painting kits, tempera paints, tattoo books, how-to-draw books, and build-your-own foam dinosaur kits. It's also a premier shopping spot for professional artists and craftspeople.

SANTA ROSA JUNIOR COLLEGE PLANETARIUM $
2001 Lark Hall, 1501 Mendocino Avenue, Santa Rosa
(707) 527-4372
www.santarosa.edu/planetarium
Star-studded shows feature various astronomical phenomena, with the night sky projected (with

special effects) onto the dome by state-of-the-art equipment. Offered only during the school year, shows are scheduled at 7:00 and 8:30 p.m. on Friday and Saturday and at 1:30 and 3:00 p.m. on Sunday. Cost is $5 for adult general admission and $3 for students and seniors, all on a first-come, first-served basis. Children younger than 5 are not admitted.

THE TOYWORKS   **FREE**
531 College Avenue, Santa Rosa
(707) 526-2099

2724 Santa Rosa Avenue, Santa Rosa
(707) 576-8609

6940 Sebastopol Avenue, Sebastopol
(707) 829-2003
www.sonomatoyworks.com
A store of educational toys, Toyworks claims 15,000 different items, from European toys, Lego blocks, and science and nature items to educational books and Lionel trains. Store hours are 10:00 a.m. to 6:00 p.m. Monday through Saturday and 11:00 a.m. to 5:00 p.m. Sunday.

LAKE SONOMA FISH HATCHERY   **FREE**
3333 Skaggs Springs Road, Geyserville
(707) 433-4533
www.parks.sonoma.net
Here's a chance to peek in on all phases of fish life, depending on the season. In summer you'll see the small, young fish; later in the season, from late October through March, you'll be able to watch the coho salmon and steelheads return to spawn and climb the fish ladder. The coho salmon will die after spawning, but the steelheads will live to return to the sea. Once the eggs have been laid and fertilized, the fish hatchery starts collecting them once a week. Year-round hours are 8:30 a.m. to 3:45 p.m. Wednesday through Sunday. There is no charge. Visitors also will enjoy a display of Native American artifacts, plus information on local geology.

OUTSIDE WINE COUNTRY

These three big attractions are technically just beyond the borders of our two-county wine region but might be worth the extra time and the short distances to reach them if you have children in need of large-scale diversions.

SIX FLAGS DISCOVERY KINGDOM   **$$$**
1001 Fairgrounds Drive, Vallejo, California
(707) 643-6722
www.sixflags.com/discoverykingdom
Rare is the Wine Country parent who hasn't succumbed to the splashy fun of this theme park. Run by the Six Flags Corporation, the park has occupied its present 135-acre spot since 1986. The park is classified into three areas: land, sea, and sky. The long bill of shows includes performances by whales and dolphins, sea lions, cheetahs, and humans on water skis. The ongoing attractions are too numerous to list, but don't miss the 10-story roller coaster called Roar and the V-2 Vertical Velocity Spiral Coaster, one of only a handful like it in the world. Tamer rides include the Frog Hopper and Safari River Journey. One-day tickets are $49.99 for humans over 48 inches tall, $29.99 for those under 48 inches, and children 2 and under get in free. From Napa, go south on Highway 29, then east on Highway 37 for just more than a mile. Days and hours of operation vary by season, so call ahead.

JELLY BELLY FACTORY   **FREE**
One Jelly Belly Lane, Fairfield, California
(800) 9-JELLYBEAN (953-5592)
www.jellybelly.com
You love 'em, you crave 'em—now see how these addictive little candies are created. The free 40-minute tour shows how more than 150 jelly bean varieties are made, along with gummi critters. The tour ends in the visitor center, when your kids get to do their own kind of "tasting," at the candy sampling bar. A cafe serves jelly bean–shaped pizza and hamburgers for the little ones, and espresso drinks for Mom and Dad. The visitor center is open daily year-round 9:00 a.m.

to 5:00 p.m. (closed on major holidays). Tours begin every 15 minutes, with the last one starting at 4:00 p.m. Reservations are not necessary. The factory is located approximately 20 minutes from the city of Napa, off Interstate 80.

NUT TREE THEME PARK $$$
1681 E. Monte Vista Avenue, Vacaville, California
(888) 448-6411
www.nuttreeusa.com
After stuffing your face with Jelly Bellies (see previous listing), travel eastward on I-80 just a little farther, to a historic icon of the interstate. The Nut Tree began in 1921 as a fruit stand and quickly became a favorite stopping point for visitors and locals. Its popularity—and its size and attractions—thrived over the decades as freeway traffic increased. The attraction closed for a few years in the 1990s, then was reborn in 2006 with carnival rides, cafes, and a railroad system sized just for kids. There are lots of rides, including one ominously called "I-80 Traffic Jammers," and a vineyard balloon tour. Tickets are sold in packages, starting at 10 for $8.50; a wristband for unlimited rides for one day is $18.95. The kids can also feed fish in a koi pond, ride on colorful hobby horses, and pose for photos atop painted animal figures. Days and hours of operation vary by season; call ahead or check the Web site for the latest. The Nut Tree is located just off I-80 at—what else?—the Nut Tree Parkway exit.

KONOCTI HARBOR RESORT & SPA $$$
8727 Soda Bay Road, Kelseyville
(707) 279-4281, (800) 660-LAKE
www.konoctiharbor.com
Big kids come here mostly for the musical entertainment—more than 100 concerts a year featuring classic rock bands, hot country artists, and other performers. But it's also a terrific place to bring the family for a day or two of boating, fishing, and swimming. Located on the shores of Clear Lake in Lake County, the 120-acre resort is a 60-minute drive north of Calistoga. It has tennis and volleyball courts, miniature golf, a playground, water craft rentals, and even a spa for mom and dad. Just about every type of lake-skimming vessel is available for rent: fishing boats, kayaks, pedal boats, pontoons, wave boards, and more. The two Olympic-size swimming pools can substitute for the lake, if the family prefers chlorinated water to the natural kind (with two wading pools nearby for toddlers). Here's another bonus for parents: the Konocti Kids Club Program, a child-sitting service (for an extra charge) that keeps your 4- to 13-year-olds occupied with activities while you boogie with Journey or the Doobie Brothers at the amphitheater. If you choose to spend a night or two, Konocti has apartments and cottages specifically sized and furnished with families in mind. Concert-night lodgings can sell out quickly, so plan ahead if you want the full experience.

DAY TRIPS

Have a map of Northern California handy? You'll see that Wine Country encompasses only a small region of this huge half of the state. Beyond Napa and Sonoma Counties are other intriguing destinations, and you might want to veer off the wine trail long enough to experience another taste of the Golden State. That's fine with me—I respect your wanderlust and encourage you to broaden your travel horizons. Fortunately, several exceptional locations are within a few hours' drive of our two-county area. To the south, the Marin Headlands, part of the Golden Gate National Recreation Area, offer scenic drives and hikes and the best views (usually above the fog) of the Golden Gate Bridge and San Francisco. Nearby Sausalito and Tiburon are charming burgs with bayside dining and lodging, phenomenal views, interesting shops, and convenient ferries across the bay to San Francisco. Berkeley is still funky, and farther east the Gold Country towns of the Sierra foothills are rich in history. All of these are suitable excursions, and so are the four destinations outlined in this chapter. Depending on where you start, the spots I'm recommending may be enjoyed as long day trips (a couple of them *very* long). But if you have the time, plan for an overnight or weekend getaway.

POINT REYES NATIONAL SEASHORE

Just southwest of Wine Country, Point Reyes offers miles of windswept beaches and magnificent palisades. Walk along cliffside trails (not too close to the edge, please), roll down lofty dunes, explore tidal marshes, and wander through a foggy forest. You're equally likely to bump into a tule elk, a sea lion, or a cow.

Dividing Point Reyes from the bulk of Marin County is the long, skinny arm of Tomales Bay and the infamous San Andreas Fault—the active demarcation line between the Pacific and North American tectonic plates. Point Reyes is moving away from the rest of the mainland, heading toward Alaska at the rate of 2 inches a year.

To get to the park, take Petaluma-Point Reyes Road southwest from Petaluma for about 20 miles. A good place to start your excursion in the 71,000-acre park is the Bear Valley Visitor Center, a big barn of a building just off Highway 1 near Olema. Close to the center you'll encounter Morgan Horse Ranch, Kule Loklo, and several hiking trails. Morgan Ranch is the only working

horse-breeding farm in the national park system. Kule Loklo is a re-creation of a Miwok village, with traditional domed shelters. If you visit in July, you might get to witness the annual Native American Celebration, during which Miwok-descended basket makers, stone carvers, singers, and dancers bring the exhibit to life.

While some visitors simply want to flop down on the pearly sand for a good read or nap, others come to explore the diversity of fascinating natural attractions. Limantour Estero is an estuary where most of the bird-watchers flock; McClures Beach has excellent tide pools; the windy Great Beach, one of the longest in the state, gets high marks from beachcombers; and Drakes Beach (which, like Drakes Bay and Drakes Estero, is named for Sir Francis Drake, the English privateer who supposedly landed here in 1579) is a Northern California rarity: a safe swimming beach. Of course, hiking routes abound, including 70 miles of trails in a big chunk of park set aside as wilderness area.

Probably foremost among the attractions is Point Reyes Lighthouse, built about 1870 to help prevent the many shipwrecks that had plagued the treacherous, rocky shoreline for centuries. It is also one of California's best spots for whale watching. In the fall gray whales migrate from Alaska to their breeding grounds in Baja California. In spring they return north with their young. The peak watching season is Christmas through the end of January, when it's not uncommon to see 100 or more spouts rise in a day.

Even the villages are pretty here. Point Reyes Station and Inverness, in particular, have remained undisturbed by the masses of visitors. Both towns have interesting shopping, dining, and lodging options too. Note that the local microclimate is highly unpredictable—except at the actual point, which is the foggiest place on the West Coast. For more up-to-date information, call the Point Reyes National Seashore at (415) 464-5100 or visit www. nps.gov/pore. (Always call ahead to inquire about weather at the lighthouse. Visitors who make the long trek out to the point are sometimes disappointed—myself included, a couple of times—to discover that rangers have closed the stairs down to the lighthouse because it's too windy to safely make the descent.)

THE MENDOCINO COAST

For many people, the journey to the Mendocino Coast is half the fun of getting there. Routes are limited but beautiful, though twisty in places, and all can be pokey. If you drive Coast Highway 1 from Bodega Bay to the village of Mendocino, allow at least three to four hours, with occasional stops to enjoy the views and a steaming bowl of clam chowder.

Gualala, pronounced "wah-LA-la," is the southern gateway to the Mendocino Coast. Along with Anchor Bay, 4 miles to the north, it forms what locals call the Banana Belt, a relatively warm and fog-free pocket of coastline. Gualala is an arts community, with resident painters, sculptors, photographers, writers, and musicians.

About 16 miles north of Gualala is Point Arena. With about 474 people, it's one of the smallest incorporated cities in the state. Once a lumber and fishing center, Point Arena now sticks mostly to the tourist trade. Surfers say the harbor

is one of the best surfing spots in Northern California. Moving up the coast, Albion (between Whitesboro Cove and the Albion River) and Little River (near the waterway of the same name) are further possibilities for weary drivers and white-knuckled passengers.

Most people who stop there are heading for the village of Mendocino, a National Historic Preservation District with about 1,000 residents. It's a delightful mix of gingerbread architecture, steep gables, and white picket fences that seem straight out of an Edward Hopper painting of New England.

In the 1960s the village blossomed as a center for artists and bohemians seeking freedom of style and life on the cheap. William Zacha came up from the Bay Area to open an art gallery, then conceived the Mendocino Art Center, a rambling collection of buildings on a rise at the edge of town. It was this art colony that first attracted a more affluent breed of visitor, seeking escape from urban living. They came to stroll the boardwalks and sniff ocean breezes. With them came a blossoming of gourmet restaurants and some uncommonly civilized inns. It is this ambience that sets Mendocino apart from other North Coast villages.

The fact that Mendocino looks a lot like the coast of Maine has not escaped the notice of filmmakers. Yet some people have been critical of Mendocino's "perfection"—one local scoffs that it is "more of a movie set than a town." A few of the more outstanding architectural structures include the Mendocino Hotel, the Ford House, and the Presbyterian Church of Mendocino, all on Main Street. The latter building is the oldest continuously operating Presbyterian church in California.

Away from the coastline, Mendocino County is also a world-class wine-growing region with casual and inviting tasting rooms. While not as well known as Sonoma or Napa, Mendocino County is getting the word out about the Anderson Valley's extraordinary wines. Originally an area of orchards and sheep and cattle ranches, it was discovered during the 1970s as an exceptional growing area for wine grapes. This rolling land, drained by the Navarro River, has quickly become braided in long rows of Pinot Noir, Chardonnay, Gewürztraminer, and Zinfandel grapes.

Today there are more than 35 wineries in the Mendocino County grape-growing regions, producing an abundance of award-winning vintages. Of the county's 2.25 million total acres, just 14,000 acres are planted to vineyards—and 25 percent of that acreage is certified organic. Mendocino's wine regions are divided into six valley areas, each noted for the different varieties of grapes produced under slightly different climatic conditions.

i **Legendary racehorse Seabiscuit, subject of a best-selling book and a blockbuster movie, lived out his retirement years at Ridgewood Ranch, south of Willits, and is buried beneath a giant oak tree on the property. For information about tours of the ranch, call (707) 459-5992 or visit www.seabiscuitheritage.com.**

THE BIG TREES

California's legendary redwood forests have inspired poetry and major awe (and more than a little avarice) during the past 200 years. Though they are often confused with their inland cousin, the giant sequoia, the redwood—or coast redwood as it is called—is a variety unto itself, with a coastal range that extends from Monterey to southwest Oregon. Santa Rosa considers itself the capital of the Redwood Empire, and several Wine Country parks are home to these noble giants (see the Parks and Recreation chapter). But if you really want to behold these extraordinary trees in all their grandeur, you have to drive north to Humboldt County. There you will find the last large stands of California's coast redwoods.

Sequoia sempervirens covered some two million acres when Archibald Menzies first gave them botanical classification in 1794. The state government created several parks around individual groves in the 1920s, but by 1965 logging had reduced the redwood ecosystem to about 300,000 acres. This prompted the U.S.

government to consolidate various state, federal, and private holdings into Redwood National Park in 1968.

More land was added to the park in 1978, after bitter wrangling between environmental and proindustry groups and deterioration of virgin growth due to upstream logging along Redwood Creek. The 110,000-acre national park is the destination of many visitors, along with three remaining state parks: Jedediah Smith Redwoods, Del Norte Coast Redwoods, and Prairie Creek Redwoods. All four parks are adjacent and, in fact, comanaged by the National Park Service and the California Department of Parks and Recreation. The national park is a World Heritage Site, the only one on the Pacific coast of the United States. Prairie Creek, meanwhile, is home to the last herds of Roosevelt elk in California.

The 7,500-acre Headwaters Forest Reserve is the most recent entry in the list of protected ancient groves. The reserve, made famous by the tree-sitting, old-growth activist Julia Butterfly, came into being as part of a $480 million controversial deal struck between the U.S. government and the Pacific Lumber Company.

Farther south, between Garberville and Ferndale, is the famed Avenue of the Giants, a 33-mile stretch of roadway that parallels U.S. Highway 101 and offers up the most majestic succession of trees on the planet. The avenue follows the Eel River and cuts through 51,000-acre Humboldt Redwoods State Park, the largest state park in Northern California. Along the road you'll encounter a hollow redwood (the Chimney Tree), a redwood trunk made into a domicile (One-Log House), and a redwood you can bisect without leaving the car (Shrine Drive-Thru Tree, one of the state's oldest surviving tourist attractions).

What are the big groves like? It's like walking into one of Europe's grandest old cathedrals, only with better ventilation. The huge trunks absorb every trace of sound, with the exception of the occasional notes of a Swainson's thrush or Wilson's warbler that float down from the branches above. The forest bed, soft with many layers of needles, crunches under your feet, and the lush ferns lend a primordial feel to the place.

The trees are indeed ancient, with the oldest dated at approximately 2,200 years. And big? Three of the six tallest trees in the world, including the grand-champion, the 379-foot Hyperion, are in the national park. At least 137 redwoods in this region have been identified as 350 feet or taller. What is the secret to their great size? Moisture, and lots of it. The 50 to 80 inches of annual rainfall that drenches coastal California quenches most of the redwood's tremendous thirst, while fog, almost a daily occurrence, keeps the trees damp and cool when the rains subside.

All the attractions mentioned here are accessed via US 101 between Garberville and Crescent City, just south of the Oregon border. From Wine Country, simply continue north on US 101 through Mendocino County; Garberville is about 10 miles past the county line. Admission to the state parks is $6, which will get you into all of them. There is no charge to enter the national park. Camping and hiking options abound. For more information, call the northern parks at (707) 464-6101 or Humboldt Redwoods State Park at (707) 946-2409 (www.parks.ca.gov/default .asp?page_id=425).

LAKE TAHOE

Nature has lavished on Lake Tahoe the bluest waters, the most majestic pines, handsome mountains, and the most brilliant cloud-studded skies you'll find anywhere—all that and keno too! Mark Twain was the first travel writer to tour the Lake of the Sky. A thousand equally dumbfounded travel writers who can scarcely describe the indescribable have since quoted his awestruck commentaries. Photos simply don't capture this cobalt-blue beauty (I know from personal experience), nor do paintings. The colors are right, but oddly, they seem too perfect, too vivid.

Lake Tahoe lies half in California and half in Nevada (the south shore is a two-hour drive from Sacramento, on U.S. Highway 50), which gives impetus for pilgrimages by a swarm of weekend gamblers. But Tahoe's best bet is the lake itself. At 12 miles wide and 22 miles long, it offers all the water-oriented fun one would expect from the largest alpine lake in North America (in the Western Hemisphere, only Lake Titicaca is larger). At 97 percent pure—the same as distilled water—Lake Tahoe is as clean as it is beautiful. Fortunately, the Sierra Club and other environmental groups are fighting to keep it that way.

Lake Tahoe is North America's second-deepest lake (maximum depth 1,645 feet). If all the water were somehow released from the lake—and if water behaved very differently than it does in real life—it would cover the entire state of California to a depth of 8 inches. Look out across the waters, and you might see colorful hot-air balloons rising from a barge in the middle of the lake just as the sun makes its appearance over the edge of the Sierra Nevada. Two-masted sailboats cut a leisurely path across the waves, while yachts hurry on their way. Couples in canoes or kayaks paddle through the shallow waters. Anglers, waiting patiently for the trout to find them, sit in their fishing boats, unimpressed by the brave soul hovering above them, dangling from a rainbow-hued parasail.

In addition, the M.S. *Dixie II* takes passengers on two, sometimes three, cruises a day—an afternoon run that crosses the lake to Emerald Bay (with its turquoise waters), and a morning cruise that features a big breakfast while following the shoreline. A second boat, the *Tahoe Queen*, also makes daily cruises, departing from Ski Run Marina in South Lake.

For a look at the lake as a whole, nothing beats the spectacular 72-mile perimeter drive. It takes about five hours (with scenic stops) on a good weather day. Plan to begin your drive early. In summer, pack or buy a picnic lunch for a brief sojourn in an adjacent park. In winter, include a midday pit stop at a ski area.

Options exist for numerous side trips while traveling around the lake. Heading clockwise from South Lake Tahoe, you'll soon climb a steep grade to a point overlooking the breathtaking vistas of Emerald Bay State Park. Below is the 39-room Vikingsholm Castle, a 19th-century mansion built by Laura Knight, who fell in love with Norway and sent craftsmen there to copy museum pieces for her home. Tours are available to those who walk the half mile down the hill, which is the only visitor access except by boat. Vistas along the entire west shore are so stunning, you'll be maxing out the megapixels on your digital camera before you know it. Heading northeast, you'll pass what has essentially always been the residential zone of Tahoe. San Francisco's early social elite spent their summers here, and millionaires put up huge estates. Hollywood has come calling more than once, and one of these homes figured prominently in the filming of *The Godfather II*.

Tahoe's oldest permanent settlement is Tahoe City, on the northwest shores of the lake. Three shopping complexes and several condominium projects give this town a year-round population of 2,000. Near the site of the bridge over the Truckee River (called Fanny Bridge because of the people hanging over its floodgates), there's a wonderful collection of Indian lore at the Gatekeeper's Museum. Tahoe City is also the take-off point for three-hour rafting trips down the Truckee River, and it is a favored location for fishermen who head out to deep water with a guide in search of mackinaw and cutthroat trout.

The lake's north shore abounds with interesting geological formations—immense boulders and tiny carnelian stones. Along the north shore you'll cross the state line into Nevada, where gambling is legal. One of its more famous casinos, the Cal-Neva, once belonged to Frank Sinatra. Those were the days when Hollywood luminaries filled the lobby. At the northeast corner of the lake, you'll find Incline Village, with its shopping center, fine art galleries, craft shops, restaurants, and, for culture vultures, drama, opera, Shakespeare, and mime.

South of Incline Village lies one of Tahoe's best beaches—Sand Harbor State Beach, strewn with giant boulders, the refuse of Tahoe's ice age. Paths climb to the top of one of the granite outcroppings, allowing a view down into turquoise waters so clear that submerged boulders as high as a house can be seen in full detail. Facilities for picnicking and barbecuing in a wooded setting are unusually pleasant.

Most of Tahoe's east shore is privately owned, but there is a small area (recognizable by a proliferation of parked cars) where sun worshippers thread their way down a footpath through the forest and spread out nude on the massive rocks to achieve that all-over tan. Zephyr Cove, meanwhile, is where you set sail on the M.S. *Dixie*. It's near the state line.

And there are other options for side trips. At Incline Village, for example, there's a junction with Highway 27 that will take you to Reno or to Virginia City, the latter a lively ghost town recalling days when silver taken from its mines built San Francisco and made millionaires whose names are still familiar. Its wooden plank streets and weathered buildings are surprisingly authentic, though the usual tourist shops line the street as well. If you're lucky, stunt cowboys will be on hand to re-create a shoot-'em-up in the streets. Reno, calling itself the "biggest little city in the world," is rife with sleek, splashy gambling casinos. The city has achieved a modest fame among nearby California cities for its inexpensive hotel rooms. It is also home to the National Bowling Association, which is quartered in a massive complex of bowling lanes and offices.

In winter some of the best skiing in the world can be found at South Lake Tahoe—specifically at Heavenly Valley. If you're not on hand during the winter months, take advantage of the tram anyway; ride to the top of the mountain and stroll along the path that skirts the rim. It's a breathtaking view, and you can sip wine and have lunch at the summit's inviting patio.

i **Just because you're at Lake Tahoe doesn't mean you have to leave wine behind. Plan your visit for mid-September to attend Tahoe's annual Autumn Food and Wine Festival at the Village at Northstar. Appropriate for all ages, the festival's long-standing events include reserve wine and spirits tasting, a grape stomp, art show, and a farmers' market.**

RELOCATION

The first 20 chapters of this book may have given you plenty of reasons to make your home in Wine Country. Reading about our green and gold mountains, the Mediterranean climate, the wild coastline of the Pacific Ocean, miles and miles of lush vineyards, great wine, fabulous food, art galleries, and San Francisco only a short drive away—well, who wouldn't want to live here year-round? But let's be practical. It's one thing to be a visitor on vacation—it's quite another to become a resident. Used to the razzle-dazzle of big-city life? The slower pace of Wine Country might make you yawn. Turned off by day after day of winter fog and drizzle? You probably should settle elsewhere. Skeptical about living in a state governed by an action-movie star? I understand. As you know, there are many factors to consider when choosing a new city or state to call home. No one place is ideal for everybody, so be certain Wine Country is right for you before putting down roots. If you do decide to relocate, welcome! I hope you will thoroughly enjoy all that Wine Country has to offer. This chapter gives you a taste of what's available in real estate, retirement resources, educational opportunities, child care options, and health care.

REAL ESTATE

In the real estate industry, 2007 will go down in infamy as the year the bubble burst (exploded with a scream is more like it). Home values took a sharp tumble nationwide, not only in Wine Country. But the drops seemed more dramatic in this region, where commonplace million-dollar-plus properties were suddenly marked down by thousands of dollars to "bargain" status. Even so, finding buyers was difficult, as the mortgage crisis and subprime lending fiasco had foreclosures at an all-time high and the stock market on a roller-coaster ride.

As this is being written, the prognosis for Northern California real estate isn't much better for 2008. Local experts are forecasting—cautiously—that we've seen the worst of the crisis here. So if you're serious about moving to Wine Country, now is the time to find an affordable home before the prices inevitably start skyrocketing again. The market is saturated with FOR SALE signs, and great houses are available in all areas and price ranges. Take the median prices listed here as only a guide—the market changes quickly.

Napa County

Despite the real estate downturn, you still pay dearly for quality of life here. In spring 2008 the median sales price of a single-family detached home in Napa County was approximately $485,000. (Median price means that half of the sales were higher and half were lower.)

Bargain prices may still be found in American Canyon, just south of Napa, where the median sales price of a home in early 2008 was $462,000. But as you head north on Highway 29, the meter on home costs begins to spin faster. As a general rule, Yountville is more expensive than Napa (median price: $615,000), the Oakville-Rutherford area is more expensive than Yountville, and St. Helena is the most expensive town in the valley. The price tags drop again in Calistoga, a bit less than the Yountville level. Despite Yountville's being overrun with visitors for such a small town, its real estate remains desirable.

As you travel through Napa Valley, you will find every sort of residence imaginable: new tract homes, spectacular Victorians, modest bungalows,

i Actor, director, and activist Robert Redford, a Calistoga resident for many years, is on the advisory committee of the Napa County Land Trust, which works to protect open space in Napa Valley for future generations.

Craftsman charmers, mountaintop castles, Tuscan-inspired villas, and prefab structures.

But what you will see most as you drive along Highway 29 is vineyards. That's because the whole of Napa County is a designated agricultural preserve, a decision ratified by the county Board of Supervisors in 1968. The designation—the first ordinance of its kind in the nation—put development decisions in the hands of the board and set a 20-acre minimum for any new subdivision of land, a dimension that has increased in increments over the years.

In Napa, most of the Victorian splendor is in Old Town—located among the letter streets south of Lincoln Avenue between California Boulevard and Jefferson Street—and the Napa Abajo/Fuller Park area. Fuller Park, in fact, is a historical preservation district. The boundaries of the preservation district are ragged, but it is bordered more or less by Jefferson, Third, Brown, and Pine Streets.

St. Helena is the burg that best typifies the Wine Country dream: charming early-century stone-front buildings, modest scale, vineyard views, and well-kept flower gardens. Accordingly, the prices tend to be sky-high here, especially on the west side. In fact, in 2004 approximately 42 homes were sold for $1 million–plus in and around this small town, which puts "sky-high" into perspective.

Calistoga offers more of a mixed bag, but it does have some wonderfully restored old houses, especially on Cedar and Myrtle Streets just northwest of Lincoln Avenue. But country estates are considered the true gems, especially if they have significant acreage.

Which brings us to the price of vineyard land. If you've fantasized about owning a hobby vineyard, investing in a few acres of grapes, and living the life of a gentleman farmer, be prepared for sticker shock. Your name may not be Gallo or Gates, but you will still need a sizable bankroll to enter into the grape-growing business here. Vineyards in this region represent some of the most valuable agricultural land in America, and these values are largely unchanged despite the recent housing meltdown.

If you're willing to settle for a lower-quality parcel (less fruit density, old trellises, and no developable homesites), expect to pay at least $50,000 per acre. More modern and higher-density vineyards can fetch around $100,000 per acre. In 2007 vineyards in the heart of Napa Valley (Oakville, Rutherford, St. Helena, and Howell Mountain areas) were selling for $150,000 to $300,000 per acre. If your fantasy includes building a modest winery on that property, be prepared to wait about two years for approval of the use permits (maybe), at a cost of nearly $1 million. And that's all before you begin construction. Want a tasting room too? Good luck. Napa County officials are saying no to many new winery proposals, especially those with big plans for tasting rooms and event centers that might generate additional traffic and detract from the rural atmosphere.

Rentals

In the city of Napa, a one-bedroom apartment will cost $850 or more; a two-bedroom unit runs about $1,100. The typical two-bedroom house in Napa can set you back about $1,300 per month; the price goes up to $1,600 and beyond for a three-bedroom, two-bath domicile, depending on location. A similar home in St. Helena starts at about $1,600, while some with more amenities rent for well over $2,500 per month.

In Calistoga a studio apartment, if you can find one, might be around $800; a two-bedroom apartment is $1,000. Two-bedroom homes may be had for $1,300 to $1,500 per month.

Real Estate Companies

PRUDENTIAL CALIFORNIA REALTY
2015 Redwood Road, Napa
(707) 259-4900
www.prucalifornia.com

CENTURY 21 ALPHA REALTY
1290 Jefferson Street, Napa
(707) 255-8711
www.c21-alpharealty.com

COLDWELL BANKER BROKERS OF THE VALLEY
1775 Lincoln Avenue, Napa
(707) 258-5200

1289 Main Street, St. Helena
(707) 963-1152

6040 Main Street, American Canyon
(707) 554-2028
www.cbnapavalley.com

FRANK HOWARD ALLEN REALTORS
802 Vallejo Street, Napa
(707) 265-1600

1316 Main Street, St. Helena
(707) 963-5266
www.fhallen.com
www.winecountrygroup.com

SILVERADO ASSOCIATES
1600 Atlas Peak Road, Napa
(707) 252-4100
www.silveradoassociates.com

MORGAN LANE
944 Main Street, Napa
(707) 252-2177, (800) 511-1030

1109 Jefferson Street, Napa
(707) 252-5528

6550 Washington Street, Yountville
(707) 944-8500

1050 Adams Street, St. Helena
(707) 963-5226
Relocation services: (800) 511-1030
www.morganlane.com

HERITAGE/SOTHEBY'S INTERNATIONAL REALTY
780 Trancas Street, Napa
(707) 255-0845

3249 Browns Valley Road, Napa
(707) 258-5500

1540 Railroad Avenue, St. Helena
(707) 963-1342

1236 Lincoln Avenue, Calistoga
(707) 942-4321
www.heritagesir.com

UP VALLEY ASSOCIATES
1126 Adams Street, St. Helena
(707) 963-1222, (800) 326-6073
www.napavalleyrealestate.com

PACIFIC UNION
1009 Caymus Street, Napa
(707) 251-8805

1508 Main Street, St. Helena
(707) 967-1340
www.pacunion.com

CALISTOGA REALTY CO.
1473-C Lincoln Avenue, Calistoga
(707) 942-9422
www.calistoga-realty.com

i The Viewshed Ordinance was passed by Napa County's Board of Supervisors in 2001 to camouflage new homes and buildings that go up on the valley's scenic hillsides. All new structures must now blend better into their natural environment.

New Resident? Make an Appointment with the Department of Motor Vehicles

Modern man's least favorite chore is most likely a trip to the DMV. The scarcity of DMV offices in Wine Country only adds to the frustration level. That's why appointments are strongly encouraged (a driver's test will not be given without one, in fact) and will usually make the experience less painful. In California every new resident who plans to operate a motorized vehicle is required to take up his or her business in person with the DMV almost as soon as the moving van is unloaded.

In general, cars and trucks brought into California from other states or countries must be registered within 20 days of establishing your residency or accepting employment. (These vehicles may also be subject to additional fees at the time of registration.) Drivers should arrange to get their new Califor-nia licenses within 10 days of putting down roots. Make it easy on yourself and schedule an appointment to wrap up all of your new DMV business in one visit. With a bit of advance planning, the experience should go smoothly (just don't get too upset about the lousy photo on your new driver's license).

Statewide, the DMV information and appointment line is (800) 777-0133/ TTY (800) 368-4327. The DMV Web site (www.dmv.ca.gov) is well designed and easy to navigate, and most of your questions can be answered there.

Napa County
2550 Napa Valley Corporate Drive, Napa

Sonoma County
715 Southpoint Boulevard, Petaluma
2570 Corby Avenue, Santa Rosa

Sonoma County

Like those in the rest of the Bay Area, housing prices took a tumble in Sonoma County over the past couple of years. By early 2008, a glut of homes on the market and fewer buyers making offers chipped away at values, and median prices dropped in almost every community.

In Santa Rosa, as in most cities, home seekers will find neighborhoods of high-priced, handsome Victorian homes, a score of new modern housing developments (some still in progress), and a wide variety of medium- and lower-priced homes. In spring 2008 median prices in the northwest sector of Santa Rosa were about $320,000; in the southeast, $488,500; in the southwest, $389,990; and $457,500 in the northeast. Prices vary in towns to the north along the U.S. Highway 101 corridor. Median prices are $527,500 in Healdsburg and $523,000 in Cloverdale.

An interesting real estate situation exists in the town of Windsor. Until the late 1980s, it was a sleepy village, but then it was discovered by housing developers. They just kept building and building. As a result, almost everything in the town is of recent origin. Now incorporated, Windsor is a fast-growing city—second only to nearby Cloverdale—with median home prices at about $411,500.

The area around the town of Sebastopol on the edge of Apple Country is, in a way, an anomaly in the county—a place where many homes are set on large acreage. People who live here like the idea of country living with amenities such as extra guesthouses and plenty of room for dogs to run and horses to graze. Because of the superlarge lot sizes, Sebastopol has among the highest housing prices in the county. Estate-size lots, rambling homes, and miniranches will often top the $1 million mark. The median home price is $860,000.

Though San Francisco–bound commuters live in all parts of the county, most live in the southernmost reaches—a fact that has influenced average home prices there. Median home prices in the border towns of Petaluma and Sonoma in early 2008 ranged between $535,000 and $675,000.

There is little residential property along the Sonoma coast, which is one reason median home prices are about $826,500. The large, modern Sea Ranch development at the northeastern edge of the county offers homes on sites that range from a quarter acre to three or more acres. For people who love the ocean, life along the Sonoma coast is indeed soul satisfying.

To help in your search for a home, local chambers of commerce are clearinghouses of information. Also, the North Coast Builders Exchange in Santa Rosa, (707) 542-9502, can help with information for individuals hiring contractors or building custom homes.

Rentals

A glut of new apartment projects in recent years, primarily in and around Santa Rosa, forced landlords to make deals to fill their units, but prices have inched up nonetheless. Expect to pay from $900 for a studio apartment and up to $1,600 for a three-bedroom unit. You can generally find lower rents in outlying areas of the county, such as the communities along the Russian River.

Real Estate Companies

PRUDENTIAL CALIFORNIA REAL ESTATE
326 Healdsburg Avenue, Healdsburg
(707) 433-4150

16315 Main Street, Guerneville
(707) 869-9011

7300 Healdsburg Avenue, Suite B, Sebastopol
(707) 829-2011
www.prurealty.com

FRANK HOWARD ALLEN REALTORS
470 First Street E., Sonoma
(707) 939-2000

13651 Arnold Drive, Glen Ellen
(707) 939-2030

9200 Sonoma Highway, Kenwood
(707) 833-2881

9212 Sonoma Highway, Kenwood
(707) 833-2880

460 Mission Boulevard, Santa Rosa
(707) 537-3000

905 East Washington Street, Petaluma
(707) 762-7766

119 North Street, Healdsburg
(707) 431-9440

117 North Cloverdale Boulevard, Cloverdale
(707) 894-1555

575 Highway 1, Bodega Bay
(707) 875-2500

16203 First Street, Guerneville
(707) 869-3865

120 Pleasant Hill Avenue N., Suite 200, Sebastopol
(707) 824-5400
www.fhallen.com
www.winecountrygroup.com

COLDWELL BANKER
165 First Street, Petaluma
(707) 762-6611

600 Bicentennial Way, Suite 100, Santa Rosa
(707) 527-8567

101 Morris Street, Suite 100, Sebastopol
(707) 823-8567
www.californiamoves.com

i If you love Victorian-era homes, Wine Country has many historic areas to choose from. In Sonoma County, check out Petaluma's west side, Sonoma's east side, and most of the streets that radiate off the central plaza in Healdsburg.

RE/MAX CENTRAL
320 College Avenue, Santa Rosa
(707) 524-3500
www.santarosa-homes.com

CENTURY 21
616 Petaluma Boulevard S., Petaluma
(707) 769-9000

1057 College Avenue, Santa Rosa
(707) 577-7777

561 Broadway, Sonoma
(707) 938-5830

326 Healdsburg Avenue, Healdsburg
(707) 433-4404

114 Lake Street, Cloverdale
(707) 894-5232
www.century21.com

MORGAN LANE
500 Broadway, Sonoma
(707) 935-5777
www.morganlane.com

PACIFIC UNION RESIDENTIAL BROKERAGE
640 Broadway, Sonoma
(707) 934-2300
www.pacunion.com

HEALDSBURG REALTY
709 Healdsburg Avenue, Healdsburg
(707) 433-6555
www.healdsburgrealty.com

NORTH COUNTY PROPERTIES
21069 Geyserville Avenue, Geyserville
(707) 857-1728
www.geyserville.org

Voter Registration

Whenever you move, you must reregister to vote. The Registrar of Voters offices in Wine Country, listed here, can supply information and forms to get you signed up to vote. You may also call the toll-free number for the California Secretary of State to learn more: (800) 345-8683. The state's Web site for voting and election information is at www.ss.ca.gov/elections.

Napa County
900 Coombs Street, Room 256, Napa
(707) 253-4321
www.co.napa.ca.us

Sonoma County
435 Fiscal Drive, Santa Rosa
(707) 565-6800, (800) 750-VOTE
www.sonoma-county.org/regvoter

SEA RANCH PROPERTIES
1000 Annapolis Road, Sea Ranch
(707) 785-2321
www.thesearanch.com

RETIREMENT HOUSING OPTIONS

In the past few years, Wine Country has attracted many new retirees and seniors. To meet the demands for shelter, new senior housing projects are springing up across the region. This is particularly true in the area of independent-living apartment complexes that provide housekeeping, meals, and laundry services, while allowing for complete freedom of movement and individuality. Following are examples of this type of retirement-living option (with a couple of other independent-living choices thrown in) within our area.

Napa County

THE MEADOWS OF NAPA VALLEY

1800 Atrium Parkway, Napa
(707) 257-7885
www.meadowsofnapavalley.org

Three levels of personalized care are offered at this 20-acre residential retirement community. The apartments are available in one- and two-bedroom floorplans, augmented by the assisted-living program and a skilled nursing center with rehabilitation services in a homelike setting. A gift shop and beauty/barber shop are also on-site.

AEGIS OF NAPA

2100 Redwood Road, Napa
(707) 251-1409
www.aegisliving.com

Studio apartments, one-bedroom flats, and shared suites are offered at this community, along with Life's Neighborhood, an Alzheimer's program. A beauty salon and barber, plus pet care and personal laundry, are all on-site.

SILVERADO ORCHARDS

601 Pope Street, St. Helena
(707) 963-3688, (800) 339-1229
www.silveradoorchards.com

In a quiet, green setting between St. Helena proper and the Silverado Trail is this popular retirement community. Silverado Orchards has 80 units altogether—small studios, deluxe studios, one-bedroom apartments, and a couple two-bedroom units. It's an active population that takes advantage of the immediate area's pleasant walking routes, plus twice-a-week exercise classes.

WOODBRIDGE VILLAGE

727 Hunt Avenue, St. Helena
(707) 963-3231

Several years ago this HUD-supported retirement complex won an award for best landscaping in St. Helena, and the parklike grounds have only improved since then, the managers say, thanks in part to some resident green thumbs. Woodbridge is a series of tidy one-bedroom, one-bath apartments, most of them grouped into fourplexes. HUD defines a senior as anyone age 62 or older.

RANCHO DE CALISTOGA

2412 Foothill Boulevard, Calistoga
(707) 942-6971

Yes, it's a mobile-home park, but if all of them looked like this, they would have a very different reputation. Centuries-old oak trees tower over the big lawn area out front, and the whole community is full of flowering plants. Rancho de Calistoga has a total of 184 lots. It also has a clubhouse, recreation building, pool, and spa. Activities include bingo twice a month, bridge, poker, exercise classes, quilting, potlucks, and Wednesday-morning brunch. The park is meant for seniors 55 and older.

Sonoma County

MERRILL GARDENS SONOMA

800 Oregon Street, Sonoma
(707) 996-7101
www.merrillgardens.com

Billed as offering "all the amenities without the work," Merrill Gardens has 153 one- and two-bedroom suites, fully carpeted (bring your own furniture), with a small kitchen, private deck, or balcony and the Anytime Dining program.

MERRILL GARDENS ROHNERT PARK

4855 Snyder Lane, Rohnert Park
(707) 585-7878
www.merrillgardens.com

Although this property enjoys country views of rolling green farmlands, it is near shopping, 1 block from a large medical complex, and a short putt to the nearest golf course. A sister property of the Sonoma Merrill Gardens (see above), this complex consists of 171 apartments.

VALLEY ORCHARDS RETIREMENT CENTER

2100 East Washington Street, Petaluma
(707) 778-6030, (800) 662-7919
www.valleyorchards.com

Valley Orchards provides three meals a day (along with a daily fresh salad bar), utilities, cable TV, transportation three days a week, housekeeping services, bathroom and bedroom laundry, 24-hour emergency assistance, and yard maintenance. Valley Orchard's 104 units are split between large studios and one- and two-bedroom apartments.

FRIENDS HOUSE
684 Benicia Drive, Santa Rosa
(707) 538-0152
www.friendshouse.org
A Quaker institution, Friends House is composed of four interrelated programs for the older person: independent-living apartments and houses, an adult day-care center, an assisted-living facility, and a skilled-nursing facility. A large part of the seven-acre Friends House site contains 60 garden apartments. People live in their own homes with their own belongings and garden space. One- and two-bedroom apartments are available, and recently some three-bedroom, two-bath homes were added to accommodate couples who want more space within the Friends House community.

LODGE AT PAULIN CREEK
2375 Range Avenue, Santa Rosa
(707) 575-3722
www.brookdaleliving.com
The Lodge is set in parklike grounds with inviting courtyards. Apartments are sunny and bright, with the charm of designer fabrics, art reproductions, and handmade quilts. They range from studios to three-bedroom, two-bath units. Some dining options are offered—you can either be served graciously in the dining room or serve yourself casually from the salad and hot entree buffet. Amenities include a pool, fitness trail, billiards room, an opportunity to garden, and a calendar of day trips.

i The California Department of Fish and Game offers a reduced-fee sportfishing license for those age 65 and older.

SENIOR SERVICES

Most senior citizens who choose to live in Wine Country are spending their retirement years actively pursuing good health and happiness. Everyone, however, needs a little help and guidance from time to time to lead a satisfying life. Here are a few connections to make it easier for seniors to find their way around in new territory.

Napa County
THE VOLUNTEER CENTER OF NAPA COUNTY
1820 Jefferson Street, Napa
(707) 252-6222, (707) 963-3922
www.volunteernapa.org
The Volunteer Center does all sorts of good work in the county, and its Senior Services Program, funded by the Napa–Solano Area Agency on Aging (see listing in this section) and the United Way, is foremost on the list. Especially valuable is the Senior Guide it publishes each year. It's a well-organized catalog of write-ups and phone numbers, with suggestions on topics ranging from health services and home care to housing and transportation.

COMPREHENSIVE SERVICES FOR OLDER ADULTS
900 Coombs Street, Suite 257, Napa
(707) 253-4625, (800) 498-9455
www.napachamber.org
www.co.napa.ca.us
Administered by the Napa County Health and Human Services Agency, this program offers in-home care to the aged, blind, and disabled who can't afford to fend for themselves. The manifold services include household tasks and shopping, nonmedical personal care when needed to ensure safety, alcohol and drug counseling, adult protective services, and psychiatric case management for seniors 62 or older who suffer from mental illness or Alzheimer's disease. Comprehensive Services also assists with procurement of food stamps and Medi-Cal (state-subsidized medical insurance) benefits.

FOOD & NUTRITION SERVICES OF NAPA VALLEY

1755 Industrial Way, Napa

(707) 253-6111

This service cooks up hot, nutritious meals for people 60 years or older on a donation basis. When needed, they will transport guests to one of seven Napa County sites or deliver food to homes. Call one day in advance for reservations.

NAPA–SOLANO AREA AGENCY ON AGING

400 Contra Costa Street, Vallejo

(707) 664-6612, (800) 510-2020

www.aaans.org

People 55 and older who are mentally and physically fit, and who are looking for a little extra cash, are encouraged to get in touch with this agency. They'll help you find part-time employment.

Sonoma County

COUNCIL ON AGING

30 Kawana Springs Road, Santa Rosa

(707) 525-0143, (800) 675-0143

www.councilonaging.com

This is the overall program that provides many of the benefits that are incorporated in member organizations such as the senior centers listed subsequently. Council on Aging provides dining rooms with a hot, healthy noontime meal at many locations in Sonoma County. The Meals on Wheels program delivers hot meals seven days a week to the homes of temporarily or chronically homebound seniors. Legal consultation services are provided, as well as money management programs, health insurance counseling, and door-to-door transportation for seniors with doctor visits. The council offers an excellent Senior Resource Guide available at senior centers or by calling the listed numbers.

SENIOR ADVOCACY SERVICES

3262 Airway Drive, Suite C, Santa Rosa

(707) 526-4108

www.senioradvocacyservices.org

Covering six counties north of the Golden Gate Bridge (including all in Wine Country), this agency offers one-on-one counseling by trained volunteers registered by the California Department of Aging. They provide independent, unbiased information on health insurance, including Medicare and supplemental programs. They also help clients sort out their medical finances and make sure they are being billed appropriately for Medicare.

PETALUMA ECUMENICAL PROPERTIES (PEP)

951 Petaluma Boulevard S., Petaluma

(707) 762-2336

www.pephousing.org

In 1977 three local ministers came together to find a way to provide low-cost housing for seniors. With community backing, PEP sought out suitable building sites and developed architectural plans. The group has built and manages 11 projects and is supported by 11 churches and AARP contributions.

JEWISH SENIORS PROGRAM

3859 Montgomery Drive, Santa Rosa

(707) 528-4222

www.jccsoco.org

The wide spectrum of entertainment and educational opportunities offered through this program includes musical events, folk dancing, autobiographical writing, book discussion, parties, and trips. Want to learn Yiddish? That's an option too! The group welcomes participants from all denominations.

SENIOR CENTERS

They're social centers, educational resources, service sources, and just plain fun places for seniors with leisure time. Most of the centers publish newsletters so everyone can find out what's in store. All have an extensive, varied program of activities, and all offer services such as blood pressure and hearing testing, legal counsel, and tax assistance on a regular basis.

Napa County

SENIOR CITIZENS CENTER
1500 Jefferson Street, Napa
(707) 255-1800
www.cityofnapa.org
Older residents get one-stop shopping at this office. Nearly 60 organizations—including the Senior Friendship Club and Napa Grange—use the center as a meeting place. It's open Monday through Friday 8:00 a.m. to 4:00 p.m. Activities range from dances, bingo, and potluck dinners to arts and crafts and pancake breakfasts. Friday mornings welcome guest speakers for Senior Seminars. Call for a monthly schedule of events.

BERRYESSA SENIOR CENTER
4380 Spanish Flat Loop Road, Berryessa
(707) 966-0206
The highlands surrounding Lake Berryessa sound like a nice place for retired folks—and, well, they are. This center has a strong lineup of health, educational, social, and recreational programs. If you call for a monthly schedule, you'll discover potluck meals, bingo, crafts, Adventure College classes, trips, dances, and more.

Sonoma County
Southern Sonoma

VINTAGE HOUSE
264 First Street E., Sonoma
(707) 996-0311
www.vintagehouse.org
Staffed largely by senior volunteers, Vintage House is open Monday through Friday, serving more than 1,000 individuals each month with up to 70 classes and activities, most of them free or low cost. The choices include art classes, line dancing, tap dancing, international folk dance instruction, canasta, bridge in several forms, tai chi, mah-jongg, and exercise classes. Lessons in French, Italian, and Spanish at levels for beginning, intermediate, and advanced speakers are also offered. The Vintage House Singers choral group is coached by a professional music director

and performs twice a year. A representative from the Department of Motor Vehicles visits each month to administer driving tests, and the tax man cometh during his season. Lunch is served Tuesday, Thursday, and Friday in the dining room for a small fee.

LUCCHESI PARK SENIOR CENTER (PETALUMA COMMUNITY CENTER)
211 Novak Drive, Petaluma
(707) 778-4399
www.cityofpetaluma.net
This facility largely houses the recreational part of Petaluma's senior program—the local meal program is administered by the adjacent Petaluma People Services Center (reach that organization at 707-765-8488 or at www.petalumapeople.org). Line dancing events draw 25 to 40 participants each week, and ballroom dancing attracts 100 or more. Group exercise goes over big, along with the computer classes, eclectic discussion groups, art instruction, and creative writing classes. Many day trips and extended trips are sponsored. The center also sponsors flu shots and blood-pressure testing.

ROHNERT PARK SENIOR CENTER
6800 Hunter Drive, Suite A, Rohnert Park
(707) 585-6780
www.rpcity.org
Active seniors as well as disabled persons who can manage on their own are welcome here to chat, play cards, and watch the once-a-month movie. General activities include line dancing, bridge, basketry, Spanish classes, a craft shop, and a billiards table. Every other month an early-evening dance brings out a lively crowd. A noon meal is served daily. The center is open Monday through Friday from 8:00 a.m. to 5:00 p.m. and on Saturday from noon to 4:00 p.m.

SANTA ROSA SENIOR CENTER
704 Bennett Valley Road, Santa Rosa
(707) 542-1228
www.santarosaseniorcenter.org
Dancing is important here—afternoon ballroom

dancing once a week, line dancing, and tap dancing. Bingo, bridge, whist, chess, and pinochle games are lively, and there are three billiards tables. Watercolor painting classes are a big draw, and there's creative writing, a poetry group, and Spanish instruction. The drama group puts on shows, and a choral group attracts those who like to belt out a tune. There are also clinics for blood pressure, allergy screening, chiropractic evaluations, and even toenail clipping. Once a month the Friendship Club organizes a potluck lunch. Meals are served Monday to Friday at 4:00 p.m. The Council on Aging also uses the center kitchen to prepare meals for delivery to the homebound. Fundraising has been under way for several years to build a larger, more centrally located senior center in Santa Rosa, and the organization has nearly reached its goal.

i The Senior Center in Santa Rosa offers a multitude of free services to golden-agers, including allergy, hearing, and blood pressure screenings; chiropractic consultations; and legal aid.

Northern Sonoma

WINDSOR SENIOR CENTER
9231 Foxwood Drive, Windsor
(707) 838-1250
www.ci.windsor.ca.us

This center is surrounded by roses—45 varieties, in fact, in a lovely garden. In the artistic category, classes are available in oil and pastel painting and sculpture. Card players have a choice of pinochle or bridge, and seniors can learn to play the guitar, study genealogy, or join in a quilting bee. For the athletic, the bocce ball court is an attraction, as is the horseshoe pit. But most popular of all is the swimming pool: Windsor tends to be hot in summer, and the pool is a terrific place to cool off. It is outfitted for the disabled, who can be lowered from wheelchair to water by a special lift device.

HEALDSBURG SENIOR CENTER
133 Matheson Street, Healdsburg
(707) 431-3324
www.ci.healdsburg.ca.us

Lunch is served here Monday through Friday, and a bus service is available to bring seniors to the center as well as to take them to shopping areas and other destinations around town. Crafts are popular, with a group meeting once a week to work on handcrafts including the art of flower arranging. An unusually talented group of woodworkers has received several honors for items created at the center. Bingo brings the lucky and unlucky to play each Thursday. Department of Motor Vehicles testing also is provided. The center is open Monday through Friday from 10:00 a.m. to 4:00 p.m.

CLOVERDALE SENIOR MULTI-PURPOSE CENTER
311 North Main Street, Cloverdale
(707) 894-4826
www.cloverdaleseniorcenter.com

Weekly blood-pressure screenings, visits by an optometrist, and hearing-aid maintenance are among the services offered in Cloverdale. Line dancing is offered one day each week, and an instructor comes in to help seniors create an autobiographical record of their lives. A newsletter keeps seniors apprised of coming attractions at the center, where lunch is served every weekday.

West County/Russian River

SEBASTOPOL AREA SENIOR CENTER
167 North High Street, Sebastopol
(707) 829-2440
www.sebastopolseniorcenter.org

This center receives laudable backing from the community, and several stores and bakeries bring in day-old products to distribute among the members. Lunch is served in the dining room each weekday, and home-delivered meals are dispatched to those who cannot come in. Card games and bingo are regular sources of entertainment, and every once in a while, there's a special program by a harp and flute duo.

RUSSIAN RIVER SENIOR RESOURCE CENTER
15010 Armstrong Woods Road, Guerneville
(707) 869-0618
www.westcountyservices.org
Both on-site lunch and Meals on Wheels are provided from this center, and because this is a rural area, limited transportation is provided. Afternoon field trips and picnics are ideally suited to this vacation spot with its many scenic locales. Writing autobiographies and exercise classes are among the indoor activities.

RETIREMENT ACTIVITIES

Educational

Several agencies and area schools offer opportunities for inquisitive, mature men and women to prove there is no age limit to new intellectual experiences. In addition to the resources listed, many senior centers throughout Wine Country offer classes in writing, foreign languages, computer skills, and other subjects. In addition, retirees can look to courses offered by Wine Country colleges (see that section).

i Napa Valley College is in the midst of building the Instructional Center for the Performing Arts, specifically designed for drama and music. It will include a 500-seat theater for large shows and a 100-seat "black box" theater for experimental productions.

Napa County

NAPA VALLEY COLLEGE COMMUNITY EDUCATION
1088 College Avenue, St. Helena
(707) 253-3070, (707) 967-2900
www.napavalley.edu

NORTH BAY DRIVING & TRAFFIC SCHOOL
1878 El Centro Avenue, Napa
(707) 252-2066
www.dsac.com

Sonoma County

PETALUMA ADULT EDUCATION SCHOOL
Various locations, Petaluma
(707) 778-4633
www.petalumacityschools.org

SONOMA STATE UNIVERSITY GERONTOLOGY PROGRAM
1801 East Cotati Avenue, Rohnert Park
(707) 664-2411
www.sonoma.edu

LEWIS ADULT EDUCATION CENTER
2230 Lomitas Avenue, Santa Rosa
(707) 522-3280
www.lewisadultschool.com

SANTA ROSA JUNIOR COLLEGE
1501 Mendocino Avenue, Santa Rosa
(707) 527-4011
www.santarosa.edu

Volunteer

A number of programs are available that put to use the skills, talents, and personalities of older individuals who choose to work full- or part-time for little or no remuneration. Here are some places to start your search.

VOLUNTEER CENTER OF NAPA VALLEY
1820 Jefferson Street, Napa
(707) 252-6222, (707) 963-3922
www.volunteernapa.org

VOLUNTEER CENTER OF SONOMA COUNTY
153 Stony Circle, Santa Rosa
(707) 573-3399
www.volunteernow.org

RETIRED AND SENIOR VOLUNTEER PROGRAM (RSVP)
1041 Fourth Street, Santa Rosa
(707) 573-3399
www.volunteernow.org

SERVICE CORPS OF RETIRED EXECUTIVES (SCORE)

777 Sonoma Avenue, Suite 115-B,
Santa Rosa
(707) 571-8342
www.scorenorthcoastca.org

FOSTER GRANDPARENT/SENIOR COMPANION PROGRAM

Sonoma Developmental Center, 15000
Arnold Drive, Eldridge
(707) 938-6201
www.seniorcorps.org

PUBLIC SCHOOLS

Napa County

Anyone who questions Napa County's commitment to education would do well to look at the many charitable events devoted to private or public schools, some of them featuring ultrapremium wines generously donated by the biggest names in the valley for live and silent auctions. A fund-raiser for Trinity Grammar and Prep School in Napa, for instance, raised $60,000 in one afternoon. Among the big names donating items for auction were—in addition to scores of Napa Valley wineries—the Oakland Raiders, the Petrified Forest, and the Winchester Mystery House in San Jose. A baseball bat signed by Barry Bonds also went up for bid.

In the 2007–08 school session, approximately 17,000 pupils were enrolled in Napa County public schools, dispersed among five districts: Calistoga Joint Unified, Napa Valley Unified, St. Helena Unified, Howell Mountain, and Pope Valley.

Bilingual education is one of the many hot-button issues facing California schools. As with many areas of the state, a large immigrant population—in this case, almost wholly from Mexico—mingles with those who migrated earlier. For instance, the ethnic distribution of students in the Calistoga Joint Unified district, with approximately 820 children enrolled in its three schools, is 69 percent Hispanic, 28 percent Anglo, and 3 percent other nationalities.

On the academic side, Napa County's chartered performance remains relatively strong. SAT I scores are always well above the state average, and participation is usually high. In other testing, Napa County's students traditionally rank high on their Academic Performance Index (API) scores, with pupils in all grades showing improvement on the Stanford 9 tests that surpassed goals set for them by the State of California.

Other success stories abound: Ten school campuses in Napa County have received California Distinguished School Awards based on evaluations of their curricula, test scores, school environments, parental participation, and special programs.

Progress has also been achieved through the New Technology High School, a Napa facility where students spend most of their time online or in-lab, with minimal teacher supervision. New Tech (www.newtechhigh.org), named a U.S. Department of Education Demonstration School for its technological advances, graduated its first senior class of future Silicon Valley moguls in 1998.

Sonoma County

Sonoma County's schools have consistently ranked in the top half of the state, although they're funded at less than the state average. Thirty-eight of the county's schools have been named California Distinguished Schools, and four have been recognized as National Blue Ribbon schools. Within Sonoma County's 40 school districts, 177 schools serve students from kindergarten through 12th grade. There are 89 elementary schools, 19 junior high schools, 15 high schools, 32 special alternative schools, and 32 charter schools. Total enrollment in the 2007–08 school year was approximately 71,400.

The growth in diversity among Sonoma County students is significant. Today local schools are educating the most culturally, socially, academically, and linguistically diverse student population in the county's history. Countywide, approximately 56 percent of public school students are Anglo, followed by 33 percent Hispanic. The remaining 11 percent are other nationalities.

The public school system also is working to address the needs of teens who have problems with alcohol or other drugs. Through programs such as Clean and Sober, the dropout rate for Sonoma County is considerably lower than the state average, and it continues to go down.

While attending to the needs of students with special needs, Sonoma County schools also consistently score in the top third of the state for every grade level and subject tested through the California Assessment Program. Average SAT scores for the county are usually higher than state and national averages.

PRIVATE SCHOOLS

Napa County

JUSTIN-SIENA HIGH SCHOOL
4026 Maher Street, Napa
(707) 255-0950
www.justin-siena.com

KOLBE ACADEMY DAY SCHOOL
1600 F Street, Napa
(707) 256-4306
www.kolbe.org

THE OXBOW SCHOOL
530 Third Street, Napa
(707) 255-6000
www.oxbowschool.org

NAPA CHRISTIAN CAMPUS OF EDUCATION: A SEVENTH-DAY ADVENTIST SCHOOL
2201 Pine Street, Napa
(707) 255-5233
www.napachristian.com

ST. JOHN'S LUTHERAN SCHOOL
3521 Linda Vista Avenue, Napa
(707) 226-7970
www.stjohnsnapa.org

ST. APOLLINARIS ELEMENTARY SCHOOL
3700 Lassen Street, Napa
(707) 224-6525
www.stapollinaris.com

FOOTHILLS ADVENTIST ELEMENTARY SCHOOL
711 Sunnyside Road, St. Helena
(707) 963-3546
www.foothillselementary.org

ST. HELENA MONTESSORI SCHOOL
1343 Spring Street, St. Helena
(707) 963-1527
www.montessori-namta.org

ST. HELENA CATHOLIC SCHOOL
1255 Oak Avenue, St. Helena
(707) 963-4677
www.sthelenacatholicschool.org

Sonoma County

OLD ADOBE SCHOOL
252 West Spain Street, Sonoma
(707) 938-4510
www.sonic.net/~marcjean/oldadobe/

ST. FRANCIS SOLANO SCHOOL
342 West Napa Street, Sonoma
(707) 996-4994
www.saintfrancissolano.org

THE PRESENTATION SCHOOL
20872 Broadway, Sonoma
(707) 935-0122
www.presentationschool.com

ST. VINCENT DE PAUL HIGH SCHOOL
849 Keokuk Street (at Magnolia), Petaluma
(707) 763-1032
www.svhs-pet.org

ADOBE CHRISTIAN PRESCHOOL/DAYCARE
2875 Adobe Road, Petaluma
(707) 763-2012
www.adobecc.org

URSULINE HIGH SCHOOL
90 Ursuline Road, Santa Rosa
(707) 524-1130
www.ursulinehs.org

CARDINAL NEWMAN HIGH SCHOOL
50 Ursuline Road, Santa Rosa
(707) 546-6470
www.cardinalnewman.org

ST. LUKE LUTHERAN SCHOOL
905 Mendocino Avenue, Santa Rosa
(707) 545-0526
www.stluke-lcms.org

STUART PREPARATORY SCHOOL
431 Humboldt Street, Santa Rosa
(707) 528-0721
www.stuartschool8k.com

MERRYHILL SCHOOL
4044 Mayette Avenue (infants through
junior kindergarten), Santa Rosa
(707) 575-7660
4580 Bennett View Drive (K-8),
Santa Rosa
(707) 575-0910
www.merryhillschool.com

THE BRIDGE SCHOOL
1625 Franklin Avenue, Santa Rosa
(707) 575-7959
www.srbridgeschool.com

i California was the first state in the
nation to approve charter schools—
the first ones opened their doors here in
1993. Though they remain public institutions, these schools are free from many of
the regulations governing regular schools.
In 2007–08, Sonoma County had 32 charter
schools.

TWO-YEAR COLLEGES

Napa County

NAPA VALLEY COLLEGE
2277 Napa–Vallejo Highway (Highway 221),
Napa
(707) 253-3064, (800) 826-1077

Upper Valley Site: 1088 College Avenue,
St. Helena
(707) 967-2901
www.napavalley.edu
Napa Valley College dates from 1942 and has
occupied its current site—180 tree-lined acres
near the Napa River—since 1965. It's a two-year
community college with about 9,000 students
and associate degree programs in a spectrum of
fields, including business administration, health
care, and, not surprisingly, viticulture and wine
technology. On-campus facilities include a Child
and Family Studies and Services complex and an
Olympic-size swimming pool. The school has an
Upper Valley Campus on the outskirts of St. Helena and a Small Business Development Center in
Napa. It also shares a guaranteed transfer agree-
ment with the University of California at Davis,
Sacramento State University, and Sonoma State
University.

Sonoma County

SANTA ROSA JUNIOR COLLEGE
1501 Mendocino Avenue, Santa Rosa
(707) 527-4011
www.santarosa.edu
The scholarship program at Santa Rosa Junior
College is unique in all of America because of
an association with the county-based Exchange
Bank. In 1948 the bank's president, Frank P. Doyle,
set up a trust that in the 1950–51 school year
paid out $19,475 in scholarships to 95 students.
In 2007 dividends from the trust awarded more
than $1.1 million in scholarships to approxi-
mately 900 students in Santa Rosa high schools.
Located on more than 100 acres, the college has

a full-time enrollment of almost 7,000. Emphasis centers on general education; transfer education for students headed to four-year institutions; and occupational education in the fields of dental hygiene, radiologic technology, respiratory therapy, the culinary arts, and many other areas. A recent addition to Santa Rosa Junior College is an 87-seat planetarium, with a dome 40 feet in diameter and 27 feet high. An additional 40-acre campus in east Petaluma offers occupational training, national park ranger training, police and fire technology, and public safety.

EMPIRE COLLEGE
3035 Cleveland Avenue, Santa Rosa
(707) 546-4000, (800) 705-0567
www.empcol.com
Empire College offers several specialized associate degrees—in accounting, information technology, paralegal, medical assistance, office administration, and tourism management and hospitality. Its School of Law awards juris doctor degrees in a four-year evening program. It also offers certificates to those studying to become legal secretaries, medical administrative/clinical assistants, medical transcriptionists, bookkeepers, and travel and tourism agents. A state-accredited college, Empire has operated since 1961 and now has some 500 students.

FOUR-YEAR COLLEGES AND UNIVERSITIES

Napa County

PACIFIC UNION COLLEGE
100 Howell Mountain Road N., Angwin
(707) 965-6311, (800) 862-7080
www.puc.edu
PUC is a small (just more than 1,600 students), private, Seventh-day Adventist college surrounded by 1,800 acres of crops and forest on top of Howell Mountain, where it has been since 1906. The views are fabulous, and the education is highly regarded. *U.S. News & World Report* ranked the school the top liberal-arts college in California in 1998, and the *Right College* places it in the top 10

in the nation for the percentage of male graduates who enter medical school. The student-faculty ratio is an appealing 12-to-1.

Pacific Union is most definitely a unique experience. The student body is ethnically diverse; the cafeteria is vegetarian (in line with Seventh-day Adventist practice); and the Abroad Program offers overseas study, including full-year programs in Argentina, Austria, France, Kenya, and Spain. Service is a big part of a PUC student's commitment. Many strike out on yearlong missions, and even more are actively involved with local homeless shelters, prison ministries, and the like. The college offers associate's, bachelor's, and master's degrees in 19 academic departments, with the most popular majors being nursing, business administration, biology, behavioral science, chemistry, art, and communication.

i Napa Valley College and Santa Rosa Junior College both offer several courses—semester-long and shorter—in viticulture and winemaking. SRJC also offers classes such as Wine Industry Event Planning, Wine Marketing Fundamentals, and Media in the Wine and Vineyard Industry.

Sonoma County

UNIVERSITY OF NORTHERN CALIFORNIA
1304 Southpoint Boulevard, Suite 220, Petaluma
(707) 765-6400
www.uncm.edu
This university, established in 1993, welcomes students from around the world. It aspires to become a premier engineering and scientific university with substantial programs in the liberal arts. Students enjoy small classes with ample individual attention from professors dedicated to quality teaching. Interdisciplinary studies are encouraged, and all academic programs emphasize the importance of effective communication for success in the modern world. The university focuses on programs in biological technology, and its degree programs include the B.E., M.S., and Ph.D. in biomedical

Public Libraries

Napa County
3421 Broadway, American Canyon
(707) 644-1136

580 Coombs Street, Napa
(707) 253-4241

6548 Yountville Avenue, Yountville
(707) 944-1888

1108 Myrtle, Calistoga
(707) 942-4833

Sonoma County
755 West Napa Street, Sonoma
(707) 996-5217

100 Fairgrounds Drive, Petaluma
(707) 763-9801

6250 Lynne Conde Way
Rohnert Park-Cotati
(707) 584-9121

Third and E Streets, Santa Rosa
(main branch)
(707) 545-0831

150 Coddingtown Center, Santa Rosa
(707) 546-2265

6959 Montecito Boulevard, Santa Rosa
(707) 537-0162

9291 Old Redwood Highway, Windsor
(707) 838-1020

Piper and Center Streets, Healdsburg
(707) 433-3772

401 North Cloverdale Boulevard
Cloverdale; (707) 894-5271

7050 Covey Road, Forestville
(707) 887-7654

14107 Armstrong Woods Road
Guerneville; (707) 869-9004

73 Main Street, Occidental
(707) 874-3080

7140 Bodega Avenue, Sebastopol
(707) 823-7691

---

engineering, the B.A. and M.B.A. in applied linguistics, and the B.A. in Chinese.

SONOMA STATE UNIVERSITY
1801 East Cotati Avenue, Rohnert Park
(707) 664-2880
www.sonoma.edu
This university was established on 270 acres of farmland in 1960. Today it offers undergraduate liberal arts and science curricula and 13 master's degree programs to a student population of about 7,000. Its computer engineering graduates walk directly into high-paying jobs, and similar results are expected for those completing the new wine business program. The school's Sonoma Plan is

considered a model nursing program throughout America. The new three-story, 215,000-square-foot Jean and Charles Schulz Information Center—named in honor of the renowned Peanuts cartoonist and his wife—is home to both the university library and the campus information technology department. In 2004 a $15 million recreation center opened, equipped with a rock climbing wall and indoor soccer, volleyball, and basketball courts. Performing arts get top billing at the campus, with plays from the pens of local writers and international favorites performed year-round, along with dance recitals and musical concerts (see the Arts and Culture chapter). A new center to showcase the performing arts is under construction.

Sonoma State University launched the nation's first MBA program focused on the wine industry in 2007. Plenty of schools teach students how to grow grapes and make wine, but few teach the business side of wine. SSU also offers a B.A. in wine business strategy and professional development courses for people already in the industry.

OTHER INSTITUTES OF HIGHER LEARNING

Napa County

THE CULINARY INSTITUTE OF AMERICA AT GREYSTONE
2555 Main Street, St. Helena
(866) 569-4137, (800) 888-7850
www.ciachef.edu/california
A learning institution devoted to the gustatory arts is one of the perks of living in Wine Country. The CIA at Greystone is the only center in the world dedicated exclusively to continuing education for professionals in the food, wine, health, and hospitality fields—and it's a beauty. It's also an attraction for visitors just passing through to check out the well-equipped culinary store and have their photos taken next to giant wine barrels (see the Attractions chapter).

It all began some years ago, when executives of the Culinary Institute of America, that factory of chefs in Hyde Park, New York, looked at about 50 potential sites to establish a West Coast center for continuing education. Their logical choice was Greystone, the majestic winery built in 1888 and used by the Christian Brothers to make sparkling wine from 1950 to 1989. After a massive gift from the Heublein Corporation (then owner of the property) and a $14 million renovation, the CIA opened for business in Napa Valley in 1995.

Inside, the facilities are almost as impressive as the 22-inch-thick tufa stone walls that frame Greystone's exterior. The third story is an immense teaching kitchen with 15,000 square feet of undivided floor space, 35-foot ceilings,

and clusters of exquisite Bonnet stoves. In the middle of the space is a dining area where students sample the various assignments they and their cohorts have handed in.

The building also houses a 125-seat amphitheater used for cooking demonstrations and lectures; the Wine Spectator Greystone Restaurant (see the Restaurants chapter for more on that); and the Spice Islands Marketplace with its preponderance of cooking equipment, books, and uniforms. Outside the old winery are garlic and onion beds, seven terraces of herbs, an edible flower and herbal tea garden, and, off-site, 15 acres of Merlot grapes and an organic fruit and vegetable garden.

Courses vary in length from three days to the 30-week, two-semester Baking and Pastry Arts Certification Program. (The average class duration is one week.) The faculty is drawn from three sources: the small but talented core of resident instructors, visiting teachers from Hyde Park, and guest instructors.

More than 50 Napa Valley wineries take part every year in an event called Taste for Knowledge, a wine tasting and wine auction usually held in November. Sponsored by the Napa Valley Unified Education Foundation, to date the event has raised more than $1 million for direct classroom enrichment in local schools.

Sonoma County

UNIVERSITY OF SAN FRANCISCO—SANTA ROSA CAMPUS
416 B Street, Santa Rosa
(707) 527-9612
www.usfca.edu
This outpost of the University of San Francisco offers several undergrad degrees (applied economics, information systems, public administration) and graduate degree programs in similar subjects. You can also get a teaching credential and a registered-nurse degree. The nine classrooms are in downtown Santa Rosa, and

seating is "seminar" style with tables and chairs grouped for better interaction between students and instructors.

CHILD CARE

Whether you're visiting for a few days or putting down roots for several years, finding qualified child care can be a daunting task. Each county has at least one organization that will help you sort out all the factors, free of charge. These agencies are able to quote prices, describe individual providers, and refer you to ones in which you might be interested.

Napa County

COMMUNITY RESOURCES FOR CHILDREN
5 Financial Plaza, Suite 224, Napa
(707) 253-0376 (general information),
(707) 253-0366 (referrals),
(800) 696-4CRC
www.crcnapa.org

Sonoma County

COMMUNITY CHILD CARE COUNCIL OF SONOMA COUNTY
396 Tesconi Court, Santa Rosa
(707) 544-3077
www.sonoma4cs.org

RIVER CHILD CARE SERVICES
16300 First Street, Guerneville
(707) 869-3613
www.rccservices.org

WALK-IN/PROMPT-CARE CENTERS

Napa County

EXPRESSCARE/URGENT CARE
Queen of the Valley Medical Center
1000 Trancas Street, Napa
(707) 257-4008
www.thequeen.org
This walk-in center, an adjunct of Queen of the Valley's emergency room, is open 10:00 a.m.

to 10:00 p.m. daily and can address a variety of nonlethal illnesses, allergies, and injuries. Board-certified physicians are on hand to treat you, and they will make referrals or deliver follow-up care if needed.

Sonoma County

ST. JOSEPH URGENT CARE CENTERS
Rohnert Park Healthcare Center
1450 Medical Center Drive, Rohnert Park
(707) 584-0672

1287 Fulton Road, Santa Rosa
(707) 543-2000
www.stjosephhealth.org
Both of these convenient clinics, operated by St. Joseph Health System–Sonoma County, are for people who need to see a medical professional but whose injuries or illnesses are not emergencies. The doctors and nurses can patch up your minor medical problems quickly and efficiently and provide diagnostic and lab services too. The Rohnert Park location is open daily 8:00 a.m. to 9:00 p.m.; the Santa Rosa clinic is open daily 9:00 a.m. to 8:00 p.m.

HOSPITALS

Napa County

QUEEN OF THE VALLEY MEDICAL CENTER
1000 Trancas Street, Napa
(707) 252-4411
www.thequeen.org
www.wellnesscenternapa.com
With 179 beds, QVH has a community cancer center, a high-end imaging department, home-care services, maternity services (including an intensive-care nursery), occupational health services, a regional heart center where open-heart surgeries are performed, and a respiratory-care department. It also features an upgraded vascular and interventional radiology lab, an expanded maternity unit, improved MRI technology, and a new 59,000-square-foot wellness center. Queen of the Valley is the designated trauma center for Napa County, with a 24-hour emergency room.

The Acute Rehabilitation Center offers comprehensive physical, occupational, and speech therapies for people who have experienced trauma (such as a stroke or spinal cord injury). Queen of the Valley is part of the St. Joseph Health System, which emphasizes dignity, service, justice, and excellence. The Queen celebrated its 50th anniversary in 2008 with a major fund-raising gala headlined by the Smothers Brothers.

> **i** If you are a Kaiser Permanente member staying in Wine Country, note that the hospital group operates a medical center in Vallejo, only 15 miles from Napa, and another in Santa Rosa.

ST. HELENA HOSPITAL
10 Woodland Road, St. Helena
(707) 963-3611,
TTY/TDD: (707) 963-6527
www.sthelenahospital.org
This full-service community hospital, off the Silverado Trail about 2 miles northeast of St. Helena, dates from the 1800s. St. Helena Hospital, with 181 beds, has a wide range of specialties, including cardiac surgery, cardiovascular rehabilitation, pulmonary rehabilitation, oncology, obstetrics, pain rehabilitation, sleep disorders, and preventive medicine. A member of the Adventist Health network of facilities, St. Helena is known for its cardiovascular lab—a major heart center for Northern California. Recently added to the hospital is the Center for Health, offering weight loss and smoking cessation programs. For personalized attention there is One, an intensive one-day health assessment that includes a complete workup of your overall being, from cardiac stress tests to blood work to vision and hearing tests.

Sonoma County
SONOMA VALLEY HOSPITAL
347 Andrieux Street, Sonoma
(707) 935-5000
www.svh.com
When Sonoma Valley Hospital was created in

1946, the vision was to combine the best of medicine with a warm and caring staff. Since then, tremendous advances in research and diagnosis have changed the face of medicine. But the hospital remains a warm, caring, family-oriented hospital with the same small-town spirit that permeates the community from which it draws its patients. Today's 83-bed facility serves 40,000 people in Sonoma Valley. The credentialed medical staff numbers approximately 90 active, consulting, and courtesy physicians involved in all major specialties. There's 24-hour emergency care too. A full range of cardiopulmonary testing equipment is available, along with cardiac rehab programs. A birth center provides a comfortable, homey place where labor, delivery, recovery, and postpartum phases all take place in one room with the family at hand. Plans and fund-raising are under way to build an updated hospital to replace this aging facility, but there is much debate over where it should be located.

PETALUMA VALLEY HOSPITAL
400 North McDowell Boulevard, Petaluma
(707) 778-1111
www.petalumavalleyhospital.org
www.stjosephhealth.org
With 80 beds and a couple dozen medical specialties, from cardiology to urology, this facility, operated by the St. Joseph Health System–Sonoma County, is a busy place. The attractive two-story, 24-year-old hospital is also a genuine community resource. There's a full-service emergency department with a physician on duty 24 hours a day and a helipad for emergency helicopter transport.

SANTA ROSA MEMORIAL HOSPITAL
1165 Montgomery Drive, Santa Rosa
(707) 546-3210
www.santarosamemorial.org
www.stjosephhealth.org
Memorial Hospital opened its doors in 1950 under the guidance of the Sisters of St. Joseph, founders of eight other hospitals on the West Coast since 1920. All services and programs are guided by the healing mission of the Sisters—service,

When Finding Help Is Urgent

Call 911 during any medical emergency. If an ambulance is not what you need, consider one of the following numbers. In the first group are phone numbers that apply throughout Wine Country, followed by county-specific numbers.

Throughout Wine Country
Poison Control Center
(800) 222-1222

California HIV/AIDS Hotline
(800) 367-2437

Crisis Line for the Handicapped
(800) 426-4263

California Smokers Helpline
(800) 662-8887

California Department of Drug and Alcohol Problems
(800) 879-2772

Centers for Disease Control and Prevention (Sexually Transmitted Disease Hotline)
(800) 227-8922, (800) 232-4636

Medical Board of California (Central Complaint Unit)
(800) 633-2322

Dental Referral
(800) DENTIST

Napa County
Suicide Prevention
(800) 784-2433

Napa County Health and Human Services Department
(707) 253-4279

Napa County Alcohol and Drug Services
(707) 253-4412

Napa Emergency Women's Services
(707) 255-6397

Sonoma County
Sonoma County Department of Health Services and Center for HIV Prevention and Care
(707) 565-4620

Suicide Prevention
(800) 784-2433

Crisis Line for the Handicapped
(800) 426-4263

Department of Alcohol and Drug Programs
(800) 879-2772

---

excellence, justice, and dignity for all members of the community. The hospital is the flagship facility for St. Joseph Health System–Sonoma County. In 2000 Memorial Hospital was named the designated trauma center for Sonoma, Lake, and Mendocino Counties, making it the busiest and best-equipped hospital of its kind north of the Golden Gate. In addition to cutting-edge surgical facilities and medical equipment, the 346-bed Memorial Hospital has some unique services including the mobile medical and dental clinics, which serve children ages 16 and younger from low-income families that have difficulty locating affordable health care. Care is provided by medical professionals who speak English and Spanish.

To give new parents extra peace of mind, the hospital partners with the University of California–San Francisco Medical Center to operate an intensive-care nursery for ill newborns on-site. It also converted in 2007 to an electronic ICU system, by which doctors can check on patients remotely through a camera/microphone setup.

In 2000 the St. Joseph Health System added another dimension to its services: a palliative care unit, across the street from Santa Rosa Memorial Hospital. One of only a handful of its kind in California, this acute-care service focuses on providing end-of-life pain management and improving the quality of life for those with life-threatening illness. In 2003 the hospital opened a $20 million ambulatory surgery center across the street from its main campus, where outpatient surgeries of all types are performed. In 2008 the hospital opened new state-of-the-art Heart Institute.

SUTTER MEDICAL CENTER OF SANTA ROSA
3325 Chanate Road, Santa Rosa
(707) 576-4000
www.suttersantarosa.org
A hospital was first established on this site in 1866, and the Sutter system took it over in the mid-1990s. As a teaching institution affiliated with the University of California at San Francisco School of Medicine, Sutter is regionally recognized for its wide range of specialty services, including a high-risk maternity department and an emergency trauma care program. It offers other special services too. The 244-bed facility's major expansion in 2001 was to its cardiovascular services. The Heart Center provides a complete range of cardiac services, from open-heart surgery to cardiac rehabilitation. This hospital's future is uncertain. In early 2007 it announced that it would close completely within a year, but by early 2008 it had reversed itself, saying it would stay open after all.

HEALDSBURG DISTRICT HOSPITAL
1375 University Avenue, Healdsburg
(707) 431-6500
www.nschd.org
Today the hospital is a far cry from the World War I era, wood-frame building that burned to the ground in the 1930s. It's now a pleasant facility with 38 beds. Services include 24-hour emergency care, physical therapy and occupational medicine services, a same-day surgery

center, and a fully modernized imaging center. The emergency department and intensive care unit were significantly expanded in 2008, thanks largely to contributions by major donors who ponied up $6 million for the project.

PALM DRIVE HOSPITAL
501 Petaluma Avenue, Sebastopol
(707) 823-8511
www.palmdrivehospital.com
Palm Drive's future as a small community hospital has been tested during the past few years. In 2007 it nearly closed for good, saved by a generous benefactor and changes in management. The hospital filed for bankruptcy protection and has remained open while it reorganizes its business plan. It intends to launch a fund drive to raise $10 million. Currently the hospital has 37 beds and one operating room, and its emergency room is staffed 24 hours a day.

HOSPICE CARE

Napa County

NAPA VALLEY HOSPICE AND ADULT DAY SERVICES
414 South Jefferson Street, Napa
(707) 258-9080
www.napavalleyhospice-ads.org
If the time comes to end the aggressive search for a cure and to focus instead on comfort and symptom alleviation as death approaches, hospice care is the appropriate choice. Hospice of Napa Valley is a nonprofit organization serving the county since 1979. In 2008 it renamed itself to reflect the growing importance of its adult day services, which it added in 1997. The frail elderly and younger functionally impaired adults are the focus of the day services program. Daily hot lunches, caregiver respites, social activities, and transportation assistance are all provided.

Sonoma County
HOSPICE OF PETALUMA
416 Payran Street, Petaluma
(707) 778-6242

MEMORIAL HOSPICE
821 Mendocino Avenue, Santa Rosa
(707) 568-1094
www.stjosephhealth.org
www.memorialhospice.org
Working in tandem as part of the St. Joseph Health System–Sonoma County, these agencies provide support and care for persons facing life-threatening illnesses so that they may live as fully and comfortably as possible. Hospice of Petaluma (working with Memorial Hospice of Santa Rosa) benefits the community served by Petaluma Valley and Santa Rosa Memorial Hospitals. A counseling and social work staff offer emotional support, counseling, and information about community resources. A hospice chaplain provides spiritual support, and grief services are also offered.

ALTERNATIVE HEALTH CARE

Alternative forms of treatment and prevention proliferate and thrive in this region. Why? First of all, this is Wine Country, where health and quality of life are paramount. And second, this is California, where people tend to be open-minded in their decision making. So if you're in search of a less traditional cure for what ails you, you're in luck. Within a short drive you can find homeopaths and naturopaths, ayurvedics and herbalists, acupuncturists and acupressurists, chiropractors and yoga gurus, reflexologists and hypnotists—and practitioners of reiki, rolfing, and biofeedback. You can even find a few shaman healers if you try hard enough. If you want to verify a license, call the Medical Board of California at (916) 263-2382.

MEDIA

I know—you're in Wine Country to forget about the outside world for a few days, to escape from the 24/7 onslaught of the media. But when you do feel like emerging from your little corner of our nirvana—or if you're a new or soon-to-be resident—the local media stand ready to enlighten you. In addition to daily and weekly newspapers and niche publications, this chapter lists radio and TV stations. *NOTE:* Anyone needing their daily fix of the *New York Times, Wall Street Journal,* or the nearby *San Francisco Chronicle* can find racks for these newspapers and more in most Wine Country communities. Wireless Internet access is probably available in your hotel or motel, too, and wi-fi hotspots have popped up in many areas of our cities.

DAILY NEWSPAPERS

Napa County

NAPA VALLEY REGISTER
1615 Second Street, Napa
(707) 226-3711, (800) 504-6397
www.napavalleyregister.com
Napa County's only daily dates from 1863, though it has gone through a few changes of ownership since Abe Lincoln's administration. The paper is now owned by Lee Enterprises.

The morning *Register,* with a circulation of 18,500, ably handles the entire county with a lot of local reporting, such as a multifaceted 1997 series about the valley's farmworkers that garnered much acclaim. The *Register* prints its community calendar on Thursday and Sunday. The calendar lists upcoming musical performances, lectures, and fund-raisers. Also worth noting here is its monthly news-rack supplement: *Inside Napa Valley,* a tourist-aimed tabloid with features on art, food, wine, and coming events. The supplement is free. The paper's online site was significantly revamped in 2008, along with its affiliated site aimed at visitors, www.insidenapavalley.com.

Sonoma County

PRESS DEMOCRAT
427 Mendocino Avenue, Santa Rosa
(707) 546-2020
www.pressdemocrat.com
For many Sonoma County residents as well as readers in adjoining counties, the morning *Press Democrat* is the paper for local, national, and international daily news, with a circulation of about 93,000 (104,000 on Sunday). The *P.D.,* as locals call it, is owned by the *New York Times* but has been serving the Sonoma County area since 1857. Although the paper's name includes the word *democrat,* the editorial stance is more middle-of-the-road. A strong sports section features popular columnists such as Bob Padecky and Lowell Cohn. Columns by Chris Smith and Gaye LeBaron also offer colorful, behind-the-scenes coverage of Sonoma County people, places, and history. The Wednesday edition carries an "á la carte" column that gives suggestions for food and wine fun for the current week. On the entertainment scene, John Beck is the gonzo reporter, keeper of a witty blog for the paper's online edition.

OTHER NEWSPAPERS

Napa County

AMERICAN CANYON EAGLE
3860 Broadway, Suite 202, American Canyon
(707) 553-8240
www.americancanyoneagle.com
Published every Tuesday, the *Eagle* documents what's happening in the predominantly residential community of American Canyon, south of Napa. This paper is owned by Lee Enterprises.

YOUNTVILLE SUN
6505 Washington Street, Yountville
(707) 944-5676
Calling itself "a newspaper for the new millennium," the independently published *Sun* covers the small town in an edition printed weekly on Thursdays. An "Out & About" column wraps up some of the community gossip, including congratulations to new parents and grandparents, while a sports columnist runs down local amateur action and tidbits about Bay Area major league teams. A calendar of events is also included.

ST. HELENA STAR
1200 Main Street, St. Helena
(707) 963-2731
www.sthelenastar.com
St. Helena's well-preserved Victorian charm even extends to its newspaper, the *Star*, owned by Lee Enterprises. The paper attempts to stay within the city limits, plus Angwin and its Howell Mountain environs. The *Star* astutely covers the important local issues—growth, tourism, elections—and its wine coverage is comprehensive. (There is a special wine edition every October.) But even the editors will admit that the feature best known for reeling in readers is the precious police log. You don't really know St. Helena until you have studied this compendium of barking dogs, double-parked cars, and nosy neighbors.

WEEKLY CALISTOGAN
1458 Lincoln Avenue, Calistoga
(707) 942-4035
www.weeklycalistogan.com
This might be the only newspaper in the nation whose motto is longer than some of its features. And I quote: "Published at the Head of the Napa Valley, a Beautiful and Fertile Section of Country, Possessing a Climate that for Health and Comfort is Not Surpassed on Earth." Amen. The *Calistogan* is owned by Lee Enterprises, and like its sister paper, the *St. Helena Star,* comes out each Thursday.

Sonoma County

SONOMA INDEX-TRIBUNE
117 West Napa Street, Sonoma
(707) 938-2111
www.sonomanews.com
Established in 1879, the twice-weekly *Sonoma Index-Tribune* has been in the same family since 1884. Serving the Sonoma Valley—a region approximately 18 miles long that extends from San Pablo Bay north to Kenwood—the paper publishes every Tuesday and Friday, with a paid circulation of 9,000. The *Index-Tribune* is an award-winning community newspaper, covering all aspects of local news—schools, city government, the fire and water boards, the wine business, prep and youth sports, adult recreational sports leagues, even bake sales and spaghetti dinners.

ARGUS COURIER
1304 Southpoint Boulevard, Petaluma
(707) 762-4541
www.arguscourier.com
Published each Wednesday, this publication (now owned by the *New York Times*) has been in business since 1855, making it the oldest paper in Sonoma County. It focuses on Petaluma community news and information on arts and entertainment. Circulation is 8,500.

COMMUNITY VOICE

100 Professional Center Drive, Rohnert Park
(707) 584-2222
www.thecommunityvoice.com

The *Community Voice,* published every Friday, is the local newspaper for residents of Rohnert Park, Cotati, and Penngrove. It tells them what is going on in their schools and neighborhoods. Columnists write up the news about anniversaries, birthdays, and other small-town happenings. The paper's well-designed sports section covers local recreational activities—especially youth sports. The *Voice* works closely with the Rohnert Park and Cotati chambers of commerce, is involved in promoting local business, and beats the drum for many local events and institutions.

NORTH BAY BOHEMIAN

847 Fifth Street, Santa Rosa
(707) 527-1200
www.bohemian.com

Before becoming the *Bohemian* in 2000, this free weekly tabloid was known as the *Sonoma County Independent*—and before that it was the *West Sonoma County Paper.* In 1994 the paper joined a Bay Area group of alternative weeklies, Metro Newspapers. Formerly serving only Sonoma County, the *Bohemian* now covers Napa and Marin Counties, featuring news stories relating to civic issues—from an indy perspective—as well as a voluminous culture and entertainment department. This weekly comes out each Thursday, with numerous distribution points in the three counties.

SONOMA COUNTY HERALD-RECORDER

1818 Fourth Street, Santa Rosa
(707) 545-1166

Published twice a week with a readership of 5,000, the *Herald-Recorder* covers real estate, business, and legal news, with statistical information from the county recorder's office and the county clerk, plus news affecting local attorneys and real estate interests.

SONOMA-MARIN FARM NEWS

970 Piner Road, Santa Rosa
(707) 544-5575
www.sonomacountyfarmbureau.com

The Farm Bureau has been distributing its monthly agricultural newspaper to the ranchers of Sonoma County and adjoining Marin County for more than 25 years. The publication covers laws and regulations that affect farmlands and disseminates information on wetlands and tree ordinances that apply to vineyards and dairy and cattle ranches. There is also general farming and viticulture news. Circulation is 4,500.

NORTH BAY BUSINESS JOURNAL

5464 Skylane Boulevard, Suite B, Santa Rosa
(707) 579-2900
www.busjrnl.com

The *Business Journal* publishes strictly business news, focusing on new startups, expansions of existing firms, and information on relocations. Circulation is more than 10,000. Usually the 40-page-plus journal, owned by the *New York Times,* will include a profile of a top-level executive, describing the company, its history, and anticipation of future progress. Published weekly, the *Business Journal* covers Sonoma, Marin, and Napa Counties. It also prints a monthly wine industry *Business Journal* and a year-end *Book of Lists.*

HEALDSBURG TRIBUNE AND WINDSOR TIMES

5 Mitchell Lane, Healdsburg
(707) 433-4451
www.sonomawest.com/healdsburg
www.sonomawest.com/windsor

The *Tribune* has had different owners since its inception more than 130 years ago, but it is now part of the Sonoma West Publishers newspaper group, which also publishes the *Sonoma West Times & News* (see listing). This is a well-rounded weekly, covering all the news of Healdsburg and Geyersville: community affairs and events, legal matters, and local personalities. The paper also prints occasional special sections. The *Windsor Times* too is strictly locally oriented—and owned by the Sonoma West Publishers. Both the *Healdsburg Tribune* and *Windsor Times* print on Wednesday. Together, the newspapers' circulation is approximately 9,000.

CLOVERDALE REVEILLE
207 North Cloverdale Boulevard, Cloverdale
(707) 894-3339
www.cloverdalereveille.com
This community newspaper is published on Wednesday and covers community and school news. Records stacked away in old files indicate the *Reveille* was first published in 1879. Present circulation is 2,400.

BODEGA BAY NAVIGATOR
(707) 875-3574
www.bodegabaynavigator.com
A weekly newspaper established in 1986, *Bodega Bay Navigator* ceased producing a print edition in 2006. The "paper" is now exclusively Web-based. It focuses on both community news and global issues and has tackled some controversial or unusual stories in its past. For example, the *Navigator* has produced stories on teen pregnancy services, violence, and the plight of the Navajo nation.

SONOMA WEST TIMES & NEWS
130 South Main Street, Suite 114, Sebastopol
(707) 823-7845, (707) 869-3520
www.sonomawest.com
Locally owned and intimately focused, this paper covers Sebastopol and the Russian River area. The publisher says the *Times & News* is "about our families, our towns, about the guy next door." Those towns are primarily Sebastopol, Bodega Bay, and Guerneville. Look for the paper each Wednesday.

i Spanish-language newspapers have proliferated in Wine Country in recent years, many available free at newsstands. The best of these include *La Voz*, the *Sonoma Sun*, and *Hispanos Unidos*.

MAGAZINES

NORTH BAY BIZ
3565 Airway Drive, Santa Rosa
(707) 575-8282
www.northbaybiz.com
Norman Rosinski publishes and edits this glossy monthly magazine, impressive with its well-designed cover and artistic inside pages. It has provided more than 30 years of business intelligence in Sonoma County, covering technology, real estate, and wine and other industries. The magazine's annual wine issue also doubles as the official program of the Sonoma County Harvest Fair. Circulation is more than 7,000.

SANTA ROSA MAGAZINE
427 Mendocino Avenue, Santa Rosa
(707) 526-8585
www.santarosamagazine.com
This slickly produced quarterly spotlights people and places that represent "the good life" in and around Santa Rosa, complete with lush photography. Published by the *Press Democrat* and sold at selected newsstands, bookstores, and upscale grocers, each edition typically includes a restaurant review, recipes, profiles of interesting residents, and a "getaway" travel piece.

RADIO STATIONS

Station List
Adult Contemporary
KNOB 96.7 FM
KMHX 104.1 FM
KRSH 95.9 FM
KVYN 99.3 FM
KZST 100.1 FM

Christian
KLVR 91.9 FM
KNDL 89.9 FM
KSHC 106.5 FM

Country

KFGY 92.9 FM

KRPQ 104.9 FM

Jazz

KJZY 93.7 FM

News, Talk, Sports

KSRO 1350 AM

KSVY 91.3 FM

KVON 1440 AM

Public Radio

KRCB 91.1 FM

Rock

KVRV 97.7 FM (CLASSIC ROCK)

KXFX 101.7 FM (ALTERNATIVE ROCK)

Spanish

KBBF 89.1 FM

KRRS 1460 AM

KSRT 107.1 FM

KTOB 1490 AM

KXTS 100.9 FM

TELEVISION

Station List

ABC: KGO CHANNEL 7 (NAPA, SONOMA)

CBS: KPIX CHANNEL 5 (NAPA, SONOMA)

NBC: KNTV CHANNEL 11 (NAPA, SONOMA)

FOX: KTVU CHANNEL 2 (NAPA, SONOMA)

PBS: KQED CHANNEL 9 (NAPA, SONOMA); KRCB CHANNEL 22 (SONOMA)

CW: KBHK CHANNEL 44 (NAPA, SONOMA)

INDEPENDENTS: KFTY CHANNEL 50 (SONOMA)

Local Broadcast Channels

KFTY TV 50 (INDEPENDENT)
533 Mendocino Avenue, Santa Rosa
(707) 526-5050
www.kfty.com
Started in 1981 by Wichard Brown, then owner of the *Marin Independent Journal*, this station is now owned by Clear Channel Communications. KFTY broadcasts to a large part of the Bay Area, with general programming that includes movies and sitcoms.

KRCB TELEVISION 22 (PUBLIC TV)
5850 Labath Avenue, Rohnert Park
(707) 585-2000, (800) 287-2722
www.krcb.org
This public television station was started in 1984 and now reaches the counties of Sonoma, Napa, Mendocino, and Lake, plus portions of Alameda, Marin, Solano, and Contra Costa Counties. It even broadcasts to San Francisco. Programming is typical public television fare: *Sesame Street, Nova, This Old House*, news programs, and the Emmy Award–winning *Natural Heroes*.

CABLE TV

Napa and Sonoma Counties

COMCAST CORP.
(800) 266-2278
www.comcast.com
If you live in one of these two counties, this is your cable TV provider. Comcast has the monopoly in Wine Country, and reviews of its service are mixed. (At press time, AT&T was busy making inroads in this region to compete with Comcast, but its progress has been slow.) Comcast offers standard cable and digital services in several packages. In 2008 the company upgraded its aging infrastructure in many areas of Wine Country to offer new features and services.

WORSHIP

In Wine Country, where a certain sense of spontaneity dominates the culture, an amazingly eclectic assortment of houses of worship has taken root and prospered. In Sonoma County alone, with a thinly spread population of about 482,034 (no larger than a good-size American city), the Yellow Pages list nearly 60 different faiths. That would be in line with figures gathered at the turn of the 20th century, when it was revealed that Sonoma County had more churches than any other county in the state except San Francisco. The zeal of the early religious organizers and preachers sustained the pioneers and laid a firm foundation for church building of the future.

NAPA COUNTY

The story of spirituality in Napa County—or, more accurately, of European-rooted religion—is sprinkled with visionaries, hard knocks, and roustabouts. Fittingly, the tale more or less begins with the gold rush. Among the starry-eyed prospectors who gravitated to California in 1849 was James Milton Small, an ordained minister of the Cumberland Presbyterian Church. In the fall of 1850, Small gave up on gold and moved to Napa to save souls, preaching to early settlers in the dining room of a boardinghouse. Three years later the national Presbyterian Board of Missionaries sent Rev. J. C. Herron from Philadelphia to the Napa Valley. He sermonized in the old courthouse, a trying experience, according to church records.

It was in reaction to the poor conditions in the courthouse that the Presbyterians built the first church in Napa city in 1855, at a time when white settlers were true pioneers. After the congregation moved its facilities a couple years later, the old edifice was reduced to service as a paint shop. In 1858 it was purchased by a group of black Methodists, who splintered from their white congregation, moved the structure to Washington Street, and called it the African Methodist Church.

Rev. S. D. Simonds is said to have been the first Methodist Episcopal preacher to reside in

Napa Valley. That was about 1851. A year later Rev. Asa White delivered a sermon in a grove of redwood trees known as Paradise Park. The grove was part of the Tucker farm, about halfway between St. Helena and Calistoga, and it became the site of the first church in Napa Valley in 1853. The Methodists built a separate church in Napa in 1856. They also laid the foundation for a church in Calistoga in 1868, but construction didn't go much further. The railroad wanted the land, and there wasn't much the railroad didn't get.

In 1917 a new Methodist church opened in Napa. During the dedication service, it was reported that $31,000 had been raised for building the church—$5,000 short of the total cost. Addressing the congregation, Bishop Adna Leonard said, "A collection is now in order. This is a courteous congregation. I am going to ask you to remain until the benediction is reached." Leonard's lock-the-doors-until-we're-solvent strategy worked. He marked pledges on a blackboard and eventually reached the $36,000 goal. That building stands today, a registered landmark of English Gothic architecture.

The Christian Church appeared in the valley in 1853, when J. P. McCorkle preached under a madrone tree in Yountville.

The Roman Catholics held occasional services in Margaret McEnerny's boardinghouse on Main Street in Napa in the mid-1850s. (The priest would ride over from the Sonoma mission.)

Napa merchant George Cornwell, a non-Catholic, donated land on Main Street, and St. John the Baptist Church was erected in 1858. The first Catholic church in St. Helena was built in 1866; actually, it was the remodeled home of a Mrs. Sheehan at Oak Avenue and Tainter Street. When the local parishioners got a new church in 1878, they paid $72 for the old bell from the Napa courthouse.

The Seventh-day Adventist Church held its first meetings in 1873, in tents at the site of what is today known as Fuller Park in Napa, and a church was dedicated in the winter of 1873–74.

The history of Calistoga, meanwhile, is inexorably entwined with the Church of Jesus Christ of Latter-day Saints, for Sam Brannan, that iconoclastic founding father and California's first millionaire, was a Mormon. After sailing around Cape Horn with a church group in the 1840s, Brannan hung onto the collected tithings. He wanted San Francisco to be the center of Mormon culture, not Salt Lake City. Brigham Young saw otherwise, and he eventually excommunicated Brannan for absconding with those funds. The first Latter-day Saints church in the valley was in St. Helena, adjacent to where that town's current Mormon church stands on Spring Street.

By 1963, Napa County counted some 37 separate churches, representing 20 denominations. Today it's more like 80 churches and 45 denominations, not to mention the many spiritual individualists who defy traditional classification.

i One of the most interesting churches in Napa Valley from an architectural standpoint is St. Simeon Russian Orthodox Church in Calistoga. Built in the 1950s, the small church is topped by the characteristic onion-shaped dome found in Byzantine design. See it for yourself at 1421 Cedar Street.

SONOMA COUNTY

A zealous young Spanish priest, Father Jose Altimira, was the first to bring Christianity to these parts. He came to what is now Sonoma County in 1823 to establish the Mission San Francisco de Solano, northernmost in a chain of missions spaced along California's coast. Despite the overthrow of the Spanish rulers in Mexico, Altimira was nothing if not enthusiastic, and he convinced his colleagues in the church that the area would be a better climate than San Francisco for the Native American converts.

A small Russian Orthodox chapel was built on the coast in western Sonoma County about the time the Spanish secularized their missions. The wooden chapel was a part of the Russian American Company's settlement at Fort Ross (see the History chapter). The Russians abandoned the fort in 1841, taking all the icons from the chapel with them, leaving behind only a large bell, candelabra, candlestand, and a lectern.

The Russians had come and gone by the time other church activity began to stir in the established city of Sonoma. In approximately 1859, Congregationalists founded Cumberland Presbyterian College, a learning center where services were also sometimes held. But some distance from the village there lived a rancher named Edwin Sutherland, who decided he would start his own church under the protecting branches of a large live oak tree on his property. He had five children, his sister across the road had six, and with the children of a few neighbors he established the Big Tree Sunday School in his own backyard. Within three years Sutherland began forming a church in the village. It would be called the First Congregational Church of Sonoma. That church still stands today, though in a different location, at 252 West Spain Street.

For years one of the lesser-known secrets about First Baptist Church in Santa Rosa was that it had been built out of a single 3,000-year-old redwood tree. The tree, 275 feet high and 18 feet in diameter, came from a ranch near Guerneville. The congregation had been unaware of the church's unique status until 1900, when a member, attorney Thomas Butts, told his story. He had been employed by a Guernevillle mill at the time the tree was felled. The mill's owner, knowing the intended purpose of the tree, personally monitored every step of the milling process to ensure the wood wasn't mingled with other lumber.

In 1939 Robert Ripley, a church member, featured the church in his "Believe It or Not" column and gave it instant fame. For many years, the Church of One Tree, at 492 Sonoma Avenue in Santa Rosa, housed the Robert Ripley Museum. Although it started as a Baptist church, One Tree became a church for many faiths, and on any given Sunday as many as 5,000 people worshipped there—as many as 10 services were offered there each week.

The 1870s and 1880s saw tremendous expansion of church activity in Sonoma County. Denominations sprang up like dogs to the dinner bell, including Methodists, Baptists, Presbyterians, Episcopalians, and a sizable number of fundamentalist groups.

One of the most renowned preachers of Sonoma County was Rev. James Woods, who established a Presbyterian church in Healdsburg in 1858. His first congregation included Cyrus Alexander, who owned the entire valley north of Healdsburg and was himself a minister. In fact, it was Alexander who proposed that if the church could raise $1,000, he would put up $800 to secure the Methodist property on the plaza, which was up for sale. The lot was eventually purchased and the church was renovated and occupied.

In Santa Rosa, the first semblance of a Catholic church (a wooden building with eight pews) was erected in 1860 on a lot donated by one of General Mariano Vallejo's relatives, Julio Carrillo. For the next 15 years, a priest came up from Marin County once a month to offer Mass at St. Rose. Finally, in 1876, a new parish formed that included Sebastopol, Healdsburg, Cloverdale, and Guerneville.

Today St. Rose parish serves as the mother church in Santa Rosa, with a seating capacity of 500. The church that was built in 1900 still stands as a historic monument, but it is empty and unused, declared unsafe in earthquake conditions. Still grand, it is now surrounded by a new church that wraps around it like a boomerang. The new building at 398 10th Street is stunning, with walls of colored glass.

Churches that once fell neatly into a half-dozen denominations—mainly Methodist, Baptist, Catholic—have now splintered into dozens of churches. It started during the Civil War when Southern Methodists and Southern Baptists started their own congregations to denote their sympathies with the South. Today there are Independent Baptists, Fundamental Baptists, and GARBC Baptists. We have various branches of Presbyterians including Korean Western. We have Buddhist and Soto Zen centers, and we have Pentecostal, Orthodox Eastern, new age churches, and a group called Metropolitan Community, plus a Church of God of Prophecy and the Foursquare Gospel.

INDEX